Cases in Managemer

Cases in Management

Kenneth R. Thompson
Nicholas J. Mathys
DePaul University

Houghton Mifflin Company Boston
Dallas Geneva, Illinois Palo Alto Princeton, New Jersey

Cover photography: Skolos, Wedell, and Raynor

Printed in U.S.A.

Library of Congress Catalog Number: 89-80938

ISBN: 0-395-52934-4

ABCDEFGHIJ-AH-99876543210

Contents

To the Instructor

Although this book of cases has been developed as a companion volume to *Management,* Third Edition, by Ricky W. Griffin, it can be easily adapted to other popular principles of management texts. See the section Using This Casebook with Other Textbooks, which includes a table that cross-lists topic areas and texts.

This book of cases is based on the notion that the application of course-related material to an actual situation offers an effective means of learning: an active process rather than a passive one. As both students and teachers, we have found that such a process of discovery has been a particularly effective learning, and consequently teaching, device. To help you get the most out of this casebook, we have provided a table detailing the types of industries and topics covered by cases (Table 1) and a list of cases and their learning goals (Table 2).

The use of cases allows the student to apply and practice the skills and concepts learned in class. The cases provided here portray a wide variety of problems and situations faced by contemporary managers. Unless otherwise noted, these cases are fictitious and based on the experiences of real-life companies.

Acknowledgments

Many people have assisted in the preparation of this book. Although we cannot acknowledge all of them individually, we are nevertheless grateful for their assistance. We particularly appreciate the case materials and critiques provided by Wayne Hochwarter and Thomas C. Head. Jeff Sartori, graduate assistant, and Shefali Trivedi, research assistant at DePaul University, assisted in the compilation and preparation of manuscript material. Thanks are also due to Dianne Cichanski and Andromeda Banks for transforming many scribbled notes into readable form.

Finally, it must be said that although many have helped in useful ways, as authors, the final responsibility for the book rests with us.

KENNETH R. THOMPSON
NICHOLAS J. MATHYS

TABLE 1 Types of Industries and Topics Covered by Cases

This table identifies each case by several dimensions—topical coverage, size of the organization, type of organization, and at what organizational level the cases focuses—which may be helpful in identifying when and how you can use it most effectively.

Case #		Industry	Level	Size	Planning	Organizing	Staffing	Control	Leading	Behavior	Communications	Multinational focus	Operations	Ethics
1.1.	New Job Dilemma	R	F	M		X	X							
1.2.	Summer Job (Before)	S		S	X	X		X						
1.3.	Matter of Time	M	T	M	X	X								
1.4.	Economy Food Mart	R	M	M		X	X		X	X				
2.1.	Management Principles	S	T	L	X	X	X	X	X					
2.2.	Mary	M	T	L						X			X	
2.3.	Granger Inn	S	T	S	X									
2.4.	Setting Standards	A	F	M	X					X			X	
2.5.	Sears in the 1940s	R	F	L	X					X				
3.1.	Location for Fast Food	S	T	S	X									
3.2.	Hospital's Market Area	S, N	T	S	X	X								
3.3.	Kansas Railroad	S, T	T	S	X								X	
3.4.	Berry's Business	M	T	S	X	X								
3.5.	Depletion of Ozones	M	T	L	X									X
4.1.	What to Do with the Gift?	S, N	T	S	X					X				X
4.2.	Reliance Insurance	S	M	M	X					X				
4.3.	Too Many Stations?	S	T	S	X									
4.4.	Location Decision	M	M	L	X								X	X
5.1.	Dept. of Management	N	M	M	X			X	X					
5.2.	Reinforcements and Goals	M	F	S	X	X				X				
5.3.	Quantifying Goals	R, S	F	M	X	X		X		X				
5.4.	State Rehab. Service	S	F	M	X	X		X		X				X
5.5.	Airports vs. Trains	S, T	T	L	X	X								
6.1.	Purchase Sense	S	T	S	X					X				
6.2.	Wide World of Travel	S	T	S	X									
6.3.	Summer Job (After)	S		S	X	X								
6.4.	Harrington Holding	S, F	T	L	X	X								

7.1. St. Andrew College	N	T	S	X									
7.2. Omega Supermarkets	R	T	M	X									
7.3. Mary Maloney	S	F	S	X	X	X							
7.4. Electronic Systems	M	T	L	X						X	X	X	
8.1. NorthStar Mfg.	M	M	M	X	X	X			X				
8.2. Illinois Best	R	T	M	X	X	X						X	
8.3. Developing Manager	R	M	L		X	X			X				
8.4. Org. of University	S	T	M		X	X	X		X				
8.5. Big Blue	M	T	L		X	X	X					X	
9.1. Sibley Plastics	M	M	M		X	X	X						
9.2. Tech. Innovations on RR	S, T	T	L		X	X	X					X	
9.3. National Bldg. Products	M, C	T	L		X	X			X			X	
9.4. Toronto Advertising	S	T	M		X	X			X			X	
9.5. Businesses and Ethics	V	T	L		X	X	X		X				X
10.1. Impire Corp.	M	T	L			X					X	X	
10.2. Southwest Metalworks	M	M	M			X			X				
10.3. What Went Wrong?	C	T	M			X			X				
10.4. Who to Promote?	M	F	M			X			X				
11.1. Mississippi Air	S, T	T	S		X				X				
11.2. Org. Development at AT&T	S	T	L		X				X				
11.3. Survey Feedback at GM	M	T	L		X				X				
11.4. Gender Equality in Japan	V	T	L						X		X		X
11.5. GE's Crotonville	M	T	L		X			X	X			X	
12.1. Cheryl and Computer Co.	S	F	S					X	X				
12.2. Ken-Ray	M	F	M					X	X				
12.3. U Lucky Dog	S	F	S					X	X				
12.4. Comstock Foods	R	F	S					X	X			X	
12.5. Customer Feedback	S	F	M					X	X			X	
13.1. Realty Crossing	S	F	S					X	X			X	
13.2. Lyon Advertising	S	F	S					X	X			X	
13.3. Mrs. Loomis Case	S, N	F	M					X	X			X	
13.4. Leaders Self-Destruct	V	—	—					X					
14.1. Data Processing	M	F	L		X		X		X	X	X		
14.2. Automatic Electric	M	F	L					X	X				
14.3. Advanced Electronics	M	F	M		X	X		X	X				
14.4. Office Allocation	S	M	M		X	X		X	X	X			
15.1. Bryant Pharmaceutical	M	F	L		X	X			X	X			X
15.2. St. Francis University	N	T	M							X			
15.3. Who Should Be Secretary?	S, F					X			X	X			
15.4. Damon Mfg.	M	F	M			X			X	X			

Case #		Industry	Level	Size	Planning	Organizing	Staffing	Control	Leading	Behavior	Communications	Multinational focus	Operations	Ethics
16.1.	Beloit Marine	M	F	M		X		X					X	
16.2.	First Bank & Trust	S, F	F	M		X		X						
16.3.	General Homebuilders	C	T	M				X						
16.4.	Controlling for Performance	G	T	—				X						X
16.5	Harold's Hamburgers	S	T	S				X		X			X	
17.1.	Lextronix Radio	M	M	M			X			X			X	
17.2.	Black & Decker	M	T	L	X	X						X	X	
17.3.	Fremont Appliance	M	M	M						X			X	
17.4.	Sun 'N Surfboard	M	T	S						X	X		X	
18.1.	Pittsburgh Supply 1	S	T	S	X			X					X	
18.2.	Pittsburgh Supply 2	S	T	S	X			X					X	
18.3.	Pittsburgh Supply 3	S	T	S	X			X					X	
18.4.	Pittsburgh Supply 4	S	T	S	X			X					X	
18.5.	Pittsburgh Supply 5	S	T	S	X			X					X	
19.1.	Midwest Tool & Die	M	T	M	X			X					X	
19.2.	Wyoming Wonders	R	T	M	X		X						X	
19.3.	Route 23	C, S	T	M	X			X					X	
19.4.	Cole International	—	M	L			X	X		X		X	X	
19.5.	Sears and Retail Ind.	R	T	L				X					X	
20.1.	Hamburger Haven	S	T	S	X	X		X	X					
20.2.	Leather Shoppe	S	T	S	X	X		X	X					
20.3.	Allegré Fashions	R	T	S	X	X								
20.4.	Schiller's Ski House	R	T	S		X		X						
21.1.	Plastic Suppliers	M	T	M								X	X	X
21.2.	Kolbe Foods	W	T	L								X		X
21.3.	World-Class Competitor	M	T	L					X			X	X	
22.1.	Business out Front	V	—	—										X
22.2.	Part-Time Lawyers	S	T	S			X			X				X
22.3.	Shakeup at Sears	R	T	L				X				X	X	X
22.4.	Helping Customers?	R	T	L										X
22.5.	Futures Industry	S, F	T	L				X		X				X

Industry: A = agribusiness; C = construction; F = finance; G = government; M = manufacturing; N = not-for-profit; R = retail; S = service; T = transportation; V = various; W = wholesale
Management level: F = first-level; M = middle-level; T = top-level
Size of organization: L = large; M = medium; S = small

TABLE 2 Learning Goals for Each Case

Case	Learning Goal	Page Number
Part 1: An Introduction To Management		
Chapter 1. Managing and the Manager's Job		
Case 1. The New Job Dilemma	To explore some of the dilemmas and letdowns a recent college graduate faces in a first managerial position	9
Case 2. The Summer Job (Before)	To clarify the management process and managerial roles required in even the simplest of enterprises	12
Case 3. A Matter of Time	To explore some of the detailed decisions that a manager makes and to raise issues of appropriate delegation and management of one's time	13
Case 4. Economy Food Marts	To analyze the management training program of a regional food chain and the types of skills and abilities needed by store management personnel	15
Chapter 2. The Evolution of Management Thought		
Case 1. Early Management Principles	To show how management (delegation of authority and span of control) was important thousands of years ago	19
Case 2. Mary	To give some idea of the possible perceptions of subjects of the Hawthorne experiments	21
Case 3. The Granger Inn	To consider how each organization is a part of the larger environment that must be considered in making managerial decisions	24
Case 4. The Importance of Setting Standards	To show some of the applications of scientific management to current problems; to show how objective setting can improve performance	26
Case 5. Human Relations Research at Sears, Roebuck in the 1940s: A Memoir	To review the early methodology used to understand employee attitudes and the role of leadership and organizational structure in affecting satisfaction	28
Chapter 3. Organizational Environments and Effectiveness		
Case 1. Finding a Good Location for a Fast Food Franchise	To describe the demographic analysis of census data as a tool to determine market location	47

Case	Learning Goal	Page Number
Case 5. More Airports Versus Fast Trains	To demonstrate how a government organization has difficulty setting goals because of the various publics that it serves and because of the differences in philosophies between old and new administrations	85
Chapter 6. Strategy and Strategic Planning		
Case 1. Does the Purchase Make Sense?	To require the student to go through the strategic decision-making process involved in acquiring a business	93
Case 2. Wide World of Travel	To require the student to develop short- and long-term business strategies for a small business	95
Case 3. The Summer Job (After)	To encourage the student to develop marketing strategies and identify key environmental factors for a small business	96
Case 4. Harrington Holding Company	To determine how funds might be allocated among business units in a diversified holding company	97
Chapter 7. Tactical and Operational Planning		
Case 1. St. Andrew College	To explore potential barriers to instituting long-range planning in a small liberal arts college	99
Case 2. Omega Supermarkets	To consider the appropriateness of using management by objectives as a planning tool	101
Case 3. Mary Maloney	To highlight the need to anticipate potential barriers to a program during the planning phase	103
Case 4. Electronic Systems, Inc.	To consider the operational strategy of a large multinational organization; to emphasize the need to resolve conflicting goals of functional departments	105

Part 3: The Organizing Process

Case	Learning Goal	Page Number
Chapter 8. Components of Organizational Structure		
Case 1. Job Design at NorthStar Manufacturing Company	To help the student apply the job diagnostic index (JDI) model, job enrichment, and job enlargement	109

Case	Learning Goal	Page Number
Case 2. Lyon Advertising Agency	To show how the environment can affect the appropriate leadership style used and how it can shape leader behavior	212
Case 3. Mrs. Loomis Case	To expose the reader to some of the practical problems associated with being in a leadership position; to relate some of the theories of leadership and power to a real situation	214
Case 4. Leaders Who Self-Destruct: The Causes and Cures	To show how a person's changing environment when he or she becomes a leader can affect on-the-job effectiveness	220
Chapter 14. Interpersonal Processes, Groups, and Conflicts		
Case 1. Data Processing Equipment Company	To explore some of the conflicts between manufacturing and quality control that can hinder the timely completion of a project	233
Case 2. The Informal Group at Automatic Electric	To show the effects that an informal work group can have on productivity if its needs are not met	235
Case 3. Advanced Electronics	To expose the student to some of the difficulties a new employee faces in trying to become an accepted member of an informal group, and how it affects performance	237
Case 4. The Office Allocation Committee at BCW	To emphasize the obstacles a newly appointed leader needs to overcome to resolve conflicts within a group	240
Chapter 15. Communication in Organizations		
Case 1. Bryant Pharmaceutical	To show how organization-based communication problems can lead to dissatisfaction and misunderstanding among the sales force	243
Case 2. St. Francis University	To show the effect that an organization's growth and formalization can have on the communication process	245
Case 3. Who Should Be the Secretary?	To show the importance of communication and feedback on interpersonal behavior	246
Case 4. Damon Manufacturing Company	To show how barriers to effective communication affect organizational and interpersonal relationships	249

Case	Learning Goal	Page Number

Part 5: The Controlling Process

Chapter 16. The Nature of Control

Chapter 17. Operations Management, Productivity, and Quality

Chapter 18. Managing Information Systems

Case	Learning Goal	Page Number
Case 3. Pittsburgh Supply—Part 3: Distribution Information System	To demonstrate some of the information needed and problems in defining information needs when designing a system for obtaining distribution information	282
Case 4. Pittsburgh Supply—Part 4: Productivity and Quality Control Information Systems	To demonstrate some of the information needed and problems in defining information needs when designing a system for obtaining data on quality control and productivity	285
Case 5. Pittsburgh Supply—Part 5: A Comprehensive Management Information System	To demonstrate some of the information needed and problems in defining information needs when designing a system for obtaining data for the company	288
Chapter 19. Control Techniques and Methods		
Case 1. Midwest Tool & Die: A Division of RayCor	To show how rigid adherence to a budget may not be appropriate	291
Case 2. Wyoming Wonders	To show how to use financial ratio analysis	294
Case 3. Route 23	To demonstrate the use of a PERT network for planning and control	299
Case 4. Human Resources Management at Cole International	To show various control measures used in a human resource management department	302
Case 5. Sears and the Retail Industry	To look at techniques to control and monitor marketing aspects of the organization	305

Part 6: Special Challenges of Management

Case	Learning Goal	Page Number
Chapter 20. Entrepreneurship and Small-Business Management		
Case 1. Hamburger Haven	To examine the entrepreneurial qualities exhibited by a successful franchise operations; to emphasize the need for sound management principles	309
Case 2. The Leather Shoppe	To emphasize the need to have a sound business plan before establishing a business venture	311
Case 3. Allegré Fashions	To explore the difficulty faced by an entrepreneur who does not properly assign tasks or delegate responsibility	313
Case 4. Schiller's Ski House	To highlight the need to decide on specific goals; to define specific roles to improve organizational performance	315

Case	Learning Goal	Page Number
Chapter 21. Managing in the International Sector		
Case 1. Marketing Angel Dolls	To show how differences in laws between countries can cause ethical problems for businesses when marketing products	317
Case 2. Plastic Suppliers, Inc. (PSI)	To demonstrate some of the issues involved when producing in a foreign country; to demonstrate managerial and strategy principles that still hold true for the international company; to demonstrate the maquiladora program in Mexico	319
Case 3. Kolbe Foods, International	To consider how the Foreign Corrupt Practices Act restricts U.S. organizations versus foreign competitors	328
Case 4. Becoming a World-Class Competitor	To present one view of how to build a company that can compete worldwide	331
Chapter 22. Managing with Ethics and Social Responsibility		
Case 1. Business Out Front on Schools: Unprecedented Activism, from Execs through Ranks	To provide an example of the larger role of business in society	335
Case 2. Can a Good Lawyer Work Part-Time? Women Lead Push for Alternative	To discuss the social role of business with respect to worker accommodation	339
Case 3. Shakeup in Sears Family: New Format Changes Old Suppliers' Relationships	To discuss the responsibility that a business has to its suppliers	342
Case 4. Helping the Customers or Killing the Town?	To consider different viewpoints on the social responsibility of store location	346
Case 5. Tradeoff in Futures Industry: Customer Safeguards Sacrificed to Growth, Critics Say	To discuss socially responsible actions in the stock and stock futures trading industry	349

Using This Casebook with Other Textbooks

This casebook was designed to be used with Ricky Griffin's *Management*, Third Edition; hence the chapters match those of the text. However, the cases can also be used with a host of other principles of management texts. The table on the following page indicates which chapters in other leading texts in the field are comparable to our casebook chapters. For example, Chapter 6 in the Aldag and Stearns text (see column 1) corresponds to Chapter 6 in this casebook, entitled "Strategy and Strategic Planning." Books that are not listed in the table can be compared to our casebook in a similar manner. For the reader's convenience, the purpose of each case is briefly stated in Table 2.

Comparable Chapters in Other Popular Management Texts

Chapter Title	Other Management Texts (see key below)											
	1	2	3	4	5	6	7	8	9	10	11	12
1. Managing and the manager's job	1	1	1	1	1	1	1	1	1	1	1	1
2. The evolution of management thought	2	2	2	2	—	3	2	2	2	2	2	3
3. Organizational environments and effectiveness	4	3	3	—	2	3	3	3	3	3	3	6
4. Managerial decision making	16	7	6	5	16	4	6	6	4	17	6	7
5. Organizational goals and planning	5	5, 6	4	3	4	5	3, 4	4	5	4	4	4, 5
6. Strategy and strategic planning	6	4	5	4	5	6	5	5	6	4	5	6
7. Tactical and operational planning	7	8	7	6, 7	6, 18	6	7	5	7	5	7	5
8. Components of organizational structure	8	9, 10	8	8	7	7	8	7	8	6	9	8
9. Organization design and culture	9	10, 11	9	9	7	8	9, 11	8	3, 9	7	10, 11	9
10. Managing human resources	10	13, 15	10	10	9	9	12, 14	9	18	9	12	10
11. Organization change, development, and revitalization	11	12	11	11	14	16	15	14	15	8	13	15
12. Motivating employee job performance	3, 12	16	13	14	10	11	16, 17	11	11, 12	10	15	13
13. Leadership and influence processes	14	17	12	13	12	13	18	13	10, 13	11	16	12
14. Internal processes, groups, and conflict	15	18	14	15	11	12	10	12	11	12, 19	14, 17	14, 15
15. Communication in organizations	13	19	15	12	13	10	19	10	14	18	18	11
16. The nature of control	17	20	16	16	8	14	20	15	16	13	20	16
17. Operations management, productivity, and quality	20	—	18	17	3, 15	15	22	17	19	16	8	17
18. Managing information systems	19	22	17	18	17	14	23	16	17	15	22	16
19. Control techniques and methods	17	21	16	16	19	14	21	17	16	14	21	18
20. Entrepreneurship and small-businesses management	22	—	—	—	—	—	—	—	—	—	—	—
21. Managing in the international sector	21	24	19	20	21	18	25	19	21	22	23	19
22. Managing with ethics and social responsibility	24	23	20	19	20	17	24	18	20	23	3	20

Key to text titles

1. Aldag and Stearns, *Management* (Cincinnati: South-Western Publishing), 1987.
2. Bedeian, *Management* (Chicago: Dryden Press), 1986.
3. Boone and Kurtz, *Management*, 3rd ed. (New York: Random House), 1987.
4. Certo, *Principles of Modern Management*, 4th ed. (Boston: Allyn & Bacon), 1989.
5. Donnelly, Gibson, and Ivancevich, *Fundamentals of Management*, 6th ed. (Plano, Texas: BPI), 1987.
6. Hodgetts and Kuratko, *Management*, 2nd ed. (New York: Harcourt Brace Jovanovich), 1988.
7. Koontz and Weihrich, *Management*, 9th ed. (New York: McGraw-Hill), 1988.
8. Kreitner, *Management*, 4th ed. (Boston: Houghton Mifflin), 1989.
9. Robbins, *Management*, 2nd ed. (Englewood Cliffs, N.J.: Prentice-Hall), 1988.
10. Schoderbek, Cosier, and Aplin, *Management* (New York: Harcourt Brace Jovanovich), 1988.
11. Stoner and Wankel, *Management*, 3rd ed. (Englewood Cliffs, N.J.: Prentice-Hall), 1986.
12. Van Fleet, *Contemporary Management* (Boston: Houghton Mifflin), 1988.

Cases in Management

How to Analyze a Case

The case method can be an enriching experience for a student. Before beginning, however, it is important to gain a clear understanding of what the case approach is all about. This section explores the purpose of using cases in a course, some methods of analyzing a case and preparing one's analysis for presentation, and several other aspects of an effective written or oral presentation. Once there is a clear understanding of why cases are being used and what can be learned from using them, it becomes much easier to analyze and apply the course material.

The Purpose of Case Analysis

Case analysis serves three purposes: it can be helpful in bridging the gap between theory and reality, it tends to reinforce concepts, and it improves analytic thinking.

First, a case can be viewed as an important means of bridging the gap between theory and practice. Most teaching approaches stress the obtainment of knowledge as the major indicator of achievement. However, obtaining knowledge is really only part of the educational process; having the ability to use that knowledge is also essential. That is where some courses fall short. Getting a solid education is difficult, and the burden of transferring knowledge taught in class is often left to the student. In some situations that burden is considerable.

Consider the various courses that you have had over the years. How many of them were simple memory courses in which you were asked to memorize facts and repeat those facts on a multiple choice or even an essay exam? That is a fine educational approach if the objective is to pass along facts and concepts. However, it does not help you develop a working knowledge of the subject material—it simple expects you to do that yourself. If you have already had experiences that you can relate to the theory, you may have less difficulty than if you have had a limited background.

The case approach can help bridge the gap between theory and reality. A case is a simulated environment in which a concept can be demonstrated. It can have a variety of formats. One of these formats, a computer simulation, has the advantage of being interactive: that is, it responds to your recommendations and changes the environment so that you have a new environment in which to make a subsequent decision. The more traditional case format is a written description of an environment that is used to demonstrate a particular concept. It may also demonstrate an environment in which a concept might be applied; these kinds of cases just establish the environment and then give subtle references to a specific problem or set of problems. Complex cases such as those provided by the Harvard Business School are examples of cases that focus more on building an environment than on demonstrating a concept.

Each of these types of cases helps meet certain goals. A short case that is written to demonstrate a specific concept is best suited to reinforcing that concept for an audience that has had no experience with it. The case is designed to provide an uncluttered environment for illustrating an idea. A more complex case is designed to show how a concept can be used in a multifaceted environment. This sort of case is targeted for a more mature audience, those who have some understanding of the concept and are ready to try it in a situation that reflects reality more closely than the shorter cases.

A second purpose for case analysis is to reinforce concepts. Simply put, there is some value in redundancy, and the case format provides that redundancy. You get a chance to hear about a concept again, but this time to deal with it in a practical way. Moreover, by forcing you to relate theory and practice, case study helps you consider the concept in much more detail than would otherwise be possible. It is one thing to memorize a concept or theory, but it is a far different matter to know the concept well enough to be able to articulate how it should work in a practical setting.

A third purpose for case analysis relates to an educational goal that goes beyond concept learning to analytic thinking. Case analysis expects you to analyze an environment and make recommendations to resolve problems in that environment. Shorter cases are less suited to the development of analytic ability than more complex cases, but both challenge you to go beyond learning concepts to developing your own thinking and reasoning ability.

The analytical process has several stages. First you must diagnose a situation. Then you must recommend some solutions and explain why those solutions will work. Lastly, you must consider how to effectively present these recommendations and the rationale for them. Thus there are three basic steps in solving cases: identification of the problem, analysis and evaluation, and recommendations. To facilitate our explanation, we will now present a case, after which we will discuss how to analyze this case using our format.

A Sample Case: Will the Tax Plan Help Reduce Chlorofluorocarbons?[1]

"Congress is getting set to impose a punishing new tax on chlorofluorocarbons that would double the cost of processing of the ozone-depleting chemicals next year and could quadruple prices by the mid-1990s."[2] The proposed tax is the way that the U.S.

1. Adapted from *GM Public Interest Report*, 1988, 1989; and Michael Arndt, "Tax Plan Clouds Research on Coolant," *Chicago Tribune*, September 25, 1989, Sec. 4, pp. 1, 4.
2. Arndt, p. 1.

Congress wishes to deal with the problem of ozone depletion. Some industry officials think that the approach will not help create a substitute for the product but will instead retard the development of an alternative.

An official of Carrier Corporation has maintained that the industry is already doing everything possible to find a substitute material to replace chlorofluorocarbons. A Ford Motor spokesperson believes that the tax may have the opposite effect than the Congress expected. Brian Geraghty, manager of strategic technology planning for Ford Motor Company, believes that a tax will only retard the search for a substitute because money will be siphoned from research and development to pay for the higher tax. The tax would make sense if there were a replacement material that could be used. Then the tax would provide a better incentive to switch from the less desirable material to the now cheaper material. But there is no substitute; hence a tax would only hurt, not help, the situation. General Motors agrees; it strongly favors the Montreal Accord, which recommends a long-term phaseout of the use of chlorofluorocarbons with restrictions on the production of the product. The longer time duration would help the industry find some substitutes for the product.

Chlorofluorocarbons are used in several important products. Forty percent are used for refrigerants in automobile, home, and industry air conditioners in addition to freezers and refrigerators. Twenty-eight percent are used for foams in insulation material and for padding in car and truck dashboards. Another 28 percent are in the solvents that wash the electronic circuit boards of computers, that sterilize medical equipment, and that serve as degreasing agents. Twelve percent of chlorofluorocarbons are used as propellants for aerosol cans in some consumer products; the propellants help to push the material out of the can. Worldwide production of the material is 2.3 billion pounds. Major production facilities are in Western Europe and North America.

The goal of Congress seems to be to retard the production and use of the material. But critics complain that Congress might reach its goal more by supporting research and development than by penalizing users.

The problem that Congress faces is that it is trying to balance public policy. On one hand, consumers desire the products that use chlorofluorocarbons. On the other hand, research shows that chlorofluorocarbons are harmful to the ozone layer. There is evidence that a loss of the ozone layer could lead to a global warm-up and an increase in harmful radiation. A global warm-up could lead to disastrous changes in climate and rainfall and to flooding of coastal areas caused by a meltdown of the polar ice caps. Increases in solar radiation have been linked to skin cancer.

Company leaders realize the problem but are also motivated by a desire to stay in business. Increased costs may or may not be passed to consumers depending upon the competitiveness of the industry. Substitute products, in some cases, are not available; hence the leaders face massive worker layoffs if they cannot produce their product.

Congressional leaders may agree with the position of the company leaders, but they also suspect that company leaders may not have sufficient motivation to make an effort to improve their research and development. The tax would increase the motivation and at the same time help to halt a growing concern that the environment is something that Congress does not seem to care about. In addition, it would give the impression that Congress is doing something to reduce the destruction to the ozone layer and to avoid future world economic and climatic disaster.

Problem Identification

Problem identification may be the hardest part of case analysis. Once the problem has been correctly identified, the other components readily fall into place. However, identifying the problem is sometimes difficult, for a number of reasons. First, you must understand the perspective of the decision maker. As you analyze a case, you need to know what perspective you are going to use in resolving it.

For example, in this case, there are three perspectives that you might use. You could look at the case from the perspective of an industry executive. The executive has an obligation to the company and to its shareholders, employees, and customers. Or you could take the perspective of a member of Congress. A member of Congress has a responsibility to his or her constituents, a desire to be reelected, and a desire to serve the country. A third perspective that you might use is that of social justice and responsibility. The question then would be what is better for society as a whole.

Differentiating between a problem and a symptom is also crucial in defining the problem. In many situations people tend to treat what they believe to be the problem when in essence they are only treating its manifestations. It is obviously important to determine the true problem, not the symptoms. For example, U.S. law enforcement officials have focused most of their attention on the drug-producing countries and the drug sellers and transporters as a way to reduce the drug problem in the United States. It would seem more appropriate to focus attention on those that create the demand for drugs in this country or the conditions that precipitate the desire to take drugs in the first place.

Congress seems to be defining the use of chlorofluorocarbons as a problem because this family of chemicals is linked to a reduction of the ozone layer that protects this planet. This would seem to be an appropriate definition if you were in Congress or were concerned with the social good. However, if you were an industry leader, you might define the problem as Congress trying to increase the cost of a raw material through taxation. Without considering the perspective of Congress, you might try to take steps to keep Congress from raising the tax. If, on the other hand, you tried to understand what Congress wants done, you could attempt to work with Congress to reach its goals without increasing taxes. Instead of building a confrontational strategy, you might try to solve Congress's problem while still advocating your own interests.

In defining the problem, the case analyst also needs to look for structural versus behavioral sources of problems. We have been told by company leaders that 80 percent of their problems are people problems and that only 20 percent are related to the structural dimensions of the organization (technology, policies, work relationships, reinforcement systems, and work process). We have found the opposite to be true. Eighty percent of the problems we have encountered have been structural problems, with only 20 percent what might be called people problems (personality, individual differences, and work ethic). What you might see in an organization are people not getting along, but that may be the result of structural parameters that create conflict.

For example, one car manufacturer had problems between the stamping division and the assembly division. The plant managers of these two divisions never seemed to get along, regardless of who had those jobs. On closer inspection by a consultant it was determined that the bonus reinforcement system helped create the conflict. Each plant received a bonus based on lower scrap loss (wasted material). What was the reinforcement of each manager of this system? The stamping plant was reinforced to send marginal parts to the assembly plant. The assembly plant manager wanted perfect parts to reduce the scrap loss rate. The end result was that the assembly plant viewed the stamping operations plant as its major foe in reaching its scrap loss rate. The company, on the basis of the consultant's recommendation, changed the reinforcement system so that a bonus was paid on the loss rates of both plants combined. Within a month after the change, both managers were working together as old friends. Five years later, using the same principle, the company realized that it should not have been reinforcing scrap loss as much as producing quality cars; hence both goals are now reinforced but with the emphasis on quality production standards.

Relating this concept to the sample case, it is helpful in sorting out problems to realize the motivation of each of the principals in the case. A member of Congress will have a different motivation than an industry executive because a different behavior is being reinforced. These different motivations or reinforcements will help in sorting out the behaviors of each party.

To summarize, three elements need to be considered. First, you must identify the perspective that should be used as the problem solver. This affects how you look at the problem and how you define it. Second, you need to identify the problem and not just a symptom of the problem. Too many symptoms are solved without solving the core issues that have created the problem. Third, you must find the structural elements of the problem. It is not enough to just focus on the behavioral or personality dimensions because behaviors are a function of their consequences; hence motivation is the result of expected consequences. Many problems we see are the result of the organization reinforcing the wrong behaviors.

Analysis and Evaluation

We are never quite sure if analysis and evaluation should come before the problem identification or after. So do not be concerned if you have a problem with that either. Through the analysis and evaluation of the facts and the situation, you can develop a sense of the problems (problem identification), and through the analysis of the case you can obtain some clearer definition of the problem and a rationale for the solutions that you will propose.

An analogy here may be helpful. Charges are made in a criminal investigation by a state or federal attorney's office. The charges are taken before a grand jury so that a discovery process can begin. The discovery process looks at the evidence to determine if there is sufficient evidence to support the charges. If there is, the grand jury recommends that the case should be prosecuted. In the same way, you make a discovery process in the initial stage of the case analysis that helps you determine the major problems. However, once you have made a cursory identification of the problems, you need to make a more extensive analysis of the facts to further define and refine the problems and to offer solutions that might make the most sense given the environment of the case. Hence, the analysis is really part of the whole process from initial problem identification to the choice of recommendations. Analysis has three aspects: justification of the problem, identification of the major issues in the case, and assessment of the tolerance for change.

Justification of the problem This involves bringing together the facts in the case that led you to identify the problem, and then justifying that choice. For example, using our sample case, let's define the problem as how to provide the best incentive for industry to move from chlorofluorocarbons to other materials in a way that will not cause too much disruption in the marketplace. In the analysis section you should provide the data that support that choice. You could justify your choice by citing the desire of Congress and society to reduce the use of chlorofluorocarbons to protect the environment and to *thereby* protect the world economy. Hence, you would show that Congress wants to balance economics with the desire for ecological safety. This kind of justification of your position is essential because it forces you to articulate reasons.

Identifying the major issues Knowing the major issues helps you develop a recommendation that considers not only the main problem, but also the environment in which the problem evolved and where the solution will be attempted. Identifying these issues helps further bring reality to the process because you have to consider the total case environment.

In our sample case we identified the problem as eliminating the production of chlorofluorocarbons without too much economic disruption. The identification of that problem considers some of the following major issues:

- The problem of chlorofluorocarbons in the atmosphere
- The problem of finding substitute products
- The potential loss of jobs resulting from a production shutdown of those industries that use chlorofluorocarbons in their products
- The need for Congress to respond to a mounting concern of the electorate.

These issues will tend to shape the framing of a recommendation or set of recommendations that should guide us toward a resolution.

Determining the tolerance for change We think this step is important because it tends to frame the recommendation. For example, in our sample case, the tolerance for change is high for society because there is a concern that something needs to be done. The tolerance for change may be low with the producers because they feel it may mean a loss of jobs and profits. Similarly, the users of chlorofluorocarbons may be resistant to change until they are assured that there is a cost-effective substitute.

The analysis section, therefore, is a very important step in the case analysis process. It forces the student to provide a rationale for the identification of the problem and helps identify the other factors described in the case that will influence the success of any recommendation that might be advocated.

Recommendations

The recommendation section is critical because it provides the link between theory and practice. You must do three different things in this step: (1) you must define a set of possible recommendations, including a selection of the choice recommendations; (2) you must link the theory to the recommendation; and (3) you must consider the possible consequences of using these recommendations.

There is seldom one ideal recommendation for a situation, in cases or in life. Most environments provide us with a host of choices, and it is best to consider all the alternatives. When you choose a recommendation or set of recommendations, you should be able to articulate why you chose that strategy over others and what those other options were. This helps you realize why different decision makers may make different decisions and why those decisions might be just as good as others.

In our sample case you might define three alternative recommendations:

- Tax the use of the product with the tax going into a joint research program to find alternative sources.
- Reject the tax and simply curb production on a long-term basis.
- Halt production of chlorofluorocarbons immediately.

You might select the first alternative on the basis that it will provide a motivation for producers and users to find substitute products. In addition, it meets the concerns of those who feel that the tax would not help find a substitute. You might reject the second alternative because it does not act fast enough to reduce chlorofluorocarbon output, and you might reject the third because it may be too disruptive to the economy and industry.

Next you need to link your recommendations to the theory that is being demonstrated or one with which you are familiar. This is an important step because case analyses tend to degenerate to "I feel" or "I think" without showing a grounding in the concept or concepts that you are trying to demonstrate. That defeats a main purpose of case analysis. If you are using a case to demonstrate a concept, then you had better make sure that the person analyzing the case has grasped the relationship.

In this example, you would relate the case to the concept being demonstrated: using reinforcement theory in public policy decisions. Hence, you should be able to relate reinforcement theory to changing the production and consumption patterns of chlorofluorocarbons through the use of public policy.

The last step in the recommendation section is to identify the negative and positive consequences that might follow if the choice recommendation is adopted. This step is important because it forces you to look at the consequences of a decision. This again relates the theory to reality.

In this sample case you would indicate that the decision might lead to higher costs to the users of chlorofluorocarbons made in the United States. Users of foreign-produced products might then have a competitive advantage. In addition, reduced consumption might lead to layoffs in the affected industries. You might therefore make additional recommendations to try to gain an international agreement governing the use and production of chlorofluorocarbons that provides the same additional costs to all producers and users. If that is not possible, an import tariff might be levied on products brought into this country while allowing no tax on those units being produced for export.

The recommendation section is important in linking reality and theory. It is imperative that you feel challenged in this section to get the most from the exercise.

Oral and Written Case Presentations

Once the case is analyzed, it is ready for presentation. However, the same order of steps used in the analysis is not appropriate for case presentation. We like to use a business style in presenting cases—that is, one that focuses on the recommendations of the analysts. Hence, the recommendations come first, and the justifications for the choices follow. The alternative recommendations and consequences are presented last. This approach works best with oral as well as written presentations. Whereas the inductive approach may be appropriate for case analysis, the deductive approach is desirable when presenting the case. We find that presenters often lose their audience if they do not begin with their proposals. In oral presentations students sometimes run out of time before they get to their recommendations; then they hastily go over them in a cursory fashion. This is unacceptable because the recommendations ought to be the core of their presentation.

Written presentations should be well organized and make liberal use of headings and subheadings to help guide the reader. In addition, they should give only a short, almost executive summary of the case and include exhibits detailing any technical or involved proposals. This approach gives training in the process of business writing. Of course, grammar and spelling should be flawless. Again, it is most important to take a mature approach to education and professional preparation.

Chapter 1 Managing and the Manager's Job

Case 1. The New Job Dilemma[1]

Earl's Food Stores is a chain of grocery outlets principally serving the northeastern United States. The corporate headquarters is located in upstate New York. The organization works in a typical corporate manner in that many of the store decisions, such as what items are going on sale, their prices, and what new items should be presented, are made at the corporate level. Conversely, many decisions are made at the store level: hiring of new part-time employees, scheduling, and other personnel-related decisions. The stores offer a fresh fish market, an on-site bakery, and a pharmacy, as well as other products and services attributed to a typical food store. The gross sales of each store range from $75,000 to $275,000 per week.

John Myers worked part-time at Earl's for two and a half years while completing his bachelor's degree in business administration. He generally worked twenty hours per week while in school and roughly thirty-five hours per week during holidays and school breaks.

John was offered the job of assistant manager contingent upon his graduation from college. This position, as seen in Exhibit 1, put him third in charge at the store. While completing the requirements for his degree, John received on-the-job training that was designed to incorporate all the knowledge and skills he would need as assistant manager. Also, John was put into situations that would be similar to conditions he would encounter in his new position.

This training program consisted of John spending his part-time hours in the functional areas of produce, dairy and frozen foods, customer services, and general merchandise. Each stint lasted between six and eight weeks. During this time, John was responsible for ordering the product, displaying the product, and making sure that the department was well stocked and that its two or three employees were kept busy. These departments had full-time managers who were accountable for their individual areas. Consequently, John's responsibility was limited to the actual time he was at the store.

Upon graduation, John was promoted to assistant manager. With the change in position came a raise in pay, from $9.00 per hour to $11.00 per hour. Moreover, his responsibilities increased. From the hours of 4 p.m. to midnight, he was solely

1. This case was written by Mr. Wayne Hochwarter of Florida State University.

EXHIBIT 1 Organization Chart for Earl's Food Stores

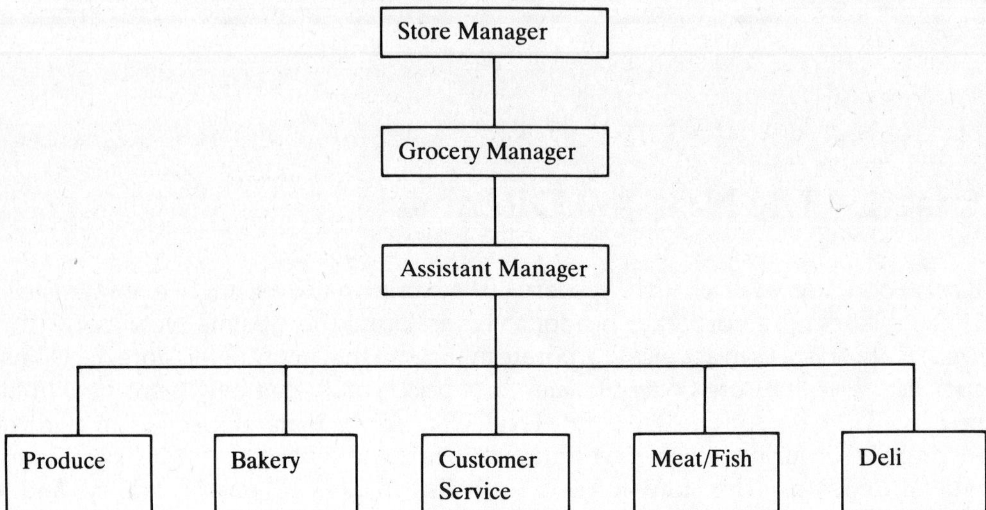

accountable for all components of store operations, as well as for the twenty or so employees that worked during these hours.

As time passed, John's eight-hour shifts became ten-, eleven-, and even twelve-hour shifts. John's store, like all stores in the chain, had a payroll budget to meet. This working and not getting paid posed the first major dilemma for John. Logic would dictate that an employee that works twelve hours should be paid for twelve hours. On the other hand, John's future with Earl's Food Stores could be damaged if he was viewed by upper management as consistently exceeding his payroll budget. Consequently, John's timecard read eight hours per shift when in reality he had worked eleven or twelve hours.

This dilemma continued for about two months. John's frustration increased until it affected his relations with vendors, employees, customers, and his wife, Karen, whom he had only recently married.

John arrived home from work, tired and depressed at 4:15 a.m., to find Karen asleep in front of the television.

KAREN. I must have dozed off. What time is it?
JOHN. Almost 4:30. Why don't you go to bed?
KAREN. I was worried about you. Why are you so late?
JOHN. I'm sorry, I should have called. I was about to call when two guys scheduled to work at ten o'clock called at five to say they were sick. By the time I got hold of someone else, I thought you'd be asleep.
KAREN. How much longer are these twelve-hour days going to go on? Can't you get more help so you won't have to work so many hours?

JOHN. I talked to my boss. He said we had more than enough help in the evenings. I guess he's right. We have enough people; it's just we don't have the right people. Most of the employees who work for me are high school students. The management hires them because there are many of them and it's inexpensive. Let me tell you, the last thing on these kids' minds is work. It's mostly parties. I feel like more of a baby sitter than a manager.
KAREN. Don't worry. It's bound to get better. Are you coming to bed?
JOHN. In a little bit. I'm gonna grab a bite to eat first. I haven't eaten all day.
KAREN. I'll fix something for you.

As John was eating, he took last week's paycheck to figure out how much he actually made per hour.

KAREN. What are you figuring out?
JOHN. Taking into account all of the hours I work, I make only $6.75 an hour. There are some cashiers that make $9.85 an hour. They didn't even go to college. This sure isn't what I had in mind when I took this job!

Analysis

1. If you were John, what would you do?
2. What management skills are needed by John in his position?
3. Analyze John's training and education as preparation for this position.
4. What factors caused this dilemma?

Case 2. The Summer Job (Before)

Harry Nelson is a sophomore at a large midwestern university majoring in marketing. His sister Joanna is a freshman at a small private college in the prelaw program. They both have been looking for a summer job to pay for school and personal expenses for the next academic year. They both enjoy the outdoors and would like a job that gives them the opportunity to be their own boss. After some discussion they decided that they both would enjoy painting houses and commercial buildings. Their analysis shows that many of the homes in their suburb are wood and frame and that some show the effects of the harsh midwestern winters. An added plus is that few competitors work in the area. A majority of the homes are owned by professionals.

They plan to create a partnership. Before proceeding, however, they want to determine the specific roles that each would have. Harry recently took a course in the principles of management and would like to apply his knowledge to this venture. As they plan for the summer, they are trying to decide how to divide up their roles.

Analysis

1. Identify specific managerial roles and skills that will be important to this venture.
2. The management process includes functions such as planning, organizing, leading, and controlling. Indicate the key factors in each of these functional areas that the siblings should consider.
3. Being both a "manager" and a painter results in a dual role that raises the possibility of conflict. What possible problems or conflicts might arise from this dual role?

Case 3. A Matter of Time

Phil Weber, president of Medford Manufacturing Company in Detroit, arrived at his desk early in the morning and found the usual stack of papers for his attention. He asked his secretary, Robert, what these papers contained. He told him that they had arrived in the mail late yesterday afternoon. Most of them were requisitions and letters for authorization from the Kentucky plant. Since Robert had screened them, Mr. Weber asked him to tell him briefly what each request contained. He thought this approach could save time. The conversation went as follows:

ROBERT. The first letter is a request for approval for the purchase of five acres of land adjoining the Lexington plant that amounts to $200,000.
WEBER. Okay, I'll sign it.
ROBERT. The next one is a request for approval to purchase an additional word processor for $895.
WEBER. I don't know anything about this one. Ask them why it's needed. If they absolutely need one, can they get one cheaper?
ROBERT. This requisition is for a new sign, which costs $650, at the entrance of the plant.
WEBER. Okay, I'll approve.
ROBERT. The next request concerns an ad for $50 as a contribution to the local Police Ball.
WEBER. Why not? Okay.
ROBERT. This one's for $100 to help cover the company's bowling league expenses.
WEBER. Absolutely not! Get more information on that one.
ROBERT. This needs your approval also. The offices need to be painted and the contractor's estimate is $985.
WEBER. Signed without comment.
ROBERT. This one's for the purchase of stationery and factory work order forms costing $450.
WEBER. Signed without comment.

On and on it went. Finally, after nearly one hour Weber was done with the requisitions, and all the incoming mail, including several express letters and faxes, were placed on his desk.

As Phil started in on these, he received a phone call from Theresa Ramos, the plant manager of the Indianapolis plant. It was already 8:45 a.m., and he would soon be late for a 9:00 a.m. meeting that he had scheduled with some of the department heads. Weber had just gotten off the phone with Ramos when Robert informed him that Jerry Kinsler, the local plant superintendent, had a crisis in the factory and wanted him to come out immediately. Weber immediately left for the floor and returned after half an hour. Weber was wondering why Jerry couldn't have solved the problem on his own. Weber thought to himself, "No matter how many decisions I make, things just seem to pile up. It looks like I'll be late for dinner again."

On his way home that evening, Phil Weber asked himself, "Why am I so busy? I don't know where all the hours go in a day. I'm always busy putting out fires and don't seem to have any time to look ahead. Most of my people think being president of this company is a piece of cake."

Analysis

1. Taking into consideration the management process, what's going on here? What would you recommend that Phil Weber do?
2. How can a manager learn to better manage his or her time?
3. How can a secretary help his or her boss manage more effectively?

Case 4. Economy Food Marts

Bruce Butler was not especially interested in going to college but had been continually told about the importance of a college education by his parents. Only his mother had attended college, and then only for one year, before going to work full-time. Bruce's dad had been an electrician for most of his life. He had gone into an apprenticeship program right after high school and had continued on in electrical work; for the most part he earned a good living.

Eventually, Bruce decided to go to a local community college program that would require only two years for completion of an associate arts degree. This enabled Bruce to work part-time to gain experience and earn some money. While at the community college he started looking for a job and had what he felt was really good luck: he was accepted into the Economy Foods student intern program. Economy Foods was a large regional supermarket chain with over one hundred stores in six states. Its student intern program had the dual purpose of providing needed experience and money for the student while giving both store and student a chance to consider permanent employment possibilities.

Bruce was first assigned to a store, and he really enjoyed it. He had a variety of jobs and met people with whom he enjoyed working. When Bruce received his certificate of arts degree, he had already received a new assignment to Economy's administrative and warehousing centers. Management was pleased with Bruce's work and offered him the opportunity to join the management training program. Since it had a good reputation and seemed to offer a step to more meaningful work while also paying more money, he gladly accepted.

During his first two years in the program, Bruce was assigned to several different stores and locations to build his familiarity and confidence in dealing with a variety of situations, customers, and managerial problems. Before taking over his "own store," Bruce received an assignment as night manager at a store located in a changing neighborhood of a large city.

The organization of the store (see Exhibit 1) was typical of other Economy Food Marts. The night manager was "second in command" and assumed responsibility for the evening store hours and closing at midnight. The supervisors who worked evenings had similar responsibility to those on "days," except that there was no meat preparation and extra people were assigned to help restock shelves and supplies for the next morning's opening.

In some ways the night manager's job was more difficult than that of the store manager. Less help was available if things went wrong, there was no one around to check records, employees were harder to retain, and many night customers were different than those who usually shopped during the day.

Economy Food Marts had developed a comprehensive set of work rules and procedures for all store operations. It also had policies in areas such as customer relations, stocking, advertising, theft, returns, store displays, pricing, purchasing, and store appearance. In addition, it had many personnel rules covering such things

EXHIBIT 1 Typical Economy Food Mart

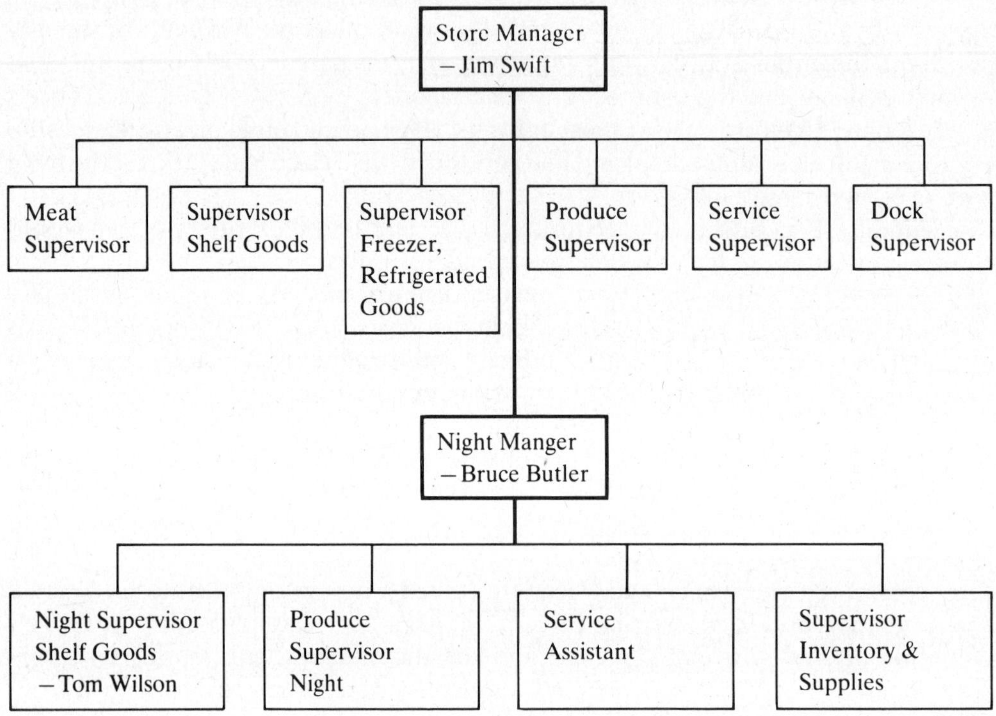

as working hours, employee behavior and dress, making out reports, and reporting how time is spent. All employees were expected to punch a time clock whenever they finished an assignment or were reassigned to a new responsibility. Standard operating procedures were used to ensure consistent performance. Finally, several years ago all important store jobs had been analyzed and standardized job descriptions and specifications had been developed. These documents provided detailed descriptions of employee work responsibilities and many details of how various tasks were to be done.

When Bruce was first assigned to the store, he was told that the store had serious employee problems. Jim Swift, the store manager, confirmed the difficulties in an especially troublesome area: "Bruce, one thing you'll have to really watch for is to make sure your crews put in a full night's work, especially the 'shelf goods' crew. They'll give you a hard time. I think it's because their supervisor, Tom Wilson, is soft and really doesn't push them. We've also had a lot of turnover in the group: of the four crew members only one has been here more than six months. I know their work is tough, moving all those cartons and goods around, but they're getting paid good money."

The next week Bruce made a point of getting to know the shelf goods crew better. Tony was the senior member of the group and often took it on himself to assign minor duties to the other three. He had worked in the store about a year and was twenty-eight years old. Jim, Roberto, and Paul were the other members of the crew. Jim and Paul worked full-time evenings to put themselves through college. Roberto was thirty-three, a bachelor who found little in common with the others and generally left right after work. Tony and Paul had become friends and would often go out for a drink after work.

After Bruce had been at the store for about a month, Jim Swift asked him, "I'd like to get your thoughts about improving the evening operation tomorrow, now that you've seen it in operation for a while!" Bruce responded, "That's great! I've been trying to work more closely with the shelf goods crew. I think they're starting to come along."

As fate would have it, that evening Tom Wilson, the shelf goods supervisor, stopped by and remarked, "It looks like we're going to need someone; I hear Roberto is looking around for another job." Bruce was dumfounded. He thought things were starting to go well. Now what would he tell Jim Swift?

Low Pay - High Stress monotonous job
Too Structured for 2nd Shift types.

Analysis

1. From an overall management perspective, what is the nature of the authority structure, policies, and regulations used to achieve store performance?
2. What are some of the factors that might affect how workers and crews respond to employment at the store?
3. What are some critical managerial skills and abilities of a store manager? A night manager?
4. From the standpoint of management training, how would you evaluate the store management training program at Economy?
5. How would you diagnose the evening shelf goods crew problem?
6. As Bruce, what do you tell Jim Swift?

Chapter 2 The Evolution of Management Thought

Case 1. Early Management Principles

Management was not created; it evolved through the needs of people. The Bible records early management principles at work.

> The next day Moses was settling disputes among the people, and he was kept busy morning till night. When Jethro (Moses' father-in-law) saw everything that Moses had to do, he asked, "What is all this that you are doing for the people? Why are you doing this all alone, with people standing here from morning till night to consult you?"
>
> Moses answered, "I must do this because the people come to me to learn God's will. When two people have a dispute, they come to me, and I decide which one of them is right, and I tell them God's commands and laws."
>
> Then Jethro said, "You are not doing this right. You will wear yourself out and these people as well. This is too much for you to do alone. Now let me give you some good advice, and God will be with you. It is right for you to represent the people before God and bring their disputes to him. You should teach them God's commands and explain to them how they should live and what they should do. But in addition, you should choose some capable men and appoint them as leaders of the people: leaders of thousands, hundreds, fifties, and tens. They must be God-fearing men who can be trusted and who cannot be bribed. Let them serve as judges for the people on a permanent basis. They can bring all the difficult cases to you, but they themselves can decide all the smaller disputes. That will make it easier for you as they share your burden. If you do this, as God commands, you will not wear yourself out, and all these people can go home with their disputes settled."
>
> Moses took Jethro's advice . . .
>
> (Exodus 18: 13–24, GNB[1])

The problems of the day called for solutions that enabled Moses to concentrate on more long-term planning issues, such as how to move large numbers of people across barren deserts. These issues would not and could not be considered under the

1. Scripture quotation identified as GNB is from the *Good News Bible,* the Bible in Today's English Version. Copyright © American Bible Society, 1966, 1971, 1976. Quote used by permission of American Bible Society.

day-to-day workload that Moses had. Hence, the solution to appoint judges over the people helped to improve the quality and quantity of the work that needed to be done. A judge over 10 individuals would handle day-to-day disputes. An individual could appeal these decisions to the judge over 50, then to the judge over 100, and then to the judge over 1,000. Moses would handle only those cases that the judges over 1,000 could not handle or that were appealed.

This management of the situation was designed to bring greater satisfaction to the people and to the leaders. The leaders were able to focus on other issues. The people had their differences resolved without lengthy waits to see Moses. The end result was a system that helped everyone.

Was there a theory behind the proposed changes made by Jethro? No, not really—it seemed to be a reaction to a problem. Much of what we see in management is a reaction to resolve a problem. We learn how to manage the situation so that people can get things done and reach their objectives in an orderly fashion. Management principles have evolved more from writers and researchers observing what is going on than from theories guiding behavior. Hence, what is studied in management courses is designed to help individuals learn from what has worked in the past in addition to what researchers and writers are learning about the present and the relationships between phenomena that are currently being discovered.

Analysis

1. What management principles, as outlined by Henri Fayol, would apply to the changes that Jethro suggested?
2. Why was it essential to have capable and honest leaders to handle the workload?
3. How would this change help the people? Shouldn't the effectiveness of management be judged by how well it helps both the leaders and those who are being managed? What about those who are clients of the system (customers, users): do they have a stake in the effectiveness of the management of the organization?
4. Why was teaching the people about the laws important for improving management in this situation?

Case 2. Mary[1]

INTERVIEWER. Mary, tell us about yourself.

MARY. I have worked for this company for ten years. This has been a good job for me. It has been the only job I have had since I graduated from high school in 1920. I lived with my family then. My dad worked for the city of Chicago in the Streets Department. My mom took care of me and my five brothers.

I guess I could have worked at better places, but this was the first job I could find and the family needed all the help it could get. Now that my dad has passed away, my income is even more important to the family than ever. I am the oldest, and all of my brothers, except one, are still in school. Jack is in the third year of high school. My youngest brother, Eric, is in fourth grade. Mitchell, the oldest brother, works down the block at the Chicago, Burlington, and Quincy railroad in the yards. He is called a car knocker. A car knocker checks over the railroad cars to make sure it is safe to move them to another location. He also attaches the air hoses so the train will have the brakes that it needs once it gets out in the main line.

We live right off Cicero Avenue, only about five blocks from the railroad yard. It is only a short walk for me to get to the plant. I think it takes only about twenty minutes even in the snow. That is a real plus because some of my friends who work downtown in the Loop have to take two buses and it takes almost an hour.

INTERVIEWER. Mary, please tell us about your job.

MARY. What is there to tell? It is kind of boring. I work on an assembly line. All day long I take one part out of a bin. Then I use a soldering gun to heat the wires that I attach to a frame for a part that is then used to make relays. That is basically all that I do for the nine hours a day that I work. And let me tell you, the job is not that exciting. Every time that you solder, the smoke comes up and hits you in the face. It smells. Sometimes the hot molten solder will splash on your hands and burn you. If it wasn't for the friends I have on the job, it would be a terrible job.

Luckily, I can talk to a couple of people that are at the same bench I am. Our portion of the plant, although smelly, is not too noisy. So we can talk. Both girls are my age and we have one older woman, in her fifties, that does the same job we do. Someone brings us parts in a bin and another person takes them away. I see my supervisor many times each day. He is a nice man, but he really doesn't bother us unless we are not getting the job done. In fact, he really did not know my name for the first six months I was here.

We are paid on what is called a piece-rate incentive system. Although we have a quota on what we should get done each day, I am also paid by the number of parts that I turn out—I guess I should really say the number of good parts that I turn out, since an inspector checks my work after I am through. I only get paid for correct solders.

Overall, I really don't have many friends on the job besides the two at my table. You really don't get much of a chance to socialize while you are at work, and the

1. This is a fictional account of the Hawthorne experiments from the viewpoint of one of the employees.

bosses only seem to take the time to tell you that you are doing OK or if there is a problem. More often than not, you hear only when there is a problem. Not much has changed in the ten years I have been here, except for the past two years, when the boys from the university have been here conducting some studies.

INTERVIEWER. Tell me about the studies.

MARY. Well, this whole crew of boys from MIT were here with a former university professor to test some management principles and changes in lighting. I am not sure about all the different things they were doing throughout the plant, but they did some tests in our room, the relay assembly room. They were really a nice bunch of fellows. They really seemed to care about what we thought about things. They wanted to know about me. Think of it, some big-shot college student spending time asking me about my job. They really cared. It was fun while they were doing their studies in our room. Some of them were kind of good-looking. On days that I knew they would be around, I would dress up some.

You could tell that we were special in the company. We had a special room for the test and the big bosses in the company would come down into the test room, and, although they didn't talk to us, they seemed to be quite interested in what the college boys were measuring. We also knew that we were special because they had us take physical exams and asked us a lot of questions about how we felt and how we thought the job might be improved. It was really fun. I really wanted to do something special for these people. For once, someone took an interest in us, our jobs, and how to make them better. At least for a couple of years, I felt we were doing some things that might have made a difference.

INTERVIEWER. What sorts of things were done in the studies?

MARY. They changed the way we got paid. It was based more on how well the group produced. In addition, they kept changing the hours that we worked, the rest periods, the number of days we worked per week, and the length of the lunch periods. In any event, we were really treated as special by the group.

INTERVIEWER. How long did the study last?

MARY. I heard the study lasted six years, from 1927 to 1933. However, I was only involved in the study for two years, from 1930 to 1932. In 1932 I was laid off because of the depression. By the time I was rehired the experiments were over and the place was back to normal.

INTERVIEWER. Normal? Didn't things change as a result of the studies?

MARY. No. At least I didn't see much change. We went back to the same work rules as before.

Analysis

1. Why would Mary be so appreciative of having someone pay attention to her at work?

2. Would putting the experimental group in a special room with special treatment possibly affect the outcome? Why? The effect that distorted the results of the study has come to be called the "Hawthorne effect."
3. How could one measure the effects of different rest periods on productivity without producing a "Hawthorne effect?"
4. The Hawthorne Studies have been considered the beginning point for the human relations movement. Why?

Case 3. The Granger Inn

Ralph and Dotty Granger were concerned about why their business was off since they moved their restaurant one block down from their previous location. The food was the same and was cooked by the same chef, yet business was down by almost a third. It sure was scary, because a third of the business made the difference between profit and loss.

The Granger Inn was started in 1966 in a small, rather plain building. There were twenty tables that were covered with plastic tablecloths. Ralph worked in the kitchen, and Dotty worked the tables with one or two other waitresses. The restaurant was crowded on weekends, with lines most weekends out the door. On football weekends (the University of Michigan was nearby), the place was crowded from after the game was over until closing, with even longer lines out the door. There was a bar at one end of the room. Behind the bar was a cooler that had windows to the bar. Through the windows, patrons could see the beef and other meats and poultry hanging in the cooler. Although Ralph worked in the kitchen most of the time, he made many tours of the tables to chat with the patrons and make sure that they were having a good time. Most of the customers were local residents of the area, and many were farmers and blue-collar employees from the nearby factories and railroad yards. Since Ralph used to own a farm and had a boy working at one of the railroad yards, he knew many of the customers by first name and took pride in that accomplishment.

The success of the restaurant was much greater than Dotty and Ralph had ever dreamed it would be. Within ten years they had paid off the mortgage on the building and had saved enough to create the restaurant that they had always wanted. Then just down the street, they found a very nice building that was owned by a building designer. The designer had made the building a showcase of classy modern design. As you came into the office, you saw a thousand-dollar chandelier with a winding staircase to the second level, which overlooked the foyer. Ralph and Dotty loved it. It could really bring some class into their dream restaurant. Although the building was more than what they wanted to pay, they felt that business would be so good that they could afford the huge monthly mortgage.

They purchased the building and moved in. They sold their old building in a matter of months. A week after they opened at their new location, another restaurant opened in their old location. Ralph and Dotty kept the same name for their new restaurant. They kept the same chef, but both their waitresses decided that they were ready to retire. Hence, the restaurant had a whole new set of waitresses. The new restaurant was twice the size of the old restaurant and was split into several rooms. This and the desire to have a greeter at the foyer kept Dotty busy and away from the eating areas. The increased complexity of the kitchen kept Ralph busy in the kitchen most of the time. In addition, he felt he didn't want to go into the eating area because he was too messy from food preparation. They had to increase prices about 20 percent over what they had at the old location, but they felt few would recognize the price changes because the menu was much more specialized than at the old location.

Hence, instead of having basic steak, they had several different kinds of steak, seafood, and poultry.

The decline in business was a real surprise to both Dotty and Ralph. Some of the regulars they had seen for years came in only a few times and never again. It wasn't because of the food. Dotty heard comments such as "the place just isn't the same, and it just is cold—not like it was in the old location."

The restaurant that took their new location had really good crowds. Even though the food was not as good as when Dotty and Ralph ran the place, it still seemed to do well.

Ralph and Dotty were really perplexed. They really didn't know how to interpret comments such as the above, and they had no idea why people weren't coming to their new restaurant. They were getting very concerned. They even tried to buy back their old restaurant, but the new owners refused. Ralph and Dotty were getting quite worried about their life savings that were in the new building, and they feared that if things didn't change they might lose everything. From their calculations, they only had about three months to improve things.

Out of desperation and a lack of ability to pay for management consultants, Ralph and Dotty called a school nearby to see if they could find some help. They wanted someone to design and give out a questionnaire to people in the community and to customers of the restaurant to find out their perceptions.

The team of students from a university market research class decided not to use a questionnaire but to try to find answers to Ralph and Dotty's questions through the use of several focus groups. A focus group is a group of individuals that are brought together as a qualitative research tool to explore individual attitudes and ideas about a particular problem. The market research team selected a group of customers as one focus group. Then they selected two groups of customers that were regulars at the old restaurant and had visited the new restaurant at least once. A final focus group was composed of those who had heard of the Granger Inn yet had not visited it.

The focus groups' discussions led to the following conclusions. First, the service in the restaurant had declined. The personnel didn't seem to care about the customers as they used to. Second, the atmosphere of the location was too upscale for the former customers, yet to noncustomers the restaurant was a "very casual dining environment."

Analysis

1. How might Ralph and Dotty react to the results?
2. Discuss the importance of looking at a restaurant from a systems perspective. What are some related variables that are important in the success of a restaurant?
3. Are physical facilities a variable in question 2? Why?

Case 4. The Importance of Setting Standards

Denzel Markham was concerned about the performance of his truck drivers. Denzel had a fleet of trucks that hauled lumber from the forest to the mill. A truck driver received an hourly wage. Denzel felt that there really was not much incentive for the truck drivers. They made only a dozen trips a day, whereas Denzel felt that twenty trips were possible. But he wasn't sure. However, the company gave Denzel a bonus based on the performance of his unit, and Denzel was going to try his best to improve performance.

Denzel first wanted to get a measure of what was possible. As a former truck driver, he knew about what it takes to load a truck, how to safely drive it down the mountain, and how to get it unloaded. After watching for a week and making some time charts, Denzel knew that twenty round trips were indeed possible. However, the current average of twelve round trips had been the average performance for the past several years. Denzel knew that just demanding it would not work; he had to try to set the conditions that would lead the truck drivers to want to meet Denzel's goal.

First, Denzel changed the pay system so that a truck driver received payment based on the number of trips that were made. The result of this action was an increase in the number of trips but a decrease in the amount of lumber carried each trip.

Denzel's second change was to modify the pay system so that a truck driver received an incentive for the amount of wood carried each day, for safe driving, and for having a truck that met safety standards as set forth by the company. A bonus was paid for reaching the various standards that were specified. In addition, a group bonus was given to each shift based on the group's performance toward meeting the standards. Denzel thought the group standard would encourage the rest of the group to try to influence the driver that was not meeting standards. He set up a pay system that gave a set amount to the driver for approaching, meeting, or exceeding each of ten standards that were established. The compensation received for each standard varied. The amount of lumber carried per day was worth much more than reaching the safety standards. However, reaching each standard was important in making a good day's wage.

Denzel's salary system was first met with a lot of hostility by the drivers. They felt that even though reaching standards would mean a 20 percent increase in pay, the level of effort needed to reach that pay level was asking too much compared with the previous wage system. Nearly ten of the hundred drivers quit. The others were slow to respond to the new system. Performance even dropped.

Denzel was perplexed and angry. He knew that standards could be reached, but he also knew that he would need the support of the drivers to do it. So he had to try something else. Denzel modified the pay system again. He reinstituted a basic day wage similar to what was in effect before he made the changes. Next, he offered additional incentives based on the weight of wood shipped and safety. An additional bonus was paid once the standard was reached. Hence, drivers could work under the old system and earn the same amount of pay they did before, but they could also work to meet the daily standard and receive additional pay with an additional bonus once the standard was met. Denzel hoped this system would reduce driver dissent while still motivating drivers to reach the standard. Without the special bonus there would still be an incentive to work toward the standard, but Denzel thought the bonus would add an additional incentive. The results were gratifying. Performance reached the standard within two weeks.

Analysis

1. How would scientific management have helped Denzel learn about an appropriate standard?
2. Why do you think that there was worker resistance to the change in the way of calculating compensation?
3. Why do you suppose the final change resulted in worker acceptance of the program?

Case 5. Human Relations Research at Sears, Roebuck in the 1940s: A Memoir[1]

Abstract

During the 1940s, Sears, Roebuck conducted extensive research on organization behavior. This paper discusses two important features of that work: employee attitude surveys, and the Sears "X-Y Study" dealing with the impact of organization structure on employee behavior and the influence of executive attitudes on organization structure.

I. Background

A significant amount of human relations research was conducted by Sears, Roebuck and Co. during the decade of the 1940s, with some carryover into the 1950s. Much of this was done in cooperation with the Committee on Human Relations in Industry of the University of Chicago and with Social Research, Inc., a private consulting firm headed by the two principals of the Committee on Human Relations, W. Lloyd Warner and Burleigh B. Gardner, and largely staffed with personnel trained by the committee. The origins and accomplishments of the committee are recorded in the companion paper to this one by David G. Moore, a member of the Sears personnel staff during the period under review and the chief liaison between the company and the committee. The purpose of the present paper is to record Sears' participation in these collaborative efforts.

Sears, Roebuck Management

The Sears organization built by General Robert E. Wood was remarkable in many ways (Worthy, 1984). Wood was an Army man, trained at West Point and with a distinguished record as head of supply and manpower services in the building of the Panama Canal and as chief of the Army Quartermaster Corps during the First World War. Because of his experience in large-scale procurement, he joined Montgomery Ward in 1919 as merchandising vice president, a post from which he was summarily fired in the fall of 1924, chiefly for his insistent urging that the company add retail stores to its mail order operations, a course adamantly opposed by Ward's president.

1. James C. Worthy, "Human Relations Research at Sears, Roebuck in the 1940s: A Memoir," in *Papers Dedicated to the Development of Modern Management, Special 50th Anniversary Issue of the Proceedings of Academy of Management*, ed. D. A. Wren and J. A. Pearce II, 1986, pp. 36–44. Used with permission.

The head of Sears, Roebuck, Julius Rosenwald, recognizing his good fortune in thus having a man of Wood's experience becoming unexpectedly available, hired him immediately, with a commitment to support his radical retail notions. Early in 1925, Wood opened his first Sears store, and others followed. The venture was eminently successful, and three years later Wood was named president and chief executive. Under his leadership, Sears not only survived the Great Depression but learned from it many lessons that enabled Wood to build in a few years' time the largest and most profitable merchandising business the world had ever known.

Strong Personnel Function

For an Army man, Wood had a curious distrust of authoritarian direction and control from above. His store managers, and to a considerable extent the department managers within the local stores as well, had wide discretion in the selection of merchandise to be carried, the quantities to be ordered, and the prices to be charged. To Wood, it was fundamental that managers at all levels worked best if they were held accountable for results but left free, within broad limits, in the ways they accomplished those results (Worthy, 1984, chapt. 7, "Organization Policies"). But Wood did not believe in blind delegation. For this kind of organization to work, special care had to be taken in the selection and placement of people, and this called for a strong personnel department.

Wood was also well aware that a widely-dispersed system of mail order plants and retail stores, each functioning with considerable autonomy, required that positive measures be taken to avoid friction and divisiveness between employees and management, to maintain high levels of morale, and to provide motivation for superior individual and group performance (Worthy, 1984, chapt. 9, "Employee Policies"). This, too, called for a strong personnel department.

In Clarence B. Caldwell, one of his best store managers, Wood found the man he needed to head that critical function. Appointed director of retail personnel in 1934, his responsibilities broadened in due course to include the entire company and he became one of the most influential and respected of all Wood's lieutenants. Encouraged by Wood to develop rational and soundly-based policies for all aspects of Sears' personnel operations, Caldwell in 1938 established a research and planning function within his department, and it was my great good fortune to be hired for that responsibility.

With college majors in English and economics, I was not a trained management or research person. However, I had been an assistant deputy administrator of the National Recovery Administration, deeply committed to the humane values of the early New Deal, and after aiding in writing the history of NRA following its demise had served as personnel manager for a Milwaukee department store. I was attracted to Sears because it was obviously a fast-growing company with good opportunities for advancement, and because it was already gaining a reputation for excellence in management-employee relationships. I was also intrigued by the fact that General Wood was one of the few big businessmen who had been a strong supporter of

President Roosevelt before breaking with him over his war policies. It seemed to me that Sears was the kind of company I wanted to work for. I was not disappointed.

II. Employee Attitude Surveys

One of the first undertakings of my new unit in the Sears personnel department was the design and implementation of a standard compensation plan for all retail employees. Other activities included studies of employee turnover and the demographic characteristics of company personnel, projections of future executive and employee requirements, designing better methods of selection and training, analyzing the operations of employee benefit plans, and exploring possible means for improving them.

Initiation of Attitude Survey Program

A particularly significant phase of the work undertaken by the research and planning unit was the development of systematic means for assessing employee attitudes and morale. By 1939, General Wood and other senior Sears officers were growing increasingly uncomfortable with the fact that they no longer had the close touch with day-to-day affairs of the rapidly expanding retail system they once had had, and Caldwell and I were directed to come up with a means for providing "a reliable and continuing flow of information about . . . how we are getting along with our people" (Worthy, 1984, p. 152; see also Jones, 1952).

It seemed clear from the outset that the best way to find out what employees thought about their jobs and the company was to ask them, and for this purpose an outside firm, Houser Associates, was retained to design and administer questionnaires which employees answered anonymously (Houser, 1938). By the end of 1939, a number of experimental surveys had been made of representative stores, and the results were encouraging. Wood and his fellow officers felt that a good start had been made and that the surveys were giving them at least some of the information they wanted. The project continued on a gradually expanding basis until Pearl Harbor, when it was suspended for the duration of the war.

Houser's approach was essentially that of traditional market research: count the number of people who respond in different ways to a series of questions. The results were interesting and useful as far as they went, but enigmatic in many respects. Clearly, something more than counting was needed. As my staff and I studied the numbers, we became more and more convinced that social influences of some form were at work and that a sociological approach to the data might prove useful.

Interpretation of Survey Results

By fortunate coincidence, early in 1941 a young man with a master's degree in sociology from the University of Illinois applied to me for a job. He was David G. Moore, at that time a member of the personnel research staff of Western Electric Company. I was impressed by his ability to describe work relations phenomena in terms that seemed to make sense. I hired him at once and put him to work analyzing the data our employee attitude surveys were beginning to produce.

Moore organized the Houser data in new ways, with interesting results. While within all groups there were relatively normal statistical distributions, there were significant variations by age, sex, length of service, type of work, level of authority, size of store, size and economic base of city, geographical region, and so on. The data began to be more meaningful, but raised even more intriguing questions as to why there should be such large differences in the attitudes of different groups toward precisely the same thing.

As the survey data were studied further, it became increasingly clear that store organizations, and probably commercial and industrial organizations in general, were "social systems," and that parts of the systems were closely interrelated. Compensation was not an independent variable, any more than hours of work, working conditions, or quality of supervision, and changes in any of these or in other significant elements in the working situation could not be made without affecting other elements and without modifying the whole. The importance of relationships and the analysis of attitudes and behavior in terms of group identity and organizational status loomed increasingly large in our thinking (Worthy, 1943).

During this period, Moore often spoke to me about Dr. Burleigh B. Gardner whom he had come to know at Western Electric. Gardner was a social anthropologist on the staff of William J. Dickson doing research on the Hawthorne counselling program, and Moore had been one of his assistants. From Moore's own training and from what he had learned from Gardner, he was convinced that some of the concepts of social anthropology, particularly those related to status and social class, would be useful in what we were trying to understand at Sears. Sometime in late 1942 or early 1943, Moore arranged for the three of us to have lunch at the Palmer House. That was the beginning of a long period of fruitful collaboration.

Shortly thereafter I met with Gardner and W. Lloyd Warner, who were then in process of organizing the Committee on Human Relations in Industry at the University of Chicago. I was as well impressed by Warner as by Gardner, and the plans they had in mind held intriguing possibilities. Sears became one of the first corporate supporters of their new venture.

Post-War Planning

During the war years, General Wood directed his corporate staff departments to utilize whatever time they could spare from otherwise pressing duties to prepare for the period of peace that would eventually come. Among other things, the personnel department addressed the subject of improving the employee survey program, and the services of the Committee on Human Relations were engaged for that purpose.

The new survey program drew heavily on Warner's and Gardner's comprehensive grasp of the concepts of social anthropology and their experience with the methods of field research. Gardner's involvement in the non-directive interviewing program of Western Electric was also useful. Because Sears planned to use its program company-wide rather than at a single plant as at Western Electric, reliance could not be placed on non-directive interviewing alone; there were simply too many people and too much ground to cover.

The program as it finally emerged ready for use as soon as the war was over combined questionnaires and interviews. A simplified questionnaire was administered to all employees in a store or other company unit, and the statistical results analyzed to make tentative identification of areas which appeared to represent problems. A team trained in non-directive techniques then interviewed executives and employees in the unit itself, and others likely to have knowledge of the problems, to learn more about what caused them. The questionnaires were used somewhat as "geiger counters" to locate areas meriting closer investigation, which might be certain departments, or particular classes of employees, or some aspect of company policy or local practice, or perhaps some recent event. In addition to locating areas of difficulty, the questionnaires also gave some indication of what the difficulties might be. Armed with information such as this, the interviewers knew where to look and what to look for (Worthy, 1947, 1950).

Although Gardner was deeply involved in designing the survey program and he and his committee staff in training survey teams and interpreting survey results, most of the actual survey work was conducted by members of the Sears personnel staff. Gardner was convinced from his extensive contacts with Sears employees in the course of developing the program that their level of confidence in the integrity of the company was sufficiently high that it would not be necessary for the questionnaires to be administered and the interviews conducted by staff of the Committee on Human Relations or by an outside firm, as had been done before the war with Houser Associates. This was a wise move because work as a member of survey teams proved to be valuable training for future personnel executives.

The New Survey Program

By this time Moore, under my general supervision, headed the Sears personnel research and planning staff and was in immediate charge of the survey program. His training as a sociologist, his experience with the personnel interviewing program at Western Electric, and his continuing collaboration with Gardner and Warner enabled him to provide the creative direction the program required, including training the program staff and interpreting survey results. Under Moore's leadership and with Gardner's aid, the staff developed high orders of analytical skill, and learned to use the questionnaire results much as a doctor uses tests as part of his procedure in diagnosing patient ills.

At one point, thought was given to the possibility of developing "a typology of the malfunctioning of organizations" which might be useful in diagnosing organizational problems. This possibility was suggested by the frequency with which profiles of questionnaire and interview data tended to form patterns which began to grow familiar, and the tendency for certain kinds of problems to occur in identifiable syndromes (Worthy, April 1950). Unfortunately, because of other research demands this possibility was not systematically pursued, although recognition of regularities definitely enhanced the skills of the interviewing teams.

The survey program was undertaken initially for the straight-forward purpose of finding how well employees liked their jobs and whether there were factors in the work situation causing dissatisfaction. The assumption was that once any such factors were discovered, necessary corrective action could be taken and all would be well. This assumption proved only partially valid, because in the new survey program we soon learned that many employee relations problems could not be understood, much less influenced, except in terms of the broader context of the organization in which they had developed.

Gradually, the scope of the surveys was expanded to include the functioning of the unit (store, factory, etc.) as a whole and the entire pattern of technical processes and formal and informal relationships which comprise the unit. In recognition of this broader scope, the name of the program was changed from "morale surveys" to "organization surveys," and rather than simply discovering causes of employee dissatisfaction the purpose became to analyze strains or cleavages without operating units which might impede their functioning. In this context, determining levels of morale served chiefly as an aid in locating problem areas for further study by a field survey team (Worthy, January 1950).

A major early conclusion of the survey program was stated in a 1949 memorandum to Clarence Caldwell: "High morale is a by-product of sound organization. It is not a result that can be achieved by and for itself; above all, it is not a result of 'being nice to people' or plying them with favors. High morale is not something to be achieved at the expense of good operating results. The same policies, attitudes, and practices which are best calculated to produce good operating results are precisely the policies, attitudes, and practices which produce high levels employee morale" (Worthy, 1949).

Findings of the Survey Program

Both internal and external factors were found to influence morale. Factors internal to Sears included job status, work pressures, tensions arising from differences in job goals and interests, tensions arising from hierarchical relationships, and disruptions caused by changes in management, company policies, job methods, and systems of rewards.

Significant influences on the quality of management-employee relations external to the company itself were also found, and while these were beyond the reach of management control it was important that management understand them. For example, the higher levels of morale generally prevalent among women employees as compared with men appeared to be explainable by differences in the social roles, expectations, and demands of the two sexes. (This was in the 1940s; the comparisons are probably different today.) Other differences could be associated with social roles related to race and ethnicity. Levels of morale in retail stores were higher than those of warehouses and factories, apparently because of greater ideological agreement between salespeople and management. Closer ideological affinity also helped explain the fact that higher morale was found in the rural south than in the industrial north, and among employees with higher- rather than lower-ranked jobs. Morale tended to vary inversely by size of unit and size of city in which the unit was located. (For a typology of social factors, see Moore, 1950.)

At a broader level, we learned that human organizations tend to hold together to the extent that they have meaning to the people in them, and ceremonials such as service anniversaries, retirement banquets, award presentations and the like provide opportunities for shared experiences which help people identify with each other and with the organization. A great deal has been written about Sears' famous profit-sharing plan, but its importance as a positive factor in employee relationships became better understood when its role was recognized as expressing the unity of interest between employees, management, and shareholders, in effect a unifying symbol about which the entire organization revolved.

Another valuable insight gained from the surveys was the fact that around any technology—store, mail order plant, factory, whatever—there develops a set of subfunctions, departments, and jobs which determine to a great extent the kinds of relationships that will develop among employees in various activities. The importance of the job and job relationships in determining employee attitudes was particularly apparent to the survey team since jobs in the stores, while not uniform, were generally similar from unit to unit. Work on the selling floor, or the receiving room, or the auditing department varied little from one store to the next, and the survey team reached the point where it could anticipate how appliance salesmen, repair servicemen, office employees, and others would express themselves simply because of the nature of their jobs. This insight proved valuable in diagnosing organizational problems.

One of the most important things gained from working with Gardner and Warner and with the staff of the Committee on Human Relations, including William Foote Whyte who succeeded Gardner as executive director of the committee, was the ability to explain complex human behavior to hard-nosed executives in terms they could readily understand. People who had learned to recognize the difference between a corner office and one down the hall readily grasped the concept of status symbols. The idea of social class and differences in class behavior made sense to them, and made it easier to explain some of the problems disclosed by the surveys.

In a field unrelated to employee behavior, I will never forget a meeting of Lloyd Warner with a group of senior merchandising executives in which he explained something that had bothered them for a long time: the fact that while Sears appliances enjoyed wide popularity among the rich and famous, even the wives of company executives were reluctant to buy their dresses from Sears. Warner pointed out that whereas a refrigerator or a power saw is relatively neutral in terms of social class identification, the clothes a woman wears are far more personal and an important way of expressing her idea of the place she considers herself to hold in society. The look of enlightenment that lit up faces in the audience was amusing to see.

Ancillary Values

In addition to its other values, because of the manner in which it was organized and administered the survey program developed into one of the company's most effective general executive training tools. Care was taken from the outset to keep the program from being perceived as threatening, and in point of fact the surveys were conducted primarily for the benefit of the manager or other executive in direct charge of the unit involved. Surveys were concerned not merely with identifying the existence and origin of difficulties; their primary purpose was problem-solving, and to this end great reliance was placed on the local executives themselves rather than on the survey team. The central objective was to give the responsible executive a better understanding of the way his organization was functioning, the various influences at work in his particular situation, and the ways these were impacting the attitudes and behavior of his people. At the same time, an effort was made to give the executive a more effective way of looking at his organization and its problems, with the expectation that with a better way of thinking about both he would be in a better position to take constructive action directed at the root of difficulties rather than at their superficial symptoms (Worthy, Gardner, and Whyte, 1946–47).

After a survey was completed and its results analyzed, the member of the personnel staff under whose direction it had been conducted would meet with the executive responsible for the unit and his staff. After reviewing the survey findings, the local executives would be questioned as to what interpretation might be put upon them, and a discussion would follow as to the best means for dealing with whatever problems had been uncovered. The survey "report" generally consisted of a memorandum to the manager saying, in effect, that "in our meeting we agreed that such and such things required attention and that such and such action would be taken." The local executives were thus intimately involved both in identifying problems and in designing solutions. It was an interesting example of the "case method" of teaching, with the considerable pedagogical advantage that the "case" was not some abstract problem but the company unit for which the executive himself was personally responsible. The learning results were impressive.

The program proved valuable in many other ways as well. It provided management with insight and understanding it could have gained in no other way of the actual state of affairs within the very large and widely-dispersed organization into which Sears by the late 1940s had grown. It produced a comprehensive body of factual material by which management was able to refine and improve personnel policies under the rapidly-changing conditions of the post-war period. In some ways, its most valuable contribution was the message it carried to employees of management's genuine concern for running the business in ways that would serve their needs as well as the company's.

The survey program developed into an invaluable administrative tool, and with modifications is still being used by Sears as a significant feature of that company's widely-admired personnel system.

III. Social Research, Inc.

Sears' work with the Committee on Human Relations in Industry went far beyond the survey program, and heavy demands were placed on the committee's resources. We at Sears became increasingly impatient with the difficulties and delays of working through university channels. Our primary interest was in solving problems, and sometimes fast action was needed. But to start a project, it was necessary first to prepare a detailed written plan, which then had to be reviewed by university authorities and finally converted into a contract to be signed by appropriate officers of the university and the company. Weeks and sometimes longer were required to get projects under way, and while this might have been fast by university standards it was often exasperatingly slow by our needs. Early in 1947, therefore, I urged Gardner and Warner to establish an independent consulting firm with which we could deal. With Clarence Caldwell's and General Wood's ready approval, I offered them a contract that would underwrite the basic expenses of their new firm for its first two years of operation.

Thus was born Social Research, Inc., with Warner as chairman and Gardner as president. Warner continued for several years longer as professor at the University of Chicago, until moving to Michigan State in 1959 to introduce the study of social sciences into that university's School of Business. Gardner severed his formal connection with the university to devote himself full time to SRI, as the new firm quickly became known. He was succeeded as executive director of the committee by William Foote Whyte who served in that post until 1948 when he accepted a professorship at Cornell University.

With Whyte's leaving, the Committee on Human Relations in Industry was disbanded. It had operated for a total of only five years, but those years had been remarkably productive, particularly in demonstrating the utility of applying the concepts of social anthropology to the practical problems of business and industry. And those concepts themselves were greatly enriched by exposure to modern forms of economic organization rather than to those of primitive societies which had previously been the discipline's primary focus of attention.

Work with Social Research, Inc.

The work and influence of the committee did not die with it. Relieved of the burden of university red tape, Sears' work with Gardner and Warner through Social Research, Inc. grew apace.

Some of the more significant of that work during the years 1947–52 included studies of special problem groups such as low status employees, commission salesmen, warehouse workers, and veterans returning from military service. A study of relationships between the company's sources of supply and its buying organization was particularly useful, as was an analysis of internal relationships within the buying organization itself. A study of the social class background of upwardly mobile employees proved useful in refining the company's recruitment and executive development policies.

In the course of several studies on a variety of subjects, attention was given to factors shaping the size and structure of administrative units within larger components of organization, and the influence of such factors on decision-making processes (Worthy, 1952). All told, an extensive number and variety of projects were undertaken in cooperation with Gardner and Social Research, Inc. for the purpose of improving the effectiveness of the company's organizational and managerial practices and for enhancing the quality of management-employee relationships.

While some of the results of this work were published, most of it was not. Unlike studies conducted under university auspices, which typically have publication of some kind in view, studies conducted in collaboration with SRI were basically done for administrative purposes, that is, to provide officers and executives with information and proposals that would be helpful in the discharge of their managerial responsibilities; many "reports" were simply in the form of memoranda. When a study had served the particular purpose for which it was made, it was usually filed away and attention turned to other more immediately pressing projects. Sponsored work with the Committee on Human Relations was essentially "scholarly," while that done with SRI tended to be much more along "consulting" lines. Fortunately, some of the more important results of this work found its way into Moore's doctoral dissertation (Moore, 1950), and to that extent has a measure of permanence it would not otherwise enjoy.

IV. The Sears "X-Y Study"

In retrospect, one aspect of the collaborative research conducted by Sears and SRI during the late 1940s is of particular interest and significance. This was the study of the reciprocal effects of organizational structure on manager and worker behavior and on the dynamics and quality of working relationships within organizations. Because this study has been alluded to from time to time in various connections but has never been fully reported before, it merits presentation here in salient part (Worthy, 1959, 1984).

In the spring of 1949 a sharp recession hit the retail industry, and General Wood with his customary decisiveness moved quickly to deal with the resulting problems. As one phase of this effort, the corporate personnel department was directed to investigate how representative store managers were coping with the problems of falling sales and profits and what could be learned from their experience. Other appropriate action, of course, was taken along lines of merchandising and expense control, but the personnel department was asked to make its own study, paying particular attention to staffing and organizational matters. The machinery of the employee survey program, by this time operating smoothly and the staff well-skilled in field research techniques, proved of great value for purposes of fact-finding and analysis. The resources of Social Research, Inc., and particularly the counsel of Gardner, were also called upon.

This study is described in detail in a manuscript written by me in 1952 and expanded in 1953, but because of the pressures of other work never completed for publication. I have a copy in my personal files, and another is on file in Sears Archives. An early draft was loaned to William Foote Whyte and summarized by him in his *Modern Methods in Social Research* (Whyte, 1952), and again in *Man and Organization* (Whyte, 1959).

"Tall" vs "Flat" Organization Structures

Studies previous to this had given indication of the superiority in many respects of relatively simple as compared with more complex forms of organization. It was Gardner who first called attention to the fact that Sears often violated the dictum that spans of management control should be kept as short as possible. For example, rather than the five or six subordinates per superior generally considered in the literature as the desirable limit, Sears had at this time nearly fifty senior merchandising executives reporting to a single merchandising vice president, with no intervening level of supervision; contrary to standard theory, the system seemed to work very well. Similar broad spans of control existed in other parts of the Sears organization, including some of the retail stores. Gardner coined the term "flat" and "tall" organizations to characterize the two types of structure.

Under General Wood's highly decentralized plan of management, executives at each level were given wide latitude as to the manner in which they set up their organizations. For many years, Wood forbade the use of organization charts for the stores, saying to us in the personnel department that "If you publish a chart, managers will think that's the way you want them to organize their stores. But I want them to organize their stores in the way they feel they can get the best results, and they can tell that better than you can." After repeated requests, Wood finally gave me permission to prepare organization charts to give to professors and others outside the company who asked for them, but with strict admonition that they were to have no circulation within the company.

Because of this latitude given store managers, many otherwise similar stores were organized differently: some, for example, were "tall," while others were "flat." The study on which the personnel department and SRI was now embarked undertook as its first objective an examination to determine whether either of the two types of organization was superior to the other, and if so in what ways.

"X" Stores and "Y" Stores

Two groups of stores, carefully matched for comparability in all respects but one, were selected for study. Sears retail stores were classified as "A," "B," and "C," depending on size and lines of merchandise carried. All stores included in the study were medium-size "B" stores located in the same general geographic area and in communities of approximately similar size and economic base. They carried the same lines of merchandise, and were roughly comparable in number of employees and volume of business. They differed in only one important respect: structure of organization. Because all were "B" stores, for convenience of the study those with "flat" structures were designated "X" and those with "tall" structures "Y."

Stores in the "X" group had a minimum number of staff and supervisory employees and simple structures. There was a store manager at the top, a single assistant manager, and approximately 30 managers of merchandise departments—"divisions," in Sears' terminology. There were, in addition, the usual non-selling or "service" activities such as shipping and receiving, customer service, maintenance, unit control, etc. In theory, all heads of the merchandise departments reported directly to the store manager, with the assistant manager usually responsible for the service functions. In practice, the store and assistant managers usually worked together as a team, dividing responsibilities on a more or less informal, ad hoc basis. There was no level of supervision between the two at the top and approximately thirty-five heads of selling and non-selling activities.

Stores in the "Y" group were set up on a more hierarchical basis. Instead of all functions reporting directly to a two-man management team, the organization was broken down into a series of sections. Instead of a single assistant manager, there was likely to be a hard lines merchandise manager supervising the hard lines departments, a soft lines merchandise manager supervising soft lines, and an operating assistant supervising service activities. In some cases there was also a personnel manager, who typically reported to the operating assistant.

In separating out these two groups of stores for purposes of study, the investigators had been prepared to find differences between them. They did, in fact, find differences in payroll costs and profits as percentages of sales—in favor, as expected, of the more simply organized "X" group with fewer higher-paid supervisors. But they found other important differences as well.

Differences between "X" and "Y" Stores

For one thing, the department managers in the "X" stores tended to be more skillful merchants than those in the "Y" stores, a trait apparent not only from personal interviews but from the merchandising results of their departments. Morale as measured by attitude surveys was higher in the "X" than in the "Y" stores, and this was especially true at the department manager level. Finally, a review of the records of the two groups going back over a period of several years disclosed that larger numbers of people had been promoted out of the "X" than the "Y" stores to higher levels of responsibility. Differences such as these between the two types of structures had not been expected, and a search began for explanations.

To the team of investigators made up of men and women experienced in the methods of field research, the answers were not difficult to find. For one thing, in the "X" stores, the manager and his assistant—the "management team"—were spread very thin. The number of department heads reporting to them was such that the amount of time they could devote to any one of them, on average, was small. Under these circumstances, the only possible way for them to accomplish their own jobs was to have high quality people heading their departments. For example, the only way a store manager could be sure of having a good hardware business was to find—either from within the organization or elsewhere—a good hardware merchant; and so on through all the other departments. Precisely because they themselves were spread so thin, the manager and his assistant were compelled to seek out people of initiative and ability, people who could take responsibility, who could be trusted to use good judgment, who could move ahead on their own without having to clear everything in advance. By and large, the department managers in the "X" type stores measured up to these specifications, and their results showed it.

The situation tended to be rather different in the "Y" stores. Here, people at the merchandise manager and operating assistant level tended to be of fairly high caliber, but those at the department manager level tended to compare rather less well with their opposite numbers in the other group of stores. The investigators found that managers with specialized assistants tended to look to these for results and were not under the same compulsion to build high levels of competence at the individual department level. The differences in caliber of department manager personnel were thus the direct consequence of differences in organization structure and of the styles of management the structures tended to call for.

But the explanation for the differences in capabilities did not stop here. In addition to pressures on the managers of the "X" stores to staff their departments with superior talent, those placed in department manager positions in such stores were exposed to a kind of experience that tended to develop their capacities in a particularly favorable manner. Because the store manager and his assistant could give only a limited amount of time, on average, to each department, the heads of those departments were forced to assume responsibility. To a rather remarkable extent, they had to make their own decisions on running their departments, and stand or fall by the results.

The task of their counterparts in the "Y" stores was considerably less demanding. The head of the hardware department submitted his merchandising plans to the hard lines merchandise manager, and because this individual would be held responsible by his store manager he typically would review the plans in great detail, make numerous changes as his judgment dictated, and the final plan would be *his* and not the department head's. The learning environment in these stores was much less favorable than in the other.

Close observation of the way the two types of stores functioned indicated that one of the definite disadvantages of the more complex organization was that it safeguarded people too closely against making mistakes. It was difficult for department managers to get far off base or to stay off base very long. But precisely for this reason, they were deprived of one of their most valuable means of learning. Much of the superiority of department manager personnel found in the stores with the flat organization structures was clearly attributable to the fact that the nature of the structure within which they worked tended to force them to accept responsibility, to exercise initiative, to develop self-confidence, and to learn from experience.

Structure and Behavior

Note has already been taken of the larger number of promotable people originating in the "X" stores. This was due in part to the greater necessity in such stores for picking high quality personnel and the more stimulating environment for personal growth in which they worked. But beyond these factors were marked differences in the styles of leadership typically found in the two types of stores.

Because managers and assistants in the more simply-organized stores did not have time to supervise in detail, their leadership tended to be chiefly in terms of setting goals, leaving much of the task of determining the means for achieving them to the department managers themselves. In stores with the taller, more hierarchical organizations, the managers and their intermediate staffs generally not only set the goals for the various departments, but worked out in considerable detail the manner in which the goals were to be accomplished. Much more than those in the "X" stores, department managers in the "Y" stores had the task of carrying out plans others had made and striving for goals they had little part in setting. Leadership in the "X" stores tended to be "goal oriented," whereas that in the "Y" stores was primarily "means oriented."

The two styles could be characterized with equal validity as "people oriented" and "system oriented." In the "X" stores, the very nature of the organization structure tended to force managers to concern themselves primarily with *people*. Store problems had to be looked upon essentially as problems of people rather than problems of things. If the performance of a department was unsatisfactory, the way to improve it was to strengthen the management of the department, for only in this way could the improvement be lasting. This kind of organization structure not only placed a premium on selecting well-qualified personnel in the first place; it also placed pressures on the manager and his assistant to work with people as their individual needs required to bring them to levels of competence where they could be entrusted with larger measures of personal responsibility.

Most emphatically, this type of structure did not involve blind delegation. Managers had to have good judgment as to which individuals could move ahead largely on their own and which required help. A considerable part of the time of the manager and his assistant was devoted to the newer department managers or to those whose performance was not up to par or who otherwise needed assistance. Throughout, the emphasis was on building individual competence, bringing people along to the point where they could run their departments with a minimum of direction and supervision.

In the "Y" stores, on the other hand, the emphasis was quite clearly on the manager and his immediate staff doing the thinking and planning and depending on close supervision and essentially mechanical controls to ensure proper execution at the department manager level. The intervening layer of supervision, moreover, tended to deprive department managers of direct contact with the store manager, which in the "X" stores was an important factor in their development.

A Second Look

The findings of the study to this point were fairly clear; equally clear, apparently, was the course of action the company ought to take. If the differences in the performance of the two types of stores were related so directly to differences in organization structure, the logical step seemed to be to convert the "Y" stores to the "X" structure. But in part because of General Wood's well-known reluctance to interfere with the way the managers ran their stores, those conducting the study thought it wise to check further.

The stores in the two groups were revisited, and this time particular attention was paid to the personalities and ways of behaving of the store managers themselves. Although each store manager was very much an individual with personal characteristics all his own, managers of the two groups of stores tended to group themselves roughly into two fairly distinct personality types. The differences between them were particularly apparent in their general attitude toward employees as revealed in the way they talked about their people and in their behavior in face-to-face relationships.

Managerial Personalities

Managers of the "X" stores generally took a great deal of pride in their employees. Walking through the store with managers in this group, they were likely to pause frequently to introduce the visitor from the national office to department managers, salespeople, and others, making complimentary remarks about their performance or relating some recent incident of merit. They tended to take special pride in their promotable younger people, and would often recount their history, their special qualifications, what was being done to further their training, how soon they would be ready for promotion, etc. These managers were not indiscriminate in their praise. They held their people to high standards and were critical of those who failed to measure up. They were usually good judges of people, able to evaluate the strengths and weaknesses of subordinates and to deal with them accordingly. In part because of their skill on this store, they usually *did* have people in whom they could take pride.

Managers of the "Y" stores tended to be rather different. They had much less of the warm, outgoing orientation of the "X" men. They were often distrustful of people, and at some time during the store visit they were likely to make remarks to some such general effect as: "It's hard to get good people these days," or "They've been spoiled by the government and the unions," or "There's something wrong with the education system—people just don't believe in doing a fair day's work anymore, they're out for all they can get and give as little as they can get away with," or "Young people have lost their ambition; you don't see many of them these days who are willing to *work* to get ahead the way we had to." These managers often seemed to expect the worst of their people, and not infrequently their fears were justified. They felt that people had to be watched, that their work had to be checked closely—else no telling what might happen.

This sketch of the two types of managers has been deliberately overdrawn to emphasize their differing orientations. But there was a definite difference in their general outlook on life and in their basic attitudes toward people. *This difference was reflected in the kinds of organizations they set up and the ways they related themselves to the people in them.*

Personalities and Structures

As has already been noted, Sears under General Wood in the 1930s and 1940s was administered with a remarkably high degree of decentralization. Individual store managers were vested with wide latitude and discretion, and this extended, within limits, to the manner in which they set up their organizations. As the study of the two groups of stores proceeded, it became clear that the two fairly different types of managers had tended to create the kinds of organizations with which they could work comfortably. The "Y" managers, who tended to have little confidence in their people, felt that employees had to be closely supervised, that someone (i.e., themselves and their key staffs) had to do the "real thinking," and that close controls had to be imposed to make sure that those further down the line followed through as they were instructed.

Managers of the "X" stores, on the contrary, tended to have more confidence in the capacity of their people, and enough skill in evaluating them to be rather sure in their judgments as in whom and how far they could place their confidence. They relinquished none of their responsibility for guidance and direction or for final results, but they sought to capitalize on the initiative and good sense of their subordinates rather than trying to do the "real thinking" for them. Their primary method of solving problems was to work with the people involved, to the end of solving not only the immediate problem but to strengthen the ability of their subordinates to deal with other problems in the future. To this end, they liked to work directly with their department managers rather than through an intermediate staff which they were likely to feel would only get in the way. The "X" managers no less than the "Y" had tended to create the kinds of organizations with which they could work comfortably.

Viewed in this light, the task of changing organization structures loomed as by no means the simple matter it had first appeared. With all the apparent superiority of the "X" structure, there was a real question as to whether the "Y" type manager could function effectively within it. This doubt was reinforced by what often happened following store manager changes. It was not uncommon to fund that a manager transferred from a "Y" store to one organized on an "X" basis would soon begin reconstituting the organization along lines more nearly like that to which he was accustomed.

These changes were usually not begun immediately nor, once begun, accomplished rapidly, but the direction was often unmistakable. Always, of course, the changes were quite "logical"—inventory problems, the need for building up, say, the soft line departments, the scarcity of high caliber people for department manager jobs, and so forth. Whatever justification there might have been for the moves, the end result tended to be an organization structure of the manager's new store not too different from that he had left (assuming, of course, that the two stores were approximately the same size and type).

The reverse process was equally pronounced. An "X" manager transferred to a "Y"-type store (again assuming reasonable comparability) was likely before long to report to his regional office that as he had become familiar with his new store he had found he had more merchandise managers than he needed. Sometime later, he might report that as soon as he could make certain moves to strengthen some of his department managers he would probably have another merchandise manager available for transfer. Here too, the end result was likely to be conversion of the organization of the manager's new store to correspond more closely with that of his old.

The task of changing organization structures thus appeared to be considerably more complicated than issuing directives or re-drawing organization charts. In the light of the study it was clear that, given some degree of latitude, the way an organization is structured is likely to reflect the personality and temperament of the key people in it—above all, the personality and temperament of the person at the top.

For Sears' purposes, the results of the study were inconclusive. It appeared unwise to try to change organization structures arbitrarily, without regard to the styles and personalities of incumbent managers. On the other hand, it was obvious that personality changes of any magnitude in managers are extremely difficult to bring about and likely to require the equivalent of psychoanalysis or religious conversion—both well beyond normal administrative capabilities. The chief lesson Sears drew from the study was recognition of the importance of selecting people for key positions who exhibited "X" rather than "Y" characteristics.

V. Conclusion

This study was in effect the climax of the collaboration between Sears, Roebuck and Social Research, Inc. as successor to the Committee on Human Relations in Industry.

Social Research continued under Gardner's leadership to operate as a successful consulting firm until 1985, but did little further work of importance for Sears in the areas of organization structure and employee behavior. To a very large extent, the close collaboration that had characterized the 1940s had depended on the personal relationships between Gardner, Moore, and myself, and while the three of us to this day enjoy each other's friendship we have had little opportunity to work together for many years.

Moore left Sears in 1950 to complete his doctorate at the University of Chicago, and went on from there to a distinguished academic career. At the beginning of 1953 I joined the Eisenhower Administration as Assistant Secretary of Commerce. By this time, Clarence Caldwell's health was failing, General Wood was soon to retire, and there was a change in the leadership of the personnel function. In light of the results of the study just described, it came as no surprise that important changes in managerial style ensued. The new style was effective in many ways, and served Sears well for many years thereafter. But it left no room for the kind of objective research in organizational behavior which had characterized the preceding ten years. It had been a productive ten years, and perhaps had gone as far as it was practical to go.

References

Gardner, Burleigh B. and David G. Moore, *Human Relations in Industry*, 2nd ed. (Homewood, Illinois, Richard D. Irwin, 1950).

Houser, J. David, *What People Want from Business* (New York, McGraw-Hill Book Company, 1938).

Jones, Virginia, "Sears Employee Attitude Program," *Personnel Report No. 52* (Sears, Roebuck and Co., Personnel Department, February 1, 1952, Sears Archives). Jones was a member of the employee survey staff from its earliest days.

Moore, David G., "Proposal for Ph.D. Dissertation," 1950 (Sears Archives).

______, *Managerial Strategies and Organizational Dynamics in Sears Retailing* (The University of Chicago, unpublished Ph.D. Dissertation, 1954).

Worthy, James C., "Social Aspects of Industrial Relations" (Sears, Roebuck and Co., Personnel Department, August 4, 1943, Sears Archives).

______, "Discovering and Evaluating Employee Attitudes" (New York, American Management Association, *Personnel Series Number 113*, October 1947).

______, "Factors Contributing to High Morale among Sears Employees" (Sears, Roebuck and Co., internal memorandum, February 18, 1949, Sears Archives).

______, *Attitude Surveys as a Tool of Management* (New York, American Management Association, 1950).

______, "Factors Influencing Employee Morale," *Harvard Business Review*, vol. XXVIII, no. 1, January 1950.

______, "Organization Structure and Employee Morale" (*American Sociological Review*, vol. 15, April 1950).

______, "Some Aspects of Organization Structure in Relation to Pressures on Company Decision-Making" (*Proceedings*, Industrial Relations Research Association, Fifth Annual Meeting, 1952).

______, *Big Business and Free Men* (New York, Harper & Brothers, 1959).

______, *Shaping an American Institution: Robert E. Wood and Sears, Roebuck* (Urbana and Chicago: University of Illinois Press, 1984).

Worthy, Burleigh B. Garner and William Foote Whyte, "Methods and Techniques for Building a Cooperative Organization" (The University of Chicago, Industrial Relations Center, Executive Seminar Series on Industrial Relations, April 1, 1947).

Whyte, William Foote, *Modern Methods in Social Research* (Washington, D.C., Office of Naval Research, 1952).

______, *Man and Organization* (Homewood, Illinois, Richard D. Irwin, 1959).

Analysis

1. Why would external factors influence employee morale as found in the Sears survey programs?
2. What was the value of the Sears profit-sharing program to the employees? To the company?
3. Explain the differences between "X" and "Y" stores. Relate them to the notion of tall and flat organization structures.
4. Why were managers most likely to be promoted from "X" stores than from "Y" stores?
5. How could the organization structure in "X" and "Y" stores lead to different styles of managerial behavior?
6. Could an "X" manager survive in a "Y" store? Could a "Y" manager be as effective in an "X" store? Why?

Chapter 3 Organizational Environments and Effectiveness

Case 1. Finding a Good Location for a Fast Food Franchise[1]

We just don't plunk down a franchise and say let's see what it will do. The costs of mistakes are just too great. So we want to collect a bunch of data to determine the market potential of the area. These data are virtually free because they are generated by the federal Bureau of the Census. Any library that is a federal depository has most of the data that we begin with, and some of the universities even have the data already on the computer. Let me tell you, what we learn from that data source is a real bargain. But let me tell you how we do it.

First, we have some good data on our current customers. We have four market segments that we attract in numbers: families with young children, young adults ages twenty to thirty-four, teenagers, and the "tween" market (ages ten to twelve). Forty-nine percent of our business comes from families who frequent our restaurant. Twenty-two percent of our customers come in alone and make a purchase. A third of our business comes from nonfamily groups. Fifty-four percent of our customers are male. Let me put this in demographic terms for you.

Let's compare the demographics of our customers with the demographics of the United States. First, we have a lower percentage of customers nine years old and younger than does the U.S. population. Fifteen percent of our customers fall in the age group of ten to fifteen years. Ten- to fifteen-year-olds constitute 11 percent of the population. Eighteen percent of our business is with sixteen- to nineteen-year-olds, whereas this age group accounts for only 8 percent of the U.S. population. Persons twenty to twenty-four years old account for 17 percent of our business, whereas they account for 9 percent of the U.S. population. We are also strong with ages twenty-five to thirty-four; they account for 22 percent of our business and only 15 percent of the population. Older age groups do not frequent our outlets much in comparison with their percentage of the population. Hence we primarily attract people ten to thirty-four years old.

Why do people come to eat? Lone individuals are primarily men who are younger (twenty to twenty-four years old) or older (above fifty years old) than our other customers. They most often come in for breakfast, least often for dinner. Families

1. This is a simulated demographic analysis.

come in more often for dinner, least often for breakfast. The teen market is strongest during the day but is a mixed blessing. Too many teens becoming rowdy will scare off the family and older age crowd. The tween market is strongest also during the day, but they normally come with an adult. Nonfamily groups are strongest at breakfast and lunch, mostly groups from nearby work sites.

So what does this all mean? If you know the relationships between sales and a demographic group, you can establish goals of what a particular spot might generate. For example, let's say we want to locate an outlet near Des Plaines, Illinois. Demographically, that community is composed of older adults. We know we aren't strong with that market. However, there is a good concentration of businesses nearby, white collar and blue collar, that can generate good lunch business for us. In any event, we don't go by feelings; we go by numbers. We plug in the demographics and they tell us what expected demand should be on a daily basis. We now compare that with the demographics of Hanover Park, Illinois, as a second potential site. We crank in the demographic data for Hanover Park. Des Plaines and Hanover Park are on different census tracks and are reported separately even though they are only ten miles away from each other. I won't show you the actual formulas that we use because we figure they are worth a million dollars to us. Anyway, we calculated that Hanover Park has better numbers. Our next job is to find a good location.

Three things are important in real estate: location, location, and location. Where we locate our unit is critical to its success. We want to be on a road that has good traffic. However, it can't be a pain to access. In addition, we don't want too many hassles from local residents because we don't want the adverse publicity. However, we will fight it if the demographics of the location really show some clear advantages to being there.

We are willing to work with a community to build a unit that "fits" in with the area. Units in some of our areas—for example, Grosse Pointe, Michigan—cost us over one million dollars more than our standard "off the rack" design. However, the potential there was so great and the need to create the proper image and relationship with the community so important that we knew we would have to make a big effort. And it worked.

What else do we use demographic data for? Well, we use it to compare expected sales at an outlet with actual sales. If our model indicates that we should have 1,000 customers and we only have 750, then we start looking for reasons. We survey our customers, and we canvass the community to find out why people aren't coming into our outlet. We then use the results to develop a marketing plan, and, if we think it is necessary, we revise our demand model.

If we do enter a market with a concentration of a specific type of individuals, we may alter our marketing efforts to meet demand. For example, in our Des Plaines outlet, we knew we would have trouble with generating dinner traffic because of the greater percentage of residents in the area over fifty, which we haven't had good luck attracting into our outlets. So in Des Plaines we have advertised Bingo Nights and senior citizen breakfast specials in order to attract that segment of the population.

We have stressed breakfast and dinner specials because the lunch crowd has been sufficient.

So, that is how we determine outlet locations and how we use demographic data. We are happy with this approach and find that it is much superior to just using gut reactions. Of course, it is always hard to tell because we can't afford to locate an outlet in an area where our analysis says we shouldn't. I guess that would be the real test of our approach. But don't expect us to try that out in the near future.

Analysis

1. What environmental variables are considered in an outlet location? Why are they important?
2. What are the limitations of using demographic data for determining site location?
3. Why is keeping local good will important in the fast food industry?
4. Could there be a method of determining whether the increase in the cost of the Grosse Pointe outlet was worth it? What might it be?
5. Why is an analysis of the environment important to the fast food industry?

Case 2. Determining a Hospital's Market Area

CEO, Memorial Hospital

There is no question that the hospital industry is overbuilt in most urban areas of the United States, and we are no different here in Eagle Harbor. We at Memorial Hospital knew that we were in a lousy location, with several competing hospitals in better locations than we were. We knew under DRGs (diagnostic related groups) that the federal government instituted that all the hospitals in the area could not continue to be all things to all people. There would have to be some specialization. We wanted to position ourselves in the best situation in the market. However, we had no idea how to assess the market and the environment that we faced. Hence we turned to the North Star Agency to give us some guidance.

Team Manager, North Star Agency

We at the North Star Agency wanted to help Memorial Hospital find a market niche to guide its strategy for the next decade. To find this niche we had to find out about the population in the effective market area, the demographics of the population, and the nature of the competition. We had a team of five individuals assigned to the project. Two would handle the competitive analysis, two the demographic analysis of the population, and the project director, Jennifer Chang, would work to coordinate and meet with the hospital staff to assess the strengths and weaknesses of the existing hospital.

The demographic team first had to determine the effective market area for the hospital. They tabulated the past two years of inpatient and outpatient records and plotted the patients' residences on a map. They found it helpful in later analysis to then segment the map into primary, secondary, and tertiary draw areas for Memorial Hospital. Primary areas were areas with a high percentage of the population that used Memorial Hospital. Secondary areas were geographical areas in which Memorial still had a strong market draw but clearly not as strong as in the primary market areas. Finally, the areas where Memorial still had some patients residing, but not many, were defined as tertiary areas.

Hospitals use two main approaches in determining their market area; both make use of patient origin (residence) data. The first relies on what is known as a *commitment index*. This index is determined by taking the total number of patients admitted to the hospital and then identifying how many and what percentage come from each community. In this case, census track divisions were used to compare hospital patients' residences with the demographics of the area. A *census track* is a subdivision of census data. A track, in this case, was a subdivision smaller than a town yet larger than a block (for which data were also available for the Eagle Harbor area).

A second approach uses what is called a *relevance index*. A relevance index is calculated by taking the total number of hospitalized patients from a community and then identifying how many and what percentage of them have gone to each hospital in the surrounding area. Usually, only a commitment index is used because the data needed to do a relevance index are more difficult and costly to obtain. However, obtaining the relevance index is much more meaningful for a hospital that wishes to determine its competitive advantage in an area. Luckily, there was a health system state agency in the area, so we could obtain the data needed to construct a relevance index.

Demographic data were obtained for the effective market area of the hospital because studies have shown that the demand for hospital services can be predicted from knowing the demographics of an area. For example, there is a relationship between education, age, occupation, income, patient's gender, and family size and the number of visits to a hospital and the nature of the visit. Obviously, a community with a greater percentage of people over fifty-five would have a greater need for oncology (cancer treatment), heart and stroke disease, and bone and joint treatment than a community with younger people.

A chart was constructed that indicated all the specialties of the competitive hospitals and in which of those specialties the hospital excelled. These data were obtained through interviews with the chief operating officer (COO) of each hospital. The group head determined the strengths and weaknesses of Memorial Hospital and where the chief executive officer (CEO) of Memorial thought the hospital should be directed in the future.

The results of the study were quite interesting. It showed that Memorial Hospital was geographically rimmed by competitors. The primary draw of Memorial was several communities that had an older blue-collar population. Most of the patients from these areas were going to Memorial for some of their illnesses even though Memorial was not the best institution in that disease specialty area. However, many residents of Memorial's primary market area were going to competitive hospitals that were known for their specialty work. This was particularly troubling because when competition intensifies and patients become more knowledgeable and demanding, Memorial could lose even more patients to competition.

CEO, Memorial Hospital

On the basis of the analysis of the North Star group, we decided to specialize in what we might call older individual diseases. We are phasing out child care and obstetrics and reducing the emphasis we had on sports medicine. We also opened a unit that deals with physical rehabilitation. We attracted a surgeon team with a specialty in disorders of the ear (primarily deafness) and an eye surgery team (cataracts). Using existing space, we also opened a substance abuse floor of the hospital.

The end result is that we feel that we are better prepared to meet the needs of the public and to be competitive into the twenty-first century. Bed censuses (occupancy rates) have increased, and general revenues have improved. We are also improving our relevance index, which is important because we seek state approval for additional programs and equipment purchases.

Analysis

1. What aspects of the environment are important to a hospital? Why?
2. Rank the list you generated for question 1 by the degree of importance each has for the survival of the hospital.
3. What did the North Star team do right? How could they have improved their study?
4. Why is the relevancy index better than the commitment index?
5. Why should a not-for-profit hospital be concerned with its environment?

Case 3. The Kansas Railroad

The creation of the Kansas Railroad in 1984 was a result of the Staggers Act passed in the U.S. Congress several years before. The Staggers Act allowed railroads to more readily abandon unprofitable branch lines or sell them to other companies. As a result, the number of short-line railroads (small regional railroads) in the United States increased. The Kansas Railroad is one of these short lines.

The Kansas Railroad is composed of 250 miles of single-track main line and several small yards. The main line was part of a major railroad between Missouri and Colorado until mergers made it redundant. There is very little bridge traffic (traffic that does not originate or terminate on the line) to support the line; hence, it is what most experts would call marginal. Between 1970 and 1984 car loadings decreased from an average of two hundred cars per day to fifty. The major trunk carrier, which is required by union contract to carry five crew members on the line, believed that the line had little possibility of becoming much more than marginally profitable and expected that it would become unprofitable within a year or two. However, a short line without the union restriction might have enough traffic and low enough costs to stay profitable.

Hal Naper, president of the Kansas railway, was originally very optimistic about his railroad. He felt he could offer better service by offering more trains and being more closely in tune with the needs of the area. Today, after five years, he is frustrated but still optimistic. In a recent interview he said, "You know, there is potential for railroads. I know it. However, I am really at a loss here. I own 250 miles of main line. Now, I can tell shippers on the line that I can offer them personalized service and that I will respond to give them cars or pick up their loads. But once I cart the loads up to KD junction, I lose control over what happens. KD junction is where our line ends and a major railroad picks up the cars and ships them on their way.

"My shippers want to know when their customers are going to get their shipment. I can tell them that I will pick up their load within four hours of when they call, but I can't tell them how long that load will wait at KD junction or in Kansas City, Chicago, or Saint Louis before it gets to its final destination. You know, we are living in what I call the Federal Express Age—you can give someone a package by 7:00 p.m. one night and it can be virtually anywhere by 10:30 a.m. the next day. Yet I am telling shippers that I can't say if it will take one, two, or three weeks for the railroad to haul a carload of logs from Mountainburg, Kansas, to Kansas City. That is the most frustrating part of the business. Now I can't blame the railroad that we interchange cars with because they are pretty dependable. They say they will pick up cars at 10:00 p.m. every night and they do it. But the connections between other railroads are not as predictable once you interchange over several railroads through several train yards.

"I can see why trucks are so popular and how intermodal traffic (trucks on trains) has really grown. With an intermodal train you can offer service from one point to another with a nearly guaranteed schedule because the train does not get switched in several yards along the way. Instead of promising a shipment in one to four weeks, I can make a promise that will be accurate within a day or two. However, it is just as quick for a shipper to haul a load to Smith, Kansas, or Springfield, Missouri, as to bother with my railroad. Hence, I am moving to offer more intermodal service from a central spot on my line while still promoting all-rail service to commodities that are less time sensitive. However, even the types of goods that are not time sensitive are decreasing. For example, it used to be that scrap metal was not a shipment that you could call time sensitive. But with changing prices on scrap and the amount of money that is tied up in a load of scrap, even some scrap dealers prefer the speed of an all-truck routing.

"We are marketing passenger service on our railroad again. This time, it is based on attracting tourists and those who want a unique dining experience. We are running a weekend day train and a summer and autumn dinner train on Saturday night and Sunday afternoon. So far, that has been a commercial success. We have some very pretty scenery in northern Kansas, and we have a good menu on the train. However, the state of Kansas is planning to extend one of the major roads in the area to make it four lanes. Part of the new road will be in some of the valleys in which we now operate. I'm afraid the wilderness environment we promote will be destroyed if the passengers only see cars and trucks roaring by at sixty-five miles per hour instead of deer and ducks on pristine streams.

"We improved car loadings and unloadings over the past few years from fifty cars a day to one hundred cars. But future growth seems to be limited. The intermodal program has only added ten or so trailers per day. That has some future potential, but we are unsure how great it is.

"We are considering approaching the local communities along the line to try to get some degree of relief from property tax assessments. The cash we might get from any such relief would be used to improve the track and equipment we have. We currently have twelve engines, six that work, and we use the others for spare parts. We have three coaches, one diner, and a caboose. We do not own any other rail cars. Our greatest need is to purchase new engines and improve our track so we can increase speeds up to the fifty miles per hour that are allowed on unsignaled main lines.

"Overall, I think there is a lot of potential in this railroad. But there are many factors outside our control that will dictate if it will be a success in the future."

Analysis

1. What are some of the environmental factors that are affecting this railroad? How do they affect it?
2. What do you think are the main factors that will affect this railroad's future? Why?

3. Do you agree with the statement that the "Federal Express" mentality has resulted in shippers' demands for faster service? Is this an environmental factor that has affected the railroad?
4. In what three ways has the government influenced or might influence this railroad?
5. How might Hal Naper get better control of some of the external factors that affect his railroad?

Case 4. Buffering Berry's Business

Berry's Business was a manufacturing company that made parts for small engines. The company had been in business since 1957 outside Marietta, Georgia. The company made basically one part that was used by a number of manufacturers. It was a complex part of the engine assembly that involved three separate processes in its construction. The parts were then shipped by truck to the various plants across the country that produced and assembled small engines.

Berry Foster was the founder and president of the company. He had built the company from a two-person operation to its current size of two hundred employees. The company started out in the garage of Berry's best buddy Bill. It now was housed in a 50,000-square-foot plant, including office space. The total assets of the plant have increased from $5,000 to over $15 million. Although Berry prefers to use his own funds to operate the organization, he did finance about 10 percent of the total assets of the company at the beginning of 1989. The equipment needed to make the engine parts was relatively specialized and costly. One machine cost $1 million; the other machines cost much less.

Berry had two major concerns. He wanted to gain greater control over factors that affected the organization but yet were not part of the organization, and he was also concerned with internal aspects related to operational and nonoperational issues. Even with these internal matters, Berry believed he lacked control, and he felt frustrated.

External problems seemed to relate to three issues: customers, suppliers, and other forces. The problems with customers related to the cyclical nature of the demand for his product. Berry could not seem to stabilize orders. Because of the nature of the industry, there was a rush to make small engines for lawn mowers and a second, though slightly smaller, rush to make snow blowers. These demands occurred during a two-month period, and the rest of the year was at a much lower level of production. This meant layoffs and idle equipment, which bothered Berry.

Second, because there were only a few customers for Berry's parts, the customers seemed to take advantage of him. They were slow to pay for parts received and sometimes took six months to pay. This cost Berry money because he had to pay suppliers and employees when the parts were made.

Suppliers were a problem too. Berry found that it was difficult to obtain shipments on a timely basis and the quality of shipments was sometimes very poor. Currently, Berry was working with suppliers who gave only the best price for parts. But he was considering a different approach because he seemed to spend too much time trying to get quotes for each order. Some days he had to send employees home without pay because there were no parts to produce. This created ill will between Berry and the employees, and Berry didn't blame them—he didn't like it either.

There just had to be a better approach. At one time Berry considered making long-term contracts with a supplier, but he was afraid that he might not get the orders that would match the long-term contracts and would end up with too much unused raw material at the end of the year.

Other external factors affected his business. Berry didn't like the degree of fluctuation in the short-term interest rate that faced him whenever he tried to get a short-term loan at the bank. He wanted to stabilize the interest rate but didn't know how.

In addition, his work force didn't seem to have much loyalty to the company. Turnover was about 200 percent in the company per year. It was hard; whenever he had to lay off employees, about half of them would never come back because they would find other jobs in Atlanta or elsewhere before they were called back to work. The additional cost of hiring new employees and the time it took bothered Berry. He thought there must be a better way, but he didn't see any. Once he thought about guaranteeing a core of employees permanent employment, but with orders as cyclical as they were, that didn't seem to be a very good idea.

Internally, Berry had problems with work flow. Some machines would run out of parts when another machine would be under repair. Raw materials were not always in the right place at the right time, so employees would have to leave their machines to find raw materials. When one machine was down, it was only a matter of minutes before they all would be out of parts. Hence, sometimes 150 employees would be standing around waiting for one person to find additional raw materials. That didn't seem right to Berry either, yet he didn't know what to do. He wondered if he could design a compensation system that would encourage more employees to work together.

Berry wondered about all these issues as he drove over to Atlanta to talk with another supplier. He really used to have fun in this business, but now he felt the job was just one problem after another. Although Berry liked to be a parts producer, he did not like to be a manager.

Analysis

1. How might Berry reduce some of the uncertainty with customers?
2. How might Berry build some buffers to reduce the problems he is having with suppliers?
3. Propose a compensation system that would improve worker cooperation.
4. How might Berry stabilize the work force?
5. How might Berry reduce the uncertainty of interest rates?

Case 5. Stratospheric Depletion of Ozones[1]

The 1987 General Motors *Public Interest Report* discussed in some detail the problem of the potential loss of ozone from the stratosphere caused by emissions of certain chlorofluorocarbons (CFCs). Since then, new scientific data have been gathered and an international agreement to control CFCs has been signed and now must be ratified. As a result, the subject merits another look as a continuing public issue. The issue is of particular interest to GM because CFCs are used in many of GM's products and processes.

The Problem

In high concentrations, ozone is undesirable at ground level where it may have harmful respiratory effects on humans. However, ozone is beneficial high in the stratosphere where it shields the earth's surface from ultraviolet light. Excessive exposure to ultraviolet light can cause skin cancer or cataracts, reduce the yield of some crops, and damage materials like vinyl plastics.

In the 1970s, scientists began to worry about the effect of CFCs on ozone in the stratosphere. CFCs are a class of chemical compounds made up of chlorine, fluorine, and carbon atoms, and, in many cases, hydrogen atoms. They are used as refrigerants in household appliances and air conditioners, as industrial solvents, as blowing agents in the manufacture of foam products, and (outside the U.S.) as propellants for aerosol sprays.

Introduced some 60 years ago by General Motors, CFCs were then considered desirable industrial chemicals because they are highly stable, unreactive, and non-toxic. When released, however, some of them rise into the stratosphere and may remain there unchanged for years. There they could be broken down by sunlight to liberate chlorine, which could then react with ozone to convert it into ordinary oxygen. Oxygen lacks ozone's ultraviolet-filtering characteristics. It should be noted that not all CFCs cause problems. CFCs containing hydrogen atoms tend to react low in the atmosphere and do not reach the stratosphere; compounds containing no chlorine do not contribute to ozone depletion, even if they reach the stratosphere.

CFCs are most often mentioned in connection with ozone depletion, but the international agreement also controls certain Halons, bromine-containing chemical compounds used in specialized firefighting equipment.

A few years ago, scientists observed a loss of ozone in the stratosphere over the South Pole each springtime—temporary reductions in ozone concentrations of over 40% have been recorded. According to some measurements, the amount of ozone in

1. "Stratospheric Depletion of Ozone," *General Motors Public Interest Report, 1988* (Detroit, Mich.: General Motors Corp., 1988), pp. 42–45.

the stratosphere worldwide has been dropping slightly. Although they were not sure of the cause of this ozone depletion, many of the scientists suspected that CFCs were responsible for at least part of the loss.

In addition to ozone depletion, the scientists feared that because CFCs, like certain other gases, absorb and retain heat in the atmosphere, their continued release could contribute to a gradual warming of the earth through the so-called "greenhouse effect," which could result in severe climatic changes.

Scientific Investigation

To resolve some of these concerns, the U.S. National Science Foundation for the past several years has been investigating the annual ozone depletion in Antarctica.

In 1987, some 150 scientists and support personnel from 19 organizations and four nations conducted the most extensive study yet, the Airborne Antarctic Ozone Experiment. This $10 million experiment was coordinated by the U.S. National Aeronautics and Space Administration (NASA). The scientists' complete findings are expected to be available near the end of 1988.

An interim report, issued by NASA in March 1988, indicates that stratospheric loss of ozone may be more serious than previously thought. Following publication of this report, E. I. du Pont de Nemours & Company, the world's largest producer of CFCs, announced plans to phase out production of the chemicals. Du Pont set no target date for ending production.

In a preliminary assessment of the NASA research, the *Scientific American* (January 1988) states:

> The data suggest that the extraordinary seasonal loss of ozone at the South Pole may well be a regional peculiarity that will not repeat itself in warmer climates, but this assessment is not conclusive. One thing is clear: chlorofluorocarbons are capable of altering the levels of atmospheric ozone. Moreover, the chlorine that has already been introduced into the stratosphere will interact with ozone for decades to come.

Although CFCs appear to play a major role in ozone depletion in Antarctica, other factors, such as weather and atmospheric dynamics, are also involved. Scientists studying the phenomenon agree that what is happening to ozone over the South Pole is a complex—far from completely understood—stew of physical and chemical events.

Early this year, scientists of the National Oceanic and Atmospheric Administration began studies of potential ozone depletion over the North Pole. So far, there is no evidence of a problem and scientists do not expect any because climatic conditions at the North Pole are very different from those at the South Pole.

Montreal Protocol

Meanwhile, the United Nations Environment Program has been engaged in ongoing discussions about placing international controls on CFCs. In September 1987, 31 nations signed an agreement—the Montreal Protocol—to control CFC-11, -12, -113, -114, and -115, and Halons 1211, 1301, and 2402. The signatory nations—which include the U.S., U.S.S.R., Japan, and the Common Market countries—together account for 70% of all CFC use. The agreement must be ratified by at least 11 nations before it goes into effect (at the start of 1989 at the earliest). The 11 nations must include those accounting for at least two-thirds of world CFC consumption and production. The Protocol was ratified by the United States in April 1988.

The Protocol requires developed nations to freeze consumption at 1986 levels by the middle of 1989, and to cut use 20% by mid-1993 and an additional 30% by mid-1998, which would put CFCs at 50% of their 1986 level. In addition, beginning in 1992, production and consumption of Halons would be frozen at 1986 levels. Also, the United Nations has agreed to review all scientific data every four years, beginning in 1990. If additional information comes to light that warrants further consideration, that information will be brought before the U.N. for review.

The Montreal Protocol allows developing nations to increase their use of CFCs 10% a year for 10 years if that is thought vital to their economies. They can increase their consumption up to 0.3 kilogram per capita. By way of comparison, per capita use in the U.S. is about 1.1 kilograms. These few exceptions allow developing countries to catch up in basic technologies like refrigeration. In addition, the Soviet Union will be permitted to finish CFC plants already under construction in its current five-year plan, providing per capita consumption in that country does not exceed 0.5 kilogram.

EPA Proposal

In December 1987, the U.S. became the first nation to take formal steps to carry out the Montreal Protocol when its Environmental Protection Agency (EPA) proposed a freeze and phasedown of certain CFCs and Halons in the United States in accordance with the Protocol. The EPA hopes to publish its proposed rules in final form by August 1988. As specified in the EPA proposal, U.S. restriction would occur only if the Montreal Protocol becomes effective. This recognizes the international scope of the problem.

Under the EPA proposal, quotas reflecting the allowable levels of production and consumption will be allocated to each of the U.S. firms that produced CFCs in 1986. Trading of allocated quotas would be permitted. EPA is also considering whether to develop specific regulations limiting CFC and Halon use for particular industries. Other considerations include imposing a regulatory fee in addition to allocated quotas, and auctioning (instead of allocating) rights to produce and consume CFCs and Halons.

Where GM Stands on Controlling CFCs

GM supports U.S. ratification of the Montreal Protocol and, to some degree, the proposed method of implementation of the Protocol's provisions by the EPA. The EPA's proposal eases one of industry's major concerns in controlling CFCs—that U.S. industries not be placed at a disadvantage with their overseas competition. It is important that EPA's implementation plan mirror the Protocol in timing and the amount of reductions of CFC production and use so as not to alter this competitive balance.

GM strongly supports the market-oriented approach of the EPA proposal. In contrast to the traditional "command and control" approach, using market incentives to control CFCs helps assure that available supplies will be directed to their most valuable uses where adequate alternative substances are not available.

However, GM does not support EPA's proposal of giving marketable permits to CFC producers. Giving permits only to the five major CFC producers compensates only one industry for the costs and inconveniences created by the limits on CFCs. Another concern is that the proposal could, in effect, create a producer cartel, which may find it profitable to lower production below the levels established by the Protocol, further aggravating the shortage. Or, producers could allocate production to favored users.

GM prefers that permits be given to users, or, failing that, be sold at auction. Allocating permits to users would either assure supplies to individual firms or compensate them if they could no longer remain in business.

Although no CFC substitutes are readily available today for most U.S. applications, specific controls on individual user segments, or additional market fees, are not needed to solve this significant engineering challenge. The freeze at 1986 levels in mid-1989 will create an immediate 15% drop in production and is incentive enough for industry to seek alternatives since this initial reduction will cause CFC prices to rise. These prices will continue to rise as each additional reduction date becomes effective. Government involvement, beyond implementation of the Protocol, is unnecessary, in GM's view.

GM's Contribution to CFC Reduction

GM uses CFCs as refrigerants in automobile air conditioning systems, as solvents for removing solder flux from silicon chips and electronic substrates, and for degreasing parts. GM's Inland Division has been using CFC-11 as a blowing agent in manufacturing urethane foam for seat cushions, but will discontinue this operation at the end of the 1988 model year. The foam will be obtained from outside suppliers who will initially use CFC-11, but are developing alternatives for it.

Because of its concern with the CFC issue, General Motors is undertaking a coordinated corporate effort to control CFC emissions and evaluate potential substitutes.

GM's Harrison Radiator Division, which uses CFC-12 as a refrigerant in mobile air conditioners, has taken a number of steps over the past few years to reduce the weight and improve the efficiency and performance of its air conditioning systems. The factory charge of CFC refrigerant has been greatly reduced from what it was in the 1970s. Significant improvements have also been made in refrigerant containment—new hose material that reduces leakage rates and improved seals, hose couplings, and connections.

Harrison is searching for new refrigerants, which involves also developing suitable lubricants, and elastomers for hose materials and seals, compatible with these refrigerants. Developing replacements for mobile air conditioning refrigerants, coupled with the time required for redesign and testing of the systems, could take seven to ten years.

Harrison is also working on improving air conditioning system integrity, and is assisting corporate and industry efforts to develop refrigerant-recovery systems for use when cars are serviced or scrapped. The standard industry practice in servicing air conditioning units has been to discharge the system to the atmosphere and recharge it after servicing. The GM Service Development Center in Detroit is evaluating equipment from outside suppliers that will recover refrigerant for recycling. Two hurdles that need to be overcome involve the anticipated high costs of such equipment and what to do with the refrigerant after it is collected.

In the summer of 1988, the Harrison Radiator Division will be cooperating with the Environmental Protection Agency in a nationwide study of CFC-12 recovered from different types and ages of vehicles in different parts of the country. The goal of the study is to set standards for reuse of reclaimed mobile air conditioner refrigerant.

Several GM component divisions that use CFC-113 as a parts-cleaning agent are investigating alternatives for this solvent, improved CFC containment, and the expanded use of aqueous washers. A number of technical issues still need to be resolved by GM and its suppliers. GM estimates that it may take up to ten years to develop and implement alternative cleaning processes that do not require CFC-113 for the many components manufactured by GM.

Efforts Elsewhere

Several industrial and trade association groups are looking at the CFC situation.

The American CFC-production industry has announced its support of rules to cut output of these compounds. A consortium of CFC manufacturers has been formed to develop alternatives to CFCs—materials with no adverse effect on safety, human health, and the environment. The industry is especially looking for substitutes for CFC solvents. The growing use of these solvents has offset gains made by a 1978 EPA ban on CFCs in aerosol sprays. A consortium of CFC producers is supporting the extensive toxicological testing of several alternative compounds.

The Motor Vehicle Manufacturers Association, the Society of Automotive Engineers, the Mobile Air Conditioning Society, and the American Society of Heating, Refrigerating and Air Conditioning Engineers are also investigating ways to minimize CFC emissions from automotive air conditioners during servicing.

An Important Job

The use of CFCs has continued to grow, particularly outside the U.S. It is estimated that 70% of the world's CFC use now occurs beyond American borders. In view of this, any unilateral American action to further restrict CFC production and use would have only a limited impact on current global emissions. For example, the U.S. banned the use of CFCs in most aerosols ten years ago, but because most other nations did not join this ban, CFC emissions from aerosols on a global scale continue to be significant. CFC restrictions must be international to be effective.

Reducing CFCs in the atmosphere is vital to human health and environmental integrity. It is an important international job. GM is working diligently to be a leader in this effort.

Analysis

1. What environmental groups other than scientists have influenced GM's activity with respect to ozone?
2. Why should GM support an international treaty on the banning of chlorofluorocarbons (CFCs) if it uses them in its production process? Why might GM not support a U.S. ban if there is no international ban on limiting CFCs?
3. Why doesn't GM just immediately stop using CFCs on its own? How might that affect GM's environment?
4. Why should GM be concerned about the EPA's proposal to give marketable permits to CFC producers instead of users? How might that affect GM's environment?

5. What are the benefits of a market-oriented approach to limiting CFCs over a command-and-control approach? What are the benefits to GM of this approach? What are the disadvantages to GM?
6. Why should GM care that CFCs could cause changes in the world's environment?

Chapter 4 Managerial Decision Making

Case 1. What to Do with the Gift?

"What a windfall!" These words expressed the feelings of most members of the chamber of commerce of a large southeastern city that had just received a $300,000 gift from an anonymous donor. The only requirement made by the donor was that the money be used to improve the community.

The fifteen dedicated members of the chamber of commerce were quite excited about the unforeseen gift. Usually much time and energy was spent in getting the needed funds for the operating budget alone. Not a year went by without many deserving projects going unfunded, to the dismay of some of the volunteer members. It was natural, therefore, to think of many ways to spend the money.

At one of the meetings one member even introduced brainstorming in hopes of deciding how to best use the money. However, after several fruitless meetings, members realized that there were too many differing views on the issue. The atmosphere at meetings also had changed from initial excitement and commitment to irritation and disgust. Members seemed more concerned with having their proposals accepted than with finding alternative ways to allocate the gift.

Finally, Alice Shaw, the president of the chamber of commerce, felt it was time to expedite the decision-making process. She said, "I think it's time we take a look at what's been going on here. This is our fourth meeting on this issue. The brainstorming process has given us numerous ideas. All of us, including myself, seem to be pushing our own pet programs without trying to resolve the donation question. Also, other important chamber business has gotten bogged down. Does anyone have any insights or recommendations into how we can settle this dilemma?"

Analysis

1. Assume you are a member of the chamber of commerce. How will you respond to Ms. Shaw?
2. What specific behavioral issues might be at work here?
3. Discuss some of the advantages and disadvantages of group decision making as applied to this situation.
4. How could this decision have been handled better?

Case 2. Reliance Insurance Company

The Reliance Insurance Company, which is a medium-sized regional insurance company located in the Northwest, specializes in automobile and homeowner's coverage. Recently, the company has been experimenting with a four-day workweek at a few of the regional offices.

Regional office personnel currently work a 40-hour week. The bulletin sent from the home office has suggested that four 10-hour days be scheduled for each employee. The schedule that has proved most effective is 7:00 a.m. to 6:00 p.m., which includes a half-hour for lunch and two 15-minute coffee breaks.

Janet Downs has been a manager for the Seattle, Washington, office for six months. For the previous three years, she had been an assistant manager for a larger branch office. After graduating from college with a degree in business, she started with Reliance eight years ago as a claims adjuster. Janet is twenty-nine, single, and looking forward to a career with Reliance. Each regional office is open five days a week, and it is the manager's responsibility to schedule his or her employees. Janet has eight employees, who are described in Table 1.

Janet is trying to decide whether to experiment with the four-day workweek. She is discussing the matter with her assistant manager, Dick Minton.

TABLE 1
Employees of Seattle Regional Office

Employee Name and Title	Age	Sex	Marital Status	Number of Dependents	Time with Company	Education
Dick Munter Assistant Manager	34	M	Married	Wife	4 years	3 years college
Harry Johnson Claims Adjuster	23	M	Single	None	1 year	1 year college
Alice Pela Clerk-Typist	38	F	Married	Invalid mother, 2 children	5 years	High school
Sandy Wheeler Claims Processor	35	F	Widowed mother	2 children	6 years	High school
Ann Hunter Clerk-Typist	18	F	Single	None	6 months	High school
Sam Darnell Claims Adjuster	36	M	Married	Wife, 1 child	5 years	2 years college
Roberta Young File Clerk and Typist	19	F	Single	None	9 months	High school
Lynda Merrill File Clerk and Typist	20	F	Married	Husband	1 year	High school

"I think I should let the group decide whether they want to work the four-day week. After all, they have to live with it. They may as well decide on the hours and schedule too. What do you think?" asked Janet.

Dick replied, "Are you crazy? You won't be able to get this group to agree on anything. They're too different. Besides, you're being paid to make the decisions."

Analysis

1. Do you think the situation calls for a group decision?
2. List the advantages and disadvantages of a four-day workweek.
3. What other information would you like to have if you were Janet?
4. If you were Janet, what would you do?

Case 3. Too Many Stations?

Steve Robinson owned and managed a service station in Indianapolis, Indiana. The station was in an excellent location adjacent to an interstate highway and on a main business artery. The traffic flow was considerable. Steve had previously owned two other stations in another city and had been an auto mechanic for some twenty years before fulfilling his dream of becoming his own boss.

The station had been in existence for over twenty years when Steve bought it three years ago. The previous owner had built up a loyal clientele, and Steve felt that his own experience and mechanical expertise would help him keep the old customers and add new business.

Everything Steve hoped for came to pass. Within a few years his sales had increased nearly 70 percent. Much of the sales increase came from repairing disabled vehicles from the nearby interstate. The remainder came from increased gasoline prices. However, profits had increased only 40 percent because of lower margins on gas sales.

Steve first became concerned about changes in competition when a new service station opened two years ago on the same highway within two blocks of Steve's station. A year later another station opened two blocks in the other direction. Both of these were major brand dealerships, and neither sought to engage in price competition. As a result, gas margins remained satisfactory. Despite a slight downturn in gasoline sales, Steve's repair business kept his profits at a stable level.

Steve's real concern was that someone would open a station that sold gas at discount prices. Rather than wait for this to happen, Steve contacted a local contractor and convinced him to build a discount gas station to be leased to Steve on a nearby vacant site. The station would sell gas, oil, and convenience items and go by the name Gas Mart.

Land was bought and construction on the new outlet was about to start when a larger contractor announced the building of a discount station across the street from Steve's discount location. To make matters worse, the competitor's discount station would be finished and in operation some four months before Steve's new station.

Steve was in a real predicament. Then the second construction company surprised Steve by offering him the new station, which also included a contract with a fuel supplier. But Steve had already agreed to lease the discount station he himself had planned. He also had his own station to operate. He wondered whether things were getting too much out of control.

Analysis

1. Identify the alternatives available to Steve.
2. Weigh the advantages and disadvantages of each alternative.
3. If you were Steve, which would you select? What are the risks involved in each?

Case 4. The Location Decision: Whose Best Interest?

Carlotta Rios is a regional manager of the Eastern Division of Computer Components Corporation (CCC), a producer of electronic parts for many computer and electronic companies. Carlotta has been with CCC for sixteen years. She joined the company right after getting an undergraduate degree in electrical engineering from Princeton. She completed an MBA degree while working in R&D and worked in several administrative positions while advancing in the company to her present position.

CCC enjoys an excellent reputation in the industry as a quality producer of component products. Carlotta was instrumental in helping the company gain that reputation because she was responsible for many of the early electronic developments that put CCC "on the map." Although she is known to expect much from her people, she has the reputation of being fair.

Carlotta has been highly committed to the organization's emphasis on quality control. Quality control is the key to success in component electronics, where the stakes are especially high. Even minor errors in computer components can lead to major problems in the finished product. Carlotta's region has been the leader in quality control at CCC for years, and her performance in his area has become legendary in the industry.

Because of a change in strategy at CCC, a decision was made to manufacture complete personal computers under CCC's own name rather than simply providing components to other manufacturers. This move, of course, is not without a great deal of risk. Of most importance is the amount of competition. There are many manufacturers in this area. Not a week goes by, it seems, without an announcement of a new technological breakthrough. These breakthroughs take two forms. A computer will be made with more technical capability—it can do more things. Or, a computer will be made more efficient. Each breakthrough can result in price reductions and therefore pose real concerns for any computer manufacturer.

CCC selected Carlotta Rios to head this new division because of her impeccable track record, especially in the area of quality. The first major decision concerned the location of the new facilities for the division. After much discussion with a number of experts in the industry, three viable locations were identified. The major factors considered important in the location decision included the supply of competent labor and the proximity to reasonable transportation, both to the market and to component supplies.

Although the number of possible locations had been reduced to three, controversy continued over which location should be chosen. Each location had its particular advantages and disadvantages. Each location had been studied carefully by a site selection committee formed especially to address this problem. The committee's recommendation submitted to the board of directors and the CEO did not specifically exclude any of the locations. However, it did prioritize them in the following order:

1. Best location: Cleveland, Ohio
2. Second best location: Albany, Georgia
3. Third best location: Tacoma, Washington

The selection committee's recommendations were provided to Carlotta Rios along with reports from various experts and consultants and other relevant data. Since Carlotta was to head the new facility, it was decided that she should have the final say in the location decision. She was asked to make a final decision within five days.

Carlotta's promotion to head the new division was a cause for celebration in the Rios household. She has two children, one starting high school and the other in sixth grade. Although they were sad about moving, they were thrilled with their mother's promotion. Carlotta's husband, Peter, was also very pleased with her promotion. Peter has been an accountant for a small CPA firm for the past eight years. The extra money from the promotion will mean that the family will be able to afford more luxuries.

The choice of the location was very difficult for Carlotta. She studied the recommendation of the selection committee at length and also carefully reviewed numerous reports. On the basis of this information, she decided that the committee's recommendation of priorities was accurate—at least she thought that until last night.

Last night, while Carlotta was reviewing the selection paperwork in the den, Peter came in with a cup of coffee and asked her what she was working on. She told him that the choice for the plant's location had essentially been left up to her. In fact, Carlotta explained to Peter that she thought that whatever location she recommended would be accepted by CCC's board.

It was with this revelation that Peter became very interested in the possible places to which they might move. Carlotta briefly outlined the three locations. Peter had assumed that location decisions were made by others in the organization and that Carlotta had little say in the final choice. Peter then told Carlotta that she should have discussed the site selection with him before making her final choice.

In fact, he explained that he didn't like the idea of going to Cleveland, Ohio (the first choice). He was very concerned about the typical big city problems and even more concerned about the education the children would receive. He also didn't relish the prospect of going to Albany, Georgia (the second choice), because he would have difficulty finding a reasonable accounting job. On the other hand, Tacoma, Washington (the third choice), appeared to be a nice area of the country. The schools there were highly regarded and there should be sufficient employment possibilities. Peter ended the discussion by making it clear that he would be upset if they had to move to Cleveland or Albany.

Analysis

1. If you were Carlotta Rios, what would you do?
2. How do organizations ensure that only relevant business-related factors are considered in location decisions?

Chapter 5 Organizational Goals and Planning

Case 1. The Department of Management

The following discussion took place at the spring management department meeting of State University:

WIL. Well, I think we can't really decide on the new major in service-sector management until we really decide what our mission is as a department.

BOB. Come on, Wil, that will just delay the process. We can decide without having to go through all that nonsense.

RON. What difference does it make what we think? We really have to be concerned with how our proposed major fits in with the dean's master plan. However, we don't know what that is.

SAL. No. No. No. All three of you are wrong. It is up to the provost whether this program is going to make it. It is the university mission statement that we need to address.

TOM. Fine, maybe we should be concerned with all three mission statements. But for golly sake, how are we going to sort out all of that? Usually, these statements are just a bunch of nebulous statements that you could park a Concord Jet in and still have room to do whatever you want. If we want to offer a service management program, let us do it. Who needs a mission statement to do that? A mission statement should only be a public relations statement anyway. If we need to, we will change our mission statement. The mission statement should not be something that binds us, but something that guides us.

RON. Don't you think you might be a shade callous on the purpose of a mission statement? Don't forget that we agreed as a department on a mission statement two years ago. That mission statement reflects agreement of the department on the direction we, as a department, should take. In addition, we agreed that resource allocation, including staffing decisions, ought to follow that mission statement. I don't see in our mission statement where it says we want to branch into a new major. It clearly states that we want to develop our human resource management major and our operations management track. Where does service-sector management fit in that mission?

WIL. Well, does that mean that we can't reconsider our mission statement? Is it a guide or is it a rope that is binding us?

SAL. I don't think a mission statement ought to be looked at as a binding statement. However, the statement does indicate where we want to allocate our resources. It is guiding us. Sure, we can change it, but also realize that we need to think the whole thing through. When I was at the provost's office, she said that she wants to see how any proposal fits in with the master plan of the department and the master plan of the college and the university. She also indicated that there is a relationship between the three, or at least there should be a relationship.

The mission statement of the university was established by the board of directors. This mission statement reflects the priorities of the university. Further, the provost said that there was agreement between the mission statements of each of the colleges and the university mission statement. It was expected that each department statement would be congruent with the college statement.

RON. So, Sal, what are you telling us? Are we in for another long and endless debate in revising our mission statement before we can make a change for the better? This is one of the things that bugs me about university life: the endless debate over trivial matters. Industry was never like this. They got things done.

TOM. Ron, you are right, and the shame of it all is that other departments could care less what we are doing. So what difference does it make to the university?

WIL. OK. Let's plan this thing out. First, we will have the subcommittee draft a modification to the proposal that demonstrates either how the proposal fits the mission statement or how the mission statement needs to be modified so that the proposal will fit. If the mission statement needs to modified, the subcommittee will propose that modification to the full department. If not, we will have a statement that should meet the provost's concern and help get this proposal past both the department and the college and the rest of the university.

RON. It still sounds like a waste of time to me.

TOM. Not if it means this thing can get passed. In fact, if we can demonstrate that we are consistent with our plans, I think it will help get faculty support. If not, then I think we ought to think it through by modifying the mission statement or withdrawing the proposal. We worked hard to get this department to think as a team. I would like to keep it thinking as a team—or at least keep the warfare down to a professional level.

They all laugh as they head off to class. The proposal is resubmitted the next month at the next meeting. It is passed by the department two months later. Three months later, the college curriculum committee passes the proposal. Six months later the proposal is returned unapproved on grounds that there is insufficient evidence of demand for the major. Wil, one of the creators of the proposal, is disgusted with the entire process and vows never to propose a curriculum change again. He says that it consumes too much time and energy. He blames the administration for capricious and arbitrary acts. The provost tells the department chair that proposals need to be justified showing estimated revenues and costs. The university can't afford more programs without sufficient student demand.

Analysis

1. What is the relationship (if any) between mission statements at different levels of the organization?
2. What should be the role of a mission statement? Is it a guide or a "rope that binds"?
3. Is coordination important in a university, where the units are not that interrelated, or is there an interrelationship?
4. Should the department make the decision on the major, or should that be the responsibility of the provost?
5. The proposal was denied not because it didn't fit with the mission statement but because there was insufficient evidence of student demand. Is that reasonable? How could one assess student demand for a major?

Case 2. Matching Reinforcements with Goals

The Terre Haute Soft Drink Company hired a new MBA to improve its productivity. Nancy, the new MBA, started out trying to improve the productivity of the truck drivers that haul the soda pop from the bottling plant to the stores.

Each driver had a route that involved stocking displays at grocery stores, filling pop machines with the product, and providing bulk sales to larger companies and institutional clients. Bulk sales were of two kinds. About half the bulk sales were large sales of cans or bottles. The other half of the bulk sales were sales of canisters of pop that would then be connected to dispensing machines.

Routes were determined by the manager of the bottling company. The drivers were paid on an hourly basis, and most drivers took eight hours to complete their route. Kevin, the plant manager, believed that drivers could, if provided the right incentive, improve productivity. Kevin wanted to reduce the cost of the product to meet the intense competition caused by the price war being waged by the large producers. Since handling the product was a major cost, Kevin believed that he could reduce the cost of the product if the drivers improved their productivity. This would help Kevin reduce the price of the soda that was sold. Hence, Kevin hired Nancy to apply some sound management techniques to improve the performance of the company and its employees.

Nancy was fresh out of a local university; however, she did not have much experience with setting up performance systems. She did know that using certain principles of behavior reinforcement can motivate an individual to behave in ways that lead to more desired outcomes. "That is no problem," Nancy thought, "I will just reinforce having the drivers complete the routes in less time."

Nancy then established an incentive system whereby drivers were rewarded not by hourly pay but by the number of clients that they called on in a day. The new system seemed to work at first because the number of clients increased dramatically. Productivity was increasing. However, after a number of weeks she started to receive complaints that the drivers were not really doing much when they called on a client. Stores would complain that the products were just dumped in the storeroom and were not stocked on the shelves. Institutional customers complained that the drivers did not help them set up the canister with the dispenser, and vending machines seemed to be ignored. Machines were not well stocked nor very clean. In addition, there was an increase in breakage, suggesting that the drivers were breaking bottles of soda through careless handling. The truck maintenance staff complained that the drivers were driving the trucks in a manner that reduced the life of the clutch and brakes. In essence, the drivers were much harder on the trucks under this sort of compensation system.

Nancy decided that reinforcing the number of customers called upon in a given day might not be the answer. So she decided on a second type of reinforcement approach. Under this system the driver would be paid a flat amount based on the quantity of product that he or she sold. Nancy believed that by reinforcing in this manner, the drivers would improve the quality of interaction that they had with the customer. In addition, productivity would increase because the drivers would be selling more of the product.

Again, sales did increase and Nancy was delighted. However, customer complaints increased again in a few weeks. The problem this time seemed to focus around two issues. First, the drivers were providing insufficient bottled soda to the grocery stores. Second, soda sold in machines was still being ignored. It seemed that the machines were too much bother for the drivers. Bottled soda was being ignored because it was harder to handle and the drivers would also have to handle the return bottles, which meant extra work and time.

Nancy decided to try a third incentive system. Under this system, drivers were paid a commission on the sales of the product but the commission would vary depending on the nature of the product. Canisters would have a lower rate than cans or bottles because they were a volume sale. Cans were placed at a lower rate than bottles. Service to the vending machines would be reinforced through the use of spot inspections. Inspectors would see that the machines were clean and correctly and fully stocked. Generous bonuses would be paid for appropriate servicing.

Although commission rates of bottles, cans, and canisters had to be adjusted a couple of times, Nancy finally felt she had found a system that worked. Performance improved. The customers seemed satisfied, and so was Kevin. Drivers now had much more autonomy in determining their delivery schedules. They had an incentive to service the customers, so they were more apt to do it well. In addition, instead of just delivering the products, the drivers had to be good salespersons. Finally, they had an incentive to improve the displays of the product because they gained from any increases in sales that occurred.

Nancy next looked at the bottling operations to see how changing the reinforcement system might affect performance there. There were two 8-hour shifts of ten people on the bottling lines. The bottling operation was highly mechanized. A key process that involved worker labor was loading enough containers (bottles or cans) to keep the line moving. In addition, filling the syrup and carbonated water vats was important. Adequate supplies were essential, but so was ensuring that the machine was working right so that the pop was not too sweet or had too much carbonation. Unloading the product was important as well because the machine would shut down if too much product backed up on the line. Nancy wondered about how to reinforce the bottlers' effort. She didn't think it would be easy.

Analysis

1. Why wouldn't pay by the hour be a good way to support a goal of improving performance?
2. Why didn't the first incentive system work?
3. Why didn't the second incentive system work?

4. What does it mean to match a behavior reinforcement system to the goals of the organization?
5. What kind of incentive system would you propose for the bottling operation?

Case 3. Quantifying Qualitative Goals

Marian Walsch was the manager of a discount store. The store, called Sam's Mart, had a strong commitment to "aggressive hospitality." This meant that the store employees worked very hard to ensure that the customer has a positive experience while in the store. One of the goals of the founder was to translate aggressive hospitality into specific sorts of actions: having very clean stores, helpful salespeople, and attractive merchandise and displays. In the early 1980s, a new facet was added to the notion of aggressive hospitality. A store employee, in uniform, would greet each customer as he or she came into the store. The customer would be welcomed, offered a shopping cart, and asked if he or she needed help finding particular merchandise.

The hourly employee that was assigned the job was normally someone new to the job. However, in some cases a retired person was hired just for the job. In Marian Walsch's store she normally used new employees because this would give them a chance to start learning the store and the culture at Sam's Mart.

When Marian went to a management training program that the company paid for at Southern University, she learned about the importance of translating even qualitative goals into specific employee behaviors. According to the speaker, this would improve the clarity of what the employee should do and would provide more specific behaviors that management could use to measure an employee's performance. Although this made sense at the training program, it wasn't until Marian got back to her store that it really became evident. Marshall was a new employee that had been the store greeter for only a few days. However, Marian was not pleased with what she saw. Marian had had several problems with new employees like Marshall in that they did not seem to "get into the job." In essence, they were shy and didn't seem to know what to do. In the past Marian had just attributed that to being a teenager. However, after the training session, Marian started to wonder whether it was because no one had really told them what they should do.

Marian sat down one day in her office and defined ten separate behaviors that were important to the store greeter's job. She communicated these separate ten behaviors to the employee and made spot checks during the day to observe how well the employee was doing. In addition, other store personnel made random checks of the greeter's performance. At the end of the employee's shift, the store manager reviewed the greeter's performance, praising good performance and working to improve performance that was less than adequate. Once the employee was doing well, the number of checks and performance review sessions was reduced. However, the results of any spot checks were included in the employee's personnel file for consideration in deciding pay increases or promotions. The system seemed to be quite effective.

Several months after Marian set up her system, she had dinner with a manager of the local bank. They talked about each other's work and business problems. In the conversation Marian talked about the system. The banker laughed and asked her if she was crazy. The idea of spending that much time on an employee's making such a marginal contribution to the store seemed inappropriate to the banker.

"Listen," Marian said, "here is an employee that is the first person that the customer meets. If that interaction comes across as indifferent or negative, the customer will probably have a negative image of the whole store. Customers that feel good about where they shop are going to buy more and come in more often. They will also tell their friends about the store. And friends are potential customers."

The banker at first didn't agree. However, the longer he thought the more it scared him. He remembered the survey that his bank had done on customer perceptions about his bank and about those of his competitors. The results showed that his bank was perceived as efficient but cold. The tellers did not seem to care. The banks that had higher ratings on the items "caring for the customer" were increasing their business faster than the other banks. "Maybe there is something to what Marian says," the banker thought. "But how do you make a bank have greater 'warmth'?" The tellers, in most cases, were the only people that the customer came in contact with, yet the bank had no program on customer relations or even any mention on the performance evaluation that rated the employee on the quality of his or her interactions with the customer. Mostly the bank reinforced the accuracy and speed with which the employee worked. But how do you judge the quality of a teller's interaction? How do you measure warmth? The banker was confused and called Marian.

Marian was surprised that what had been said several weeks ago was still in the banker's mind, particularly since the banker had scoffed at her approach. However, after some ribbing, Marian recalled some of what was said at the training program and repeated it over the phone: "When you talk about the quality of an interaction, management normally uses nebulous terms such as *attitude*. But telling an employee that he or she has a bad attitude does not do much to guide the employee. A bad attitude can mean one thing to one individual and another to a second person. A more effective manager will try to articulate what should be done in a role, with respect to both the duties and the quality dimensions of the job. Although not all aspects of the job will be articulated, at least there is less potential for confusion."

The banker said, "That is all well and good, but surveys indicate that our bank isn't warm enough. What should I do?"

"Turn up the heat," Marian said.

"Do you hear me laughing?" the banker said.

"OK. Warmth must be translated into behaviors or activities that you or your employees can demonstrate. What can be done to improve customer perceptions? Warmth is really just a generic word for a host of behaviors and activities."

Analysis

1. What sorts of behaviors might Marian have identified as part of the store greeter's performance?

2. Why is this approach called "quantifying qualitative aspects" of performance?
3. Identify five activities that the banker might do to improve the environment of the bank. However, do not include any changes that might be made in the tellers' performance.
4. What changes might be made in the tellers' performance? Identify five behaviors.
5. How might qualitative aspects of the bank manager's job be measured?

Case 4. The State Rehabilitation Service

Ann Wong was the supervisor of a rehabilitation service office in South Dakota. Ann had just finished working with a team of university professors to develop a means of quantifying performance standards for case-workers.

A case-worker works with individuals who might have one or more of three different kinds of disabilities: physical, mental, and retardation. In addition, the case-worker is concerned with training programs for convicts once they leave the institution. There are several levels of severity for each kind of disability. The rehabilitation service had classified various disabilities as severe, and "employable after rehabilitation" (EAR).

It was the job of the case-worker to meet with the client and then develop a plan that would help the client enter the work force. So, for example, if a client had lost an arm in an accident, the case-worker would develop a plan that would provide therapy for the client to learn how to use an artificial arm. Once that program was over, the case-worker would develop a plan for the client to enter a more sheltered work situation and to receive additional training. The long-term goal was to have the client secure employment in a regular job within the community. The case-worker, therefore, worked with clients as well as with potential employers. Training centers and sheltered workshops were another important aspect of the case-worker's interactions.

Ann wanted to improve the methods of reinforcing good performance among case-workers. The old system was a simple system that really did not provide much feedback to the employee nor protect the employer if the employee felt the system was discriminating against the employee. The evaluation system was composed of a dozen questions that a supervisor could use to rate the employee on twelve aspects of the job. Worker attitude was one aspect. Other aspects were personal appearance, ability to communicate, accuracy of paperwork, timeliness of reports, and so forth. The rating scale had five ranks: excellent, better than average, average, needs improvement, and needs much improvement.

Ann believed that these sorts of evaluations did not give much direction to employees and allowed them to feel that they "had to be the boss's favorite" to rate well. This was personally repugnant to Ann, and she wanted to develop a system that was performance based or at least based on measurable behaviors. Employees would excel because of their effort, not because of some correct or incorrect perception by the supervisor. Part of the university team was devoted to creating these performance-based measures. The team also worked with the employees themselves because they realized the importance of getting input in the process.

The team set twenty-five different standards of performance. The standards measured both qualitative and quantitative aspects of the job. Quantitative aspects included the number of case loads of each counselor. In addition, a tracking system measured the progress of each client during the period. Often more than six different plans were written for each client as family conditions changed or as they found that the program as originally designed was too hard or too easy for them. The number of clients that were rehabilitated was calculated. A rehabilitated individual was one who remained in his or her new job for sixty days.

Paperwork was considered as both a quality and quantity dimension. The correctness of the plan and the appropriate classification of the client were essential to the agency because several individuals were involved in the client's progress. They had to have correct information so they could provide correct services at the appropriate time. For example, client financial planning was conducted by the staff specialist. She had to know when the clients were almost ready to enter the work force. If they entered too early, the training program would be forgotten; if too late, they could be in financial problems because they would not have the ability to budget their resources.

The case-worker's performance was measured partly by the quality of his or her interaction with the client, outside agencies, and the internal staff. This was measured through the use of a survey, and, if performance was poor on this dimension, a focus group might be used. The focus group was composed of the case-worker's internal and external contacts so that the agency could decide how to improve interactions in the future.

Ann really liked the system, and so did all of the better case-workers. However, Ann had some nagging feelings that she shouldn't just let the evaluations go "on automatic pilot." She believed that although the system was good, she had little opportunity to encourage someone who might be improving or to send a message to a person who was starting to get sloppy in the job. In reality, Ann believed that there ought to be some personal and professional discretion in the system. Although the system gave her and the employees good guidance, it also needed to include some intangible dimensions. However, this imprecision disturbed Ann, because she had been taught in school that performance improves if it is quantified and if specific goals are used instead of general goals. Performance goals also should be hard, not easy, to reach, but not too hard to make an employee give up. Little in her formal education seemed to suggest that a supervisor should not go by the books and consider unmeasurable dimensions of performance. The law staff also supported the notion that following clear objectives would be easier to defend in court. However, one supervisor from the sand hills area did agree with Ann. She told Ann that all the systems in the world cannot perfectly measure an employee's performance.

Analysis

1. What are the benefits of measuring performance in the evaluation of an employee?
2. Can we measure an employee's performance perfectly using performance-related objectives?
3. Should professional judgment enter into performance evaluations?

4. If one allows professional judgment of intangibles to affect performance ratings, how can the employee be protected so that the supervisor is not acting in a capricious or arbitrary manner?
5. Should individual performance goals be linked to the organization's goals? How?

Case 5. More Airports Versus Fast Trains[1]

Trains Could Cut Demand for Short Air Trips—For Every 3 Flying NY to Wash., 2 Now Ride Amtrak

> 'Our business is moving people,' consultant J. Lynn Helms, a former head of the Federal Aviation Administration (FAA), told a group of aviation experts recently. 'We must not let our personal desire [to fly] overshadow our responsibility to the traveling public. We must include high-speed rail transportation in our planning.' (*Governing*, November)

> Given airport overcrowding, would it make sense to encourage trains rather than airplanes for trips between nearby cities? The department [U.S. DOT] is simply incapable of making such a choice among modes: The FAA wants to build more airports, regardless of whether the airplane is the most efficient way of getting from here to there. (*The Journal of Commerce*, editorial, Nov. 9)

> We cannot expand airports fast enough to stay ahead of the inefficiencies of hub-spoke operations. The congestion can be relieved by using ground transportation on shorter routes and bringing back long, non-stop flights. For oil conservation and travel efficiency between cities less than an hour apart, railroads . . . are better bets than airports [in] the East and West Coast corridors, St. Louis–Kansas City and others. (Frederick C. Thayer, in *USA Today*, July 8)

Many people ask *The Journal of Commerce*'s above question. The case for more use of rail is strong: modern trains, on now-under-used rights-of-way, would have competitive trip times, more reliability and—in bad weather—safety, greater energy efficiency, and less environmental cost.

New airports use too much land (up to 30,000 acres each), worsen suburban gridlock by generating much auto-dependent development (as around Washington's Dulles Airport), take too long to plan and build (20 years for Dallas–Ft. Worth, our newest big airport, opened in 1974), and cost too much—$3 billion each.

Pressure is growing for more restrictions on noise and nighttime flights at airports nationwide. Students in schools near the Los Angeles airport reportedly have above-normal blood pressure. "Environmentalists across the country have brought new airport and runway construction to a halt," says American Airlines Chairman Robert L. Crandall (*J of C*, Nov. 22).

Meanwhile, Amtrak's Seattle-Portland and Chicago-based short-distance trains are too slow to be air-competitive. Last year Amtrak nearly rerouted Chicago–St.

1. News from the National Association of Railroad Passengers: "More Airports vs. Fast Trains," *National Association of Railroad Passengers News*, Vol. 23, No. 2 (February 1989), 1–4. Used with permission.

SKINNER'S 200 MPH THRESHOLD: TOO HIGH!

Secretary of Transportation Samuel K. Skinner said after his Feb. 6 confirmation that 200 mph trains would be an alternative to flying. But, even with a top speed of only 110 mph (Metroliners 125), Amtrak carries 2 people from New York to Washington for every 3 that fly (7 for every 3 that fly, if one includes intermediate points). Even overseas, top speeds are well under 200: 149 in Japan, 168 in France.

Louis trains, bypassing Bloomington and Springfield (the state capital), due to deteriorating tracks.

Rail dollars are scarce, but DOT has billions for aviation, thanks to the quaint U.S. practice of earmarking user funds (in this case, the airline ticket tax and fuel taxes paid by general aviation) for reinvestment in the collecting mode of transport, even where another mode (i.e., rail) could do the job better.

What Is the Problem?

To air advocates, the problem is simple: air travel more than doubled in the past decade; strong growth will continue; more and bigger airports are needed. Critics say the magnitude of recent growth is overstated (see "Air Travel Growth"). They say traffic projections *must* reflect some 'slowdown' factors aviation people ignore . . . and *should* reflect a new public commitment to rail.

The *FAA* is sponsoring a Transportation Research Board (TRB) study of *airport* needs. This epitomizes what's wrong with federal transport policy: the *transportation secretary* should have sponsored a TRB study of *intercity* travel needs.

TRB's preliminary report mentions rail only briefly. For air, the report says "demographic trend data indicate 2 to 3 times the 1986 traffic by 2050" but, due to "uncertainty . . . as projections extend into the future," says that, "for long-range airport planning and land reservation, it is safer to emphasize the upper range. . . . The working group therefore concluded that airport system planning for 2050 should [assume] 2 to 6 times the 1986 traffic."

The air lobby will say TRB's report "proves" we need many more airports. TRB, however, is only as good as its funding sources, none of which are connected with intercity passenger rail.

Aviation Advocates' Solution

Frustrated at resistance to new airports near big cities, air experts are touting "remote transfer airports" (a.k.a. "transfer-only airports," "wayports") far beyond the suburbs, serving primarily transferring passengers, but also perhaps connected to the nearest metro areas by "surface modes—highway or rail operating at a speed competitive with short-haul air travel" (TRB's words).

Today, aviation receives extensive, often-ignored subsidies from general funds ("Aviation Subsidies," next page; "Big Airline Subsidies," *NARP News*, Dec. '85).

But "wayports," with revenue only from connecting passengers, may need even more non-user subsidies. As TRB delicately put it, "The institutional and financial issues of ownership, capital investment, and operation would be paramount. To gain airline acceptance and patronage, the [wayport] would have to offer operational and competitive business advantages to compensate for the loss of originating passengers who now board flights at hub airports within metropolitan areas."

Some still hope for new hub airports, though the Denver flight . . . suggests even these will require more non-user subsidies. TRB says new big-city airports have often been rejected "because of cost, lack of suitable sites, environmental impacts, or adverse effects on surrounding communities. Nonetheless, as the pressure of demand increases, the feasibility of building large new airports in metropolitan areas that serve as major traffic hubs will need to be reconsidered."

**AIR TRAVEL GROWTH:
UNDER HALF WHAT YOU THOUGHT**

"Industry spokesmen consistently point out that passenger boardings have almost doubled since 1977. But they rarely mention this: The actual number of passengers has risen only about 40% over the same period, estimates the industry's own trade group, the Air Transport Assn. . . .

"At least 2 boardings are usually counted when one person takes a connecting flight. And airlines today—with their new 'hub' airports—have far more connecting flights than before. . . .

"Are airports being used by people who are flying more often—or by people who simply are taking more connections? 'You have to wonder whether some airport congestion could simply be relieved if airlines had more non-stop service,' says Harold Seligman, president of Management Alternatives, a travel-consulting company in Stamford, CT."

The Wall Street Journal, Sept. 15

FEDERAL AVIATION SUBSIDIES: HIGH; MAY SKYROCKET

The FAA estimates "private-sector users are responsible for about 85%" of FAA spending and "have received a general fund subsidy of $17 bill" since the trust fund's 1970 creation.

"Proposals by the Nixon Administration in 1971 to restrict capital spending from the trust fund, while fully funding FAA operations from it, led the Congress to restrict trust fund spending to only the capital costs of the aviation system. . . . These limits [though later modified] have restricted the trust fund to financing an average of only 27% of FAA operations since 1980. As a result, the general fund of the Treasury finances nearly half of total FAA spending for the aviation system."

Under present law, federal air taxes will be cut in half in Jan. 1990 if aviation capital spending does not reach certain levels. The levels are not likely to be reached and "the result would be a $10.1 billion reduction in taxes for private-sector users of the aviation system."

One policy option would require private-sector users to pay their full costs, recognizing "that the accumulated surplus in the trust fund is the result of past general fund subsidies and is not in fact owed to private-sector users of the system. [Compared with present law,] this would increase aviation excise tax revenue by $19.2 billion 1990–1994, thus reducing federal budget deficits by $14.4 billion, and would divide aviation system financing more equitably between private-sector users and general taxpayers."

The Status of the Airport and Airway Trust Fund,
A Special Study by the Congressional Budget Office, December

Indeed, TRB found 13 locations in major metro areas "to have high potential for either expanding the existing airport or developing a new secondary site by conversion of general aviation or military facilities."

The already-powerful air lobby last Apr. 12 launched a $15 mill., 2-year nationwide p.r. campaign to persuade air passengers and Congress to support big increases in air-system spending. The campaign ignores aviation subsidies and focuses on the "outrageous" air trust fund surplus and the "need" to spend more money faster.

Another Solution

You can help rail get more attention by including information from this newsletter in communications with your public officials!

If the gasoline tax is raised for deficit-reduction purposes, some of the increase likely will go for highways, since many legislators oppose use of gasoline tax revenues for *non-transportation* purposes. Urge your legislators to see that Amtrak and mass transit together get 4 pennies of any such increase!

America may yet follow the recommendations of Carnegie-Mellon University's Richard A. Rice, who said the U.S. could almost double transport output in 20 years while *reducing* transport energy consumption! (Key departures from past policies: a 2,600% increase in intercity rail passenger-miles; no growth in short-distance air travel.) (*Technology Review*, Feb., 1974)

Pricing could ease airport congestion. . . . TRB—of all organizations!—treats this like a hot potato: "Economic measures, such as peak-hour pricing or differential pricing of access for certain airport users, can also be employed, although these measures are often controversial. In particular, commuter airlines, charter operators, and private business aircraft operators argue that increases in landing fees would effectively deny them access to the airports of choice."

Note the parallel between highway and airport gridlock: in both cases, developing rail alternatives and pricing today's congested facilities would benefit the public at large—minimizing environmental and community impacts; in both cases, the dominant forces ignore rail and pricing and rely mainly on the laying of more concrete!

Some Calls for Sanity

- If ideas of dramatically increased use of fast trains in the U.S. "seem visionary, it's not because they are, but because of the paucity of thinking done in this country by those—in government, in business, in academia—who, out of indifference or powerlessness or ties to entrenched economic interests, content themselves by chuckling at those nostalgic cranks who still believe the Iron Horse has a future."—*The Sacramento Bee*, editorial, Jan. 15.
- "Railroads could again become the transportation choice for short trips. At Detroit's Metropolitan Airport, for example, nearly 25% of daily flights connect with cities within 120 miles."—David Morris of Knight-Ridder Newspapers, article in *The Atlanta Constitution*, Nov. 27.
- "Between 13 and 50% of current air traffic at Chicago's O'Hare International Airport could be relieved if Amtrak's midwest corridor were fully developed. . . . A recent street survey conducted by the *Chicago Sun-Times* showed that 3 of 4 respondents would prefer using improved Amtrak midwest corridor trains to flying. . . . 27% [of O'Hare] flights serve destinations within 200 miles of Chicago.

. . . Fully 50% . . . goes to points within 400 miles of Chicago."—Illinois ARP News Release, Dec., 1987.

- "Re your June 1, page-one article 'At LaGuardia Airport, Passenger Surge Causes Delays and Congestion': There is one solution to relieving the traffic congestion at LaGuardia. That is the expansion of rail passenger service in the Northeast."—Richard P. Duffy of the Empire State Passengers Assn., letter in *The Wall Street Journal,* July 6.
- "Re 'Aviation Experts Warn of Gridlock at U.S. Airports' (front page, June 19): Before this country begins to pave over what's left of the countryside, an alternative must be examined. In the last decade, faced with similar problems of overcrowded airports, Germany and Switzerland decided to integrate their intercity rail systems with major airports at Frankfurt, Geneva, and Zurich, using rail service to distribute passengers to smaller cities, thus reducing airport congestion caused by connecting flights. . . . The potential to reduce the number of planes using U.S. airports by this approach is enormous. . . . The cost of [developing rail service] would be a mere fraction of the $57 bill. projected for expanding our airports. . . ."—Michigan ARP Chairman Alan J. Gebauer, letter in *The New York Times,* July 6. [New facilities at Orlando Airport include reservations of rights-of-way—including tunnels—intended for fast intercity and local trains.]

(Single copies of CBO special study, "The Status of the Airport and Airway Trust Fund," available from CBO Publications, 202/226-2809, House Annex #2, Room 413, 2nd & D Sts., SW, Wash., DC 20515. "Future Development of the U.S. Airport Network: Preliminary Report and Recommended Study Plan" is $5 prepaid—VISA and MasterCharge accepted—from TRB, 202/334-3214, 2101 Constitution Ave., NW, Wash., DC 20418.)

Analysis

1. How might the federal government get some sense in its approach to allocating funding for transportation projects? In essence, this question might be rephrased to "Given the various clients to be served, how can the federal government set its own objectives to guide its allocation of resources among various modes of transportation?"
2. How does public opinion affect this allocation process?
3. Should public opinion affect this allocation process, or should the federal government develop some more rational or quantitative model of allocating resources?
4. How might a change in administration affect the goals of the Department of Transportation?

5. Does the long-range view suffer in a political environment that is subject to reelection every four years?
6. How might the long-term perspective be maintained in the political environment in Washington, particularly with respect to transportation policy?

Chapter 6 Strategy and Strategic Planning

Case 1. Does the Purchase Make Sense?

"I think that we have done as much as we can do in the hotel industry, and frankly, I'm starting to get a little bit bored with the whole thing," replied Hub Ellis at the monthly board meeting of the Bargain Beds hotel chain.

It was Hub's dream to acquire a struggling hotel chain and to get it back on its feet, so when the Confederate Inn hotel chain was put up for sale in 1985, Hub accumulated all the money necessary to purchase the ailing chain and assumed the majority of its debt. The thirty-eight hotels were located primarily in northern Georgia and Alabama and had lost money for six consecutive years before Hub and his backers purchased the business.

Before operations began, Hub thought it was necessary to change the name of the hotels and appoint himself president and chairman of the board. Having spent twenty-three years in the hotel industry, he felt he was qualified to run the organization. The management team of Bargain Beds consisted of other seasoned hotel administrators who also sought the same challenges as Hub. The organization shifted its marketing and media attention to salespersons, truckers, and others who would usually stay for only one night. The chain offered no-frills lodging by concentrating on clean rooms at low prices. None of the outlets had indoor swimming pools, restaurants, weight rooms, or any of the other amenities that are found at most hotels. This emphasis proved to be very successful. The chain was now making a substantial profit and had recently paid off all of the debt assumed upon acquisition of the hotels.

Before the most recent directors' meeting, Hub came upon a rather intriguing investment opportunity. A chain of seven movie theaters located in central Georgia came up for sale. All of the theaters were located in towns serving between 25,000 and 40,000 people, employed about twenty-five part-time employees, and were situated in strip malls near a major thoroughfare. Usually, these strip malls consisted of one large department store, one drug store, and seven or eight specialty shops.

An analysis of the theaters' balance sheet really got Hub's attention (see Exhibit 1). It showed that the chain had lost money over the last four years—just what Hub needed, a new challenge. Hub also concluded that the chain had a very good chance of making money with the right "management philosophy."

When Hub went to visit the chain in the role of movie patron, he got the impression that a conflict existed between management and theater employees. This notion was

EXHIBIT 1
Three-Year Income Statements for First-Run Productions

	1986 ($000)	1987 ($000)	1988 ($000)
Revenues	$2,392	$2,410	$2,425
Cost of Goods Sold	1,107	1,106	1,106
Gross Profit	$1,285	$1,304	$1,319
Expenses			
Building and Maintenance	$ 761	$ 767	$ 765
Advertising	70	73	73
Utilities	151	152	152
Wage Expense	337	363	381
Miscellaneous Expense	51	51	52
Total Operating Expenses	$1,370	$1,406	$1,423
Total Profit (Loss)	($85)	($102)	($104)

confirmed after speaking with both sides. It appeared that almost all of the theater employees wanted a part-time job, but management wanted the part-time employees to be as committed as full-time employees without the salary that came with this commitment. Although the organization had some provisions for overtime pay (hours over sixty), few workers embraced this philosophy. In fact, the troubles between the workers and management had reached the point where the workers had begun to initiate union representation. Being well versed in resolving employee disputes in the hotel industry, Hub thought this was a problem that he would have no trouble straightening out.

Hub felt that this was a good time for the hotel organization to diversify its interest. At next month's directors' meeting, he intended to propose the acquisition of First-Run Productions.

Analysis

1. Do you think that this acquisition makes good strategic sense? Why or why not?
2. What barriers may have an effect on whether the board decides to purchase First-Run Productions? Internal? External?
3. Discuss Hub's management philosophy in this context. Will it work?

Case 2. Wide World of Travel

Wide World of Travel could be described as a mom and pop travel agency. Originally started over twenty years ago by Art and Kathy Wilson, it has provided a comfortable living and helped put two children through college.

For the past several years, the Wilsons have generated over 75 percent of their revenue by booking three- and four-day trips for individual clients to the major gambling areas in New Jersey and Nevada. As Kathy says, "It may not be an exciting part of the business, but it's profitable."

Lately, the Wilsons have begun to worry about the many changes forecasted for the travel industry. The proliferation of discounting by airlines and other travel services has increased the need for automation, which would require a significant capital investment for the Wilsons. If these changes affected their core business, the Wilsons' ability to survive would be in question. But they also feel that their core business has been getting tedious—too predictable. They are afraid their boredom may eventually harm business.

These factors led the Wilsons to contact a consultant that specializes in advising small business owners in the travel industry. The consultant thoroughly examined Wide World of Travel and came to the following preliminary conclusions:

1. The three- to four-day bookings to gambling areas are cash cows. With little effort these junkets can still be counted on to provide predictable cash flow for several years.
2. The Wilsons are experts in many diverse aspects of travel. They are licensed and certified to make travel arrangements domestically and internationally.
3. Wide World has operated in a defensive mode for many years. It is profitable within a narrow segment of the travel industry and doesn't venture much outside its boundaries.
4. The Wilsons are ready for a change.

Analysis

1. What would you advise the Wilsons to do?
2. Develop a short- and long-term strategy to guide Wide World of Travel. In doing so, identify the following:
   a. Additional strategic business units you would recommend
   b. How you would judge the effectiveness of the new strategy
   c. At what time you would judge the strategy's effectiveness

Case 3. The Summer Job (After)

Harry and Joanna Nelson's summer painting business has been successful beyond their expectations (see Chapter 1, Case 2). At the end of the summer they paid back the loan from their father, covered all expenses (materials, equipment, and wages for two part-time employees), and put enough in the bank to meet their primary goal—to earn enough money to pay for school and personal expenses for their current year in college. The next summer was even better. Harry prospected for new clients and divided managerial responsibilities with his sister Joanna. All painting was done by five employees.

The Nelson's Painting Service (its formal name) developed a solid reputation in the community as an honest, reliable, and reasonably priced service venture. Several residents and business owners expressed regret at Harry's impending graduation and worried that the painting service would be disbanded. These community feelings did not go unnoticed by the Nelson's. Although Harry was busy interviewing with several large companies, he wondered whether he wasn't overlooking the opportunity in his community.

Harry decided to explore the idea of continuing the business on a full-time basis upon graduation. He found that a line of credit from the bank would be available. But more important, his research indicated a need for lawn care and snow removal that would make the Nelson's Service Co. (the proposed name) a year-round enterprise.

Analysis

1. What key general environmental characteristics should the Nelsons consider?
2. Develop a marketing strategy for Nelson's Service.
3. Why is Harry's definition of his business critical to his success?
4. What are the tradeoffs that Harry faces by going into business for himself instead of working for a large corporation?

Case 4. Harrington Holding Company

The Harrington Holding Company is a diversified holding company with major interests in transportation (it owns a regional railroad), energy (it explores and develops oil and gas fields), real estate (it owns and leases commercial and industrial real estate holdings in metropolitan areas), and tank cars (it manufactures railroad tank cars).

Harrington has four major divisions to deal with its four major interest areas: transportation, energy, real estate, and manufacturing. Each year the presidents of the divisional units have to submit a strategic business plan for the following year and for the next five-year period. The objective of such planning at the business-unit level is to determine how the particular business can succeed—to improve the competitive position of the business unit, to concentrate on those segments of the business unit that are more attractive, and so forth.

The corporate officers of Harrington classify its four operating companies according to the portfolio management strategy categories developed by the Boston Consulting Group (BCG). Unfortunately, in considering the one- and five-year plans developed by the operating companies, they have some disagreement about which business belongs in what category. There is less disagreement among the Harrington business units categorized as "stars." In their plans, these business units all agree that their business growth potential is great, that relative market share is good, and most importantly, that much money has to be invested to ensure the promised profitability in the future.

It is here that agreement ends. "Cash cow" business units agree that they make more money than they spend. However, in their one- and five-year plans, they have requested large increases in personnel and capital funds to expand their operations and develop new markets. They are not anxious to turn over large cash surpluses to develop markets and products other than their own.

The "dog" business units do not see their plight as hopeless. They have no interest in being divested, liquidated, or harvested. They argue eloquently in their one- and five-year plans that, with proper reinvestment, their market shares can be not only maintained but also increased.

Finally, Harrington has identified several business units as "question marks." However, it has also decided that the risk associated with developing a competitive stance for some of these businesses given the uncertain market share is not warranted. The operating businesses, however, see things differently. They have asked for large injections of capital and personnel to aggressively develop and capture the market share in the areas where their business growth potential is greatest.

Analysis

1. When using the BCG approach, how do you justify the reallocation of resources among various business units?
2. What evaluation criteria would you use to determine which business units are supported and which are not?

Chapter 7 Tactical and Operational Planning

Case 1. St. Andrew College

St. Andrew College is a small private liberal arts college located near St. Louis, Missouri. It was founded in 1925 and has a strong reputation for a solid liberal arts curriculum. Nearly 80 percent of its graduates go on to attain graduate degrees. Prelaw and premed are among its strongest programs. Its enrollment has been stable at about two thousand students for the past few years.

Recently, the number of freshman applications has been declining, and there are fears that academic standards may have to be lowered if this trend continues. An enrollment management task force in the admissions department has determined that many of these "lost applicants" have enrolled at nearby state universities to major in professional areas such as business and engineering. In addition, tuitions at state-supported schools are less than one-half that at St. Andrew.

The president and the board of regents of St. Andrew know that they need to modify some of their goals and objectives to meet the challenges posed by (1) the changing demographics that are reducing the number of college-age students that St. Andrew has traditionally attracted, (2) the reduced federal and state funding that has made St. Andrew less affordable to a wider range of potential applicants, and (3) a greater interest by students in a career-oriented curriculum (business, engineering) at the expense of a traditional liberal arts curriculum.

In a special session the board of regents approved the following goals for St. Andrew College: In ten years the curriculum must be redesigned to reflect a stronger career orientation so that professionally oriented courses make up one-third of the total curriculum. In addition, college resources must be in place to handle at least 30 percent professional majors and 70 percent liberal arts majors. This goal statement was based on continuing a full-time equivalency of 2,500 undergraduates after ten years.

Analysis

1. What barriers to planning might hinder progress toward this ten-year goal?
2. What resource reallocations need to take place to accomplish this goal?

3. What types of contingency plans would you recommend? What factors should be monitored and used to indicate the proper times (action points) to implement the contingency plans?

Case 2. Omega Supermarkets

Omega Supermarkets is a chain of thirty successful supermarkets in medium-sized cities in the Southwest. It has been the company's policy to have one leading store in cities with a population of approximately 50,000 to 100,000 people. In each city, large, attractive stores have been developed that provide complete product lines of food and related products sold at competitive prices. Recently, the company had to close a few poorly located stores. Over the years it has relied on the instincts of its president and founder, George Nagel, for most decisions, including where to locate stores. All in all, the company's profit record indicates that his judgment has generally been correct during the company's twenty-five-year history.

George's daughter Lesley recently graduated from a university with a degree in business administration and joined the company as assistant to the president. Her major responsibility involved developing a "system for planning."

Lesley's management courses had stressed the importance of planning. Her summers spent working at various company stores reinforced her conviction that a more formalized planning effort was needed because not a day seemed to go by without some "fires having to be put out." The more Lesley thought about it, the more she felt that management by objectives (MBO) was a technique that could be useful not only in determining new store locations, but also in planning day-to-day store operations.

Lesley discussed her ideas with her father, who responded, "MBO is nothing new here. We have always had important company objectives that everyone strives to meet. As you know, I expect $15 million in sales, a profit on sales before taxes of 2 percent, a return on investment of 15 percent, and employee turnover to be stabilized at 8 percent. In addition, an ongoing training program is to be put into effect by June 30 of this year, and two new stores are to be built by the end of the year."

"But I'm more interested in how these goals have been developed and who was involved in the decision," replied Lesley.

"Well, they were primarily my thoughts after discussing the situation with Neil Hardin, the vice president of store operations, and William Waterhouse, the controller."

In later discussions with both the store operations vice president and the controller, Lesley discovered that they felt they had little direct involvement in planning except for compiling financial information for George. This led Lesley to believe that a more formal planning process needed to be implemented that also involved store managers. However, she also realized from experience that the store managers' time commitments already were very burdensome.

Lesley was somewhat confused as to the direction to take in planning.

Analysis

1. How would you characterize the planning that is taking place currently at Omega Supermarkets?
2. Is MBO being used at Omega?
3. Would you implement an MBO program at Omega? If so, how?
4. What should Lesley recommend in regard to planning?

Case 3. Mary Maloney

After finishing high school, Mary Maloney decided to go to work "for a while." "Classes, papers, projects—they all seemed so unrelated to the real world," said Mary, "I needed some time to sort things out for myself."

Fortunately, Mary had taken some typing and "commercial" classes, so she was able to get a job quickly. She went to work as a clerk-typist for Creative Results, Ltd., a public relations and advertising firm. Creative Results performed a variety of advertising and public relations activities, including the preparation of ads for newspapers; the development of designs and artwork for posters and outdoor advertising; the design and writing of short paperback books on leisure-time subjects; and even assistance to some clients in fund raising.

Mary loved working with people at Creative Results. "The people are so alive and creative; they're just terrific!" Her own job wasn't very challenging, but she was learning something new about the business every day.

After six months Mary's supervisor, Kathy Stevenson, indicated that her work was very good and that she seemed to have potential for more demanding work. Opportunities were there, but certain qualifications needed to be met. "We have jobs around here opening up regularly, some pretty good ones," said Kathy. "The trouble is that the specialized work we do here usually requires at least some college, on-the-job training and sometimes special training in art, graphics, design, or writing."

Mary decided to take some classes at one of the state universities located near where she lived. Creative Results allowed Mary to work a 25-hour work week that permitted her to take a full class load at school. She found that she enjoyed college much more than she had thought she would because it seemed more related to matters at work.

About a year later she applied and was accepted for a job as coordinator-expeditor in the Leisure Time Books department at Creative Results. Her work involved coordinating activity between clients and in-house writers and designers to ensure that print schedules were met. She found the work interesting and demanding. "There are a lot of things to keep organized, people to keep happy, and schedules to meet."

After about a year in the job, Mary's supervisor was promoted to another unit and Mary was asked if she would like to apply for the supervisory position. Although it meant working full-time and having to go to school part-time, she decided to take the position as supervisor of coordination and planning for the Leisure Time Books department. As supervisor Mary interacted with many department heads and had overall responsibility for planning the projects that flowed through her department. The department itself was a small one: it had only four people, including a clerk-typist. However, the work was extremely important, since her responsibility was on-time completion at budgeted costs.

As coordinator Mary had run into various problems and situations that she felt could be improved on or even avoided. As supervisor of coordination and planning, she now had the opportunity to introduce some changes to improve the work of planning and coordinating the printing of leisure-time books.

One constant problem was timing and coordinating the activities of artists and writers in the company. Mary thought, "These people never seem to be able to get their work done on time." Another concern was that about one-third of the books were over budget or were delivered late to customers.

Normally work wasn't released to the printer until all revisions had been made in the project. Mary had noticed that on many book projects, only minor corrections were done after the second revision. She thought, "Why not send the material to the printer at this point so they could get started and possibly save two to four weeks' time?" Mary decided to try this experiment on several book projects, feeling that the costs of added changes would be minimized and the project would be ahead of schedule if delays occurred elsewhere.

Mary tried her plan on four different book projects, with mixed results. The approach worked well on two projects, saving about two weeks on one book and over three weeks on the other. However, things weren't as fortunate in the other two projects, where costly changes occurred. In one case a customer requested a major change in format; in the other case the editor asked for major modifications after having second thoughts regarding the manuscript.

When Mary finished her analysis of the results of her plan, she remarked to a friend, "I think it was a good idea, but everything we gained on two of the books was offset by the added costs on the others. I guess I've got more to learn about the planning and operations of this business."

Analysis

1. What are some barriers to planning that may have affected "Mary's plan"?
2. What, if anything, would you have done differently than Mary?

Case 4. Electronic Systems, Inc.

Electronic Systems, Inc., is a European-based manufacturer of highly technical products that contain hundreds of electronic and mechanical components. Although many of the subcomponents are sold to research and medical industries, the major systems are sold to the electronics and optical industries for more than $200,000 each. The company's current sales volume is $300 million; it has shown a steady 15 percent increase in sales over the past few years and is expected to increase that to 18 percent per year with the introduction of new U.S. products. The European-based parent company of Electronic Systems could not expand its physical facility significantly because of its physical location.

Therefore, Electronic System's U.S. facility was originally set up to become self-sufficient as a sales and service organization within five years. Two years ago, a manufacturing and assembly operation was begun to satisfy increasing customer demands. In addition, Electronic Systems recognized that the U.S. market in electronics was several times larger than the European market served by the parent. For these reasons Electronic Systems felt that its U.S. subsidiary could become a market force if its electronics capabilities were joined with the high-technology hardware and mechanical capabilities of the European facility. As of this year, sales of the U.S. facility amounted to only 10 percent of Electronic's total international sales of $300 million. However, the U.S. share is expected to grow from 25 to 30 percent of international sales in the next five years.

Recently, the president of Electronic Systems gave the vice president of operations, Greg Bell, an assignment to develop an operational strategy for the U.S. operation, now that it was entering a rapid growth phase. Greg started by detailing some of the problem areas related to the international operations of Electronic Systems. These included the following:

1. Wage rates in Europe are as high, if not higher, than those in the United States. This would be a consideration in the exchange of personnel between countries and would affect product costs.
2. Language and overall communication difficulties arise from cultural differences as well as from the large geographic separation.
3. Tax considerations have become more complex and have to be dealt with carefully.
4. Duplication of inventory and corporate staff expertise has become an increasing problem; both must be minimized at least during the early stages of international expansion.
5. Exchange rates often have a significant effect on profit figures.

Problems currently being encountered in the U.S. operation included the following:

1. The engineering of standard systems, which includes a document identifying each system component, its part number, and the electrical schematics to assemble the components, requires four to six weeks to complete.
2. Perpetually late deliveries of in-house (special) engineering systems, and recently poor delivery on standard and/or previously built systems, which are easily assembled by the manufacturing department, have begun to occur.
3. Recent quotations have identified a four-month time period required to order, receive, and build a standard system. Previously, systems had taken one month to assemble and two weeks to test and receive customer acceptance.
4. It takes two to eight weeks to get an order from the parent for systems engineered using items available through the European facility. Items in stock can be shipped from the parent in one to two weeks, without difficulty. Shipments coming from Europe typically are shipped by air on Friday and clear customs by Tuesday. However, the items then take up to two weeks to show up in the computer as being available for customer orders.

Problems identified by various people in the company included the following:

1. The mission of the U.S. facility must be defined so that all management personnel can understand it and have a common goal.
2. The present documentation and information transfer systems are incomplete and incompatible.
3. The inventory control system is inadequate in responding to customer orders and continually contains inaccurate information.
4. Training is poor and gets a slow response.
5. Methods of locating and selecting experienced and competent managers must be improved.
6. The integration and handling of completely U.S.-developed products that can be sold as components to systems or as complete units must be worked out.

After identifying these problem areas, Greg decided to talk to the managers of manufacturing, engineering, marketing, and systems to obtain their viewpoints concerning an operating strategy. Figure 1 details the present organization structure of Electronic Systems.

Analysis

1. What do you feel each of the managers of manufacturing, engineering, marketing, and systems would emphasize as part of an operating strategy?
2. What organization changes are necessary as part of an operations strategy?
3. Discuss some major components of an operations strategy.

FIGURE 1
Organization Chart of Electronic Systems

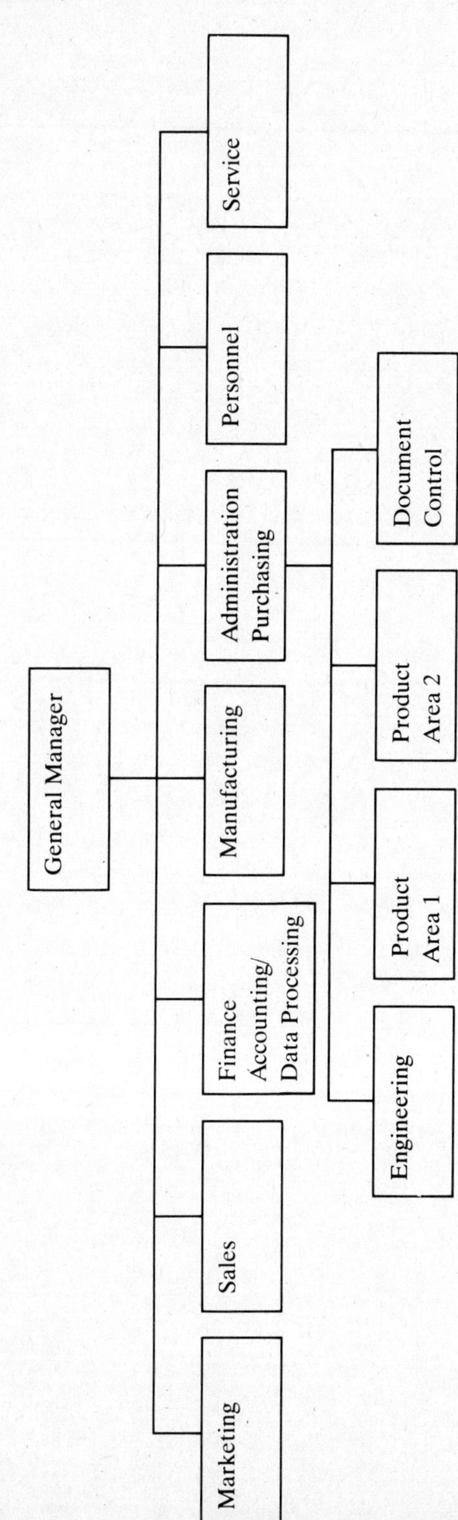

Chapter 8 Components of Organizational Structure

Case 1. Job Design at NorthStar Manufacturing Company

Ryan Cooper wanted to make changes in the operations at NorthStar Manufacturing. He believed that it would be possible to improve productivity and the quality of an employee's output through job redesign. In addition, he believed that jobs could be structured so that they would be more satisfying to the employees. Ryan first looked at the water pump operations.

Currently, water pumps were put together on an assembly line. There were ten work stations on the line and a separate employee for each operation (see Figure 1). The most complicated operation was the three-solder attachment in step 4. The ten steps are described below, and Figure 1 gives a rough layout of the work stations.

Step 1. Frame and housing are bolted together.

Step 2. Pump is bolted on frame and housing. Pump is checked to ensure that it has the proper bushings for the electric motor that will be added in a later step.

Step 3. Seat for the electric motor is attached to frame and housing. This piece is soldered to the frame.

Step 4. The electric motor is soldered to the seat. In addition, the motor is soldered on the frame in two other positions. This is done because of the high torque that can be created when the pump is under heavy use.

Step 5. Electric wires are attached to the motor and to the pump and soldered in place.

Step 6. The wires and motor are waterproofed.

Step 7. The bottom housing is bolted to the frame, pump, and motor.

Step 8. The top housing is bolted to the frame, pump, and motor.

Step 9. The assembled pump is waterproofed and painted and held twelve hours to dry.

Step 10. Labels are attached and rubber seals are placed on all external wire openings. The pump is tested.

Defective pumps were returned to a special rework area, where additional employees corrected the problem.

Ryan did not believe that any of the steps required highly specialized skills or equipment. In fact, most of the employees shifted work stations every four hours just to reduce some of the degree of monotony that occurred.

The work environment was smoky and noisy. The smoke came from the soldering process; the noise came from the fans used to suck out the smoke and from a stamping operation for another manufacturing process that occurred right next to the pump assembly line. The noise made it nearly impossible to communicate on the line. Because of the noise, each employee wore soundproofing devices, which made communication even more difficult. Hence, although most workers were within 50 feet of each other, there was very little communication between employees except at breaks and downtime.

The water pump line was considered relatively short by some standards. This means that there was little opportunity for an employee to "work up the line" to vary the pace. The employees on this line had a high degree of turnover (300 percent in the past year). Ryan believed that part of the problem was the line and the dull jobs that employees were asked to do. Pay was based on an hourly salary, which was fair given the wage rates in comparable jobs.

Ryan had the option, with the closure of one line, to move the pump line to another area away from the noisy stamping line. However, he was unsure if he should move the assembly operation as is to the new area or consider some other approach. This decision was particularly important to Ryan because he had just finished reading an article that linked increases in employee performance and satisfaction to job design. One of the approaches that seemed more comprehensive than the others was written by Hackman and Oldham. This approach, called the job diagnostic index (JDI), assessed various core dimensions of a task. The article identified various job core dimensions that helped develop positive psychological states in individuals who wanted to grow in their job.

Ryan wondered if that sort of system could be applied to the pump assembly line. After all, with turnover at 300 percent, the current system did not seem to create happy or productive workers. The notion of job enlargement and enrichment seemed to apply to this situation too. But how? It seemed that Ryan always had a problem with linking the reading he did with reality. The theories looked good, but he never seemed to have enough knowledge to know how to apply them. That was a major gap in his education, and it seemed as if he would always learn his lessons through experiences.

Analysis

1. What should Ryan do about the pump assembly line? Why?

FIGURE 1
The Pump Assembly Line

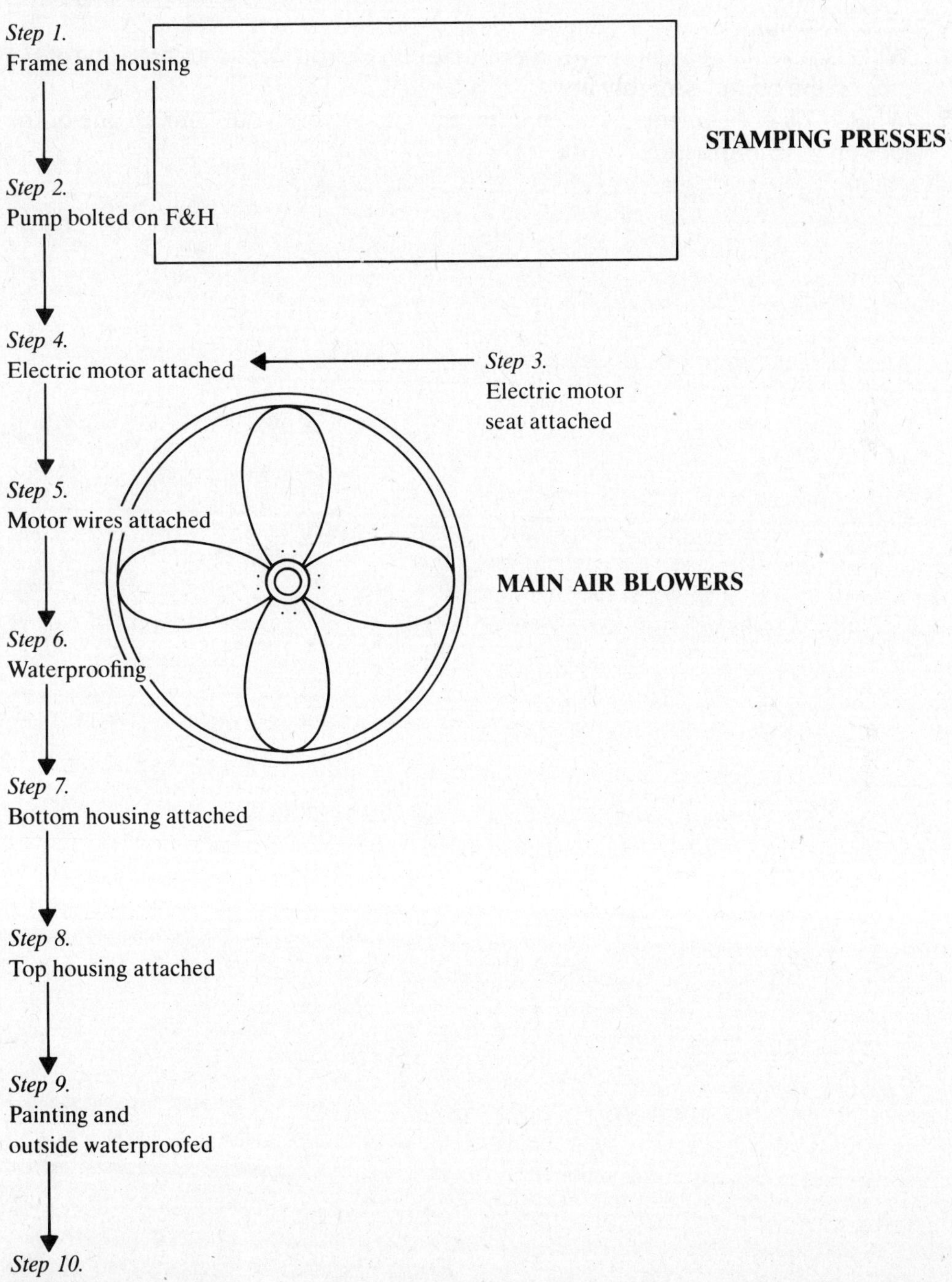

2. Make a proposal that will improve the core dimensions of jobs on the pump assembly line. Relate each change you make to one of the core dimensions.
3. Improving the core dimensions is only effective if an employee has a high growth need. Explain.
4. What is job enlargement? Give an example of how you would enlarge one of the jobs on the pump assembly line.
5. What is job enrichment? Give an example of how you would enrich one of the jobs on the pump assembly line.

Case 2. The Illinois Best Department Stores, Inc.[1]

Susan Barkley was the youngest CEO of the Illinois Best Department Stores, Inc., and was the first woman CEO of a large retail operation in the state of Illinois. She was in charge of seven stores in Illinois. Like most upscale outlets using the department store format, Illinois Best was suffering intense competition from discount stores. Wal-Mart and K mart had really hurt through their aggressive pricing policies and use of brand name merchandise. The upper end of the market was also being eroded by the various specialty stores that had blossomed in the area. The end result was that sales had been flat for the past five years. Although the chain was still viable, investors were not encouraged.

Susan was also displeased with the quality of the interaction between customers and sales associates.[2] Customers complained that common responses from associates would be "This is not my department," "I'm not sure what department that's in, try over there," and "No, I can't ring that merchandise up for you, that's not my area." These sorts of responses bothered Susan because they were not the kinds of images that kept customers coming back.

Illinois Best Stores were organized like most department stores. There were four main categories, soft goods (clothing), hard goods (most everything else), automotive, and jewelry. Automotive and jewelry were leased departments that were not owned by Illinois Best. This was common practice in many department stores.

Soft goods were divided into ten departments: ladies' dresses, sports dresses, lingerie, men's suits, men's casual wear, children's wear, shoes, baby clothes, a wedding shop, and an accessories department that included belts, ties, scarves, and tie tacks and small items of accent jewelry.

Hard goods were divided into twenty departments: paper products, specialty food items (candy), stationery, toys, sports equipment, lamps, household appliances, televisions and stereos (including computers and VCRs), garden supplies, pets, bathroom towels and equipment, white goods (sheets, blankets, and other bedroom products), outdoor furniture, indoor furniture, beds and frames, dishes and small cooking appliances and accessories, computers, clocks, records and tapes (including disk records and VCR tapes), and tools and handicrafts (hardware and arts and crafts).

Hard goods accounted for two-thirds of the space in the stores, soft goods (fashion wear and children's clothes) accounted for one-fourth, and jewelry and automotive accounted for the remainder of the space.

Although there was a higher profit margin on soft goods, Susan felt that the stores' major draw was their full line of merchandise. However, she also felt that Illinois Best could be at a crossroads. Its market share had decreased from 20 to 15 percent in the

1. This is a fictitious case but is based on a real situation faced by a number of department store CEOs.
2. Illinois Best calls their employees associates, as does the Wal-Mart chain. This demonstrates that employees are more than employees at Illinois Best—they are part of the team.

past decade. All department stores had lost about 10 percent of their market share. In the past ten years the biggest gainers in the market, at least in the effective market of Illinois Best, had been the specialty stores (their sales had increased by 50 percent in real growth). Discount stores had increased 40 percent. The increase in market share was 8 percent for specialty stores and 4 percent for discount stores. Illinois Best determined that it lost 3 percent of its market to specialty stores and 2 percent to the discounters.

In any event, the numbers did not look that good, and Susan had to determine what to do about it. There had been some innovations in the industry, but most of these changes were not suited to the image of Illinois Best. For example, some discounters were moving into the superstore concept, combining groceries with a traditional store. These stores were usually 100,000 square feet or larger. A second concept was wholesale clubs. Again, this was not in the image that Illinois Best wanted to create: it was too nonservice oriented. However, Susan believed there were three choices to consider besides trying to find a suitable merger partner.

The first option was to follow a discount pricing policy. This approach was used by Montgomery Ward in 1988 and by Sears in 1989. The second option, also tried by Sears in the early 1980s, was to develop a specialty store concept in the department store environment. For example, instead of lots of open space, separate environments were created to give the feeling that the customer was in a specialty store atmosphere. L. S. Ayres tried this approach by dividing its store into several different areas. The third option was to do nothing with the organization of the store but to devote time and attention to improving the associates' treatment of customers. The first and third options would do nothing to correct the departmentalization mentality that the associates had seemed to develop. This mentality would be less of a problem in the specialty store concept because the customers would think more in terms of separate departments than they would in the other options.

Perhaps a reorganization of departments was necessary. Or perhaps the associates should be trained in merchandising so that they could answer customer queries and ring up merchandise from other departments. A procedural option might be to move all cash registers to the front of the store. However, Susan wasn't too excited about this option because it would not fit the image she would like Illinois Best to have. She didn't know if she had a personnel or organization problem. However, she wanted to make sure she didn't have a problem.

Analysis

1. Does Susan have an organization or a personnel problem? Why?
2. How should Susan organize the stores: by product, customer, or some other division? Why?
3. How are the stores organized now? Why?

4. Propose an organization structure that would divide Illinois Best stores according to a specialty store concept.
5. How might the organization of a store be linked to the image that the CEO wants to portray?

Case 3. Developing the Manager and the Employee

Alice Quintal was concerned that the assistant managers in Tom's store did not seem to be as promotable as many of the other assistant managers of the fifty stores in Alice's region. Alice was a regional store manager for a major discount retail chain with 1,000 stores in twenty states. The growth of the chain had created a need for store managers, and Alice believed that Tom's assistant managers had good technical ability. However, they lacked the maturity needed to be successful on their own. Alice attributed their lack of development to Tom.

Tom had come up through the ranks. He had started in Plano as a stocker when he was still in high school. After finishing high school he worked full-time in the store in stocking and then moved to a position as department manager in the sports department. As department manager, Tom was responsible for ordering products, maintaining a clean area, answering customer questions, having accurate signs indicating prices, and identifying which elements were on sale. In addition, he was responsible for creating attractive displays. Tom did well in this position and was promoted to assistant store manager ten years ago.

There were five assistant store managers in a 90,000-square-foot store such as the one in which Tom worked. The assistant store manager was expected to take over when the manager was not in the store and to coordinate activities of several departments. However, the philosophy of the chain dictated that the assistant manager should be active in all aspects of the store. When a truck came in, the assistant manager was there to work with the rest of the employees to physically unload the truck. When the store was busy, the assistant manager became a cashier or bagger.

Collis E. Pitts had been Tom's manager and was one of the best managers in the region. However, Collis didn't delegate duties to his assistants to help them develop. Like Tom, he worked seventy to eighty hours a week in the store. Although Collins was on a salary, the number of hours bothered Alice, who believed that a good manager should be developing assistants so that they can make decisions in the absence of the manager. There should be no reason for the store manager to put in that kind of time. Alice wanted to see managers put in only fifty to sixty hours per week.

In any event, Tom had become a store manager last year. Alice believed that because of Collis's managerial style, it had taken Tom almost ten years to reach his new position. Now Tom was using the same sort of management style that Collis had used, and it was slowing up promotions for *his* assistant managers. This simply would not do. Alice wasn't sure how to handle the problem. In a certain respect, it seemed to be one of delegation: Tom wanted to have control over the store. Although wanting to maintain control is an important positive attribute, Alice believed that Tom could maintain control while still developing the assistant managers. But how?

Store managers were compensated primarily through a fixed salary with annual merit increases that were based on the evaluations made by the district and regional managers. The fixed component accounted for only about one-third of their compensation. The remaining two-thirds were bonuses. One-half of the bonus was based on the company's performance; the remaining half was based on the store's sales and comparisons of several cost items. The actual dollar cost value was less important than the percentage of sales that the costs represented. Hence, there was quite a strong incentive for a store manager to be diligent in maintaining control. Bonuses constructed in a similar manner were allocated to assistant managers.

Alice knew that Tom wanted to ensure that the store was run properly, and that was good. However, Tom did not seem to understand that he needed to be concerned with developing the assistant managers. The question was how to unlock that portion of Tom's responsibility. This aspect would be difficult for Alice to watch because she visited this store only once a month, since it was only one of fifty stores in Alice's region. However, Tracey might be able to help in this situation. She was the new district manager, had responsibility over only ten stores, and did visit the store once a week. However, Tracey was new at the job. She was a college graduate who had little supervisory experience and did not know the political structure of the organization.

Alice thought she might try one strategy that she had learned about when she was reading an article on Sears (see Case 5 in Chapter 2). Sears found that the managers who were better developers of personnel used a decentralized rather than centralized managerial approach. One way to introduce this approach was to load the job with additional responsibilities that would literally force the manager to delegate to get everything done. Alice thought she could load the job by putting Tom in charge of setting up some of the new stores. This would force Tom to be out of his store, which would force the assistants to make decisions. Once Tom saw that the assistants had the ability, he might be more relaxed in allowing them some latitude on the job.

A second approach was to revise the evaluation procedure for Tom to emphasize the importance of developing assistant managers. However, Alice would have to articulate very specific sorts of behaviors that Tom ought to execute to "develop" the assistant managers, and Alice herself was not sure what those behaviors should be. It seemed clear that Tom did not delegate, but how does one delegate without losing control? However, Alice was determined to make Tom a better manager.

Analysis

1. What is meant by centralization versus decentralization? How is that related to delegation?
2. Why did Alice feel that Collis was an excellent manager even though he didn't delegate?
3. Did the compensation system reinforce a centralized or a decentralized managerial style?

4. Do you think loading the job would force Tom to become more decentralized? Are there some ethical concerns with this sort of approach?
5. What should Alice do to help Tom's assistant store managers develop their skills through a more decentralized approach?

Case 4. The Organization of a University

There has been increasing concern about the quality of college education in the United States. One author, Charles J. Sykes, blames the problem on the principle of self-governance in the university. If professors are in charge of the curricular matters, academic villages of scholarly activity develop with little regard for the development of the student.[1] This lack of concern with student needs is noted by other authors. For example, Christopher H. Lovelock argues that business school curriculums have not kept pace with the changing needs for skills.[2] There may be many reasons for an apparent decrement in the quality of college education, and the structure of the university may be one of them.

A typical university structure appears in Figure 1. There are several colleges in the university, and most of these colleges are relatively autonomous. A typical college of commerce or college of business administration is divided into several departments: accountancy, finance, economics, marketing, management, business law, quantitative methods, and management information systems. Each department is relatively autonomous except that it follows the guidelines provided by the accreditation society that governs the discipline. For example, a business school is governed, in many cases, by the AACSB (American Assembly of Collegiate Schools in Business). However, the AACSB usually issues only broad guidelines for topical coverage; it does not recommend specific courses.

A second organization that influences the structure of universities is the AAUP (American Association of University Professors). At some schools, the AAUP is the bargaining agent that deals with a collectively negotiated agreement. However, at most schools the AAUP influences university policy and practices by threatening to blacklist those schools that do not follow their guidelines. AAUP guidelines specify that it is the prerogative of the faculty to decide curriculum matters.

The administration at most universities is composed of individuals who have faculty rank in some specific discipline. The end result is that the faculty establish policy regarding course content because the administration has limited expertise in the various specific disciplines in a given academic area.

The consequence of this type of organization is that little attention is paid to the development of the student. Each academic area builds its own topical areas of interest without building upon the courses taught in different disciplines. Learning content skills (the knowledge of the discipline) seems to take precedence over learning process skills (the ability to relate content skills to decision making and the ability to communicate and analyze). Marketing does not know what is covered in accounting and management. Finance is not sure of the preparation students have in accounting. Precious class time is spent reviewing material that should have been

1. Charles J. Sykes, *ProfScam* (Washington, D.C.: Regnery, Gateway, 1988).
2. Christopher H. Lovelock, "Business Schools Owe Students Better Service," in *Managing Services: Marketing, Operations and Human Resources*, ed. C. H. Lovelock (Englewood Cliffs, N.J.: Prentice-Hall, 1988), pp. 22–24.

FIGURE 1
A Sample Organization Chart for a University

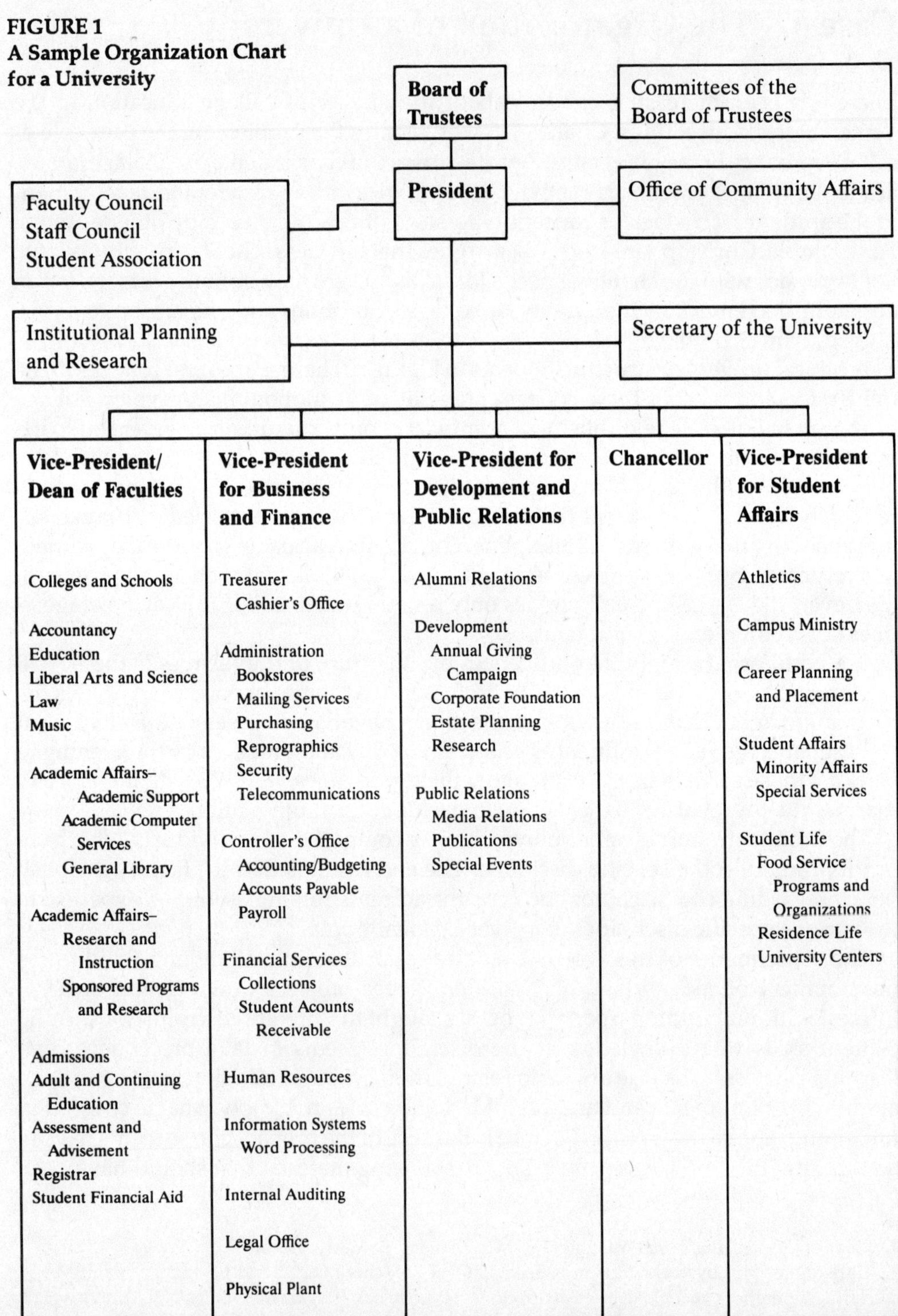

covered elsewhere. A student graduates with good content skills in various departmental areas but has never been challenged to prove his or her ability to think or to communicate verbally or orally.

The process of specialization continues to grow. Departments recruit faculty with specialized degrees in a specific area and less and less of an overview of the entire business administration needs of the student. One course, the capstone policy course, was advocated by the AACSB to pull aspects of each of the areas into a case experience for students. The trouble with the capstone course, however, is that it is harder and harder to find faculty with the eclectic skills needed to do an effective job in the classroom.

Is it as bleak as Sykes reports, or does the student still gain from this system? Is it a structural problem or a system problem? Or is it both? What is the solution?

Analysis

1. Draw an organization chart for a typical college of business.
2. Is there anything ambiguous about the organization chart in Figure 1? What is it?
3. How might the organization of the university change to meet the needs of the student? Propose an organization chart. What sort of organization type are you proposing?
4. What would you recommend beyond what you proposed in question 3 to improve the responsiveness of universities in meeting the development needs of the student?
5. Who is currently responsible for the development of students? Who should be? Why?

Case 5. Big Changes at Big Blue[1]

For 74 years, International Business Machines Corp. has had one extraordinary boss after another. Founder Thomas J. Watson had a genius for selling and for motivating other salesmen. His son Thomas Jr. had the vision to move the company aggressively into computers in the 1950s. In the 1960s, T. Vincent Learson blended aggressive marketing and clever product design into a formula so potent that it attracted a federal antitrust suit that Frank Cary and then John Opel had to defend.

But no one who preceded him had a tougher job than the one John F. Akers inherited. Watson Jr., Learson, Cary, and Opel have all told him so. Akers' struggle has been not only with hundreds of competitors, impatient customers, and carping critics, but also with IBM itself. By the time Akers took over as chairman in 1985, arrogance, inertia, self-delusion, and plain old corporate flab had left the No. 1 computer maker in no shape to cope with its worst earnings slump ever. While earlier CEOs had worried about such things as keeping growth in double digits, Akers was handed an unprecedented challenge: masterminding the turnaround of a $50 billion company that no one had expected to be in trouble.

In attempting that, Akers, 53, already has produced an IBM that's leaner, younger, more open-minded, and faster on its feet. After a flat 1986, revenues are moving up again, albeit at half the pre-slump rate, and heavy cost-cutting is boosting profits once more. What's most impressive is that Akers has accomplished this while preserving IBM's most cherished tradition: no layoffs. In this he stands far apart from his counterparts at Exxon, General Motors, and AT&T, who over the same period slashed their work forces to help reduce bloated costs. Akers has produced what Harvard business school professor D. Quinn Mills describes in a forthcoming book as "probably the most massive redeployment by a company in decades"—all without firing a single employee.

But that isn't good enough for John Akers. Dissatisfied with what he sees as temporary fixes, he has embarked on a strategy that involves nothing less than reinventing IBM. The management reorganization announced on Jan. 28, which he describes as IBM's most significant restructuring in 30 years, is only the latest step. Frustrated for years by a sluggish headquarters bureaucracy, Akers now has delegated responsibility to a half-dozen general managers. With IBM's product lines and markets expanding all the time, "there's no way that one small set of managers at the top should think they are close enough to the action to make the decisions in all these areas," Akers told *Business Week* in a rare interview. The relatively young managers who are being handed more power are being asked to do something almost unheard of in the recent annals of IBM: to bring an entrepreneurial spirit to their lines of business.

If his plan works, long before Akers reaches mandatory retirement in 1994 he'll have forged a brand-new company—in structure and outlook. Indeed, three years of

1. Geoff Lewis, "Big Changes at Big Blue." Reprinted from the February 15, 1988 issue of *Business Week* by special permission, copyright © 1988 by McGraw-Hill, Inc.

computer slumps, PC clones, and the success of rival Digital Equipment Corp. have led the company to rethink its most basic assumptions.

Moving Fast

For one thing, IBM can no longer count on its 70% share of the mainframe business to give it automatic dominance in other computer markets. Mainframes themselves, which normally produce 40% of IBM's revenues and more than 50% of its profits, will no longer be the reliable source of growth that they have been. Although the company expects double-digit growth in the best years, average revenue growth for the mainframe market is slipping to about 7% annually. That will mean that IBM minicomputers and PCs, which have frequently been pulled along by the successful mainframes, will have to compete more on their own merits. Before that can happen, the company will have to fix some weaknesses, particularly in its midrange machines. Even then, the more competitive markets for these smaller machines are unlikely ever to deliver the 60%-to-70% gross margins IBM gets from mainframes.

To reap that kind of return, Akers is orchestrating the company's most rapid move into new businesses since the 1950s. He has teamed up with Stephen Chen, the former Cray Research Inc. computer designer, to get IBM into the fast-growing, high-margin supercomputer business. And by acquiring Rolm and 16% of MCI Communications, IBM is ready to become a worldwide force in building voice and data networks.

More important to IBM's bottom line are moves into software and services. "Software enhances our margins," says Akers. Sales of it already have grown from 8% of revenues in 1985 to about 12% in 1987. IBM now has an entire new division dedicated to cranking out new packages. Analysts expect its software revenues to grow by 35% annually over the next few years. At the same time, IBM is bursting into the potentially lucrative business of systems integration—analyzing a customer's business and then installing the proper mix of hardware and software, be it IBM's or not, to make the customer most productive—all for a fat fee.

The difficulty is that IBM's historical strength in computers doesn't guarantee it a leg up. It has to compete as never before, and on all fronts at once: minicomputers, PCs, software, and systems integration consulting. Even in mainframes, the company has powerful rivals, including huge Japanese computer makers such as Fujitsu and Hitachi. With strong competitors in each of these businesses, IBM can't snare customers just by flashing its logo. IBM machines will compete for slots on computer networks with equipment from Apple, DEC, and dozens of others. "It's not an all-blue world anymore," says Edward E. Lucente, the IBM vice-president in charge of U.S. marketing.

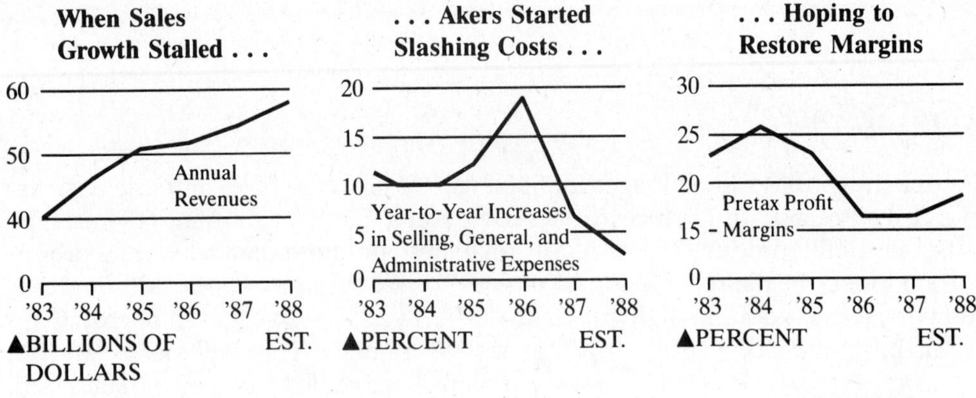

Data: International Business Machines Corp., Merrill Lynch & Co. Estimates

Data: Merrill Lynch & Co.

Hot Streak

The company was losing its competitive edge by the time Akers took over. Starting in the late 1970s, says the data processing director for an East Coast bank, IBM "got so bureaucratic they lost sight of the customer." When customers delivered specifications for a system they wanted but IBM didn't have, IBM's salespeople suggested there was something wrong with the request—not the products. "In the early days, IBM recognized that computers were used to solve problems," Akers points out. But that changed in the late 1970s and early 1980s, he concedes. IBM salespeople lost sight of the problems customers wanted solved—concentrating more on just moving machines. "I'd say we became too product-oriented," Akers says.

This shortsightedness was perhaps understandable. When IBM switched from leasing computers to selling them, it produced an incredible growth streak, doubling revenues from $23 billion to $46 billion from 1979 to 1984. By then the company owned the PC market, despite a late start and unspectacular technology. "IBM developed the feeling that it could do no wrong," says John Connell, president of the Office Technology Research Group, a consulting firm in Pasadena, Calif. "An absolute myopia developed about what was really happening out there" with customers.

Akers' first priority, when he began fashioning IBM's comeback strategy in 1986, was to fix this problem. In 1987—which the chairman christened "the year of the customer"—IBM salespeople became more solicitous. And, in an effort that one top executive calls *glasnost*, the company began opening up. Instead of designing products in secret and then surprising the market, it started talking to customers first. And it's shedding its infamous "not-invented-here" attitude toward non-IBM equipment. Says Akers: "We're more forthcoming about our plans, and ready to propose using other companies' products." Lucente says there will be even more emphasis on the customer in 1988. Instead of just talking to a few hundred, this year IBM will meet with more than 4,000 at seminars around the country.

The change is evident to outsiders. Lucente now runs a small army of 28,000 people in 284 offices who sell and install machines and otherwise assist customers. That's up 22% from 1986 and three times the force that rival DEC deploys. Says one customer: "It's almost like the IBM of 15 or 18 years ago. They've come full circle."

By comparison, fixing IBM's product problems is proving much more daunting. "I don't have any problem with the way they sell," says the data processing manager for an auto importer. "It's the products I sometimes have trouble with." In particular, the company's midrange computers continue to suffer in competition with DEC's VAX minicomputers. IBM's 9370 minicomputer, which insiders dubbed the "VAX-killer" when it was introduced in 1986, has misfired so far. This small-scale version of IBM's 370 series mainframes is the right size for running a department in a large corporation, but it lacks the right software for the job. In late 1986, IBM hinted at an order backlog for 40,000 of the 9370s. Since shipments began last summer, however, less than 5,000 have been sold. From 1985 to 1987 IBM's share of the midrange business dropped from 28% to 23%, while DEC's share jumped from 16% to 20%, according to International Data Corp. estimates.

Depressed

The results were apparent when IBM released 1987 earnings in mid-January. Its $5.3 billion in profits, or $8.72 a share, was close to what many analysts had expected. But Wall Street was sorely disappointed to see how the numbers added up. In the fourth quarter more than 80¢ of the per-share net came from items such as currency exchange, a lower-than-expected tax rate, and profits on the sale of Intel Corp. stock. Most alarming: In a year when rivals such as DEC, NCR, and Unisys had shaken the computer slump, IBM still lagged. While worldwide revenues were up 6%, U.S. sales were down 5% from the 1986 fourth quarter and off 2% for the year. Analysts read the numbers as weak acceptance of IBM's newest machines. The company's already depressed shares skidded six points to 111¾.

Even stalwart supporters did a double take. Figuring that the revenue growth needed to match or beat IBM's pre-slump earnings of $10.77 per share could still be a year away, Daniel Mandresh of Merrill Lynch, Pierce, Fenner & Smith Inc. cut his 1988 earnings estimate from $11 to $10. Until he sees signs of growth approaching 10%, he says, he will stay neutral on IBM. Adds First Boston Corp. analyst Steven Milunovich: "It's clear that with the products that they have now, which are an improvement, the company will continue to lose market share this year. It needs products."

Improving products is the primary goal of the recent reorganization. By forming five autonomous product groups and pushing much of the decision-making down to general managers in these units, Akers hopes to cut through the bureaucracy that has slowed product introductions. General managers in personal computer systems, mid-range systems, mainframes, and communications will be given latitude to develop the products they need for their particular markets. The fifth unit will be responsible for delivering state-of-the-art building-block technology such as memory chips. From among this group of general managers—George H. Conrades, Stephen B. Schwartz, Carl J. Conti, Ellen M. Hancock, and Patrick A. Toole—the successor to Akers may be selected.

One thing these executives are sure to be rated on is nimbleness. Since the 1970s, IBM has had a "contention" system, meaning that two or more product prototypes would be pursued by competing teams. Only after the company's six-member management committee heard the pros and cons would one contender get the nod. And that could take months or even years.

It's not easy for big companies to avoid this: Former DEC executives say that although the $9 billion company has trotted out a stream of new VAXs in rapid succession, its expanding bureaucracy is starting to slow things down. Akers knows what that can cost. Back in 1981 a small, independent team—sequestered in a remote Florida lab—took one year to bring out the original PC. But once the PC operation was folded into the larger Information Systems & Communications Group, work on new products slowed. Instead of arriving in mid-1985, as competitors originally feared, the Personal System/2 hit the market nearly two years later. The delay helped clones of the older PCs grab one-third of IBM's market share. Now, lacking its former market leverage in PCs, IBM is finding it harder to make the new PC an industry standard. To boost sales of some PS/2 models, it has recently cut dealer prices.

Neither the personal systems division—a $10 billion-plus business including PCs and typewriters—nor any other product division can be run like the original PC group. But Akers believes that general managers can learn to think like entrepreneurs. "I've told them to think of themselves as chief executives," says Akers. "In their markets, each one has a different set of competitors and role models." By focusing on competitors such as AT&T, Northern Telecom, and Siemens, for example, Ellen Hancock's Communications Products division hopes to identify market requirements sooner and bring out the right products faster.

Whatever the market, Akers is preaching a new religion: shorter product cycles. The company began concentrating on the issue in 1986 after a group of customers, including Honda Motor Co., urged it to do better. Since then, Executive Vice-President Allen J. Krowe has pursued a worldwide campaign to make IBM "best of breed" in product development.

Contention may still occur among IBM's product organizations in the U.S. But now it is supposed to be resolved by Terry R. Lautenbach, a trusted Akers lieutenant who has been named general manager of the newly formed IBM United States organization. Lautenbach will oversee the five product divisions and Lucente's sales organization. In short, he'll be responsible for businesses that generate about 44% of IBM's revenues.

Akers says that speedier development cycles will begin paying off this year. "By midyear we should have the fundamental elements in place for every segment of our line," he says. "For the first time in quite a while the product cycle should be playing in our favor." Major introductions slated for 1988 include a top model in the mainframe line and Silverlake, a replacement for the System/36 and System/38 minicomputers. That machine, which can replace some 250,000 computers already in use, is regarded as IBM's best bet in the midrange market now. And William C. Lowe, who heads the personal computer business, hints that by the time clones of the PS/2 begin showing up this summer he'll have new models out.

Developing the right kinds of software may be trickier, but that's where *glasnost* is helping out. At the 6,000-employee Application Systems division in Milford, Conn., "a fundamental part of the development cycle is the participation of customers," says Anthony Mondello, vice-president for office systems. Since April groups of 10 to 12 major customers have met regularly with IBM programmers to discuss specific software under development and general software strategies. Mondello says their suggestions have sparked "four or five" changes already. The advantage in dealing directly with customers instead of relying solely on his own marketing experts, says Application Systems division President Joseph M. Guglielmi, is that the information is "not filtered."

Big Help

To see how a package would compete in the market, IBM software developers have set up "usability labs." Customers and hired researchers try out software, while programmers observe through a one-way mirror. Video cameras tape everything from fingers on keyboards to screens to facial expressions of the participants. Eventually, boasts Mondello, such testing should help IBM come up with a "user interface"—a way of presenting programs and information on a computer screen—that will be even easier to learn and use than the format that has made Apple Computer Inc.'s Macintosh so popular.

That would be a big help to Guglielmi, whose assignment is to make IBM a major player in the market for applications—spreadsheets and the like. Although IBM's software revenues have climbed steadily, the biggest chunk of business continues to be mainframe operating systems, the software that controls the basic functions of those big machines. Now the emphasis is switching to applications packages that can run all across IBM's product line, from PCs to minicomputers and mainframes.

Once such software exists, the company expects to have a compelling sales pitch for customers who are trying to set up extensive computer networks. In the meantime, rival DEC has the edge. Because all its computers use the same basic architecture, software written for one size VAX can run on another. By contrast, IBM has several main architectures—for PCs, minis, and mainframes—as well as specialized hardware for work stations and transaction-processing jobs such as running a stock trading system.

To smooth over these differences, IBM has sketched out a set of specifications called Systems Application Architecture. Packages that conform to SAA rules, whether written by IBM or independent software companies, should work on IBM

HOW IBM CUT 16,200 EMPLOYEES— WITHOUT AN AX

The full-employment policy at IBM has long been the envy of Corporate America. Now, for students of the phenomenon, there's the company's experience since 1985. International Business Machines Corp. took what might have been a morale-busting campaign to cut costs and, on balance, turned it into a morale-boosting exercise in building corporate loyalty. And it learned something as well: Stay lean. "We are trying to instill what I call a hiring-avoidance mentality in all our managers," says Walton E. Burdick, vice-president of personnel.

As sales stalled, management had two goals: cut costs by trimming the work force, and eliminate thousands of production, staff, and managerial jobs while adding thousands more in sales and marketing. The company wanted to do both while preserving its no-layoffs tradition.

The first step—an extreme one for IBM—was an early-retirement plan. It was a big gamble, because this scatter-gun approach has cost other companies key employees. But it paid off. Some 80% of those who left were in jobs IBM wanted to eliminate. And since these more seasoned employees earned high salaries, the savings were big.

Retooling. Coupled with normal attrition of about 3%, the retirements cut total employment from 405,500 in 1985 to 389,300 by the end of 1987. The company also cut out overtime and temporary employees. These moves eliminated the equivalent of 12,500 more full-time jobs and, with other cuts, saved $700 million in 1986 alone. IBM did hire 23,400 workers during 1986 and 1987, but that was half the normal number. Most new hires were for high-growth businesses—software, for instance.

Then IBM fell back on the retraining program for which it's famous. In addition, 9,400 people—including many production workers—volunteered for courses lasting up to 18 months. Some 3,700 are being trained as programmers, while 4,600 others are learning to be sales agents or customer consultants. Meanwhile, IBM has computerized much of its training, cutting its education budget from $750 million in 1986 to $700 million last year.

Now the company is training people to fill many of the jobs those 9,400 left, and so on down the line. "Backfilling" is what IBM calls this less formal training, which usually takes a few months. Some 45,000 employees have been through it since 1985.

IBM's Leaner Work Force	
Employees in 1985	405,500
Took Early Retirement	15,000
Normal Attrition	24,600
New Hires	23,400
Employees in 1988	389,300
Data: International Business Machines Corp.	

While there were no outright layoffs, all the turmoil riled some workers. "It seemed a little duplicitous to encourage people to leave and then go out and hire the same year," says an executive who retired early. "Some people were pushed out the door, though not many." More than 21,000 had to change locations, including 4,600 who went from head offices to the field. Some 4,300 people had to move, many involuntarily, when their offices closed. "It's a spectrum of sacrifice," says Burdick.

Upward Paths. Still, IBM employees are more willing to move than most. The company ensures this by structuring career paths so that advancements usually accompany moves. D. Quinn Mills, a Harvard business school professor whose book on IBM's redeployment of workers will be published in May, did 100 in-depth interviews with IBM employees, plus an additional 250 through a written questionnaire. He figures that of the nearly 10% of IBM employees who took new jobs, only one-quarter thought they had made lateral moves—a sacrifice to the company. The rest saw the change as a promotion. "I expected to find that people were willing to sacrifice because of their loyalty," says Mills. "Instead, IBM took a downsizing and turned it into a career opportunity."

Whether the company really can use all these people depends on whether it can boost its growth. "If that doesn't happen, they'll have to rethink the whole thing," says Mills. But even he believes that it will take a lot more bad news before IBM lays anyone off.

By Aaron Bernstein in Armonk, N.Y.

and other manufacturers' machines in a network. The combination of SAA and improved networking has made incompatibility "kind of yesterday's problem," Akers insists. But customers and analysts alike say that SAA's payoff is several years away because the programming task is so complex. Still, major customers are looking forward to SAA. "From my standpoint, SAA is an extremely strong positive," says William H. Anderson, a senior vice-president in charge of computers at Prudential-Bache Securities, Inc. "We're committed to it."

Getting SAA moving is a top priority for Hancock's department. With such a system to smooth the way, the communications division could begin to extend networks of personal computers around IBM mainframes. Last year, IBM installed 9,000 "token-ring" local-area networks, analysts estimate. That pales in comparison with the 85,000 Ethernets that competitors have sold, but is seen as a strong showing, considering IBM's late start. Beyond that, Hancock is looking for ways to combine voice and data communications products for IBM customers.

Another Story

To provide the software that would make computer networks almost as easy to use as the phone system, IBM is marshaling an army of people. It has assembled 26,000 programmers in the U.S. alone. Among other things they are pounding out the software to tie disparate computers into a coherent network.

But the software investment should pay off—in the battle against DEC and others and also in the effort to restore profits to historic levels. IBM has had to continually push down the price per unit of computing power to match competition, both from mainframe rivals and from suppliers of smaller systems. So far software is another story. IBM has been able to raise prices by 10% to 15% annually on mainframe packages and, in some instances, by as much as 35%. William D. Easterbrook, an analyst at Kidder, Peabody & Co., estimates that gross margins on some products are near 90%.

Another potential gold mine is systems integration, traditionally the province of service companies such as Electronic Data Systems Corp. A company that coordinates the activities of many subcontractors on big projects typically commands a fee of 20% of the value of a contract. For a company that can also supply much of the hardware and software, the fee can be 80% of the total value, according to Peter Cunningham, president of market researcher Input. "It's a fabulous opportunity," he says.

'Plenty of Room'

In this area, IBM has a running start. Its Federal Systems division in Gaithersburg, Md., had been doing systems integration for the government for years. Now, IBM is the leader in the commercial market, too, Input says. The value of IBM's commercial contracts jumped fivefold last year, to about $1.5 billion, and should continue to grow rapidly, Akers predicts. "They're saying the market is so big, there's plenty of room," says Melvyn E. Bergstein, a partner with Arthur Andersen & Co., an accounting firm whose consulting practice handles systems integration projects. "But we worry about IBM."

Perhaps more important in the short run is the pressure Akers is putting on his marketers to offer tips on improving productivity to everyday buyers of computers—a return to IBM's heritage, he says. Customers seem receptive: "We need help in figuring out solutions to our business problems," says Marcel L. Gamache, senior vice-president for information services at Blue Cross/Blue Shield of Massachusetts. "IBM needs to understand how our business works."

One of the IBMers making this happen is Jack Hammond, director of customer, executive, and professional education. His group has taught hundreds of IBM salespeople a method called Information Systems Investment Strategies. Using special software, salespeople compare a customer's financial performance with that of its competitors. A relatively low inventory turnover ratio, for example, might signal the need to update inventory management. The ISIS program can estimate the costs of a new system and then plot expected benefits. "Measuring the return on information systems investments is something all our customers would love to be able to do," says Hammond. "IBM would like to see it, too." With purchases of information processing systems now accounting for nearly 40% of U.S. capital spending, "we now have to play in the big leagues when it comes to major capital investments," Hammond adds.

This kind of service and salesmanship seems bound to pay off eventually. But Akers' call for entrepreneurism comes too late to change results in 1988—or at least that's what Wall Street believes. Despite 1988's new products, analysts still foresee only about a 6% revenue gain for the year, though Akers hints that it may be higher. In any case, he adds, the company's improved cost structure will deliver disproportionately higher earnings gains on anything more than 6%. "There's leverage," he says. "Lots of leverage."

A 'Champion'

Yet until the company proves that its products can deliver, the new IBM will remain more theory than reality. There's also the question of whether the managers of IBM's five new product units—each employing tens of thousands of workers and generating billions of dollars in annual revenues—can inspire their subordinates to think as entrepreneurs.

Akers has seen IBMers do it before. "He was a great champion of ours when we were working on the PC," recalls Max E. Toy, a member of the team that developed the PC and now president of Commodore Business Machines Inc. But can he spread the entrepreneurial spirit throughout the corporation? IBMers, many of whom—like Akers—have spent their entire working lives at Big Blue, tend to share the same view of the world. "You really need to bring out the wild duck in people," says Toy. "And that's gong to be difficult to do in a culture that prizes uniformity of approach and style." Akers plays down the problem: "We're trying to change the habits of an awful lot of people. That won't happen overnight, but it will bloody well happen."

He's counting on a hidden strength of the IBM organization: its adaptability. "I have dealt with IBM for 19 years," says Michael R. Zucchini, chief information officer of Fleet/Norstar Financial Group Inc. in Providence. "They are the single greatest purveyor of change. I'm optimistic they will change—their survival might be at stake."

That's the drastic view. From where Akers sits, the worst is over and the best is about to come. "The rewards will be forthcoming," he says. "And, because of the adversity we've gone through, they'll be all the sweeter."

By Geoff Lewis in Armonk, N.Y., with Anne R. Field, John J. Keller, and John W. Verity in New York, and bureau reports

Analysis

1. On the basis of the organization design chapter, what sorts of organizational design changes would you say were made at IBM?
2. Will the organization design changes lead to greater or lesser cost efficiency?
3. What was hoped to be gained from the organization design changes?
4. In what ways did IBM change to become more responsive to the customer?
5. Why would IBM's policy of full employment help employees accept change?
6. Is just changing the organization structure enough to improve the entrepreneurial spirit, or is more needed? If you think more is needed, what additional changes do you think are warranted?

Chapter 9 Organization Design and Culture

Case 1. Down with Bureaucracy at Sibley Plastics

The new plant manager at Sibley Plastics was excited about his new promotion. Fred had been a line foreman for several years and had developed a reputation for being fair and relating well to the rest of the workers. In addition, he was somewhat of a nontraditional leader who did not like to blindly follow established procedures and policies. The operatives liked it that Fred would bend the rules to improve the morale of the group. The following is a log of some of the events that occurred in the first two and a half years that Fred was plant manager.

Day 1

Fred is announced as plant manager. During lunch, he tells the employees that he wants a more flexible work environment. Bureaucracy has no place in this plant. As long as he is manager, Sibley Plastics will be operated on the notion that workers can be trusted and are working for the company and not against it. Rules for the sake of having rules is a crazy concept and not what Fred wants in his plant. Hence, the first thing to go will be the time clock. Employees are expected to be honest and will be paid on a salary basis. Further, if any employee has a complaint, he or she should feel free to come in and see the plant manager. There is no reason for having layers of managers that will keep employees from going to the top. Further, the plant manager's office staff will be instructed to keep three hours a day open on the plant manager's schedule to meet with employees. If there is open time within those three hours, the plant manager will go out onto the plant floor to talk with the employees.

End of the First Month

There is some indication that employees are becoming more lax in getting to work on time. Although that is not a problem in most areas, it is a problem for the two assembly lines that cannot begin until all the employees are at their work stations.

Fred forms an employee task force to determine if the assembly line can be abolished in favor of a work station approach. However, as the deliberation continues, the line is only operating about seven hours in an eight-hour shift because of tardiness in getting to work, returning from lunch, and returning from the two scheduled breaks during the day.

End of First Evaluation Period

Instead of the usual evaluation form, Fred decides to use a management by objectives (MBO) approach. Under MBO, the employee and supervisor negotiate the goals for the upcoming period. There is concern that some employees have a "better deal" than others because of special projects they are involved with, such as the assembly line change group and the quality circles work group. Some supervisors are confused about how to evaluate the different goals established by each employee. Translating performance into merit increases is made more difficult. Some employees grumble that they have not been treated equitably in the process.

End of First Year

There is an increasing perception that employees are being treated unfairly. In several cases, Fred has let some employees go home early because of family situations even though each employee received a full day's pay. In addition, the MBO system has seemed to foster a perception that special deals are being made between supervisors and selected employees. The employees do not express these problems to Fred because of their respect for him. Yet pressures are building. When someone does make a comment about a program, such as the MBO program, Fred responds that it just takes a little time to work the bugs out, be patient. Because of production problems, Fred is not able to live up to his commitment to be available to meet with employees three hours per day.

End of First Year and a Half

The employees have grave doubts about the equity of the MBO program. It seems that Fred's line managers are making agreements that create some inequity with respect to workload. Employees doing the same job seem to end up with different performance expectations. Since merit increases are based on successfully reaching goals, they favor those who set lower goals. The employees seem to share the perception that Fred is a wonderful communicator with people but a lousy administrator. Fred does not meet with many employees anymore, and his office staff refer problems to the department heads. The department heads complain that there is a lack of guidance from the plant manager.

End of the Second Year

Three suits are filed against the company. One suit charges that Fred discriminated against an older employee. The claim is that merit increases were not based on a standard that was applied to all workers in a similar job classification. Two other suits are filed for wrongful discharge. Employees were dismissed because of poor performance and for not coming in on time. The employees both maintain that the firings were related to their sex and race. In the EEOC hearing, there is little documentation about the work performance and timeliness of the employees. Morale and productivity have steadily decreased, with turnover increasing to 25 percent of the work force in the past year. Fred does not know what to do. He is considering abolishing the MBO system and reinstating time clocks to regulate the exact hours that an employee is at work. However, he cannot decide what to do because both of these actions are so far removed from his management philosophy.

End of Two Years, Four Months

Fred resigns as plant manager. The grapevine indicates that Fred either had to resign or be fired. Fred is reassigned as a foreman, but he leaves that position because of personnel problems in the unit. It appears that the employees do not trust Fred and cannot work with him. The lawsuits are settled out of court for a total of $800,000. A new plant manager is assigned and institutes tough new policies on performance and tardiness. Within six months a union is voted in by the employees, leading to a contract that costs the company an additional $1 million.

Analysis

1. Define the problem that Fred had in his leadership role as plant manager.
2. Why was Fred effective as a foreman yet not as a plant manager?
3. How might Fred have been successful with the changes he wanted to make?
4. Does having a bureaucratic system ensure that there is equity?
5. Is it bureaucracy that leads to inefficiency, or the management of the bureaucracy?

Case 2. Technology Innovations on the Railroad

The railroad industry has undergone a major revolution in the past twenty years. Much of the change has been funded since the passage of the Staggers Railroad Deregulation Act. The act, passed in 1981, gives railroads greater flexibility to compete on price and service. The renewed interest in railroads by the investment community has helped fund a vast array of projects that have further strengthened the ability of railroads to be competitive. Specifically, technology has helped centralize operations, thereby improving efficiency.

Traditionally, railroad operations were organized according to geography. Each division was divided into 100-mile length divisions, which was the standard day mileage that a crew could cover in eight hours. Trains were dispatched from yard to yard using a logbook or train register that recorded which trains would be on the track in a given division. This was of particular concern because much of the track was single track. Hence dispatchers had to know where each train was so that another train was not dispatched that was going in the opposite direction on the same track.

Because this process was governed by telegraph and telephone communications, dispatchers were given a modest territory to cover so they would not be overwhelmed with the volume of trains. As a train passed a station or switch tower, the station agent or tower master would log the arrival and departure and telegraph the dispatcher. Train "meets" (when two trains from opposite directions pass or when one train passes another train on a side track) were managed by a system of train orders. These train orders would be passed up to the engineer and conductor using a wire hoop. They were passed along while the train was moving in the station but before the meet was made. The orders would state something like "Train 1 should take the siding at milepost 123 until train 4 passes." The process was quite labor intensive because each station had to be manned to record the progress of the trains and notify the dispatcher of the progress. In addition, the station agent or tower master had to pass train orders to the trains.

Several technological advances have changed much of the way that railroads operate. One of these advances is centralized train control (CTC). CTC allows the dispatcher to know where each train is in his or her area. A board of lights that depicts the track under CTC allows the dispatcher to change signals, throw switches, and manage virtually all aspects of the movement of trains over the division. The need for station agents and tower masters is greatly reduced, and, because data on train location are submitted immediately, trains flow with fewer delays than under the old train order dispatching method. Currently 25 percent of all rail lines use CTC.

CTC uses direct electrical lines to the dispatching office. For a time the complexity of wiring kept CTC dispatching centers geographically dispersed. However, in 1989 the CSX railroad dedicated an advanced form of CTC.[1] The "super" CTC operations manage all trains in the 20,000 miles of mainline track where CSX operates. Trains

1. "Railroad News Photos," *Trains: The Magazine of Railroading*, May 1989, p. 17.

from diverse locations such as Chicago, Toledo, and Baltimore are all managed from the one central Jacksonville, Florida, location. The centralized operation is possible through the use of computer displays and radio-operated communication systems. Several large railroads in the United States are planning to use space satellites for train tracking and control.

Technological advances have occurred in other areas as well. Computer software programs have been developed to improve the tracking of engines. A new diesel engine costs over $1.5 million, and it is important that the engine is used to bring the best return on equipment. Computer programs now track engine utilization and plan schedules to improve equipment efficiency. In addition, railroads are allowing their engines to stay on the same train over several railroads. Under the old system, once the train completed its trip on its own railroad, the engines would be taken off and those of the new railroad would be attached. The result was greater engine wait times and poorer utilization. Computer software helps match power (engine) requirements with the expected traffic demands over the rail line.

Computers have also been used to track shipments over railroads. Under the old system, a car list was made of each freight car in the train. This list was recorded as the train left the yard. A new list was manually created as the train entered the classification yard of its destination. Under this system a sales agent had difficulty telling a customer the current location of the shipment. Computers have improved these car location methods. Under computerized systems cars are scanned as they enter train yards. The car number is entered into a computer that is connected to a central location. A sales representative can search on the computer to find out the car's current location and its expected arrival at the customer's destination. Customers can change shipment destinations en route and so have greater flexibility in moving products to markets with higher prices. For example, wheat farmers may change a destination to take advantage of better prices at specific commodity locations.

Hence, technology changes have meant big changes in the way that railroads operate and the degree of responsiveness that a railroad might have to changing traffic patterns and customer needs. Technology has made the change possible, and competitive pressures have made the change necessary. In the future these changes may lead to a whole different way of organizing and managing the complex operations of rail companies.

Analysis

1. Do you think the use of CTC will tend to centralize operations? Why?
2. Do you think the use of computers for car tracking will centralize or decentralize operations? Why?
3. Do you think the use of computers might lead to a change in organization structure from geographical to something else? Why?

4. How might technology be linked to organization structure?
5. How might technology be linked to the culture of the organization?

Case 3. National Building Products, Inc.

National Building Products (NBP) was the name given to a conglomerate managed by W. Graham (W. G.) Johnson. W. G. developed a holding company when he decided to acquire other building supply companies in addition to his own plastic tubing company, called W. G. Johnsons' Building Supply. The tubing company made plastic pipes that were used in sewer lines in residential and commercial buildings. It also produced plastic flexible tubing that was used primarily for drainage pipe around foundations. The pipe also had extensive use in agricultural settings for drainage in fields.

In 1980, W. G. decided that he wanted to expand the company and broaden the manufacturing base. The best way to do this, in his estimation, was through acquisition. In 1981, therefore, he acquired the Saint James' Lumber Company. Saint James manufactured plywood, finished wood for flooring and detail work, and framing lumber. The company owned some forestland, but most of the raw timber came from independent suppliers. Out of these two companies W. G. created the holding company, NBP. He did this for tax reasons and to meet his long-term goal of building a more integrative company. The holding company would act as the parent company and would have a staff directed toward management of diverse entities.

In 1982, NBP acquired Illinois Glass, a manufacturer of windows and glass insulators. The company was a regional company much like Saint James and W. G. Johnson Building Supply. It had sales in fifteen states, primarily in the Midwest. Then in 1985 NBP acquired Red Ball Clay and Tile Manufacturing Company of Winnoa, Minnesota. The company was a regional producer of high-quality tile for flooring and wall applications and of clay and tile drainage pipe for use in housing and agricultural applications. Red Ball had manufacturing facilities in three locations: Winnoa and Rochester, Minnesota, and East Troy, Wisconsin. Finally, in 1989 NBP acquired Beloit Brick Company based in Janesville, Wisconsin, which produced bricks for construction and decorative paving.

The current organization chart for NBP appears in Figure 1. There has been relatively little integration of the separate organizations because W. G. does not want to change operations until a master plan is developed that can demonstrate that the changes will lead to an improvement in overall operations. Because many companies have difficulty when changes are made by an acquiring organization, W. G. wants to be sure that all changes are accepted and have a high probability of success to both the individual company and National Building Products as a whole.

As Figure 1 indicates, most of the companies in NBP are organized as separate units. Each is still known by its original name with an additional logo that reads "a fine company of the National Building Products group." W. G. feels that the companies should keep their old names because of the customer loyalty and quality reputation they have maintained over the past twenty years.

However, W. G. is concerned over several issues, primarily about current organizational practices. He is asking himself the following questions.

FIGURE 1
Organization Chart,
National Building Products, Inc.,
7/1/89

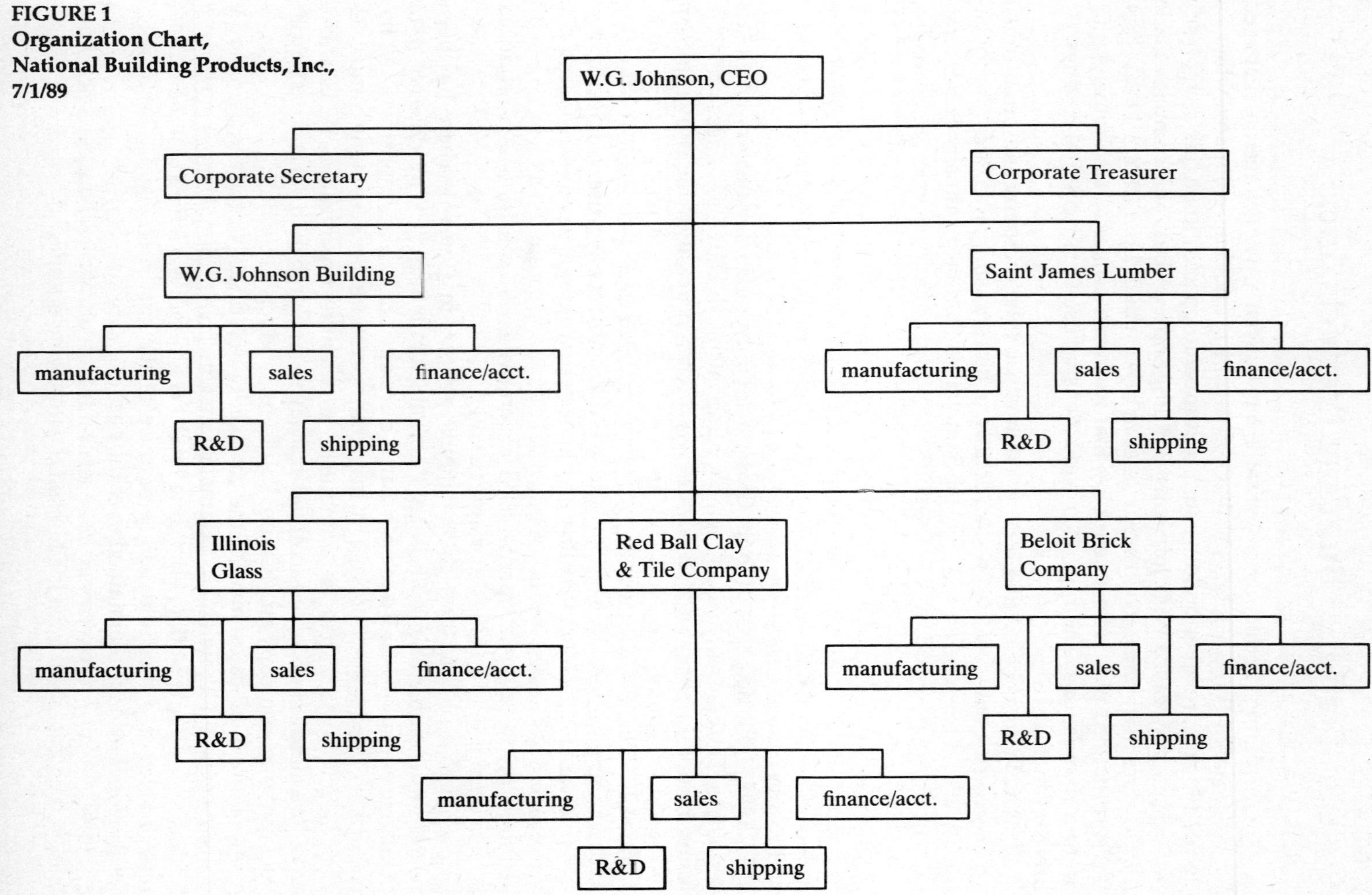

A. How can we achieve operational economies of scale? The operations of the NBP group are not very integrated. Should there be more integration, and how can it be achieved?
B. Product development seems compartmentalized. One might expect that the group of companies would exchange and integrate technologies and applications. Instead the separate groups seem to be looking to use their own products and not to solve customer problems. For example, the research staff at Saint James developed a wood framing material to handle an important client's need for a water-resistant external deck finishing wood. Several thousands of dollars went into the development of the product. However, Illinois Glass had already developed a plastic-clad wood window frame material that could have been readily applied to the client's situation. It would have cost National Building Products much less and would have had a much longer life than the finishing wood.
C. Currently, the combination has created little marketing synergy. The few sales representatives that call on construction companies represent only their own companies. Hence, it is possible to have five separate representatives call on the same client, all from NBP. Marketing efforts are similarly diffused.

Analysis

1. What kind of organization structure is NBP currently using? What leads you to this conclusion?
2. What kind of organization structure is each of the companies of NBP using? Why?
3. How might W. G. address the operating issue raised in question A in the case?
4. What recommendation would you make to address the concerns expressed in question B in the case?
5. What recommendation would you make to address the concerns expressed in question C in the case?
6. Draw a new organization chart that reflects the changes you made in questions 3 to 5.

Case 4. Toronto Advertising, Ltd.

Toronto Advertising, Ltd., is an advertising firm that employs over one hundred people in three locations across Canada. Toronto Ad, as it is called, develops advertising campaigns for film, sound, and print media. In essence, it is a general, all-purpose advertising company. It has over five hundred clients, with the top one hundred clients accounting for 60 percent of its business.

The flow of an advertising campaign from idea to execution consists of several stages. First, a client contacts Toronto Ad and expresses an interest in developing an account. An account manager is assigned to the client on the basis of the manager's specialty. Although all account managers are supposed to be generalists, through their previous work experience they may have particular skills in specific areas that may help them meet the needs of the client.

Figure 1 shows how Toronto Ad was organized before 1985. The account manager worked with a creative department to develop an advertising campaign. The creative department developed panels to describe the campaign. A presentation was then made to the client for approval. Once that was accepted, the creative department transferred the creative panels to a production department. The production department translated the panels into the media specified. (The production department at Toronto Ad is divided into video production, still photographs, text writers, sound creations, and special effects.) The account manager worked with each of the specific departments and the creative department team to develop the actual advertisement. While the production was in process, the promotion department was arranging advertising runs with various media outlets. Finally, the advertisement's location, date of showing, and cost of showing were negotiated.

FIGURE 1
Organization Chart for Toronto Advertising, Ltd., Pre-1985

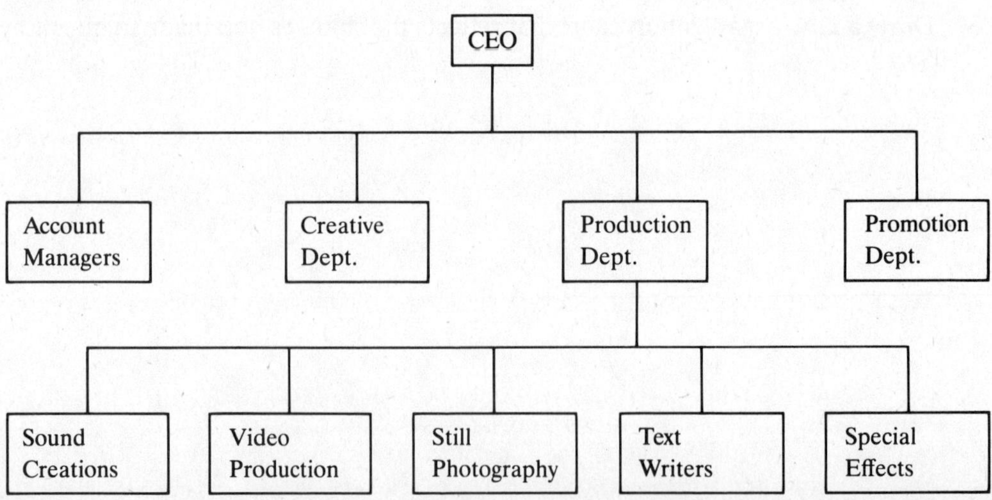

Toronto Ad recognized in 1985 that its organization was causing some conflict with the account managers, who complained that they could not move their projects along efficiently. To find out the progress of a project, they had to contact the head of the relevant department. Since the employees reported to the functional heads in each department, the account managers had no direct authority over any employees outside their own area. They therefore proposed that the organization chart be modified to describe a project form of organization. Under the project form, the account manager would have direct authority over all employees who were assigned to a specific project. In this manner, the account manager would have greater control over output and could be more responsive to the needs of the customer.

In 1985, Toronto Ad revised its organization structure into a project form. Each account manager was in charge of certain employees for the life of a project. Once the project was through, the employees were unassigned. If an individual was not called into enough work groups by the various account managers, he or she could be released from the organization. It was felt this would "keep employees on their toes" and reflect the importance of billable hours as a major driving factor in Toronto Ad's success. Account managers had been under this form of work evaluation for years.

Problems arose from using the project form. Under the old functional or process type of division there was a sense of someone in charge. Under the project form, no one seemed to care for the functional units. Damaged equipment was not repaired. There seemed to be no plan for the systematic purchase of equipment to keep the unit "on the cutting edge" of technology and special effects. In addition, unassigned personnel had little guidance on what to do, whereas under the old structure, an unassigned employee would have been learning new skills or repairing equipment.

To correct these problems, Toronto Ad, in 1989, changed to a matrix form of organization structure. Functional managers were reinstated, but the account managers still retained coresponsibility for those employees assigned to a specific project. However, jurisdictional disputes arose immediately. The functional managers, who had to manage many projects, complained that the account managers were not utilizing employees' time well. The account managers claimed that the functional managers were trying to "empire build" and to negate the power of the account managers.

Analysis

1. Do you feel the billable hours concept is a fair way to compensate an employee? Why or why not? What are the positive and negative aspects of this form of evaluation?
2. Draw Toronto Ad's organization chart that was in effect from 1985 to 1989.
3. Draw Toronto Ad's organization chart that has been in effect from 1989 to the present.

4. What would you do to correct the problems with Toronto Ad's current organization?
5. Which organization structure would you advocate for Toronto Ad? How might you reduce the problems associated with its adoption?

Case 5. Businesses Are Signing Up for Ethics 101[1]

Fraud. Price-gouging. Pollution. All these allegations made headlines in a recent week. It's not exactly the kind of image American business likes to project. Yet the frequency of such stories is leading many to wonder if American management is suffering a crisis in ethics.

The result: Corporations are rushing to adopt codes of ethics. Business schools are scrambling to add ethics courses. And hundreds of consultants are being hired to put "integrity" into corporate cultures. Kenneth Blanchard, author of *The One Minute Manager,* is coming out with a breezy book on ethical management cowritten by none other than Norman Vincent Peale.

Elements of a full-blown management fad in the making? "The market is full of hucksters, promoting quick-fix ethics programs," says Mark J. Pastin, director of the Lincoln Center for Ethics in Temple, Ariz. "I wonder where all these qualified people in ethics have come from."

The issue has also attracted attention from the Business Roundtable, composed of the chief executive officers of 200 major corporations. It has just completed a landmark study of how big business deals with such questions. Andrew C. Sigler, chairman of Champion International Corp., helped initiate the effort, and the Roundtable set up a task force that included five ethicists and consultants. The group studied ethics programs at 10 companies. "I've read so much on this subject by so-called experts who have never set foot in the real business world," says Sigler. "All we're trying to do here is lay out what companies are really doing."

It turns out some companies are doing a lot. The question is whether it's working. One rather disquieting lesson: Even companies that have long emphasized ethics can't guarantee that they will be immune from a lapse in judgment. Take Boeing Co. Since 1964 the aircraft maker has had an ethics committee that reports to the board. Besides "ethics advisers" in subsidiaries, Boeing has a corporate office for employees to report infractions. Training in ethics is done by line managers, not consultants. Yet in 1984 a Boeing unit illegally used inside information to gain a government contract.

"Sitting up here in Stamford," explains Sigler, "there's no way I can affect what an employee is doing today in Texas, Montana, or Maine. Making speeches and sending letters just doesn't do it. You need a culture and peer pressure that spells out what is acceptable and isn't and why. It involves training, education, and follow-up." The Roundtable report makes several recommendations: greater commitment of top management to ethics programs, written codes that clearly communicate management expectations, programs to implement the guidelines, and surveys to monitor compliance.

High-level corporate involvement seems essential. At Chemical Bank, for example, some 250 vice-presidents have taken part in two-day seminars on corporate values that begin with an appearance by the chairman. Managers work through 12

1. John A. Byrne, "Businesses Are Signing Up for Ethics 101." Reprinted from February 15, 1988 issue of *Business Week* by special permission, copyright © 1988 by McGraw-Hill, Inc.

HOW SOME COMPANIES ATTACK THE ETHICS ISSUE

BOEING CEO involvement; line managers lead training sessions; ethics committee reports to board; toll-free number for employees to report violations

GENERAL MILLS Guidelines for dealing with vendors, competitors, customers; seeks recruits who share company's values; emphasizes open decision-making

JOHNSON & JOHNSON A 'Credo' of corporate values integral to J&J culture, companywide meetings to challenge the Credo's tenets, and surveys to ascertain compliance

XEROX Handbooks, policy statements emphasize integrity, concern for people; orientation on values and policies; ombudsman reports to CEO

Data: Business Roundtable

case studies of such issues as loan approvals, staff reductions, branch closings, and foreign loans.

Mutual Trust

Strict enforcement of codes is also important. Chemical Bank, the report says, has fired employees for violations of the company's code of ethics even when there are no violations of law. Xerox Corp. has dismissed employees not only for taking bribes but also for fairly minor manipulation of records and petty cheating on expense accounts.

Executives at several corporations, including Xerox and General Mills Inc., believe that active civic involvement is a critical part of a corporate ethics campaign. As one General Mills executive told a Roundtable researcher: "It's hard to imagine that a person who reads to the blind at night would cheat on his expense account."

Another issue: striking the right balance between centralized management controls and giving employees enough autonomy to build mutual trust critical to maintaining a value system. Johnson & Johnson is seen as a model. With some 150 units, J&J emphasizes individual autonomy and initiative. Yet its one-page statement

HERTZ IS DOING SOME BODY WORK— ON ITSELF

Frank A. Olson, chairman of Hertz Corp., is wishing that he could handle the current scandal at the giant car-rental company the way Lee Iacocca managed Chrysler Corp.'s odometer follies last year. Through candor and charisma, Iacocca allayed concerns over Chrysler's practice of spinning back odometers on cars used by executives and later sold to consumers.

"People believe him," says Olson. "He said, 'We did it, we were dumb, it won't happen again.' But I'm not Lee. It's devastating."

Hertz isn't Chrysler either. The car-rental company admitted overcharging motorists and insurers $13 million for repairs. Hertz has an ethics code and requires its employees to sign a compliance statement, but it didn't seem to make a difference.

Olson says senior management discovered the problem in 1985, when a U.S. Postal Service inspector, acting on complaints by car insurers, found that a Boston office was creating damage estimate reports from nonexistent body shops. An internal audit, Hertz says, pointed to the company's national accidents control manager.

Claims poured in from 13 zones, all of which reported to manager Alan Blicker, five levels below the chief executive officer. Blicker claims that he is being made a scapegoat. Olson charges that Blicker was the "architect" of several fraudulent practices that led to a grand jury probe. Olson fired Blicker, cast out 18 others, and centralized control.

Retail Costs. As much as 80% of the $13 million in overcharges from 1978 to 1985 resulted from charging the retail cost of fixing cars—though Hertz received volume discounts on the repairs. Senior management approved this practice on the advice of in-house legal counsel, who pointed out that such competitors as Avis, Budget, and Alamo followed a similar practice. Unlike the competition, however, Hertz failed to disclose to customers that they would pay for damages at "prevailing retail rates."

Olson ended that policy in 1985. Now the company charges the actual repair costs. Hertz has also refunded more than $3 million to customers and insurers so far. What about the future? Vows Olson: "If I catch one guy billing at something other than cost, I'll throw him out the window myself."

of values, known as its Credo, is an exception to decentralization. "The Credo is a unifying force that keeps the individual units marching together," declares CEO James E. Burke.

J&J's Credo addresses the need for business to make a sound profit while also acknowledging the need to respect employees as individuals and to make high-quality products. Burke credits the statement for helping to guide the company through its product-tampering crises with Tylenol in 1982 and 1986.

'Challenge Meetings'

The Credo has become a central part of J&J's corporate culture. In 1975, Burke began "challenge meetings" for top managers to explore whether the 30-year-old statement was still valid. For three years more than 1,200 managers attended two-day seminars of 25 people to challenge the Credo. Burke or President David R. Clare presided at each session. J&J has been through two other major follow-ups since, and challenge meetings are now held twice a year for new top managers.

Some experts feel such an ongoing approach is essential. "You have to keep renewing the effort," says Laura L. Nash, a Harvard University ethicist who studied J&J. Unfortunately, though, such an extensive program is unusual in Corporate America. Stanford University's Kirk O. Hanson, an authority on ethics, figures only 1 in 10 companies is doing it the right way: via a continuing program that works at all corporate levels.

And there's some question just how important an issue ethics is, given the host of other problems confronting American business today. "If you asked the members of the Business Roundtable to list the five major issues they confront today, I don't think many of them would list ethics," says Paul J. Rizzo, former vice-chairman of International Business Machines Corp. That may be so, but ethics seems to be moving up the corporate priority list.

Analysis

1. Why is organization culture important in influencing ethics?
2. Sigler claims that top management cannot ensure ethical behavior by issuing statements and by keeping diligent control. Why?
3. How might the organization's structure affect its ethics and culture?
4. How might the leadership of the organization influence the organization culture and particularly its ethics?
5. What is a challenge meeting? How does that type of meeting influence the development of Johnson & Johnson's culture and its ethical posture?
6. Is ethics a control problem or an organization culture problem?

Chapter 10 Managing Human Resources

Case 1. Impire Corporation[1]

Mark Pecke returned from a week's vacation in Disneyland with his wife and two children to find the following memo on his desk:

Friday, September 8, 1989 7:20 p.m.

To: Mark Pecke: Vice President of Human Resources

From: Robert Magoulas: International V.P. of Operations

Re: Need to fill South American OPS vacancy

Mark, I just got a call from our South American affiliate. They informed me that Bob Ryan has unexpectedly quit his position as operations director. He really didn't give any reason as to why he quit, just mumbling something about "those darn terrorists." I tried to get in touch with you but your secretary told me that you were going on vacation. We have really got to get moving on filling this position. We've got orders that need to be filled right away or else I'm afraid we may lose our South American market. Attached you'll find a list of candidates that I feel would be best for the job. We don't have time to go about any of our regular usual selection activities. We need to have this job filled because the person you choose should be in Peru next Monday. Thanks.

Mark's job as vice president of human resources included selecting the management teams that made up all operations outside the United States. His employer, Impire Corporation, was a multinational corporation that had business activities in seventeen countries. The majority of these activities were in Europe and Central or South America. The company was originally a chemical manufacturer, but it soon found itself diversifying into financial services and petroleum exploration. From his Miami office, Mark had to decide who was going to be the new operations director in South America. He had to make a quick choice from the prospective candidates presented by Robert Magoulas. Background information was provided from the employee data bank.

1. This case was written by Mr. Wayne Hochwarter of Florida State University.

Pedro Gonzalez—47 years old, married. Two children. Began career with Impire in 1962 as a factory worker in Lima, Peru. Did not graduate from schooling comparable to the American high school system. His present position is assistant to the operations director. (The position of operations director was left vacant by Ryan's resignation.) His twenty-five years with the organization have predominantly consisted of production-related activities in the Lima, Peru, area. Company records indicate that he has had no discipline problems; he has adequate, not outstanding, performance, but it is solid; he does what he is told; he follows orders. Has been with the organization for a long time and knows the workers and the geographic area.

Fred Martinez—35 years old, married. No children. University of Miami BA, University of Florida MBA. Began working for Impire part-time while at the University of Miami. Hired after receiving his MBA to serve as assistant to Carl Robinson, who is vice president of operations at the Miami headquarters. Hard working, teaches a night class in operations management at Florida International University. Interested in researching operations management with colleagues at the U. of Miami. Doesn't like to work overtime. Sets aside weekends for research and time with the wife. No complaints for any disciplinary reasons, solid recommendation from Carl Robinson. Has not really expressed a visible interest to move up in the company, seems rather content where he is. Reviews indicate times of great performance and others of just getting by. Great potential. Familiar with the Miami area but has not spent any time working or vacationing abroad. Might be a good time for us to see what Fred is made of. Agreed?

Thomas Schultz—54 years old. Divorced. Three grown daughters. BA from University of New York in production management. Has worked as a production troubleshooter for Impire for the last thirteen years, meaning that he goes into a troubled area for a short time, gets operations working again, and goes on to the next assignment. Embraces that role. Has served in that capacity in Massachusetts, London, Chile, and Mexico City with good results. Great intensity, which sometimes gets him in trouble with those that have similar short fuses. Although effective, sometimes is crude and lacks tact—especially in foreign lands. I think he'd chomp at the bit for this assignment.

Wright Smith—29 years old, married. One son. BA from the University of Kentucky in industrial relations. MBA from U of Kentucky. Worked as a part-time factory worker in the Lexington branch throughout his undergrad days at UK. Worked full-time during holidays and summer vacations. Excellent performer. Originally interested in going to law school; really took a liking to the production end of the business, thus the reason for the MBA in production from UK. Presently working as the operations director for the Knoxville branch. Great performance reviews, good control of inventories. Seems well liked by most. Caught in the middle of a labor dispute three years ago when the plant was being persuaded to become unionized. A lot of ill feelings at the time, wounds seem to be healing. Not well versed in the

South American culture, but a real go-getter, actively pursuing a promotion of some kind; deserves it, I think. I'm somewhat concerned with his lack of international experience. What do you think?

Teddy Espinoza—44 years old, married, three children, only a teenage son left at home. Born and spent the first thirteen years of his life in Bogota, Colombia. Family left because father wanted a better life. Father worked as custodian during the day and as a security guard at night. Mother was also a maintenance worker for the city school system. Family immigrated to New Orleans but settled in South Miami. AA from a local junior college, BA in business management. Limited experience in operations management. Worked his way up the ladder. Originally a management trainee. Began as office manager, then shop manager, presently manager of operations in Baton Rouge. Taking a more active role in the production end of the operation. Hard working, has gone far without an advanced degree. Dedicated to the organization. Only legitimate concern is his ability to react to emergency situation.

Analysis

1. Whom would you choose for the position? Why?
2. What criteria are important for this position?

Case 2. Southwest Metalworks

Bill Massey had just been informed that a young woman named Paula Stevens had been hired for the position of vice president of manufacturing, a position that Bill had hoped to get. Paula Stevens was in her early thirties and had an undergraduate engineering degree as well as an MBA. On the other hand, Bill Massey was fifty years old and had been plant superintendent at Southwest Metalworks for seven years. He had been with the company for almost thirty years, working his way up in the manufacturing area. He started as a machine operator and then worked in quality control and as a leadman. He spent time in various foremen's positions and was promoted to assistant superintendent before being made plant superintendent.

After finishing high school, Bill had to go to work to help support his family because of his father's death. Through the years he attended several workshops and seminars on management practices. Bill was highly regarded within the company for his knowledge of manufacturing. He could work with people and was well-liked and respected by the employees.

When the president, Al Newman, told Bill Massey who his new boss would be, Bill replied, "I don't know whether I can work for a woman, much less one twenty years younger than me, especially one who has never run a machine or fixed one. What can a person like that possibly know about running a manufacturing plant?"

A few days later Al Newman met Paula Stevens in his office. "Paula," said Mr. Newman, "I think you may have some problems with Bill Massey. He's a good man, but his feelings are hurt. I think he feels bad about being passed over. What do you have in mind to win him over?"

Analysis

1. Why would Mr. Newman choose Paula Stevens over Bill Massey? Do you agree with the choice?
2. Is Bill Massey being unreasonable in his attitude toward Paula Stevens? Discuss.
3. How should Paula Stevens approach the situation with Bill Massey?

Case 3. What Went Wrong with the Selection?

"I just don't know what went wrong here," complained Charlene Madison, chairman of the board of Madison Construction Company, as she sat in the now empty conference room reflecting on the startling events of the past hour.

Madison Construction had over five hundred employees, and annual revenues from contracts surpassed $70 million. Three years ago the firm's general superintendent had died of a heart attack, leaving a large gap in the organization structure between top management and several of Madison's ongoing field projects. The superintendent had reported directly to the executive vice president. Immediately, a vigorous search was begun to find a replacement. The chief responsibility of the general superintendent was to coordinate all field projects. The assignment included serving as a liaison between the project managers and line supervisors working on the field reports.

The board felt that an immediate replacement was needed. A new superintendent, Bill Cartwright, was hired from a large corporation. Initially, the board thought that Cartwright would be able to step right in without causing any lapse in the coordination of field projects. After one year, however, it became apparent that he was not living up to expectations. The project engineers opposed him in many situations, and to make things worse, refused to report to him. Instead the engineers communicated directly with the executive vice president. Eventually Cartwright was released, and this time the board took on a vigorous search within the company to fill the general superintendent position.

Personnel files of several potential candidates were reviewed in depth by Charlene Madison and other board members. Finally, Hank Peters was selected. Hank, a high school graduate, had begun as a laborer with Madison over ten years ago. During that time he had become foreman and then ultimately general foreman. All reports from line supervision indicated that Hank was very good at the technical aspects of construction. He was also very loyal and committed to his men and seemed to get along well with the foremen and their crews. No one worked longer or harder than Hank Peters.

Peters plunged into his new job as general superintendent with even more gusto than in the past. He was on the job before seven in the morning and seldom left before putting in twelve hours of work. Each day he would make the rounds of ongoing projects. Some people in the company felt he was on his way to becoming the youngest and most successful general superintendent the company had ever had.

Recently, however, a reorganization of top-level management occurred, caused by the retirement of one of the directors of the company. At the same time, the project engineers, as a group, petitioned for Hank Peters' removal from his position as general superintendent. Feeling the pressure from below, other board members decided to prevent any similar expression by the engineers in the future. Consequently, they eliminated the job of general superintendent.

Analysis

1. Why do you think the project engineers rejected Hank Peters?
2. What basic error in selection was committed by the board in its choice of Hank Peters?

Case 4. Who to Promote: Education Versus Experience

Norm Nichols had been employed by Always Start Battery Company for more than thirty years. Despite his long service, he was only forty-eight years old. Norm started with Always Start as a mail clerk right after high school, received several promotions, and was transferred to the accounting department after three years. Norm took a number of evening courses and attended various workshops over the years in an attempt to better himself. Eventually it paid off, and he was made a supervisor in the department.

Norm was viewed by most as a valuable employee. His loyalty and commitment to the company were never questioned. His performance appraisals stressed his "good work habits." He was a friendly and gregarious sort and got along well with everyone. Norm was never one to "make waves," and when he saw a problem, he usually took care of it himself. If it was unusual, he checked with his department head, Bob Herder, for advice before addressing the situation.

Bob Herder had been manager of the accounting department at Always Start Battery for over fifteen years. During that time the department had doubled in size. It now consisted of sixty employees, five of whom were supervisors.

Recently, Bob announced his retirement, and management was faced with the task of selecting Bob's replacement. This would be no easy task, since over the years Bob and Norm had become good friends. Bob had recommended that management choose Norm. Top management, however, decided that Norm was "not good manager material" because he was not aggressive enough to be an effective leader of the whole department. Besides, another supervisor in the accounting department had caught top management's eye. Michelle Williams was only thirty-five years old and had been a supervisor in the accounting department for five years. Michelle "looked like good managerial material." She had graduated from a prominent business school and was currently working on her MBA. From the start Michelle had been an Always Start "junior executive" in the company's management training program. Although Michelle had limited experience, she seemed to make up for it with drive and originality. Many top managers who came in contact with her thought she "could go far."

Top management wanted to promote Michelle Williams to replace Bob Herder as manager of the accounting department. However, they worried what effect this choice would have on Norm Nichols, who they still considered to be a valued employee. They worried that Norm's effectiveness as a supervisor would be diminished if he were offended by the move. There was also a possible effect on other long-term employees, who might come to believe that service and loyalty to the company counted for little. Like other companies its size, Always Start Battery had rewarded long-term employees with a generous array of benefits that included incentive raises and a pension program. Now the company had to choose between old reliable Norm Nichols and bright young Michelle Williams.

Analysis

1. Who would you choose and why?
2. Identify the pros and cons of choosing Norm.
3. Identify the pros and cons of choosing Michelle.

Chapter 11 Organization Change, Development, and Revitalization

Case 1. Mississippi Air

Mississippi Air (MA) was a regional air carrier based in Memphis, Tennessee. It was acquired by Pennsylvania Airlines (PA) in 1989. PA wanted to merge the two companies, but since it was concerned that the bad image of MA would contaminate its own good image, it decided that the two companies would be run separately until MA's image improved. The job to improve MA's service and operating characteristics went to Samuel J. Hawkins, who had been in charge of passenger operations at PA before assuming the new role. He appointed Katherine Ingram Thompson as his assistant director at MA. Katherine, or Kit, as the people at MA called her, had been what you might call a rising star at MA before the acquisition. Sam wanted to find someone there who knew operations and the corporate mentality at MA yet who was not locked in the mentality that created the bad image of MA in the first place.

The bad image of MA seemed to be well founded. Equipment was kept to Federal Aviation Administration (FAA) standards; however, painting and cleaning had second priority. Hence, the planes had faded and peeling paint, and some were still painted in the same colors as when they had been bought from their previous owners. The seats and carpets were stained and well-worn. Equipment shortages were the rule rather than the exception. There were few back-up planes; hence, when one plane was off-line for heavy maintenance, some routes had to be canceled for the day. The same was true with maintenance problems that could be fixed in a few hours. MA officials would determine which route had the fewer revenue passengers and freight and would cancel that segment for the day. Passengers were then offered alternative bus service to their destination. Roughly 10 percent of the flights were canceled on any given day. On-time performance for MA was 47 percent. For PA, in contrast, it was 82 percent.

MA's reputation was poor for other reasons as well. Employees were considered unfriendly and unprofessional. Reservations were often lost or incorrectly placed.[1] Baggage damage claims were higher than the industry average for commuter airlines. The morale of the employees was generally very low, and the passengers knew it.

1. It was not determined whether this was a problem of employee error or of administrative procedure. Some employees charged that the company would deliberately "lose" reservations on overbooked flights so that it would not have to make cash settlements with those who were bumped from flights.

Probably most damaging to MA were the several well-publicized incidents involving its aircraft and pilots. In one case the pilot landed in North Dakota when he should have landed in South Dakota. In a second case, the baggage door flew open at 20,000 feet, scattering luggage over a five-mile area. In a third case, a pilot was cleared to land at Meigs field in Chicago on a charter flight. He told the control tower he had visual contact with the field and landed in Lake Michigan, three miles east of the runway. Instead of the required copilot, the pilot had had his girlfriend aboard. Luckily, there were no passengers on the flight, since the plane was going to receive a charter of forty senior citizens who were on a two-day outing in Chicago.

All these events had contributed to what might be called a disastrous image and employee morale problem. Sam and Kit had to try to clean up the mess with somewhat limited resources, since neither MA nor PA had large amounts of cash reserves even though both were profitable airlines. PA was earning 10 percent on revenues, and MA was making 1 percent. Both airlines had full aircraft. PA had 80 percent capacity, and MA was running at 70 percent capacity. PA's break-even was 50 percent capacity, and MA's was 52 percent. Both airlines relied exclusively on Beech 12 aircraft, although PA had purchased five SAAB craft with seating for nearly sixty-five passengers.

Both Sam and Kit believed that they would have to make a two-pronged attack on the problem. With employee morale as low as it was, it needed specific attention. In addition, the image of the airline would have to be changed. However, there was strong sentiment at corporate headquarters in Dayton that MA should not contaminate the image of PA. Although the corporate headquarters would be willing to fold MA into PA, they did not want to do it unless MA could operate up to PA's standards of performance. Both Sam and Kit agreed that the sooner MA could be eliminated as a corporate identity the better, but they also understood the corporate headquarter's position. But how could they create an improved image without a name change?

They decided that the name change would have to be made. However, the only way to receive permission from the home office was to have a plan that could be implemented at the same time the name change took effect. A plan was needed that could address the major problems facing MA.

The two-pronged approach would first involve employees. A nominal group technique (NGT) would be tried at several locations around the system. Employees would be asked to list and prioritize the major problems of MA. Once the problems were prioritized, the employee groups would be asked to come to a consensus on solutions to the problem, again using NGT. Image and operating problems were to be addressed.

While the NGT program was under way, Sam and Kit made their own list of problems and solutions. Obtaining additional equipment was a major issue. They believed that five additional aircraft would be needed. Sam and Kit did not know if any combination of MA and PA service could free up aircraft to be used to reduce the shortage, so they assumed that joint service would not immediately occur. Their other option was to cancel service on some routes so that the level of dependability would meet that of PA. Sam and Kit believed that no service was better than irregular service. Although they thought that reduced off-peak service might be provided, there might not be sufficient demand to make it profitable.

Analysis

1. Explain the NGT approach. How does it work?
2. How is employee involvement going to help resolve the problems? After all, aren't many of the problems caused by the employees? What principle of organization development is being followed by involving the employees?
3. What approach would you advocate to resolve the problems at MA?
4. How might the equipment shortage and management policies relate to poor worker morale?
5. Is the policy of not merging MA with PA reasonable even if some operating costs are saved?

Case 2. Using Confrontation Meetings as a Form of Organization Development at AT&T

In 1984, the Department of Justice, antitrust division, successfully argued before the courts that the American Telephone and Telegraph Company (AT&T) was violating antitrust laws and should divest itself of specific units to allow greater competition. This action led to the breaking up of AT&T. AT&T retained long-distance service while several regional phone companies maintained control of local service. Critics lamented, "Why mess with a telecommunications system that is the envy of the world?"[1]

On the fifth anniversary of the divestiture (January 1, 1989), analysts saw a company that was not falling apart as predicted[2] but one that had a way to go to solidify its long-term position in the market.[3] A new blow to the company occurred on April 18, 1988, when the leader of AT&T, James Olson, died of colon cancer. On April 19, 1988, Robert Allen was elected by the board of directors as chairman and chief executive officer of AT&T.[4] "Within a week of the appointment of Allen, the head of the computer operations—one of the company's big bets for long-term growth—quit. At the same time a joint venture with Olivetti of Italy was unraveling."[5] The big question was how AT&T would handle this additional turbulence.

Robert Allen has a much different personality than James Olson, and there was speculation that a whole different style of managing would occur. And it did. Allen felt, with just cause, that the company still had not entered into the competitive environment it had been forced into by the antitrust decision. The company still had the culture it had had when it was a monopoly. As Allen put it, "We came out of a business that had a single culture. It was very paternalistic, thorough, slow-moving, and exceptionally proficient in accomplishing its mission, but in a static environment. . . . AT&T didn't have to worry about speed in bringing out new products—it controlled the technology and the market."[6]

The new market was much more competitive and demanded quick action by competitors. Allen believed that the culture at AT&T had to change to meet the new environment or its market share would continue to erode. At the same time, he pushed to change the environment to enable AT&T to become more competitive by reducing some of the controls that still plagued it as a result of the antitrust decision. However, a major focus was to change the culture of AT&T so that the organization thought and acted like a company in a competitive environment instead of one still protected as a regulated monopoly.

1. Kenneth Labich, "Was Breaking Up AT&T a Good Idea?" *Fortune*, January 2, 1989, p. 82.
2. John J. Keller, "AT&T Is Eating 'Em Alive," *Business Week*, February 16, 1987, pp. 28–29.
3. John J. Keller, "AT&T: The Making of a Comeback," *Business Week*, January 18, 1988, p. 56.
4. Andrew Kupfer, "Bob Allen Rattles the Cages at AT&T," *Fortune*, June 19, 1989, pp. 58–66.
5. Ibid., p. 59.
6. Ibid., p. 61.

Allen has made many procedural and structural changes to modify the culture of the organization. Recently, AT&T acquired Paradyne Corp, a competitor that manufactures data communications equipment.[7] The acquisition signaled the end of a long-standing tradition that only AT&T homegrown projects were tolerated by management. The new ideas and management of Paradyne were believed to be an important move on Allen's part to shake up the culture of AT&T.

This sort of culture change can be helped through several organization development interventions. *Confrontation meetings* are one such intervention. A meeting or series of meetings are created in order to confront problems facing the organization. In AT&T's case, meetings might be called to resolve the problem that it is not competitive enough in the marketplace. Various groups might develop ideas and plans for resolving this problem. Some of the ideas might be to change the organization, and some might reflect on the changes that the organization could make to influence the environment in which it is trying to compete. These sorts of meetings might be held with top management, with the strategic business units (SBU) such as the computer division, down to functional units within each SBU. The goal is to obtain ideas for change, but that isn't the only goal—of equal importance is building a climate that will recognize a need for change. And because the ideas for change have come from the group, a stronger commitment to the change effort is possible.

Currently, there is apprehension about the changes in the organization and the specter of a shrinking work force. In 1984, AT&T employed 373,000 employees. In March, 1989, that number was pared to 304,600.[8] Having group input on the change process helps to reduce some of those fears because people have greater say in their destiny. Even in cases of unit divestiture or RIFs (reductions in force), groups that are consulted may be able to create plans to facilitate the process and reduce the disruption and trauma that will occur with the change.

Although organization development approaches such as confrontation meetings will not necessarily improve the difficulties that a company faces, they may help generate ideas and build the degree of commitment that will help make changes successful. In AT&T's case, Robert Allen cannot change the culture of AT&T alone. It will take having thousands of employees accept and adopt the culture that Allen desires. Through organization development approaches, Allen will be better able to reach the vision he has for AT&T.

Analysis

1. How can organization culture be changed using organization development approaches? Give an example using AT&T.
2. Wouldn't an organization development approach cost more in lost work time and salaries paid for people who are in meetings instead of working?

7. Ibid., p. 59.
8. Ibid., p. 66.

3. If you agree with question 2, how might you determine the costs versus the benefits of using an organization development approach?
4. Isn't it possible that a committee will make a recommendation that is not adopted? If that happens, couldn't an organization development approach create more ill will than having the CEO make the decision?
5. Regarding question 4, how might the CEO reduce the negative feelings that are caused by a decision that is contrary to the group's recommendations?

Case 3. Using Survey Feedback at General Motors to Improve Product Quality[1]

General Motors has achieved significant and positive gains in product quality as a result of dedicated efforts to make quality and total customer satisfaction—from design through delivery—its number one operating priority. The quality objective is conformance to requirements on a consistent basis to meet or exceed customer needs and expectations in such areas as workmanship, reliability, durability, performance, safety, fuel economy, comfort, and styling. This objective has been the driving force in GM's new-model vehicles and engines which are approaching world class quality levels.

To further accelerate the quality improvement process, General Motors is instituting the UAW/GM Quality Network.

Quality Network

The UAW/GM Quality Network is a joint people involvement process emphasizing teamwork and continuous quality improvement to enhance GM's competitiveness based on total customer satisfaction. The goal of the quality network—to produce the highest quality, customer-valued products—is based on a commitment to have the "voice of the customer" drive everything that GM does in engineering, design, manufacturing, marketing, and customer sales and service. GM suppliers and dealers are part of the Quality Network.

The Quality Network recognizes and utilizes the talents and resources of GM people to manage the processes that impact all elements of a customer-driven environment. Further, it provides a framework for assuring a single, consistent approach to the implementation of continuous quality improvement strategies throughout the Corporation.

The idea behind the Quality Network is to maximize the contributions of GM people everywhere. In so doing, it recognizes the vital role of the UAW and all other unions representing U.S. employees. Every hourly and salaried employee, every union member, every manager, and every executive is a full partner in the business and is to be involved in a joint effort to improve quality processes, eliminate waste, and assure continuous improvement of every task and operation at General Motors.

The motivating force for the Quality Network is the Corporate Quality Council, which is co-chaired by the President of General Motors and the UAW's Vice President/Director of the GM Department. Implementation of the strategic elements of

1. This selection appeared as part of the article entitled "First a Vision, Now the Payoff," *General Motors Public Interest Report, 1988* (Detroit, Mich.: General Motors Corp., 1988), pp. 10–12. Used with permission.

the quality program is carried out through Group, Division/Staff, and Plant Quality Councils. These Councils comprise both union and management individuals where applicable. For example, a Plant Quality Council is comprised of the plant manager's staff, local union chairman and/or president, a union-appointed plant quality representative, and a management-appointed quality representative.

At the plant level, the Quality Network process will jointly address and implement—with full employee involvement—such areas as machine capability studies, preventive maintenance schedules, and process and product quality assessment. Cross-functional, continuous quality improvement teams are to be established which will include all outside suppliers to assure receiving the highest quality products.

Central to the successful implementation of the Quality Network is a joint educational and awareness program. This program addresses all aspects of a quality business and communicates quality techniques and processes.

"Targets for Excellence" Program

Suppliers to General Motors are vital partners in the Corporation's quality-improvement efforts. To strengthen its supplier network, GM has instituted a broad-reaching, continuous improvement program called "Targets for Excellence."

The new program is a problem resolution, assessment, and development process which applies to GM suppliers of productive and service parts, and includes GM manufacturing locations. "Targets for Excellence," which replaces a variety of previously used supplier rating programs, emphasizes continuous improvement in five key assessment areas of business—quality, cost, delivery, management, and technology. Approximately 6,000 domestic suppliers will participate in the program, now under way, which ultimately will be extended throughout the nation and the world.

Supplier assessments will be conducted by GM teams from purchasing, product engineering, manufacturing, and quality control activities. The results of the assessments will be reviewed with individual suppliers, then shared with all GM operating units in North America. The program eliminates multiple visits by different GM organizations to the same suppliers, as had been done previously.

All of GM's direct supplier manufacturing locations have received a "Targets for Excellence" manual prior to participating in an assessment, and every supplier is provided an opportunity to participate in an informational session as the new process is implemented. The manuals and informational sessions, in addition to explaining key evaluation areas, also detail new procedures designed to help suppliers gain operating efficiencies. "Targets for Excellence" awards will be presented to suppliers, signifying superiority in the five assessment areas.

FIGURE 1
UAW/GM Quality Network

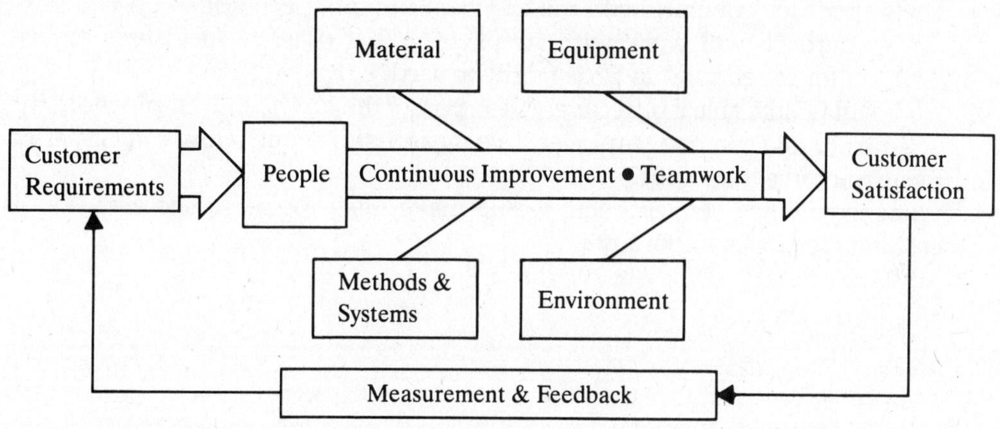

Source: "First a Vision, Now the Payoff," *General Motors Public Interest Report, 1988* (Detroit, Mich.: General Motors Corp., 1988), p. 12. Used with permission.

GM Quality Programs in Perspective[2]

A diagram of the UAW/GM Quality Network appears in Figure 1. Note the importance of the measurement and feedback loop in the program. The feedback loop reflects GM's process of assessing customer satisfaction and expectations as part of its effort to make this program meaningful. The "Targets for Excellence" program is aimed at suppliers and would link into Figure 1 with materials and equipment when equipment needs to be purchased that will perform within the quality standards developed in the Quality Network program.

2. The following section reflects the analysis of the author of this casebook and is not part of the GM original statement.

Analysis

1. Describe how GM uses the survey feedback method of organization development (OD) in its Quality Network program. Why is it valuable?
2. How has GM used teams to improve quality? Relate this approach to the organization development technique called "team building." How does GM's approach fit this OD technique?
3. Why are the suppliers an important link to GM's quality program? How does GM's approach compare with the OD team-building technique? Do you think GM's approach will work with suppliers? What other inducements besides "Targets for Excellence" awards might be used?
4. How will GM be able to effectively incorporate the on-the-line employee in this program? How can one employee give meaningful input? How can GM effectively reinforce that input?
5. What are the key elements that would make this program a success? Why is customer feedback important?

Case 4. Facing Gender Equality in Japan[1]

Japan is entering the era of equality, much as the United States did in the 1960s and much for the same reasons. Its labor shortage has given women a better chance of being taken seriously in the workplace than ever before and in jobs that have been traditionally dominated by males.

> For 13 straight years women have entered the Japanese labor market at a faster rate than men. In 1988 they made up more than 40% of the entire labor force. About half of all Japanese women hold jobs. Nor are these just singles waiting for the right man: Almost two-thirds of working women are married. Though they still are most visible as bank tellers and department store clerks, they are starting to appear in more than a token way in the paneled conference rooms where decisions are made.[2]

From 1984 to 1989 the number of women with managerial titles increased by 50 percent. Although, by U.S. standards, this may seem well behind the progress made by women in managerial jobs, the change in Japan is considered quite remarkable. In the past, there were two tracks for employees regardless of education. One, managerial and professional, was normally reserved for men. This is changing with the labor shortage and the improved education of the Japanese women. "Some 95% of Japanese women are high school graduates, and 36% have junior college or four-year college degrees."[3]

In most cases, the change in attitude by Japanese corporations has not filtered down to Japanese male-dominated workplaces. This has created a set of problems for Japanese companies and for female employees. Many men do not respond well to a woman in a traditional male-dominated role. It is therefore difficult for the female to establish credibility and for the workers to establish an effective work team. Although, in the United States, we might think that Japanese men should simply adjust, most companies realize that change does not come overnight and it is helpful to provide some sort of program that will help raise the male-female issues so that they can be considered in an open and direct forum.

Even Japanese female executives realize that part of the solution is how they approach the problem. The president of the Japan Association for Female Executives says, "There are still a lot of conservative men out there. They have not changed, even though the women have. These women must try to be easy for the men to accept."[4] This is not capitulation, but an approach to changing ingrained attitudes that allows some give and take for the company, the female professional, and the conservative

1. Adapted from Sally Solo, "Japan Discovers Woman Power," *Fortune*, June 19, 1989, pp. 153–158. Copyright © *Fortune*, used with permission. Specific quotes and general ideas related to the Japanese situation are adapted from the article. Ideas relating to the use of organization development are attributable to the authors of this casebook.
2. Ibid., p. 153.
3. Ibid., p. 153.
4. Ibid., p. 154.

male. This is where an organization development (OD) approach might help improve working relationships between male and female managers in Japan. Four specific approaches can be used: sensitivity training, team building, data confrontation, and grid training.

Sensitivity training has been used in organizations with mixed success. In the Japanese situation, male and female executives from differing companies might spend several days together discussing roles and experiencing role reversal simulations and other opportunities to discuss the feelings of men and women as they interact in the working environment. Each group obtains a better awareness of the problems and prejudices that are experienced in the work environment. Strategies to combat the experiences that reduce the effectiveness of the female leader might be discussed in this sort of forum.

Team building might be considered a second organization development approach. In this approach, the management team conducts training sessions in which members discuss how to improve the team and how to build a better team approach to problem solving. It would not be imperative to consider the male-female bias directly, only to focus upon building a working relationship. While considering team productivity, a greater sense of the contribution of males and females might surface, but the emphasis is more on experience and ability and less on gender.

Data confrontation could be a third approach to reduce gender bias. A survey could be taken that explores how men and women feel about having female executives. The results of the survey could then be discussed at a data confrontation meeting. A plan of action for resolving any problems that are indicated from the results of the survey could be constructed using input from all of the members of the group. In this way, members of the group can understand feelings of others about perceived gender differences and relate those differences to their own predispositions. Linking gender bias to problems in performance might be considered a means of showing how gender bias hurts the company and its employees. This appeal to company improvement might work well in Japan because it appears that company loyalty is stronger there than it is in the United States.

The premise of grid training is to move the leader's behavior from various positions on the grid to the optimal point on the grid, which is an effective orientation of getting the job done with a strong orientation for people.[5] Differences in treating gender might surface when various leadership approaches are discussed. These differences might be related to the needs of both genders for satisfaction in the work environment and to building an effective work team.

5. See Robert R. Blake and Jane S. Mouton, "Managerial Facades," *Advanced Management Journal*, July 1966, p. 31, for the first discussion of this approach.

Analysis

1. How is gender bias related to organization culture? How can an organization change its culture?
2. How could sensitivity training reduce the gender bias? What problems might occur when using sensitivity training?
3. What are some of the benefits of using team building to reduce gender bias? Why might it not work?
4. What are some of the benefits of using data confrontation to reduce gender bias? Why might this approach not be effective?
5. What are some of the benefits of using grid training to reduce gender bias? Why might this approach not be effective?

Case 5. GE's Crotonville: A Staging Ground for Corporate Revolution[1]

Radically altering the genetic code of a large, successful corporation requires revolutionary action. Since 1981 John F. Welch, CEO of General Electric, has been struggling to break the company's old genetic code. This code was built around a core set of principles based on growth in sales greater than GNP, with many SBUs (strategic business units), relying on financial savvy, meticulous staff work, and a domestically focused company. The new genetic code is to build shareholder value in a slow-growth environment through operating competitive advantage with transformational leadership at all levels of the organization.

After five years of this effort—which included downsizing GE by over 100,000 employees, divesting $6 billion and acquiring $13 billion in businesses (RCA being the largest), doubling investment in plant equipment and R&D, and at the same time increasing earnings and shareholder value (GE moved up to #3 in the United States in market value from #10)—Welch was asked, "What was your biggest mistake?" He answered, "I was too timid and cautious. I did not move fast enough . . . bureaucracies need quantum change, not incremental change. . . ." Three years later, in 1989, Welch was still accelerating change at GE.

To accomplish the quantum change in GE, a new breed of leader is required. These are leaders who can:

1. *Transform the organization;* that is, creatively destroy and remake an organization around new visions, supported by revamping the social architecture of the organization. This is needed at all levels of GE and is a continuous process.
2. *Develop global product and service strategies.* As GE more aggressively looks to world markets, it is faced with developing world-class products and services at world-class cost. This means changes in product and service design, production, distribution, and marketing. Leaders must be able to:
    - Create new forms of design teams
    - Make strategic use of sourcing
    - Drive world-class standards for design, service, and performance.
3. *Develop strategic alliances.* To deliver on global strategies, more and varied alliances are emerging. These alliances are partnerships that are needed to gain market entry, achieve price competitiveness, gain technology, learn more about management, and so on. The success of these alliances will be determined by a set of leadership factors: skill and prescreening of potential partners, proper

1. Noel M. Tichy, "GE's Crotonville: A Staging Ground for Corporate Revolution," *The Academy of Management Executive,* 3, No. 2 (1989), 99–106. Used with permission.

negotiation, the right condition for partnering, and good coordination and integration mechanisms.

4. *Global coordination and integration.* As the boundaries of GE span wider geopolitical and cultural diversities, it becomes increasingly difficult to integrate the organization. Better communication and cultural integration will be required since all human resource systems will be impacted by this development.
5. *Global staffing and development.* Growing world-class leaders will be the key to competitiveness. Staffing and development systems at GE are outmoded and are undergoing total revamping to develop a new brand of leader.

This article chronicles the evolution of a revolutionary agenda at GE. Crotonville, GE's Management Development Institute, is increasingly being used by Welch as a key lever in the radical transformation of the company's culture. The overall Crotonville strategy and particular developmental stagecraft will be discussed. Finally, lessons for other CEOs are articulated. This article is based on my two years as leader of the last phase of Crotonville's transformation. I was the manager of GE's Management Development Operation from 1985 through 1987.

The Crotonville Heritage as a Lever for Change

In 1956, when Crotonville launched its first 13-week advanced management program Ralph Cordiner, who became CEO in 1950, was using development as a direct lever for change. Cordiner believed that decentralization by product line would best position GE to capitalize on the post–World War II market opportunities. He hired Harold Smiddy, a former Booz-Allen consultant, to engineer a massive restructuring. Cordiner and Smiddy quickly saw that GE did not have the managerial talent—that is, multifunctional general managers—to run a decentralized company. A major effort was launched to design an advanced management curriculum and build Crotonville, a campus-like setting in Ossining, New York. The design of the curriculum drew on the expertise of academicians from around the country and resulted in the creation of a multivolume set of books on how to be a multifunctional general manager in GE. These books were referred to as the "GE blue books," which became Crotonville's "catechism." The critical point here is that Crotonville's birth was as a CEO-driven lever for change. This continued under the next CEO, Fred Borch, as Crotonville was used to introduce strategic planning to GE. Borch's successor, Reginald Jones, used Crotonville to round out the strategic planning effort and improve cash management and inflationary accounting practices. In the Welch era, Crotonville again became a centerpiece for the CEO's efforts to make change happen at GE, but on a scale unheard of since Cordiner's days.

The Early Welch Effort

The first act of a transformation is creating a sense of urgency for change and dealing with the inevitable resistance to a new order.[2] From 1981 to 1985 Welch worked closely with Crotonville and its leader, James Baughman, to delayer, downsize, and change GE's portfolio. Baughman revitalized the curriculum, faculty, staff, and the facility to get the message across to thousands of managers, to try to impact their hearts and minds. Baughman joined GE after years on the Harvard Business School faculty. He had taught at Crotonville since 1968 and was aware of its shortcomings as well as its potential. As eager as Baughman was to revitalize Crotonville, he was not prepared for the passion of Welch's challenge to him when they met for the first time in January 1981: "I want a revolution to start at Crotonville. I want it to be part of the glue that holds GE together."

Under Baughman's leadership, the first moves were to do a program-by-program upgrade of the faculty, curriculum, and staff, and set the stage for a total revamping of the Crotonville strategy. This resulted in the top-level executive programs being tied directly to the GE succession planning process; thus, there was much more selectivity with business heads accountable to the CEO for seeing to it that Crotonville development experiences were carefully planned and carried through for their managers. New programs were targeted for populations previously unserved by Crotonville. The first of these was a New Manager Program, targeted to those managers who hire, train, and supervise the vast majority of GE employees. If Welch was to "drive a stake in the ground" for the new GE culture, this was a critical population to win over.

Another very significant, substantive, and symbolic event was the change in the physical facilities at Crotonville. As GE was going through a very dramatic set of changes, including downsizing, delayering, and divesting, Welch was investing in the future not only in terms of business but also of leadership. The new facilities would provide living and development space in the 21st century. This development was Welch's second stake in the ground.

The New Manager Program began the process of shifting Crotonville's focus back toward the new college hire. In addition, during this period horizontal integration began with Crotonville's acquisition of the functional development responsibilities in marketing, finance, computer information systems, and human resources.

By 1985, the Crotonville transformation was well on its way. Two significant changes occurred that year. First, the reporting relationship of Crotonville was shifted from the employee relations organization to the executive management staff. This enabled Crotonville to be better integrated with the succession planning process and the CEO's office. Second, Baughman was promoted to broader responsibilities on GE's Executive Management Staff, and it was his suggestion that his successor be brought in from the outside to keep up the momentum for change and new perspectives. Furthermore, it was proposed that this individual would take on the assign-

2. *The Transformational Leader*, Noel Tichy and Mary Anne Devanna, Wiley, 1986.

ment as a two-year leave of absence from the academic world. Baughman would retain GE oversight of Crotonville, but the person hired would be in full charge of all educational and development programs. Thus, when my two-year assignment began, the revolution was well along the way and a new vision was emerging for Crotonville. This was a vision that embodied much more than a development agenda; it was a centerpiece in the transformation agenda for GE and its culture. The challenge of leading Crotonville during this historic period was what led me to take a two-year leave of absence from the University of Michigan and join GE.

Welch's Second Act: Crystallizing the Vision

By 1985, Crotonville was well on its way to becoming once again a lever for change at GE. Ironically, a series of evolutionary experiments and changes led to a revolutionary agenda. Although the following premises were never made explicit by Welch or senior executives in GE, they were clearly implicit, based on the behavior and actions taken regarding the role of Crotonville.

Premise 1: Revolutionaries do not rely solely on the chain of command to bring about quantum change; they carefully develop multichannel, two-way interactive networks throughout the organization. So did Jack Welch.

(a) The chain of command, with its vested interests, is where much of the resistance to change resides. Therefore, there is a need to stir up the populace of the organization and begin developing new leaders for the new regime.
(b) There is a need for a new set of values and templates in the organization.
(c) There is a need for mechanisms to implement all of these changes. Therefore, new socialization and new development processes are required.

Premise 2: Revolutionary change occurs by blending the hard and the soft issues.

(a) Welch understood this blending of hard and soft issues quite well, since it was the hallmark of his experience in building the plastic business in GE. On the one hand, he was a tough person, while on the other he invested a great deal of time and energy in coaching and developing team players and team building. He insisted those who had to depart be treated compassionately; that is, "a soft landing." Thus, the cornerstone of Welch's strategy for building an organization and a winning team is this blending of the hard issues (budget, manufacturing, marketing, distribution, head count, finance, etc.) and the soft issues (values, culture, vision, leadership, style, innovative behavior, etc.).
(b) Welch felt that U.S. leadership in general and GE leadership in particular were weak on both the hard and the soft issues from World War II through

the late 1970s, until increased competition from Japan and elsewhere led to a rude awakening.

(c) Since the early 1980s, GE has been very aggressive about getting strong leadership on the hard issues, such as downsizing, reducing levels of management, and driving productivity. However . . .

(d) Driving solely on the hard issues will only work so long as the primary focus is on bottom-line improvement—and you can only squeeze so far. The long-term need is for top-line growth via new markets, products, innovations, and so on. Driving on the hard issues also takes the excitement out of the organization and can suck the psychological reserve out of people. Thus, the challenge for GE by the mid-1980s was to be strong on the soft issues as well as the hard.

(e) Welch uses Crotonville as a lever for blending the hard and soft, for getting at the hearts and minds of thousands of high-leverage middle managers to test, revise, and inculcate new GE values. It enables him to cut through the chain of command and get at the grass roots, from new college hires up to officers.

Premise 3: Revolutionaries rewrite the textbooks and revamp the education systems. Welch did the same.

(a) The GE "blue books"—the 25-year-old Crotonville bible—were symbolically burned. Welch has said repeatedly that there are no more textbook answers; leaders must write their own textbooks.

The New Crotonville—GE's Giant Workshop for Staging Revolution

Starting in the early 1980s under the leadership of Jim Baughman, the focus at Crotonville moved from the Ivory Tower end of the training spectrum toward the practical; thus, it became a workshop for wrestling with real organizational and people issues. During this period, more and more live cases from GE were brought into the curriculum; Outward Bound-type activities were introduced for team building; and there was increased personal involvement on the part of the CEO and officers in teaching the programs.

In 1985 this trend was explicitly recognized. A new mission statement and a new management and OD strategy were articulated for Crotonville, followed by the aforementioned rapid shift toward the workshop end of the development spectrum.

The mission for Crotonville was spelled out thus:

> To leverage GE's global competitiveness, as an instrument of cultural change, by improving the business acumen, leadership abilities and organizational effectiveness of General Electric professionals.

The management and OD strategy built on a new set of concepts concerning the depth and impact of management and organization development. Out of this effort came a framework, later known as the "Tichy Development Model," which provided the concept and rationale for shifting much of the curriculum and emphasis at Crotonville.

Exhibit 1 lays out the strategic framework used to transform Crotonville. This framework conceptualizes development along two dimensions. Along the top of the matrix the focus is on depth of development experience. This ranges from one end of the spectrum, which entails developing awareness, to the opposite end, which entails developing fundamental change. The other dimension refers to the target of the development experience. Here it ranges from change targeted at individuals to change targeted at the organizational level. Historically, at Crotonville, as is true of most university schools of business, the primary focus was on the cognitive understanding of the individual. Managers from all over GE attended Crotonville programs as individuals and participated in classrooms where they learned finance, marketing, accounting, and organizational behavior largely through case studies, reading, discussions, simulations, and so on. The major impact was cognitive understanding with some skill development. The problem with this approach, as with executive education in business schools, is that when the individuals return to their organizations, they have difficulty translating their classroom experiences into the work situation because they haven't fundamentally changed and, just as importantly, their organizations often resist individuals with new ideas. These people do not have a support system—a group of co-workers—that has gone through the experience with them. This was the challenge facing Crotonville: How to move development toward the upper left-hand part of the matrix to help deal with the evolutionary agenda of transforming GE. The challenge was to take a large number of participants a year—approximately 8,000—in a 53-acre, 145-bed residential educational center and move the development experience as far as possible toward the workshop end, while at the same time dealing with the economies-of-scale issue—which meant that customized workshops were not the answer.

The shift in the Crotonville mindset from a training to a workshop mentality has led to a totally new program design: An increasing number of teams attend sessions whenever possible. Participants bring with them real business problems and leave with action plans, and representatives from various GE businesses bring unresolved live cases to Crotonville for participants to help solve. Leadership behaviors are rated by participants' direct reports, peers, and boss before the program so the change can be linked back to the work setting. Executives consult to real GE businesses on unresolved strategic issues; teams also spend up to a week in the field consulting with these businesses on these issues. As mentioned above, members of the CEO and officers come to Crotonville to conduct workshops on key GE strategic challenges.

EXHIBIT 1
The Tichy Development Model

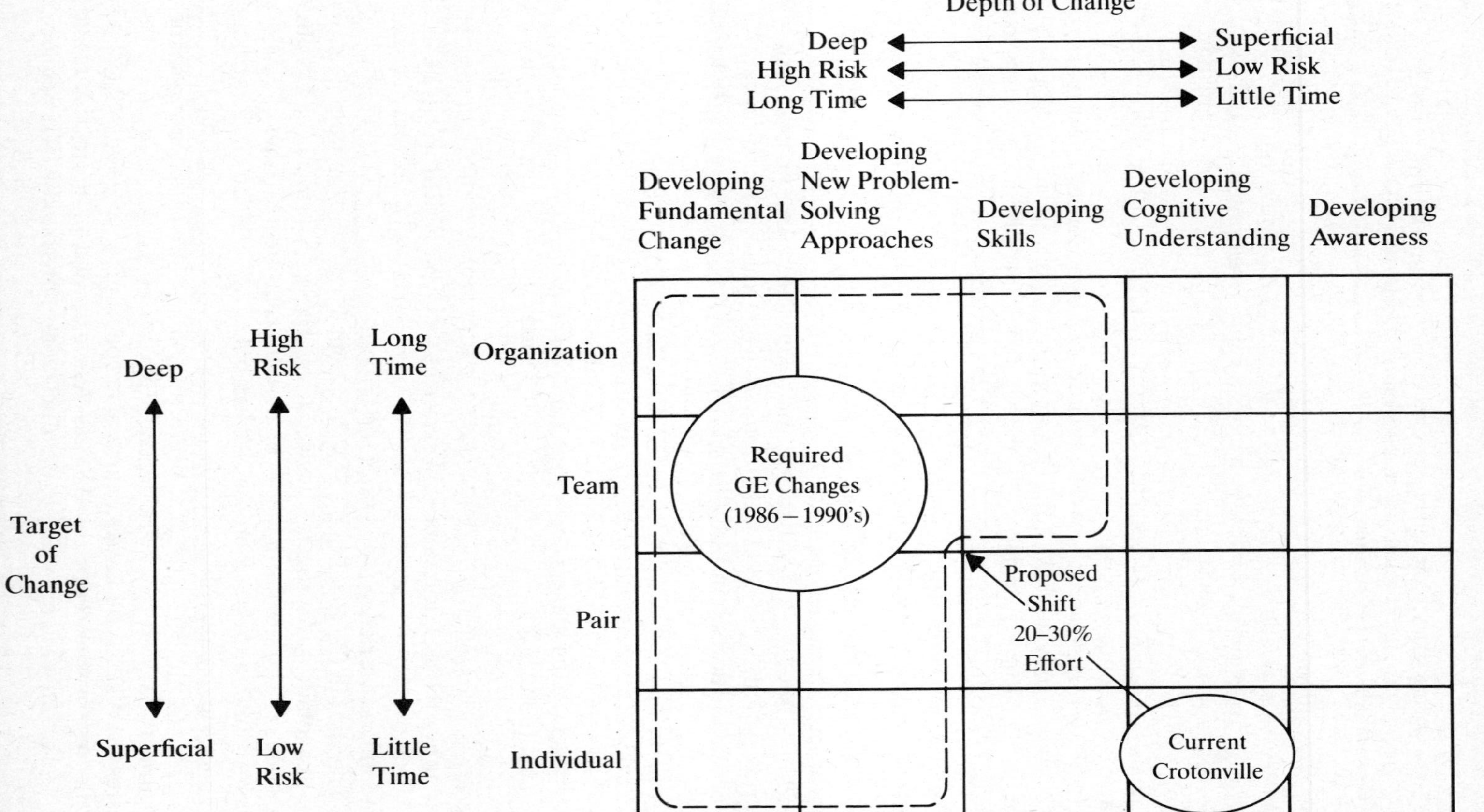

Along the way, participants find the development experiences increasingly unsettling and emotionally charged. They feel uncomfortable with feedback from their back-home organization; they wrestle with very difficult, unresolved, real-life problems, not case studies; and they make presentations to senior executives, argue among themselves, and work through intensive team-building experiences, which include a good deal of Outward Bound-type activity. The measure of program success shifts from participants' evaluation of how good they felt about the learning experience to how the experience impacted on their organization and their leadership behavior over time.

Who Gets Developed?

The other key strategic issue was deciding what populations are to participate in the Crotonville experiences. At GE the assumption is that over 80% of development is through experience; i.e., on-the-job learning. The remaining 20% consists of highly leveraged, formal development activities. With its diverse, large businesses, at GE most of this 20% of formal development occurs out in the various businesses.

EXHIBIT 2
Core Development Sequence

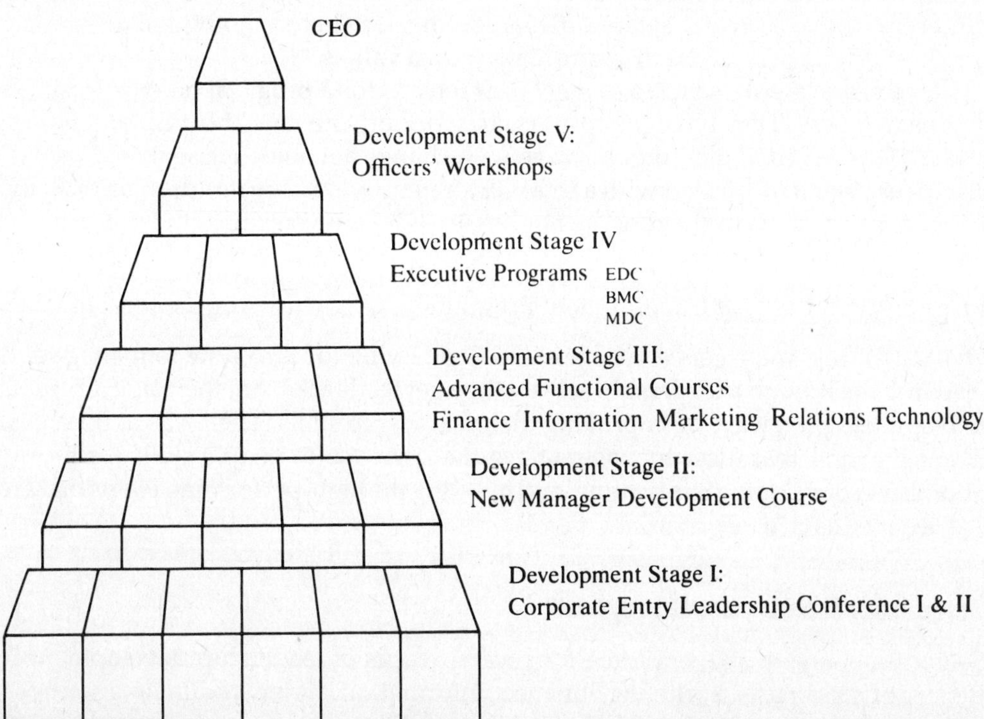

Therefore, Crotonville represents only a small percentage of the formal development resources. The critical question thus is, "Who gets to come to Crotonville and at what point in their career?"

This challenge resulted in a reevaluation of leadership development in the 1990s and beyond, from new campus recruits up through the CEO. The CEO and others worked on the career model for leadership development to identify key transition points in people's careers—that is, "moments of opportunity" (joining GE as a new recruit, becoming a manager for the first time, and so on)—where they could and should be impacted by a set of shared values and leadership characteristics. The result: By 1986, a core development sequence was implemented. This sequence extends from new college hires up through the officer population. A result of rethinking the strategy was the new, core Crotonville curriculum, shown in Exhibit 2.

Stage 1: Corporate Entry Leadership Conferences I and II

Close to 2,000 new off-campus hires come to Crotonville within three months of joining GE to learn about global competition, what it takes to win on that global playing field, GE's strategy for winning, and the changing GE values, as well as to undergo a personal examination of their core values vis-à-vis GE values. They come in groups of 100. Officers, senior human resource executives, and young managers teach and lead these programs. At the end of each year, 200 facilitators, 30 offices, and 30 human resource executives have taught in this program. All of them are the target of change. As many senior officers comment, "There is nothing like teaching Sunday School to force you to confront your own values."

Three years later this group of new hires returns for a program on total business competitiveness. They have real projects to work on, are taught by GE executives, and have to return to their organization with change agendas. These young professionals are again inculcated with a total GE strategy and value mindset. In 1989, the CELC-II program moved out of the businesses as a joint venture with Crotonville.

Stage 2: New Manager Development Program

Over 1,000 new managers a year come to Crotonville to learn how to manage and lead in GE. Through a leadership survey they get feedback from their direct reports to help them plan ways of improving their leadership skills. The focus at this stage is making sure that these managers have the right "soft" people skills for hiring, appraising, developing, motivating, and building the high-performing teams that are needed by this critical group.

Stage 3: Senior Functional Programs

Senior functional managers come for several weeks of leadership development in their specific areas—marketing, finance, information systems, human resources, engineering and manufacturing, among others. All the programs involve change projects and some actually require the participants to invite senior line managers (their bosses or major clients) to spend several days at Crotonville to tackle these change projects. Obviously, making real change happen and leadership are the agendas.

Stage 4: Executive Programs

There are three four-week executive programs for GE managers, which are taken over a five- to eight-year period. These programs integrate outdoor leadership challenge experiences, consulting team projects and CEO projects.

One program, the BMC (Business Manager Course) is organized around consulting projects. The head of a GE business presents a difficult, unresolved strategic business problem that is carefully packaged prior to the start of the program; market and industry analysis, financials, and other data are pulled together along with a clear project statement, and set of deliverables specified by the head of the business. Teams of BMC managers spend the third week of the program in the field interviewing customers, managers, and competitors, and collecting background information to make recommendations. During the fourth week of the program the heads of the businesses involved with the projects come to Crotonville for the presentations. The sessions are electric; the teams, the heads of the businesses make hardhitting business recommendations as well as advise on how to implement the recommendations, and they specially emphasize the soft, human side of change.

The participants are also given feedback on both the hard and soft issues. They debrief their own team members, providing each member with concrete behavioral feedback, based on the intense four weeks of teamwork, on how to be a more effective GE leader. The participants and business clients reconvene six months later to follow up on the progress of the implementation, recommendations, and each participant's leadership agenda.

Stage 5: Officer Workshops

Officer workshops, which are held periodically, consist of groups of 20 to 30 officers who wrestle for several days on unresolved, companywide issues. The CEO actively participates in these sessions.

Elective Programs

In addition to the core sequence described above, Crotonville provides a portfolio of elective programs ranging from courses on leading change—similar to the experienced manager program—to functionally specific courses on information systems, marketing, and human resources. This portfolio is constantly changing as the needs of the corporation change.

EXHIBIT 3
The Development Challenge—Who and What?

	Developing "Global" Maturity and Sophistication	Developing Technical and Business Know-How	Developing Leadership Abilities
For Business Leaders			
For Functional Leaders			
For Experienced Managers			
For New Managers			
For Functional Contributors			
At Entry-Level			

The Continued Transformation of Crotonville

Since 1987 Crotonville has played a key role in both transforming GE and developing a new pipeline for human resources for the future. When I left in 1987, Crotonville's portfolio was enlarged again. All the technical education at GE was brought under Jim Baughman's direction, along with the campus recruiting and early corporate training programs for targeted new college hires. Crotonville thus becomes GE's integrating device for coordinating developing from off-campus up through the office level.

Exhibit 3 summarizes the agenda for Crotonville as it enters the 1990s. The agenda has three primary development objectives: (1) help develop "global" maturity and sophistication, (2) help develop technical and business know-how, and (3) help develop leadership abilities. These objectives are worked on differently at each stage of development, from the entry-level college hire up through the head of a business.

In 1989 Crotonville is being used by Welch to spearhead an effort to liberate middle management at GE. The "old way," hierarchical bureaucracy needs to be radically altered to create the "new way," nonhierarchical, fast-paced, flexible organizations of the future. The transformation must be led from the middle. A series of workshops will provide the catalyst for mobilizing 30,000 to 40,000 middle managers, removing unnecessary carryovers from the past bureaucracy—processes, reports, approvals, measures, and meetings. These workshops will be run in every business and involve the business heads and all their middle-level managers. The process is called "work out."

Lessons for Other CEOs

Crotonville is not unique. It does not require a large campus and bricks and mortar investment to use development as a tool for both bringing about quantum change in an organization and developing future generations of leaders. For this to happen, the leadership challenge for a CEO must entail the following:

Vision. For the CEO to leverage change via development, he or she must have a reasonably clear articulated future vision for the company. This vision must include the organization culture and shared values that will likely be needed in the future. Such a vision must go well beyond the faddish articulation of values triggered by the "excellence" fad of the early 1980s, when everyone had a list of company values that read like the Boy Scout Handbook. The values must be closely integrated with the imperatives of winning in the marketplace.

Leadership characteristics. The CEO must be able to articulate the appropriate characteristics of leaders; that is, the characteristics that will fit with the culture and shared values of the future organization. All too often, companies undertake competency studies focusing on who are the successful managers and leaders of today. This will only ensure that development is focused backward on yesterday's successes, not on the harder task of thinking through what is the new template for leadership in the future. This is not a task to be delegated to human resource staff people, who often have little idea of where the industry, the business, and the company are headed. Only the CEO can lead this effort, albeit with strong staff support.

Career transition points. To maximize the impact of any formal development experience, timing is critical. The challenge here is to have a clearly articulated "theory of the case." This enables the organization to deal with the 80/20 dilemma; that is, the 80% of development that really takes place as a result of life experiences and on-the-job development, and the 20% that takes place via formal development programs. Again, this is a responsibility of the CEO, with strong human resource support. The company must have a framework that provides guidelines in blending on-the-job development and other developmental tools, such as secondary assignment activities and coaching and counseling emphases, with formal development experiences. At each career phase, what tools are to be used for what purposes must be identified.

CEO involvement. For development to leverage the kind of change and impact discussed in this article, the CEO must visibly lead the development process by participating in the overall design and architecture, delivery, and integration of the development process as it gets tied to succession planning and rewards. This is not a voluntary, open university-type approach to development. It is a very personal tool of the top leadership of the organization as well as a very central part of organization effectiveness.

CEO role model. No CEO should undertake the challenge of using development as a lever for change and as a creator of the new shared values in leadership without also understanding that such a process will put more pressure on the senior leadership to demonstrate personal adherence to those values. An open-dialogue, interactive development process also means that top management must be able to take criticism. Hypocrisy will be uncovered and a great deal of subtle pressure placed on leaders to overcome the schizophrenia often found in changing cultures; that is, where people in the middle rightfully point out that top management gives a great deal of lip service to change but in reality their practice is "Do as I say, not as I do." The CEO must lead a critical group of senior executives to undergo the same kind of rigorous self-examination as do participants in the development process. For example, if middle managers are being asked to have subordinates fill out surveys on their management practices, the CEO and the top team must also do the same.

Organizational resistance. Perhaps the final and real test of the CEO is how he or she deals with resistance to change, as well as how he or she handles the transition from the more comfortable awareness and cognitive learning portion of the matrix in Exhibit 1 to the area of fundamental change, in which a great deal of emotion and turmoil are stirred up. This means that the development and human resource staff will have to deal with the fact that the daily "smile sheet"—that is, evaluation of how happy participants are with each day of the program—tends to go up and down during a real transformation experience. Not everyone is always happy; officers have to wrestle with business problems with participants and are made to feel uncomfortable (and sometimes accused of hypocrisy), and there is a tendency for some people to think that things are getting out of hand. It is here that the CEO must stay the course. At times such as this, it might serve well to remember that no one ever gave a high rating to his drill sergeant during the middle of boot camp.

Conclusion

In this article I have laid out a challenge to those CEOs who are wrestling with the transformation of their organizations for global competitiveness. It is my contention that one of the most underutilized levers for change is the rather elaborate investment in development that most large corporations make. One reason why it is so underutilized is that there is little or no personal commitment or involvement by the CEO. Obviously, the challenges laid out here are not for everyone. Once the CEO decides to use development as a lever for change, he or she must make the commitment and follow through on the six principles outlined above. Doing so will be a real test of leadership for all involved.

Noel M. Tichy is a professor of organizational behavior and Human Resource Management at the University of Michigan's School of Business Administration and editor of the Human Resource Management *journal. He developed and currently directs Michigan's Advanced Human Resource Executive program. He is also the director of the Global Leadership Program, a senior executive Japanese, European and U.S. consortium. From 1985 to 1987, he was manager of General Electric's Management Development Institute. Formerly an associate professor at the Graduate School of Business, Columbia University, he launched and directed the Advanced Program in Organization Development and Human Resource Management. He holds a Ph.D. from Columbia University and a B.A. from Colgate University.*

Professor Tichy is the author of several books, including Organization Design for Primary Health Care *(Praeger, 1977),* Managing Strategic Change *(Wiley, 1983),* Strategic Human Resource Management (Fombrun, Tichy, and Devanna, Eds., Wiley, 1984), *and* The Transformational Leader *(Tichy and Devanna, Wiley, 1986). He has written numerous articles on organization theory, development, and change, appearing in various journals (including* Journal of Applied Behavioral Science, Organizational Dynamics, Administrative Science Quarterly, Human Relations, Columbia Journal of World Business, Sloan Management Review, *and* Journal of Business Strategy*). He has served on the editorial boards of the* Academy of Management Review, Organizational Dynamics, Journal of Business Research, *and* Journal of Business Strategy. *He is a past chairman of the Academy of Management's Organization and Management Theory division and is a member of the Board of Governors of the American Society for Training and Development.*

Professor Tichy consults widely in both the private and public sectors. Among his clients have been Exxon, General Motors Corporation, General Electric Company, Honeywell, CIBA-GEIGY, Chase Manhattan Bank, Imperial Chemicals, Inc., 3M, Lockheed and IBM.

Analysis

1. Why was Crotonville considered so important in changing the culture at GE?
2. Why was the shift from the individual change to a team or organization-wide change important to the master vision at GE?
3. What is the core development sequence discussed in the article? How does that concept relate to the organization development effort?
4. How might GE evaluate the effectiveness of Crotonville's efforts?
5. How is GE internationalizing the perspectives of its managers?
6. Why does the CEO need to get involved in the development effort? How was this done at GE?

Chapter 12 Motivating Employee Job Performance

Case 1. Cheryl and the Computer Company

Cheryl Koontz was just completing her BA in computer science from the University of Nebraska. She was working at the university's computer service as an operator at one of the remote laboratories. Her job consisted of helping students who had problems on the mainframe and PCs. She also was in charge of bursting output from the laser printer and placing it in the bins for later pickup by students and faculty.

After graduation Cheryl received a job offer from a local computer company in Lincoln. The company did most of the computer processing for the area banks and retail stores. Cheryl was hired in the position of operator I. This job entailed correcting system problems and handling emergencies when the system would fail. The job required effective interpersonal skills, since an operator had to deal with programmers from the company and clients who had varying knowledge about computers. There was some degree of stress because the work was somewhat cyclical, with peaks at the end of the month when businesses were closing their books.

The following is a chronological view of Cheryl's experience in the first year on her job. Each time period includes Cheryl's view of the situation and her supervisor's perception of her performance. The "Narrative" sections give background information. Note the changing perceptions and consider why these perspectives changed over time. Did Cheryl change, or did her boss?

First Day

Narrative

This is the first day of work for Cheryl. She has had only minor jobs before now. She is twenty-one years old and has only worked on the family farm and for the university computer center. She has traditional values that underscore the importance of working and giving your best to the employer.

Cheryl

I am excited about the new job. The money is very good compared with what I was getting at the university. The people seem nice and my boss seems to be very helpful. It is a small company, which I think is good. I will be able to learn many more aspects of the business than I would if I were working for a large organization. I really hope to have a chance to try different jobs while I am here so that I learn all I can about mainframe computers and PCs. My long-term goal is to become a programmer or a systems analyst for a company. By systems analyst, I mean I want to be able to translate a company's needs for computing into a format for generating reports.

Boss

Cheryl is a bright but inexperienced employee. We are taking a chance with her because she has limited experience.

First Month

Cheryl

I am really enjoying the job and all the different things that I have learned. The people are very nice to me. It has been strange, though. The boss says she wants us to do our best, yet she seems not to really care what we do. I see other operators here that just get by with minimum effort, yet the boss really does not say that much about performance. In fact, some of the other operators get upset at me when I work too hard. They say that I am trying to embarrass them. However, I do not feel good about not doing my best.

Boss

Cheryl is doing an excellent job. She has exceeded our expectations. We are expecting to take her off probationary pay within a month. This will move her up to other operator Is' level of compensation. We normally pay each operator the same so they will not get upset that one is getting more than the other. Pay increases are given every half-year and are normally around the cost of living. We haven't had a chance to say too much to Cheryl about her good performance. We really do appreciate the additional hours that she has spent on the job. Since all the operators are on a basic salary, it is surprising that Cheryl will put in the extra effort.

After Six Months

Boss

Cheryl has been doing well. We are pleased with her performance. She received permanent employee status five months ago, which increased her pay to that of all other operator I positions with one year of experience. We have noticed that she is less willing to spend extra hours on the job. We consider that part of the newness wearing off. I guess if I had to rate her performance, she would be considered average. She has kept more within her job duties, which I like. When Cheryl was first hired she would be doing many sorts of jobs beyond what was required in the position. That seemed to upset the other operators. So we talked to her about that.

Cheryl

You know, I used to be real excited about this job. I felt people cared about me. In turn, I cared about the company. Now, I don't know. The boss does not seem to notice or reward good performance. She does not want me to learn new skills. I don't see any point in giving forth more effort because I can get the same pay increase with or without the effort. Nobody seems to notice or care. We are just one small part of the whole picture and not a very important part, the way it seems to me.

End of Year 1

Narrative

Cheryl resigns.

Boss

Cheryl was a good employee. She told us that she found a better job. You know, it is so hard to find someone with any loyalty to the organization anymore. You train them and they quit. Doesn't anyone care anymore?

Cheryl

Sure I quit. The reason I gave was that I found a better job. And I hope I did. This company didn't care about me or even much about what it was doing. People didn't do their job well and the company didn't care. Why doesn't the company care about its employees? Why doesn't the company care more about the job that it does? Doesn't anyone care anymore?

Analysis

1. Explain Cheryl's motivation based on Maslow's need hierarchy.
2. Explain Cheryl's motivation based on Alderfer's ERG theory.
3. Explain Cheryl's motivation based on Herzberg's dual factor theory of motivation.
4. Explain Cheryl's motivation based on the need for achievement, power, and affiliation.
5. How is the company to blame for Cheryl's resignation?

Case 2. Ken-Ray Book Company

Ken-Ray Book Company publishes and sells college textbooks in the United States and Canada. The company started over one hundred years ago as two separate companies, the L. J. Ken Book Company and the Josse Ray Publishing Company. In 1969 they merged into the Ken-Ray Book Company. The company has published college textbooks exclusively since 1969, when it sold its trade book unit to Sanford & Company. Ken-Ray (K-R) Company has sixty sales representatives who cover the fifty states and each of the Canadian provinces. The organization structure of the sales division includes six regional sales managers and another six regional editors. Normally, the regional editors and sales managers are promoted from the ranks of sales representatives.

Each sales representative receives a quota for sales for the year. Bonuses are based on whether the representative meets or exceeds that quota. Sales are based on the sales of new books, since used books are marketed and sold by several other companies. Representatives must also alert the regional editors to any professors who might be interested in publishing, and they receive a separate bonus for any professor who signs with the company. The bonuses vary from region to region based on the "potential" of the region, which in turn is based on the number of books that have been previously signed in the region. This system is an attempt to reduce inequities that might occur between sales representatives' territories. Since 1979, the method of calculating bonuses has been published for all sales representatives, and regional sales figures are published on a semiannual basis.

The following three sales representatives were interviewed in the summer of 1989. Two questions were asked of each representative: (1) What motivates you to do well at K-R? and (2) What could be done to improve the motivation and performance of the sales representatives? This was part of a consulting project of Minnesota State University and was an attempt to assess the effectiveness and efficiency of K-R's sales effort. The following are excerpts of comments made by a focus group that was held in Chicago.

SUE. You know, I have worked for the company for over three years and I have yet to have someone at the home office send me any positive words about my performance. I have met quota each year, and all I get is an increase in the quota.

HAROLD. You're lucky. I haven't made quota and it isn't my fault. Yet the regional manager always says I need to do more. The Montana Book Store is killing us with used books. I get a large adoption of a new text and the sales are great for a year. By the second year, Montana Book Store is sending used copies in like crazy. New sales for an adoption drop by 90 percent in one year, and this company still clings to the notion of having a four-year cycle on books (four years between the time a new edition comes onto the market) instead of three. That isn't my fault.

BILL. Well, I'm new to the company. I want to do a good job, yet I don't think I have had enough training. What was my training program? It was two weeks in the field with the regional manager. Why, he knew almost all of the people we called on. I don't know a soul. It's going to be tough to meet the quota that they set for me.

HAROLD. I, for one, ignore the quota. I'm here to do a good job, and that means that I'm going to take the time to know the customer. I would really prefer to become a regional editor someday, and that means I need to be well known among the professors. I need to find some talent out there and work with it so I can get credit for some book contracts that are signed.

SUE. That takes too much time and the potential of getting a contract is too slim. I worked with one professor for three years just to have her move to a different school. You know what this industry is like. The only way for a professor to get a decent salary increase is to move to a different school. People move around almost as much as sales representatives. Anyway, I want to be promoted to regional sales representative. That comes from selling books, and I'm going to do that over anything else. That's what I'm good at.

BILL. I think they could increase performance by changing the way they calculate our bonuses and the way they publish books. Regarding the book-publishing aspects, first they should go to a three-year publishing cycle. Next they should make the covers out of cloth to lower the price of the book and reduce its life. Third, they should reduce the use of color pictures—they're too costly. Regarding bonuses, they make it impossible to meet your quota, so you give up. It would make better sense to lower the quotas or start counting the number of calls that we do make on professors. The system is all wrong. That's why I can't possibly do a good job.

SUE. Well, I think I get paid fairly. I wasn't sure until they started publishing the sales data and average salary increases for the regions. That gave me a bench mark. I produced over the average and I got paid over the average. Two things helped me to improve my effort and my satisfaction: first, being able to find out what average performance was for the region, and second, being able to compare my salary increase with an average. Just knowing that is important to me. If my performance is below standard, then I deserve a lower-than-average increase. If it is above standard, then I should get a compensation increase that is above average.

HAROLD. I agree, but I also am working to please myself first. I know what it takes to do the job right. If they don't appreciate me at K-R, then I'll go somewhere else. My reputation is established in the field, and there isn't any company out there that is going to have me do anything to reduce that image. I will not compromise my standards.

Analysis

1. Explain Sue's behavior using expectancy theory.
2. Explain Sue's behavior using equity theory.
3. Which individual appears to have more of an external locus of control? Why? Which has more of an internal locus of control? Why?

4. Which sales representative is governed more by intrinsic satisfiers? Why? Which is governed more by extrinsic satisfiers? Why?
5. What features do you think K-R should have in its compensation program to meet the diverse needs of its employees if the above three sales representatives reflect the views of K-R employees? Why? Identify the appropriate aspect of a motivation theory that supports your answer.

Case 3. U Lucky Dog Cleaning Service

U Lucky Dog Cleaning Service is a small business in Des Plaines, Illinois, a suburb of Chicago. U Lucky Dog employs thirty full-time cleaning staff. The staff are assigned in teams of two or three people to go to different industrial locations. The assignments are mostly at night after the plants have been cleared of employees. Supervision is minimal because the teams are dispersed over a 20-mile radius from the cleaning office. Although cleaning materials are supplied, the teams provide their own transportation to a site.

U Lucky Dog serves many different types of businesses, including a steel-processing plant, five banks, four food stores, three department stores, fifty light manufacturing plants, and over one hundred general offices. Cleaning schedules vary from service five days a week to a cycle of light cleaning once every other day and a good cleaning once a week.

The skill level of these jobs is very low; hence the salary is not high compared with that of more skilled jobs. As a result, turnover is relatively high (100 percent per year), and the quality of work varies greatly. Louisa and Carol Gomez, co-owners of U Lucky Dog, believe that their two most troublesome problems are finding good employees and retaining those employees, and obtaining consistency in performance. However, the cleaning service is very competitive and they do not think they can raise salaries to attract better employees. In fact, they believe that conditions have been getting worse over the years. Carol commented, "You know, the First National Bank used to be able to be completed by two people in four hours. Now it is taking three people five hours to do the same job. It is amazing." The number of complaints from clients confirms their problems.

Carol and Louisa decided that they would try to change things. They contacted a resource person from the Small Business Administration (SBA). The SBA turned the case over to a student consulting group that was part of a small business institute. The students' report advocated that U Lucky Dog should talk with Chris D. Claytor, who taught in the Business School and did this sort of consulting. The following presents some of Chris's report.

CHRIS. First, tell me how you pay people.
CAROL. We pay them by the hour.
CHRIS. What does that reinforce in an employee?
CAROL. Ah, being here and doing a good job.
CHRIS. Try again.
CAROL. Being here?
CHRIS. That's right! We haven't done a thing to reinforce that they do the job well.
CAROL. What reinforces that?
CHRIS. Well, only fear of being fired. How many times do you check an individual's performance, and what are the consequences of that check?
CAROL. Well, if they don't do a good job, we will get on their case.

CHRIS. What if they are doing a good job?
CAROL. Well, ah, er, nothing.
CHRIS. What are pay increases based on?
CAROL. Well, if they don't get fired or quit, they receive a 10 percent increase each year.
CHRIS. Even if they have an excellent record?
CAROL. Yes, but give us a break. It is hard enough just to keep them on the payroll, let alone cut their pay increase because of average performance.
CHRIS. So what do you reinforce?
CAROL. Average performance?
CHRIS. Give me a list of what you want your people to do.
CAROL. We want them to clean an area. You don't need a list for that.
CHRIS. So, they all know what you want them to do?
CAROL. No, the first night they go with a team, and the team tells them what to do.
CHRIS. How does the team know?
CAROL. Louisa or I go out on the job with the team and explain what needs to be done.
CHRIS. OK, somebody needs to know what needs to get done. Let's make a list and put some expected cleaning times on that list. Let's look at a bank and what needs to be done there.
CAROL. OK, here goes:

30 min	Clean ashtrays.
30 min	Clean wastebaskets.
60 min	Clean urinals and toilets.
60 min	Clean sinks, including polish faucets.
30 min	Check supply of toilet paper and hand towels.
60 min	Wash all glass doors.
30 min	Polish all doorknobs.
15 min	Water plants and cut off any dead growth.
15 min	Feed fish and clean out rabbit cage.
30 min	Replace any burnt-out lights.
60 min	Vacuum all rugs. There should be no visible loose dirt, paper, or lint on the rugs when finished.
30 min	Dust paintings.
60 min	Dust desks, and all fixtures.
30 min	Bag trash and take to dumpster.
60 min	Wipe off tables in the lunchroom area.
30 min	Refill napkin holders and condiments in the lunchroom.
30 min	Dust TV and wipe TV screen. Wash out toaster oven and microwave oven.
60 min	Wax and buff hallways and areas without rugs.
60 min	Dust lights and corners of ceilings in all rooms.

CHRIS. OK, you tell me how to set up a system that will reinforce good performance—not just showing up—and will clearly specify the duties that the team at the bank ought to be doing.
CAROL. Give me a clue.
CHRIS. Well, I am telling you, Carol, you have all the makings of a good system that will increase job performance. You may have to differentiate more between what is good and poor performance in your list, but you have what it takes if you just put it all together.
CAROL. Well, whatever you say.

Carol was excited but had no idea what Chris was talking about.

Analysis

1. What is Chris talking about?
2. Set up a system that reinforces good performance using the notion of contingent reinforcement. How does your system reinforce good performance? How is it better than the current system?
3. What behavior intervention is "fear of being fired"? Punishment or negative reinforcement? Why?
4. Is pay by the hour a contingent reinforcer? If so, what is the contingency?
5. What is the importance of specifying the activities that need to be done? Consider your answer in the light of reinforcement theory and goal-setting theory.

Case 4. Comstock Foods

Ted Comstock owned a chain of five food stores in central Ohio. The following statement of Ted's operating philosophy is based on five edited interviews over a six month period:

You know, you really have to look at managing from the perspective that the organization is a behavioral system. That is why many of the motivation theories aren't worth the paper they're printed on. I know, I have been in the business for twenty years, and I have to tell you that you cannot look at one person and apply a motivation theory to that one person in a vacuum. There is a whole environment out there, a whole culture that affects the way an employee thinks and acts. Even the company can be looked at as something that builds its own culture. This culture affects how each employee thinks, acts, and reacts to what is going on.

At Comstock Foods, we have been trying to lock into a culture that pays off for us, the customers, and the employees. Here is what we do. First, we want to have a store that is clean and filled with stock that looks like somebody cares for it. We spend more on store maintenance than other food stores because we want that perception. I don't want holes in the parking lots. I don't want shopping carts that don't work properly because that sends a message. If you don't take care of the physical surroundings, it says you don't care. If employees don't think you care, then they are not going to care. The customers will get that message real soon, and you have lost a valuable way to compete. Competing just on the basis of price is not a good way to retain much customer loyalty.

Customer loyalty hinges on receiving value and on having a pleasant experience while shopping—well, at least not an unpleasant shopping experience. Some people would argue that shopping is never a pleasant experience. However, we want to make it as pleasurable as possible. Hence stock is going to be fresh and appealing. Carts are going to work. When customers get to the check-out line, our staff are going to know what they are doing and will be friendly. We are not going to assume a customer is a crook; hence we don't waste a lot of time checking identifications to approve checks. We have automated much of that, and we instruct our employees not to make a big production out of check approvals or accepting food stamps.

People ask us how we find and retain employees that care about the customer. Heck, we work at it. We recruit employees. We screen them. We tell them what is expected on the job, and then we reinforce their behavior on the job. Part of my job as owner is to assess performance every day. In addition, when I find something I don't like, I mentally require that I find someone who is doing something right and praise that person for it. I used to carry around a host of five-dollar coupons in my pocket.

When I saw an employee do something right, I would peel off a coupon and give it to the person. The coupon meant five dollars in groceries for the employee and only cost us four dollars and fifty cents in merchandise, so I think everyone came out ahead.

Do you understand what I am trying to say? You have to consider the whole environment when you are trying to motivate employees. You have to ask, "What do you want done? What sort of work environment will facilitate reaching what you want done?" I consider those two points each day when I come into work.

If the environment matches what we want to get done, it is easier to get it done. If the employees know we care about them, they are going to do more for us. Part of showing that we care consists of setting expectations, and part is setting the tone of the environment so that the environment rewards good performance.

For example, I want baggers to greet each customer they deal with. I do not insist on one particular greeting, just some acknowledgment. I want them to load the bags properly (eggs, bread, and vegetables on top; cans, bottles, and solid materials on the bottom). I want them to ask customers if they would like to have curb-side loading (we take the cart to a loading area and put the groceries in their car when they drive up to the loading zone). The baggers should thank each customer for shopping at Comstock's. We spot-check their performance. Pay is based not on how long you have worked at the store, but on how well you perform the job.

We also want to develop the employee. This is called "cross training." It is better for me if I can use a bagger as a checker, a checker as a stocker, a stocker as a customer service desk operator, a customer service desk operator as a cashier, and so on. We will boost pay based on the number of jobs that an employee is qualified to do. Hence, our system shows that we want to develop employees and to reward them for that development and for doing the job well. That is what I call building a supportive environment and a culture that will help the store reach its goals.

This whole philosophy of treating employees is related to the experience we want customers to have in the store. I want the customers to feel at home and to know that we care about them. All of our efforts are directed toward treating the customers as we would like to be treated.

To build a climate that supports our employees, we have store meetings, a quality circle program, a periodic focus group discussion about how to improve the store, and a profit-sharing program. All employees are eligible to receive profit sharing as long as they are off the probationary period. We have a good health care plan and a retirement plan.

There is a customer suggestion box, and we respond to each suggestion either by writing directly to the customer or by posting the request in the store with a response below it. We have a small play area for children so the parents can shop in peace. Our managers try to spend some time soliciting comments from the customers each day. In this manner we try to motivate everyone in the store to create a good environment.

Analysis

1. Do you agree with Ted Comstock's view that motivation can be affected by the environment and culture of the organization and its employees? How?

2. Does a pleasant surrounding affect performance? Do you think you learn more in a classroom that is better furnished than one that is not? Why?
3. How does clarifying job expectancies show that a manager cares about the employee?
4. How might cross training affect an employee's performance? How might it be a motivational tool?
5. Wouldn't store meetings and quality circle group meetings reduce productivity in the store? Wouldn't it be better to have the employees out doing their jobs?

Case 5. Customer Feedback to the Main Office: Selling Newspapers Plot, Stock, and Bare Shelf[1]

Research concerning the improvement of customer service behaviors is one of the future directions for organizational behavior management (OBM) (Andrasik & McNamara, 1982). Behavioral training programs coupled with supervisor feedback to employees or incentive programs have increased customer assistance in a grocery store (Komaki, Waddell, & Pearce, 1977), increased friendliness in a fast-food franchise (Komaki, Blood, & Holder, 1980), increased follow-up after retail sales of furniture to ensure that customers were satisfied (Crawley, Adler, O'Brien, & Duffy, 1982), and improved customer service by airline personnel (Feeney, Staelin, O'Brien, & Dickinson, 1982; Luthans & Kreitner, 1975).

Brown, Malott, Dillon, and Keeps (1980) trained retail sales clerks in a department store to approach customers, to greet them, to be courteous, and to close a sale. Although training was minimally effective, daily feedback from the supervisor was more efficient and more cost-effective. Moreover, one sales agent, who did not participate in the training program but did receive daily supervisor feedback, showed as much improvement as those who received customer service training. Finally, performance was maintained after the sales people were simply told that their sales behaviors would be evaluated by customers. Customers were given the opportunity to return an evaluation form after purchasing items from the store. Although this allowed them to become eligible to win a $100 gift certificate, none of the customers returned the forms. In a non-retail setting of an amusement park, Zemke and Gunkler (1982) provided tokens to guests as well as managers. Tokens were to be delivered to park employees when guests found the employees to be helpful. Employees were to be reinforced by guests for friendliness, service, park cleanliness, and for the quality of shows. Guest satisfaction increased, and they spent more money in the park during the token presentation condition.

Although OBM researchers have studied sales agent training and performance as well as customer satisfaction, no studies have examined the utility of customer feedback to retailers as a procedure to improve employee performance. This may not only be an effective method to evaluate and improve performance, but its unobtrusiveness and cost-effectiveness make it appealing to retail managers.

The present study was designed to improve the stocking of a retail product in various locations in a small, north central city in the United States. The retail products, morning newspapers, were not available to the author because I lived a number of

1. C. Merle Johnson, "Customer Feedback to the Main Office: Selling Newspapers Plot, Stock, and Bare Shelf," *Journal of Organizational Behavior Management*, 7, Nos. 1–2 (1985), 37–49.

The author would like to thank Sharon Bradley-Johnson for her helpful comments and data collection as well as Jason Evans and Nicole Robertson for data collection and for carrying out reliability checks. Reprints may be obtained from C. Merle Johnson, Department of Psychology, Central Michigan University, Mount Pleasant, MI 48859.

miles outside of the city limits. This precluded home delivery for all morning newspapers except one. Understanding the economic loss for rural home delivery, I purchased issues from various stores or vendor boxes located in town when I drove to work, to lunch, or on the way home. However, frequently I would find the stores or vendor boxes sold out by noon. Somewhat irritated, often I would drive to another location until I could find the newspaper(s) I sought that particular day. If, however, I found myself driving to many locations to procure a favorite newspaper, extinction occurred. I would frequently give up and buy a different newspaper.

The impetus for the present study occurred at 10:30 one Saturday morning. After driving to a number of empty vendor boxes, I finally found one with my preferred newspaper. Purchasing the last copy in the vendor box, I turned to leave when a man on crutches hobbled around the corner. He, too, was seeking the same newspaper. I gave him this last copy saying I would find another—which I did after driving to several more locations. The following Monday I began collecting data.

Method

Subjects and Apparatus

The subjects were the various personnel responsible for the delivery and stocking of the vendor boxes of four morning newspapers in the state of Michigan. Personnel included delivery agents, circulation directors, and a local manager. Newspaper A was a statewide periodical published in Detroit. Newspaper B was a local periodical in the mid-Michigan area. Newspaper C was also a statewide paper published in Detroit. Paper D was a national periodical that was printed via satellite.

In addition, comparison data were collected on five other newspapers within the state. None were national or statewide periodicals, although all were larger than newspaper B in retail sales. Data from these newspapers were collected when the author was in various Michigan cities for other reasons.

Procedure

Data were collected in a mid-Michigan city on a daily basis six days per week, excluding Sundays and holidays. Newspaper B did not publish on Sundays, and Newspaper D had weekend editions which were not restocked on Saturdays or Sundays. Data were collected in five locations about the city. The four newspapers had vendor boxes, side by side, in each of the five locations. Three locations were in front of restaurants, one was in front of a grocery store, and the last was in front of a department store. Data from six other Michigan cities were collected in a similar fashion. Various locations in these cities that had the same national newspaper, the two statewide papers, and a local newspaper, all in vendor boxes side by side, were used to collect comparison data. One exception was city Alpha. The national newspaper was not circulated in this town, and only three papers were utilized for data collection, the two statewide papers and the local newspaper. This city was included because the local paper, Newspaper B, was the same newspaper published in the original mid-Michigan city. Comparison data were collected on five additional Newspapers (E, F, G, H, & I) in the five other Michigan cities (Beta, Gamma, Delta, Epsilon, & Zeta). All of these comparison data were collected on random days, Monday through Saturday.

Dependent Variable. The author looked at each of the four vendor boxes and noted whether or not there was at least one copy of the newspaper for sale within the box. Display copies in the front of the vendor box were typically the last issues sold. Display copies also blocked the view of additional copies, therefore, the dependent variable chosen was dichotomous: at least once issue available versus none available per vendor box. Data were collected between 5:00 and 7:00 p.m. in order to allow time for the papers to sell that day and in order to maintain consistency in the time period for data collection. Generally, data were collected from the car while the author was on the way home from work. Occasionally I would have to get out of the car because display copies were missing while additional issues remained unsold on the rack in the vendor box, because lights at night reflected off of the glass display making data collection difficult, or because trucks or other automobiles blocked the view of the vendor boxes.

Experimental Design. A multiple baseline across the four newspapers in the mid-Michigan city was employed. Intervention was administered in a staggered fashion to Newspapers A and B while Newspapers C and D remained in baseline. Data collected from the six other Michigan cities were used for comparison purposes only.

Baseline. Data were collected on Newspapers A, B, C, and D for 31 days.

Intervention. Intervention was a package of feedback to the delivery supervisors as well as feedback and backup consequences to the delivery agents. For newspaper A intervention began on day 32 with a telephone call to the local delivery service. As a customer I requested that the delivery service stock the vendor boxes in town with a few more newspapers because I had difficulty purchasing issues when they ran out early in the day. I explained that I often would purchase their main competing paper, Newspaper C, when their vendor boxes were empty. I also inquired about home delivery. The receptionist took my name and telephone number and said someone would call back the next day. After no return call, I called again two days later. The receptionist connected me with the manager to whom I repeated my request for home delivery or having more newspapers stocked in the boxes. I also indicated that I was buying their main competitor because it was easier to find stocked vendor boxes. The manager indicated that home delivery was not possible because I lived outside the delivery area, and he described the location of a few vendor boxes that were typically not sold out. On day 84, after I purchased a copy of Newspaper A from one of the vendor boxes utilized for data collection, I left an envelope under the bottom issue of the stack of newspapers left in the box. The envelope was addressed to the delivery agent and was taped to the rack. In it was a note thanking him or her for keeping the vendor boxes well stocked for the past few days because it made it easier for me to purchase the newspaper. The note was unsigned. I also had enclosed two state-administered lottery tickets as a token of my appreciation (Gaetani & Johnson, 1983). On day 94 I called the state circulation office of Newspaper A in Detroit. I learned the name of the state circulation director from his receptionist, but could not speak to him because he was in a meeting. I left a message concerning home delivery and that I would follow the call with a letter. The letter was mailed to him the next day, and it noted the problems I had subscribing to his newspaper. It also addressed the problems I had purchasing issues from vendor boxes when they sold out early. Enclosed was a copy of a graph of the multiple baseline data through day 94 with the four newspapers' names included. I pointed out how Newspaper C, their competitor, had stocked their vendor boxes with more papers and seldom sold out. Moreover, I included a copy of a second graph of Newspapers A through I in cities Alpha through Zeta and pointed out that empty vendor boxes for Newspaper A apparently was not just a local problem. On day 105 I received a reply (letter dated on day 103). He thanked me for both graphs and said that he would try to arrange home delivery for me (which never occurred). He indicated that the data were interesting and useful, yet economic cost precluded overstocking all vendor boxes statewide. On day 136 I left another envelope containing a note and two lottery tickets in another Newspaper A vendor box. This unsigned note for the delivery agent was in a box not utilized for data collection so that the five locations would not be evident to the local delivery service.

Intervention for Newspaper B was similar, but reversed in order. On day 111 two lottery tickets and a note thanking this delivery agent for keeping the vendor box well stocked were enclosed in an envelope and taped to the bottom of the rack, under the last issue. Although it is not certain that the delivery agents received the feedback and lottery tickets, the envelopes were placed under large stacks of papers after 5:00 p.m. so that it would be unlikely that another customer would take them. All envelopes were gone the next day when I purchased a paper from these same boxes. On day 120 I called the circulation director and was unable to speak to her. I learned her name and followed the call with a letter written in a similar fashion as I had done to the state circulation director for Newspaper A. Enclosed were the two graphs, except that the first graph depicted data up to day 120 rather than day 94, as had been the case for Newspaper A.

The package of feedback to circulation directors and feedback and consequences to delivery agents was only applied to Newspapers A and B. Further replication did not seem necessary since Newspapers C and D had high percentages of available newspapers during the protracted baselines.

Follow-up. Data collection was completed on day 171. One month later data were collected for six consecutive days, Monday through Saturday. This week, days 196 to 201, were used as a follow-up period. No feedback or lottery tickets had been employed for either newspaper for over two to three months, depending upon the newspaper.

Reliability. Twenty-one reliability checks were carried out when two observers would record the data either from different automobiles or independently, if in the same car. Reliability checks were taken during Baseline, Intervention, Follow-up, and during comparison data collection in the other Michigan cities. The 20 opportunities (4 newspapers × 5 locations) per day were divided into the number of agreements by the two observers and multiplied by 100 to determine percentage agreement. Results ranged from 95% to 100% agreement per day with a mean of 99% across the 21 reliability checks.

Results

The results from the mid-Michigan city, Newspapers A through D, are depicted in Figure 1. Thirty-one days of Baseline for Newspaper A revealed variable data with a mean of 46% of vendor boxes with papers available. During Intervention for Newspaper A a mean of 81% of the vendor boxes had newspapers available. During Follow-up 87% of the Newspaper A vendor boxes had papers.

One hundred and ten days of Baseline for Newspaper B revealed that 61% of the vendor boxes had available newspapers. Although the Baseline data were variable, a slight rising trend was noted. During Intervention for Newspaper B, 97% of the vendor boxes were stocked. Follow-up was 100% for Newspaper B.

The 171 days of Baseline for Newspapers C and D revealed stocked vendor boxes 92% and 89% of the time, respectively. These percentages were maintained during the one week Follow-up since Newspaper C exhibited 100% stocked vendor boxes while Newspaper D had 97% of its vendor boxes with newspapers available. A note of interest is that Newspaper D had a 10 cent price increase on day 73 which did not appear to affect these data.

The results from Newspapers A through I in cities Alpha through Zeta are presented in Figure 2. Although no intervention was carried out for Newspapers A and B in these cities, the arrows indicate when intervention started for these newspapers in the mid-Michigan city. It appears that little, if any, generalization was demonstrated by Newspaper A to cities Alpha, Beta, and Delta, even though this was after the state circulation director had been contacted by letter (day 95). Generalization data for Newspaper A after Intervention were not available in cities Gamma, Epsilon, and Zeta.

Newspaper B demonstrated more generalization by the 100% availability in city Alpha, however, the two 100% days during initial Baseline do not allow this to be conclusive. All other data in Figure 2 were used for comparison purposes only.

FIGURE 1
The percent of vendor boxes with newspapers available across days for the four newspapers, A, B, C, & D, in the mid-Michigan city. Intervention only occurred for newspapers A and B in a multiple baseline across pages. One month follow-up data were recorded for one week on days 196 to 201.

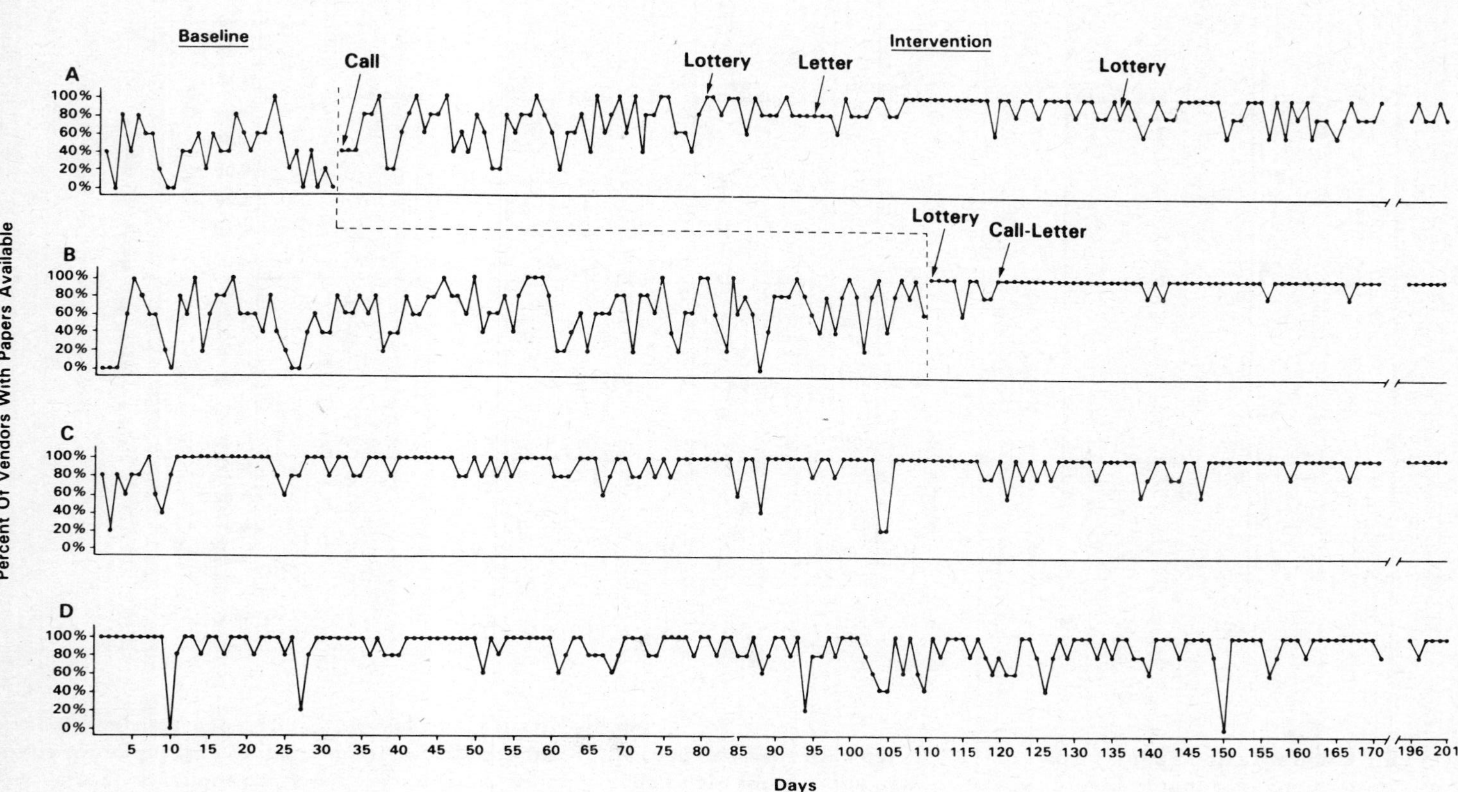

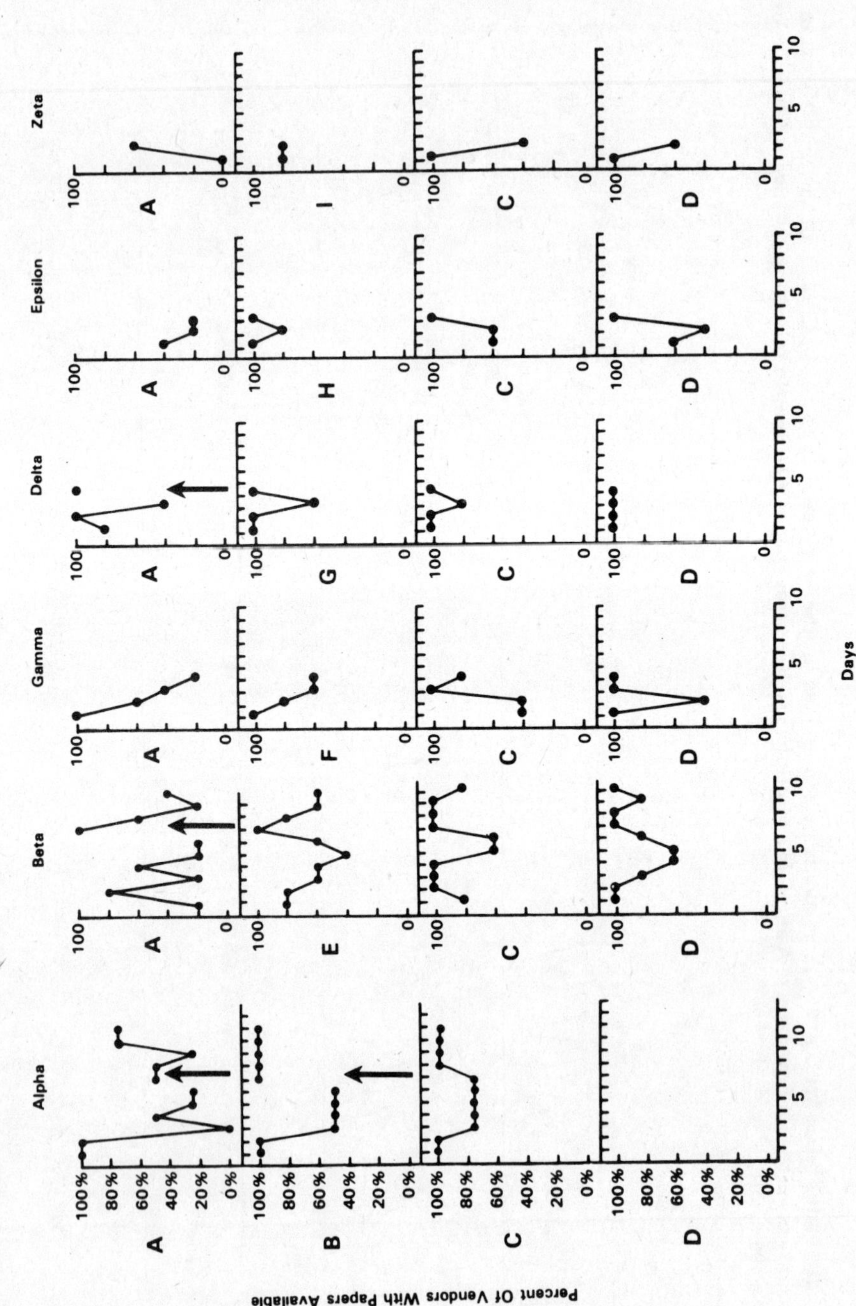

FIGURE 2
The percent of vendor boxes with newspapers available across days for the nine newspapers, A through I, in the six comparison cities, Alpha through Zeta. No intervention occurred in these cities and generalization data were recorded after the arrows for newspaper A in cities Alpha, Beta, and Delta and newspaper B in city Alpha.

Discussion

This project demonstrated that a package consisting of customer feedback to circulation directors, coupled with feedback and back-up consequences to delivery agents, can increase the stocking of newspaper vendor boxes. The telephone call to the local manager for Newspaper A did not seem very effective. He did not return the original call and two days later when he was called again he was not very receptive to stocking more newspapers. Instead he mentioned the location of vendor boxes that had not sold out that day. The lottery tickets to the delivery agents as well as calls and letters to the circulation directors of Newspapers A and B seemed to be more effective. A systematic component analysis of these intervention techniques would be useful to research in future OBM studies. Although individualized graphic feedback is a common and successful tactic for performance evaluation of sales personnel (Mirman, 1982), is it effective by itself when delivered by customers to retailers? Are other forms of customer feedback effective? Would customer feedback and appreciation to the delivery agents be effective without concurrent feedback to management? Is the contingent delivery of state-administered lottery tickets effective for delivery agents when delivered without managerial or customer feedback? Are other forms of back-up consequences effective for delivery agents?

Questions arise concerning the potential cost/benefit impact of increased sales of newspapers. The state circulation director for Newspaper A noted in his letter that harm caused by sold out vendor boxes and the value of additional sales should be weighed against newsprint and transportation costs. However, he pointed out that additional sales were important since Newspapers A and C were in a competitive marketing battle for having the largest circulation in the state.

Newspapers and other media may be receptive to customer feedback. Recently a related study by Jason, Marinakis, and Martino (1985) demonstrated that a university professor was able to prompt newspaper reporters in Chicago to write articles describing behavioral work (behavior analysis and behavior therapy). The authors suggested behavioral topics to reporters staggered in a multiple baseline across newspapers. During the prompts delivered via telephone calls Jason et al. provided feedback on articles and the reporters ". . . were generally pleased to learn that a psychologist had read and enjoyed one or more of their stories." This study, along with the present study, showed that letters to the Editor may not be the only form of reader and customer feedback to newspapers.

Questions also arise regarding the potential of customer feedback to other types of businesses. Mirman (1982) suggested that retailers continue to employ "mystery shoppers" who are trained to evaluate the performance of sales personnel. These could be staff or actual customers reimbursed for their assistance. Mirman notes that this method is unobtrusive and has been successful in the past. However, customer feedback may pose some problems. Over 500 department store customers failed to return any of the sales-persons' evaluation forms in the Brown et al. (1980) study, even though customers had the opportunity to earn a $100 gift certificate. A successful case was directed by Johnson (1981) who was able to eliminate an advertising error by a large pharmaceutical company via customer feedback. A two-page, color advertisement appearing in many major medical journals contained a headline that read, "Day Long Behavior Therapy Without Dosing Problems!" A cordial letter to the company's advertising department noted that drug therapy for reducing hyperactivity in Attention Deficit Disordered children should not be called behavior therapy. The company agreed and promptly withdrew the term from future advertisements.

Feedback in general has been reviewed by management researchers and found to be effective (Greller, 1980; Ilgen, Fisher, & Taylor, 1979; Kopelman, 1982; Nadler, 1979). OBM reviewers have also supported the utility of feedback in organizations. However, these authors point out that feedback as a technique is too broad and vague and that relevant parameters of feedback need to be researched (Ford, 1980; Kreitner, 1982; Peterson, 1982; Prue & Fairbank, 1981). Mawhinney (1984) and Peterson (1982) have supported this point by calling for more behavior analysis and basic science within OBM research. The present study did little to ameliorate the confusion concerning the discovery of relevant parameters of feedback. It did, however, point out another feedback technique that will need to be addressed by OBM researchers. Because customer service is important for retail management, and since customer feedback is one of the most logical methods of evaluating customer service, it appears that this area should not be neglected within OBM research. The potential of customer feedback for improving customer service as well as retail sales and organizational effectiveness is unknown.

References

Andrasik, F., & McNamara, J. R. (1982). Future directions for industrial behavior modification. In R. M. O'Brien, A. M. Dickinson, & M. P. Rosow (Eds.), *Industrial behavior modification: A management handbook* (pp. 428–440). New York: Pergamon Press.

Brown, M. G., Malott, R. W., Dillon, M. J., & Keeps, E. J. (1980). Improving customer service in a large department store through the use of training and feedback. *Journal of Organizational Behavior Management*, 2, 251–264.

Crawley, W. J., Adler, B. S., O'Brien, R. M., & Duffy, E. M. (1982). Making salesmen: Behavioral assessment and intervention. In R. M. O'Brien, A. M. Dickinson, & M. P. Rosow (Eds.), *Industrial behavior modification: A management handbook* (pp. 184–199). New York: Pergamon Press.

Feeney, E. J., Staelin, J. R., O'Brien, R. M., & Dickinson, A. M. (1982). Increasing sales performance among airline reservation personnel. In R. M. O'Brien, A. M. Dickinson, & M. P. Rosow (Eds.), *Industrial behavior modification: A management handbook* (pp. 141–158). New York: Pergamon Press.

Ford, J. E. (1980). A classification system for feedback procedures. *Journal of Organizational Behavior Management*, 2, 183–191.

Gaetani, J. J., & Johnson, C. M. (1983). The effect of data plotting, praise, and state lottery tickets on decreasing cash shortages in a retail beverage chain. *Journal of Organizational Behavior Management*, 5, 5–15.

Greller, M. M. (1980). Evaluation of feedback sources as a function of role and organizational level. *Journal of Applied Psychology*, 65, 24–27.

Ilgen, D. R., Fisher, C. D., & Taylor, M. S. (1979). Consequences of individual feedback on behavior in organizations. *Journal of Applied Psychology, 64*, 349–371.

Jason, L. A., Marinakis, G., & Martino, S. (1985). Prompting articles on behavioral research in newspapers. *The Behavior Therapist, 8*(3), 51–53.

Johnson, C. M. (1981). Eliminating misnomers in advertising by written feedback. *The Behavior Therapist, 4*(4), 22.

Komaki, J., Blood, M. R., & Holder, D. (1980). Fostering friendliness in a fast food franchise. *Journal of Organizational Behavior Management, 2*, 151–164.

Komaki, J., Waddell, W. M., & Pearce, M. G. (1977). The applied behavior analysis approach and individual employees: Improving performance in two small businesses. *Organizational Behavior and Human Performance, 19*, 337–352.

Kopelman, R. E. (1982). Improving productivity through objective feedback: A review of the evidence. *National Productivity Review, 83*, 43–55.

Kreitner, R. (1982). The feedforward and feedback control of job performance through organizational behavior management (OBM). *Journal of Organizational Behavior Management, 3*, 3–21.

Luthans, F., & Kreitner, R. (1975). *Organizational behavior modification*. Glenview, IL: Scott, Foresman.

Mawhinney, T. C. (1984). Philosophical and ethical aspects of organizational behavior management: Some evaluative feedback. *Journal of Organizational Behavior Management, 6*, 5–31.

Mirman, R. (1982). Performance management in sales organizations. In L. W. Frederiksen (Ed.), *Handbook of organizational behavior management* (pp. 427–475). New York: John Wiley.

Nadler, D. A. (1979). The effects of feedback on task group behavior: A review of the experimental literature. *Organizational Behavior and Human Performance, 23*, 309–338.

Peterson, N. (1982). Feedback is not a new principle of behavior. *The Behavior Analyst, 5*, 101–102.

Prue, D. M., & Fairbank, J. A. (1981). Performance feedback in organizational behavior management: A review. *Journal of Organizational Behavior Management, 3*, 1–16.

Zemke, R. E., & Gunkler, J. W. (1982). Organization-wide intervention. In L. W. Frederiksen (Ed.), *Handbook of organizational behavior management* (pp. 565–583). New York: John Wiley.

Analysis

1. Explain the change in behavior of newspaper vendors using the Vroom expectancy model of behavior.
2. Which behavior intervention was used in the study: positive or negative reinforcement, extinction, or punishment?
3. Why do you suppose the calls to the local manager were not as effective as the other interventions?
4. Why do you suppose newspapers are not more aggressive in making sure their vending boxes are full?
5. How could the local manager improve vending machine servicing by the delivery agents?
6. Explain how one might use the approach shown here to improve employee responsiveness in another situation. Be specific.

Chapter 13 Leadership and Influence Processes

Case 1. Realty Crossing, Ltd.

Realty Crossing, Ltd., was a realtor agency serving the Madison, Wisconsin, area. The office was staffed with over fifty realtors and was the second largest realtor in the Madison area. The firm specialized in commercial and multiunit residential sales; however, it also serviced all the real estate needs of its clients. It had been in business for over forty years and was owned by Douglas Allen, a real estate broker and registered investment counselor. Douglas had just taken over the business from his dad, who was retiring after being in the real estate business for fifty-five years. Douglas, who was fifty years old, had worked continuously for Realty Crossing for the thirty years he had been in the business.

The business was organized in much the same way as many realty offices. Brokers were really independent agents who were charged a fixed fee for being associated with the agency. The fixed fee covered the office, clerical, and general advertising expenses associated with the multiple listing of a property and the advertisements that were made each week in the newspaper. A broker's salary, under this arrangement, was based totally on commissions. The agency would support a new broker's fixed costs until the first property was sold and then would deduct those costs from the sale. An additional amount was deducted to build a reserve for the broker. This reserve could not be less than four months' fixed costs and could be as large as the broker desired. The reserve was to be used in months when the broker did not have enough sales to cover the fixed costs. It was placed in an interest-bearing account and was turned over to the broker when the broker resigned. In addition, the broker could ask that the reserve be reduced to the four-month limit at any time.

The situation in the office was amazingly chaotic. Obviously, the more activity the broker had, the greater was the potential revenue that he or she would make. Once the fixed costs and minimum reserves were met, all the additional revenue went directly to the broker. The incentive level was high, and so was the energy level. Brokers were there to sell real estate.

The push to sell real estate did put some customers off. Douglas had received some complaints from clients that the brokers seemed more interested in making a sale than in meeting their needs. He also did not like what he overheard sometimes in the office. Brokers were "putting on the hard sell" to clients to buy a particular property regardless, Douglas believed, of what the customer really wanted. Although Douglas could not document that this approach was hurting the agency, he wondered about the long-term survival of the business. But it would be hard to convince many others that his concern was valid because the agency was the second largest in the city and had had double-digit growth in annual sales for the past ten years.

In contrast, Realty Crossing's competition across the street, House to Sell Realtors, was based on a whole different system and one that intrigued Douglas. House to Sell Realtors was a twenty-person agency and the twelfth largest agency in Madison. It had grown at a modest 2 percent real growth each year for the past decade. House to Sell Realtors was targeted more toward residential properties—primarily condominium and single-family units. It had been in the business for thirty years and was a limited corporation under the state and federal definitions.

The internal organization of House to Sell was much different than at Realty Crossing. House to Sell brokers were paid 2 percent of the 6 percent commission that was made on a sale, with the remaining 4 percent going to the "general pot." Office and advertising expenses were deducted from the pot, and any monies left over at the end of the year were given out as bonuses to the brokers based on their years of service with the company. However, the differences between the bonuses of junior and senior brokers were very small.

Activity in the office was much slower than at Realty Crossing. Realtors talked more with each other, seemed to spend more time with a customer, and were less prone to "make a fast sale" and put pressure on a customer. There was much more mutual helping in the office, but Douglas did not see the aggressiveness that was present at Realty Crossing; hence, there were also fewer sales.

Douglas wondered which sort of office environment might be best for Realty Crossing. Although it was hard to argue with the fast-paced aggressiveness of the current operations, he was not sure if he or the customers would prefer it in the long run. Perhaps the key factor was the leadership of each firm, but in this case he felt that the main difference was the manner in which the brokers were compensated.

Douglas did not like the lack of aggressiveness in the House to Sell organization. He believed that not receiving a large personal commission on a sale might, and apparently had, reduced the incentive for brokers to be aggressive. When all brokers received an equal portion of the same pot, they put in less effort. The mentality that "Joe or Sally will make the big sale and we will profit from their efforts" could easily prevail.

However, the aggressiveness at Realty Crossing was perhaps getting so out of hand that it might hurt the organization. Douglas wanted to get a balance of both approaches, but he was not sure how. In addition, he was not sure how much the role of the leader would affect the behavior of the organization. If he, as leader of Realty Crossing, talked more about cooperating more among brokers and serving the customer, would that change the brokers, or would more have to be done?

Douglas longed for the simpler days when he worked for his dad and didn't have responsibilities to the company and its fifty brokers.

Analysis

1. How is the compensation system affecting the behaviors of the brokers?
2. What are the benefits and disadvantages of Realty Crossing's system?
3. What are the benefits and disadvantages of House to Sell's system?
4. What should Douglas do to reduce the destructive aggressiveness in the office?
5. How might Douglas's leadership style affect the behaviors of his brokers?

Case 2. Lyon Advertising Agency

When I first came to Lyon Advertising Agency three years ago, it was the first time I was a manager of the graphics production area of an agency. I had been a graphics designer myself for ten years at another agency in Chicago. The Lyon Agency needed a new manager and did not feel the department had good candidates itself. There was concern by top management that the department was not operating effectively and had too much infighting.

The previous manager of the department was a very friendly and cooperative person. I do not think I have ever met a kinder person or one that wanted so much to please. However, as a manager he may have been too nice and may have allowed things to happen that did not build the department. One group of graphic designers in the department had a free hand, in the absence of more guided leadership, to run the show as they wanted. And run it they did. I heard that they intimidated the junior employees, threatening them to either work with the senior people or find that they would not be supported for promotion by the "senior staff." The "gang of four," as I called these "senior staff," tended to control the hiring and promotion process. Under the previous department manager, all existing employees could vote on the hiring of a new employee. This policy was followed because it was important to have cooperation and an effective work team. However, the gang of four distorted the process so that no one was hired with better performance records than those of the gang. Hence, the gang enhanced their own job security and control over the department. The other staff in the department were relatively passive and allowed this behavior to continue.

This is what I was getting into. It was a challenging environment and one in which I felt I could make an important improvement. I believed that my boss understood the problems and what had to be done. I believed I had his support.

The first year, I worked on documenting the performance of all employees. I wanted to have a stronger system that would, in effect, give grounds to fire those who were not doing the job well. In addition, I hired some excellent professional graphic designers and production staff that the rest of the group supported, or at least I thought they did. One of their friends, who was not well qualified, was rated high by the group. I ranked him below the other candidates and hired, in my opinion and with strong documentation, the best qualified. The gang of four were outraged and encouraged the person not hired to file an age discrimination suit, which he did. That cost the company some money even though the Equal Employment Opportunity Commission (EEOC) refused to proceed with the complaint after the discovery process found no basis to the charges. In addition, the gang of four were working hard to spread all sorts of distortions to undermine the confidence that people had in my ability and integrity. I was appalled.

I believed that to confront this group would not be productive, since most of their activity was covert. The strategy I used was to be visible, fair, and consistent with my actions. Why didn't I fire the gang of four? Well, they were good production people and the company had a practice of retaining people who had sufficient levels of performance. Personally, I defined performance as the quality and quantity of production that occurred. I did not consider their personal conduct on the job as material for the evaluation process—at least at the beginning.

Once I established that the promotion process would be conducted in a fair and impartial manner, I found that previously passive junior employees became much more active in the affairs of the department. They were much more willing to suggest changes and add to the creative dimensions of our product. In many respects they were willing to challenge the gang of four. When the gang was critical of the promotion process, several junior staff composed a strong letter against the gang's claims.

That and other conflicts that began to occur made me realize that I had to go beyond performance measures in the evaluation process and look at an individual's total contribution. That I did, and it resulted in howls of protest by the gang of four but support from the rest of the department and from my boss.

Once the gang realized that their appeals were overruled by my boss, they had limited recourse. In addition, their somewhat unrealistic protests had reduced their own credibility throughout the company and within the department. In a word, their control over the department was over. While I was in charge, they knew that they would be treated as all the other employees, not as a special group. They would be evaluated on standards that would be applied to each employee, and these standards would include how well they worked with others and how well they worked toward building the department. An evaluation system was put into place that was centered more on objective measures of performance and less on the subjective opinions of others. The policy and procedures established would govern the department more than would personalities. With these changes, I felt the department would be more strongly protected against a gang in the future.

How are things now? I see a department that is growing together and starting to build. There is much less visible infighting and a new spirit of cooperation. Although the gang members are still here, they have been more reserved. I see them more concerned with rebuilding their damaged relations with groups than causing more problems. Although it wouldn't surprise me to see them at it again in the future, at least for now things are running very well. I think we have all learned in the process.

Analysis

1. What sort of leadership style was this person using?
2. How might a leader avoid this problem?
3. What sort of leadership style might be most effective in this sort of situation? Why?
4. What sort of power did the gang of four have? How did they obtain it?
5. Are there substitutes for leadership in place? What are they?

Case 3. Mrs. Loomis Case[1]

Background

The Student Counseling Center of Miller University had experienced considerable internal turmoil for three years. When Dr. Beth Sims took over as its new director, she knew little of the history of the Center. Having been in student counseling for nine years, she knew MU had always been considered one of the best counseling centers among midwest universities. It was especially well known for the excellent mentoring its now retired director, Bob Grimes, had given to many young professionals in the field. Many of "his" protégés had moved on to become directors and deans at other institutions.

She also knew Grimes' replacement, John Youngs, had resigned rather surprisingly after only two years in the position. The counselor with the most seniority on the staff, Carl Bearman, had been appointed as interim director while a national search was conducted.

The Center had a staff of six counselors, three men and three women, in addition to Dr. Sims. Beth had met all of them during her interviews as well as Mrs. Loomis, the secretary. Beth remembered Mrs. Loomis had told her with real pride in her voice and a tight smile on her face that she'd been with the Center for 18 years and had four years to go before retirement. Beth sensed that Mrs. Loomis was very proud of being in the middle of the activities in the Center. From the appearance of the office and especially Mrs. Loomis's desk, Beth guessed that the secretary liked to have everything in order.

Beth came into the position with a suspicion that she was not the choice of the counseling staff. During her interviews, she had sensed some staff hostility toward her. She considered many reasons for this. It seemed they were a tightly knit group. They indicated that they did many social events together. Perhaps the perceived animosity was due to her having a Ph.D. when none of the other counselors had one. At 32, she was not much older than all the staff. She had only two years of full time administrative experience as an assistant director of the counseling center at the Big Ten university where she had earned her doctorate. She also knew that the Center at Miller had never had a female as an administrator.

She mentioned her concerns about the staff to the Dean when he made the job offer. He brushed her comments aside by saying it was probably due to what had happened in the sudden resignation of Youngs. He assured her she was exactly what the

1. Roger Smitter, "Mrs. Loomis Case," in *Annual Advances in Business Cases, 1987*, ed. Cyril C. Ling (Whitewater, Wisc.: Midwest Society for Case Research, University of Wisconsin, 1987), pp. 243–256. Used with permission.

university needed. Due to the Dean's enthusiastic support and her desire to gain more administrative experience, she took the job.

Orientation to the Center

During her first week, Beth began a review of the Center files. Mrs. Loomis was proud to show her these files and Beth quickly learned why. The records were clear, precise and very complete. Beth learned that her predecessor had resigned about midway through the previous year. Two counselors had left after his first year and another resigned at the start of his second year. The records also indicated that the number of student appointments dropped considerably during the last weeks before Youngs resigned. The records contained copies of the many memos which Youngs sent to the staff. The records showed he had initiated many procedures, partly, Beth gathered, because the organization of the staff under Grimes had been very loose. Beth also noted that under Grimes, Mrs. Loomis had sat in on staff meetings to take minutes. Youngs had excluded her from these meetings.

Beth also set out to get to know her staff better. During her first staff meeting, she announced she would have Mrs. Loomis (who was again included in the meeting) make appointments for all the staff to meet with her for informal "getting-to-know-you" sessions. She also announced her goal of restoring the Center to a position of respect on campus and in the profession. She mentioned several possible ideas and programs the staff could undertake. The other counselors had little overt reaction other than "That's interesting" and "We might try that." Beth did most of the talking at the first staff meeting. She came away from it very frustrated.

Staff Interviews

Beth had Mrs. Loomis schedule Carl Bearman as the first appointment. He nervously waited outside Beth's office, talking with Mrs. Loomis. Mrs. Loomis sensed his nervousness and asked what the problem was. He said he was fearful that Dr. Sims might turn out to be too much like Youngs. As was the case in the past when one of the young counselors had a problem, Mrs. Loomis provided a willing ear to listen. After some more discussion of Beth, she added in a whispered voice, she was "disappointed in that young woman." She told him how she had baked cookies and brought them to Dr. Sims' apartment when she was moving in. She had invited her to dinner during her first week on the job. "She was nice and thanked me alright, but she's never mentioned it again. And, I've given her all the information about how we used to run the office, but I think she wants to do it her way." She then gave one of her short but tense smiles as Carl got up to go into Sims' office.

Within a few minutes, Mrs. Loomis could hear animated talk coming from the office. Then, there was some laughter. Carl's session went well beyond the 30 minutes which had been allotted. Mrs. Loomis had to tell the next staff member to wait. The staff member recalled later that it was clear from her demeanor that she did not like appointments to run long and disrupt the schedule.

After emerging from the appointment, Carl reported to Mrs. Loomis that he and Beth "had a great time together." He added, "She knows a lot about counseling. She encouraged me to go on for a Ph.D. In fact, she knows the key people in the grad schools. She's got some terrific ideas about what needs to be done to get this office moving again." Then he added, "She had guessed I had some problems when I was trying to run the office. But, she said it was a good experience and that she would help me learn more." Mrs. Loomis had been smiling in her tight little smile until the final comment Carl made. Then, her face turned to a frown.

Mrs. Loomis heard similar comments when another counselor emerged from Beth's office an hour later. At five o'clock, Mrs. Loomis interrupted Beth's appointment with the third staff person to ask if it was alright if she left even though an appointment was going on. Almost without looking at her, Beth said, "Of course, Mrs. Loomis, go ahead."

News of the sessions with the new director was the main topic of conversation among the staff counselors during the next few days whenever they met in the reception room. Because Mrs. Loomis was almost always seated at her desk in the middle of the room, she heard their excited chatter about Beth. Staff members commented privately that Mrs. Loomis seemed like her old self again, working busily and pretending not to listen to these office interactions.

During the next staff meeting, Beth learned a great deal about what had happened under Youngs and Grimes. One counselor said Youngs had imposed "a lot of rules, but I suppose they were needed since things were pretty loose with Grimes." No one noticed Mrs. Loomis looking shocked. Then the counselor added, "But, the problem with Youngs was he always made you feel like a hired hand. He thought we all had to be here at 8 a.m. sharp and couldn't leave until 5. Bob Grimes didn't care when we came in. In fact, you were the one who kept us from not abusing the freedom he gave us, weren't you, Mrs. Loomis?" Mrs. Loomis suddenly looked embarrassed and managed only a faint smile. The group quickly moved on to another topic.

Role of Mrs. Loomis

About a week later, during an informal discussion at a local coffee and donut shop with one of the experienced counselors Beth learned more about Youngs. The start of the open rebellion against him was signaled when Mrs. Loomis stopped defending him. The counselor said, "I'd never heard her say an angry word about anyone until Youngs came here. At first, she would tell us to be patient with him. 'He's inexperienced. He'll learn' she would say. She thought that since he was the director, he was right. Then, she overheard him call her a 'fussbudget' one day. She never showed any emotion outside but inside we could tell she was plenty upset. She let everyone know in her way that she was displeased to be working for him. She could be the same old gabby Mrs. Loomis one minute and then when Youngs walked in the room, she wouldn't say a word. That was when she started talking about retiring early. I'm sure glad she didn't then. What would we do in this office without her? She knows how to do so much around here."

Only once did Beth ever attempt to talk about Youngs with Mrs. Loomis directly. Beth had asked her for some files which she promptly retrieved. When Beth asked why Youngs had established these files, Mrs. Loomis said only, "He had his ideas." When Beth pressed her a little, Mrs. Loomis would only say that she was glad Dr. Youngs was gone. Then, she seemed to soften up a little in her demeanor to add: "I'm so sorry for all the grief Carl had when Dr. Youngs left. I just know Carl is a better counselor than Dr. Youngs will ever be. But, heavens, that young man knew nothing about running an office. You should have seem him struggle with the budget. It's a good thing I've been around this office since the dawn of time." Beth replied with only "Yes. He said you were helpful."

Bob Grimes

After two months on the job, Beth asked Mrs. Loomis to schedule a lunch appointment with Bob Grimes. Mrs. Loomis seemed to light up when she talked to Grimes on the phone. The former director of the Center still lived in the small town where the university was located. But, he never visited the Center. At lunch, Grimes recalled his days as Director with obvious fondness. "You know, in the early days, we just had to deal with routine stuff—like homesickness and maybe some fraternity pranks. But in those last few years, I never felt like I could be of much help with the drug abuse and alcoholism problems these kids have now. I was fortunate to have people on staff who could handle that."

Beth complimented him on his reputation as mentor. He recalled his retirement dinner when so many of his former staff people came back to give him praise. Then he paused and in a mock hushed tone said, "But, don't let that fool you. It was Mrs. Loomis who really ran things in the office. Without her, I wouldn't have had time to work with students and those young counselors. She did all the hard work. I simply let people do what they were good at. A Counseling Center shouldn't give a lot of orders to people."

He went on to praise Mrs. Loomis for helping new counselors feel at home. "She wasn't all business, you know. She would give them a meal when they moved in. She had plenty of them over for dinner, especially after her husband died. She never had any kids of her own but she sure made up for it in how she treated the staff people in my office."

Grimes also told her he had advised the university *not* to hire Youngs. "Sure, he had a fancy Ph.D. and all that, but it's important to come up through the ranks like I did. I know if someone is a 'people-person' or not. So does my staff. Youngs just wasn't that kind of fellow." Beth shared with him some of her perceptions of the university and town but let Grimes do most of the talking during their lunch.

Relationships with Mrs. Loomis

After this session, Beth tried especially hard to have a friendly but professional relationship with Mrs. Loomis. She made it a point to compliment her exactness and attention to detail. When she gave her plenty of advance notice on major typing projects, Mrs. Loomis usually replied with, "Oh, I don't mind. Heavens, Mr. Grimes was always coming in with something that just had to be done at the last minute." Beth also encouraged her to take the standard ten minute coffee break with other secretaries in the building. But Mrs. Loomis always said with a smile but firmness in her voice, "It's important to be at my desk and get your phone messages, especially in the Counseling Center. And, we have so many students coming in, it just wouldn't do for me to be away from my desk, would it?"

Indeed, there were more students coming into the office. A new image for the Center had blossomed on campus. Beth was asked to speak in residence hall meetings about a variety of topics. The counselors were also busy with appointments and campus programs. Beth seemed pleased at what had been accomplished within a few short months.

Beth's rapport with the staff carried over to the students who worked in the office as part-time clerical assistants. She got to know them on a first name basis. One in particular, Susie Dunn, had worked in the office for three years. She and Mrs. Loomis would often talk when they worked. One day, when Beth was putting on her coat to leave for a meeting, she overhead Susie say to Mrs. Loomis, "You know, for a couple of years, this was just a job. But, now, I'm really interested in looking into a master's degree in counseling after I graduate from here."

"Well, that's nice," said Mrs. Loomis, "but a nice young lady like you should have no trouble finding a handsome man and settling down."

A few minutes later, just as Beth was leaving, she said to Susie, "See if Mrs. Loomis can find a time in my appointment book. I'd like to talk with you about your interest in counseling." Susie readily agreed to do so.

Conflict

Beth returned late that afternoon about 4:45 p.m. to the office after a long and difficult meeting on the budget with the Dean. She greeted Mrs. Loomis with a casual "Hello" and then proceeded directly to her office. Once seated at her desk, she was surprised when she looked up to see Mrs. Loomis standing in the doorway, looking as if she needed permission to come in. Mrs. Loomis said, "Now, Dr. Sims, here are those important phone messages which came in while you were out." As was her custom, she began to read the messages out loud to Beth. This behavior had always bothered Beth but she had never said anything. This time she did. She raised her voice slightly and said in a firm tone, "You know, Mrs. Loomis, I can read them myself. Just give them to me."

Mrs. Loomis slumped in her posture, walked to Beth's desk and threw the messages down on the desk. "First, you ignored everything I did for you, you disrupted the schedule in the office, then you make fun of Bob Grimes, then you criticize me in front of the staff. I just don't know what to do." She walked out quickly. Beth soon heard Mrs. Loomis typing. Beth sat at her desk, stunned at the outburst of emotion.

After debating with herself for several minutes about what to do, she decided to talk with Mrs. Loomis before the work day was over. When she walked out of her office, she saw that her coat and hat were not in their usual place. Beth found in her mailbox a brief letter from Mrs. Loomis giving two weeks' notice before quitting.

What steps should Beth take next?

Analysis

1. What was Dr. Sims' most useful source of information about the history of the Counseling Center? What other sources could she have used?
2. What differences existed between the formal organizational chart and the informal structure of the day-to-day workings of the Center? Which of these were most important for Dr. Sims to know?
3. What factors made Mrs. Loomis a powerful person in the organization? What factors made her a weak person?
4. What style of leadership does Dr. Sims seem to practice? How is it different from the styles of her predecessors? How was her style in part determined by what her predecessors had done?
5. What messages did Dr. Sims' behaviors send to her staff?
6. What should Dr. Sims do at the end of the case?

Case 4. Leaders Who Self-Destruct: The Causes and Cures[1]

Why do some people derail when they reach the top? What psychological forces affect executives when they attain a position of power? Why does an executive who seems bright, likeable, and well adjusted, suddenly resort to strange behavior when he or she becomes chief executive officer?

There are no simple answers to these questions. In order to address them, we must deepen our understanding of the psychodynamics of leadership and the vicissitudes of power. A number of clinical insights from dynamic psychiatry and psychoanalysis may help in our analysis.

First, however, consider an example that illustrates the kind of irrational behavior described above. Before Robert Clark[2] assumed the presidency of the Solan Corporation, he had always been well liked. His supervisors had been impressed by his capacity for work, his helpful attitude, his dedication, and his imaginative method of solving problems. He eventually crowned his seemingly brilliant career by being selected to succeed Solan's former CEO.

In the period immediately after Clark took over, he received many accolades for his role in taking a number of long overdue steps. Gradually, however, after the initial enthusiasm had cleared up, many of his old colleagues concluded that he had apparently undergone a personality change. He had become less accessible; his once widely acclaimed open-door policy and advocacy of participative management had disappeared. He had become increasingly authoritarian, impatient, and careless of the feelings of others.

The organizational effects of Clark's transformation were quickly forthcoming. In their desire to please him, key executives would jostle for his attention and waste time and energy on power games and intracompany squabbles rather than on strategic decisions. Company morale sank to an all-time low, and the financial results were predictably dismal.

What happened to Clark—and *why* did it happen? Certain psychological forces—his own and those of his followers—came into play, creating a multitude of problems. Here are three reasons why this occurred:

- Succession to the top leadership position in an organization is necessarily isolating in that it separates leaders from others (who now directly report to them) and leaves them without peers. As a result, their own normal dependency needs for contact, support, and reassurance rise up and overwhelm them.

1. Manfred F. R. Kets de Vries, "Leaders Who Self-Destruct: The Causes and Cures." Reprinted, by permission of publisher, from ORGANIZATIONAL DYNAMICS, Spring/1989 © 1989. American Management Association, New York. All rights reserved.
2. "Robert Clark" is a pseudonym, and the name "the Solan Corporation" is fictitious. The following individuals and organizations mentioned in this article are also identified by pseudonyms or fictitious names: Peter Harris and the Noro Corporation; Ted Howell and the Larix Corporation; and Ted Nolan and the Dalton Corporation.

- Whether consciously or unconsciously, employees expect their organization's leaders to be infallible and even gifted to some degree with "magical" powers.
- Troubled by guilt feelings about their success and fearful that it may not last, leaders may unconsciously cause themselves to fail.

To some degree, every human being suffers from these reactions and feelings. History has provided us with many examples of leaders whose behavior became pathological in the extreme once they attained power: political leaders such as King Saul, Caligula, Adolph Hitler, and Colonel Quaddafi, or business leaders such as Howard Hughes.

I am not suggesting that each business leader will resort to pathological behavior upon reaching the top of his or her organization. What differentiates those who "crash" from those who don't is the latter's ability to stay in touch with reality and take these psychological forces in stride. Many leaders are very good at handling the pressures that leadership brings; indeed, some individuals who may previously have been rather colorless turn into great leaders when they attain positions of power. However, some leaders just can't manage; the regressive pulls simply become too strong. Since were are all susceptible to these psychological forces, I will discuss their dynamics.

Isolation from Reality

On June 18, 1982, the body of Roberto Calvi, Chairman of Ambrosiano, Italy's largest private bank, was found hanging under Blackfriars Bridge in London. The exact circumstances of his death may never be known; however, this was certainly an ignominious ending for one of Italy's most prominent bankers. It was also one of the saddest developments in modern Italy's largest financial scandal.

Although the extent of Calvi's involvement may never be known, he certainly carried a heavy responsibility. His secretive, control-oriented management style didn't help, and his remoteness was an added complication. In newspaper accounts of that time, Calvi was described as the most private of financiers, an individual who was very reserved and formal, a man for whom communication was a difficult task. From the various descriptions we have of him, he was apparently a person who would internalize his problems rather than confide in anyone. Here was an individual who had a very detached way of dealing with others.

Why did Calvi get himself into this situation? We cannot really answer this question; however, we do know that, in spite of the sea of executives reporting to Calvi, he apparently ended up very much alone in dealing with his problems. There was apparently no one he could turn to, which seems paradoxical in light of his contacts and his very active life. Unfortunately, this kind of isolation seems all too common among people who head organizations, and it can affect their sense of reality.

The term "loneliness of command" has been used frequently in the context of leadership. The inability to test one's perceptions, the tendency to lose touch with reality because one occupies a top position, is a danger anyone can fall victim to when in a leadership position.

For example, when Peter Harris became president of the Noro Corporation, he thought that his personal and professional lives would continue more or less as they had before. The appointment had been very routine; as one of the senior vice-presidents of his company, he had been the logical choice for the job.

In reality, however, Harris had to deal with more changes in his lifestyle than he had expected. Soon after he assumed the presidency, he realized that, in spite of his efforts to maintain his previous amicable working style, he was creating more distance between himself and his employees. Although he tried for a while to be one of the boys, he discovered that this was no longer possible. In short, Harris now had difficulty socializing with and having to make tough career decisions about the same person; life seemed much simpler if he retained some distance. He had also discovered that friendliness to an employee was quickly interpreted by others as favoritism; attempts at closeness by an employee were similarly viewed as a lobbying effort.

Although Harris simplified matters by keeping his distance, this had a price. He increasingly felt a sense of isolation, a loss of intimacy. He could talk to his wife, but that didn't seem to be enough. He wanted to confide in someone more familiar with what happened in the business, someone on whom he could test his ideas.

Sometimes he would think nostalgically of the time before he became president. Occasionally, he found himself longing for a way to resurrect the broken network of relationships, searching for a way of sharing, but this had become impossible. A side-effect was that he was becoming increasingly irritated about having gotten himself into this position; it was not what he had expected. He began to wonder if his increasing aloofness was affecting his ability to make decisions.

The examples of Roberto Calvi and Peter Harris show us one of the pitfalls of assuming the position of CEO; for some it becomes a mixed blessing. The organization's leaders are supposed to take care of their organization's existing strategic and structural needs; they are expected to articulate a vision of the future and show others how to achieve it. But there are a number of other aspects to leadership; one of these is that leaders should take care of the dependency needs of their employees. Given the universal nature of these needs, however, one must ask who takes care of the *leaders'* dependency needs? When no such person is available, some leaders may suffer from anxiety associated with loneliness and disconnectedness; some may even lose touch with reality.

When leaders reach the top of their organizations, they may be dismayed to learn that their network of complex mutual dependencies has been changed forever. Some leaders can overcome this and find other forms of gratification; others may even enjoy experiencing a certain degree of detachment. However, many leaders become upset at finding themselves in this situation and may react accordingly. They may feel frustrated and angry and may even experience a seemingly irrational desire to "get even" with those who have not fulfilled their dependency needs. The resulting scapegoating behavior can create a very politicized organization torn by interdepartmental rivalry.

However, aggression can also be turned inward, which can lead to depression and to alcohol and drug abuse. If these extreme responses continue, they can have dire consequences for the organization.

The Dangers of Transference

Apart from acting as catalysts in the achievement of their organizations' objectives, leaders can also become the embodiment of their employees' ideals, wishes, feelings, and fantasies. By transforming their subjective fantasies into objective reality, employees may imbue their leaders with mystical qualities—a phenomenon that may occur despite their leaders' attempts to resist it. Employees may consciously or unconsciously perceive and respond to their leaders not according to objective reality, but as though the leader were a significant authority figure from their past, such as a parent or teacher. When this occurs, the boundaries between the past and present may disappear.

As with any authority figure, leaders are a prime outlet for such emotional reactions. Given their position, they can easily retrigger in their employees previously unresolved conflicts with significant figures from their past. When this happens, regressive behavior may occur: Employees may endow their leaders with the same omniscience that they attributed in childhood to parents or other significant figures.

This psychological process—the distortion of the whole context of one's relationships—is called *transference* and is present in all meaningful human interactions. Although leaders may find it hard to accept, all interpersonal exchanges involve both realistic *and* transference reactions—and leaders are particularly susceptible to this kind of confusion.

Transference reactions can be acted out in several ways and can affect both leaders and their employees. One common manifestation is for employees to "idealize" their leaders in an attempt to recreate the sense of security and importance they felt in childhood, when they were cared for by apparently omnipotent and perfect parents. As authority figures, leaders fall easily into an employee's subconscious definition of a "parent" role. Employees may therefore want to endow their leaders with unrealistic powers and attributes, which in turn can inflate their leaders' self-esteem.

During periods of organizational upheaval such as cutbacks or expansion, employees are particularly anxious to cling to their beliefs in their leaders' powers as a way of maintaining their own sense of security and identity. For this reason, employees will do anything to please or charm their leaders—including giving in to their extravagant whims. Thus in times of organizational crisis leaders may conceivably be surrounded by "yes-men." This lack of critical opinion can obviously have dire consequences for their organizations. If leaders get too much uncritical admiration from their employees, they may begin to believe that they really are as perfect, intelligent, or powerful as others think. Losing one's grasp on reality in this way is a common human failing, but it can be particularly dangerous for leaders since they often have the power to act on their delusions of grandeur. When a CEO stops listening to criticism and embarks on an overambitious expansion or orders the unnecessary construction of a new company headquarters, this process may indeed be at work.

As a result of their grandiose delusions, some leaders will favor highly dependent employees who are in search of an all-knowledgeable, all-powerful leader. However, such leaders can be very callous about these employees' needs; they may exploit them and then drop them when they no longer serve their purposes.

Such employees may legitimately react angrily to this type of behavior. However, another less obvious process may also be at work: Employees may subconsciously blame their leaders for failing to live up to their own exaggerated expectations. Angry about this, and perhaps aggravated by callous, exploitative behavior, these employees may find their attitudes quickly turning from admiration to hostility and rebellion. Like children, such people tend to divide all experiences, perceptions, and feelings into unambiguously "good" and "bad" categories. Thus, although new CEOs may initially have been welcomed as messiahs, they may be surprised to find out how suddenly their employees' mood can shift. After one setback, employees may view their leader as being responsible for all the company's problems, even if these problems developed long before his or her arrival.

Faced with this transition in employee attitudes from admiration to rebellion and anger, leaders may become irritated and even develop slight feelings of persecution. But leaders have to realize that this is to a certain extent inevitable and that they must exert a certain amount of self-control.

Some leaders, however, may be tempted to retaliate—possibly by firing their critics. There are some leaders who tend to mentally divide their employees into those who are "with" them and those who are "against" them; such as outlook is liable to breed an organizational culture of fear and suspicion. Employees who are "with" their leaders share their outlooks and support them even if they engage in unrealistic, grandiose schemes or imagine the existence of malicious plots, sabotage, and enemies. Effective leaders, however, know how to contain their excessive emotional reactions and avoid being caught up in groundless fears.

The Case of Ted Howell

To illustrate how these psychological forces can affect a leader, consider the following incident. As a result of the unexpected death of his predecessor, Ted Howell was appointed president of the Larix Corporation, a company in the electronics equipment field. Howell had been found with the help of a headhunter who had highly recommended him. He had previously held a senior staff position in a company in the same line of business; Howell's knowledge of the industry had been a key factor in convincing Larix's board to take him on.

Soon after his arrival, Larix's board members saw signs that Howell was having difficulties dealing with the pressures of the job. A number of rash decisions made in his first week at the office were the first indications of trouble. But in spite of these mistakes, everything initially turned out better than expected. First, one of the company's main competitors went out of business, which freed up an important segment of the market. In addition, one of Howell's employees came up with an excellent marketing idea that he quickly adopted and that proved very successful. Some executives were disturbed because their colleague never received credit for it; nevertheless, these two factors helped to get Larix back into the black.

Unfortunately, this success apparently went to Howell's head. After the turnaround, he embarked on a dramatic expansion program, ignoring cautionary remarks made by his employees, consultants, and bankers. Other steps were taken, including the relocation of the company's headquarters to what Howell thought were more suitable surroundings and the acquisition of an expensive company plane. These two actions put a heavy strain on the company's finances. Those executives who expressed disagreement or concern about the new moves were fired; consultants who suggested that Howell change course suffered the same fate. In the end, only sycophants who were willing to share his grandiose ideas and accept his aggressive outbursts were left.

As expected, the unrealistic plans and high expenditures put the company into the red. However, Howell was unwilling to admit his role in the debacle. When questioned at directors' meetings, he would become defensive and deny any responsibility for the losses; instead, he would blame them on faulty moves made by his predecessor or on vindictive action by executives no longer in his employ. In his opinion, a turnaround was just around the corner. To an increasing number of board members, however, Howell's behavior was becoming unacceptable. Eventually, having become impatient with the continuing losses and with Howell's imperious, paranoid behavior, they managed to remove him.

As in the case of Robert Clark, here was an individual who was apparently well adjusted and who had performed well in his previous job. After his promotion, however, when he was subjected to the pressures of being a leader, this same individual began to behave irrationally.

One contributing factor was apparently the excessively high expectations that Howell's employees had for him. Overwhelmed by all the attention that he was suddenly receiving, he apparently allowed his sense of reality to become distorted. Perhaps because he couldn't withstand these psychological pressures, he may have assumed that some of the qualities ascribed to him were true and behaved accordingly. When his grandiose actions backfired and he couldn't deliver, his employees reacted with anger. Howell began to show signs of paranoid behavior and retaliated by putting the blame on others.

This distortive reaction pattern is another factor that contributes to this strange, irrational behavior we sometimes find in leaders. These reaction patterns are semi-dormant tendencies with which we all have to deal and which arise easily in leadership situations. As I have indicated, some leaders find it very difficult to withstand these pressures.

The Fear of Success

In a success-oriented society, failure is looked upon as a catastrophe, and to some extent we all fear it. But while the fear of failure is quite understandable as a reactivating mechanism for feelings of incompetence, fear of success is more of a mystery. In fact, Sigmund Freud tried to demystify some of the dynamics behind this fear in an article entitled "Those Wrecked by Success" (1916). He noted that some people become sick when a deeply rooted and longed-for desire comes to fulfillment. He gave as an example a professor who cherished a wish to succeed his teacher. When this wish eventually came true, the professor became plagued by feelings of depression and self-deprecation and found that he was unable to work.

The Case of Ted Nolan

Sometimes we can see how top executives fall victim to this form of anxiety. Reflecting on his career, Ted Nolan recalled being surprised when he was asked to succeed Larry Fulton as president of the Dalton Corporation. Like many of his colleagues, he had thought that the vice-president of marketing was the person most likely to be chosen by the board; however, he certainly didn't protest when asked.

When his appointment came through, however, Nolan noticed that he felt slightly ill at ease, a feeling that didn't go away when he took over. He became increasingly preoccupied with the question of whether he could hack it. He began to have difficulties sleeping at night, tormenting himself by wondering whether his previous day's actions had been correct. He often felt like an impostor, having just been "lucky" to get the job. To make matters worse, he also developed a full-fledged drinking problem. At work he found it increasingly difficult to concentrate and make decisions. He wondered how many of his problems in handling the top job were noticed by his board members. When were they going to realize that they had made a mistake, and that he was really an incompetent fake?

However, as Nolan said himself, he had been fortunate. His wife had been a great support to him. Because of the changes in his behavior, she had encouraged him to see a psychotherapist. As he explored the underlying causes of his anxiety with the therapist, he began to realize that he had always been anxious whenever he was put in a position of responsibility; previously, however, he had handled it better because there had always been others in a similar situation with whom he could talk. This time, however, he was really on his own.

With the psychotherapist's help, Nolan discovered the relationship between his past and his present feelings. In reviewing his life, he realized how successful he had been, having overcome tremendous handicaps to work himself up to a position far above those held by his parents and siblings. He also recognized that this success had come with feelings of guilt and betrayal of his origins. Having risen so far above his roots apparently contributed to his current anxiety. He had explored these feelings with his psychotherapist and had succeeded in becoming more objective by integrating these feelings with his current situation. Being able to see those connections and working through these insights had brought him greater peace of mind. What's more, he felt he was now doing a fairly good job in his new position.

What Nolan's experience exemplifies is that some people believe, whether consciously or unconsciously, that success can only be attained by displacing someone else. For them, success is perceived as a symbolic victory over the parents or siblings of childhood. This is particularly true for those individuals who have never resolved rivalrous feelings toward the latter. If this is the case, to be successful and to have tangible accomplishments in adulthood can turn into a Pyrrhic victory.

In a case like this, success becomes symbolically equated with betrayal. Success makes these individuals stand out and be noticed; it becomes a provocative, hostile act that not only leads to feelings of guilt but also invites retribution. As in childhood, being in such a position may arouse the envy and resentment of others. Retaliation will be feared from those individuals with whom the person is competing. Thus unresolved competitive feelings from the past become confused with present-day reality. Since success is feared to have negative consequences, these successful individuals may downgrade their accomplishments or even view themselves as impostors. They may have difficulty believing that they have achieved success through their own abilities.

In management situations, these irrational thoughts and behavior patterns may not become evident as long as the executive in question is one out of many. As long as such patterns are not particularly noticeable, the problem may be subdued. But as soon as these people reach a leadership position, they may become anxious, deprecate their accomplishments, and even engage in self-defeating behavior.

Staying on Course

I have described some of the more problematic aspects of leadership, as well as depicted a number of psychological forces that can negatively affect individuals in leadership positions. Many of these forces will often be brought to bear simultaneously; leaders who cannot withstand them will be the ones who cannot manage. Stress reactions may follow, and such individuals may lose touch with reality.

Exhibit 1 depicts the various forces at work in leadership and the potential dysfunctional outcomes. We see how leadership is part of a complex mosaic of interactive patterns that very much depends on the personality and background of the leader and the nature of the relationship between leader and employee. This all takes place within a specific situational context.

EXHIBIT 1
The Pressures of Leadership

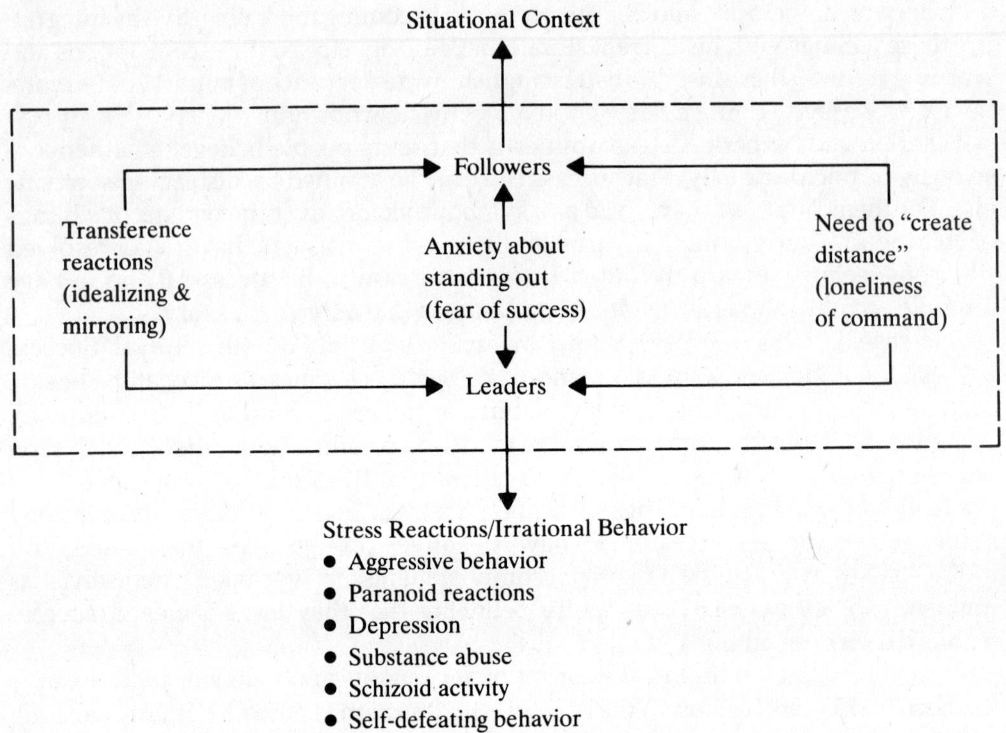

Leaders should be aware of the psychological forces and should be able to identify potential signs of trouble. To prevent stress reactions and irrational behavior from coming to the fore, leaders should engage in a regular process of critical self-evaluation. Those who are interested in the vicissitudes of leadership may want to reflect on the following questions:

- How accessible is the leader?
- How does the leader react to bad news or criticism from an employee?
- Is the leader able to discuss any problems or ideas with colleagues?
- Does the leader think of employees in terms of those who are "with" and those who are "against" him or her?
- How realistic is the leader's vision of the company's future? Is there a large discrepancy between his or her own and others' points of view?
- Is the leader willing to accept responsibility if things go wrong, or does he or she blame "the others"?

- Is the leader quick to take offense and feel unfairly treated? Does he or she have a great need to "blow his or her own horn"?
- Does the leader feel anxious and guilty when he or she is successful and have difficulties believing that his or her professional success is caused by his or her own accomplishments and not by sheer luck?

In considering these questions, we should not forget that the ability to change fantasy into reality, given the power leaders have, can be like the mythological siren's call and may cause an individual to change as soon as he or she attains a leadership position. The potential for losing touch with reality and behaving irrationally is dormant in all of us.

Paradoxically enough, it is sometimes this very irrational quality that is needed to make some leaders effective. Paranoid reactions and visionary experiences may feed very well into certain types of situations, and many political and religious leaders have acted in just this way (consider Joseph Stalin or the Ayatollah Khomeini).

However, in spite of what may have been an initially enthusiastic reception, there is a dark side to this behavior. To evoke regressive tendencies in others and to provoke aggression is to set in motion that which may be impossible to stop.

What Organizations—and Their Leaders—Can Do

This cautionary note—on a somewhat lesser scale—is also true in business situations. Here, however, it may be somewhat easier to set up safeguards against the excesses of leadership. Leaders in contemporary society have to deal with the government, unions, banks, or other stakeholders that may take on the role of a countervailing power, helping to keep the leaders in touch with reality. In many large organizations, leaders will inherit an organizational structure with different checks and balances in the form of distribution of key policy decisions over a number of individuals and various agencies that will circumscribe their behavior. Moreover, in large organizations organizational processes find their own momentum and are resistant to dramatic change. Social systems have their own way of providing a "safety belt" for individuals through their inherent structure.

Apart from the various external checks on leaders' actions that may prevent these irrational manifestations from coming to the fore, leaders themselves can take preventive action. Encouraging frank feedback from outsiders such as external directors, bankers, and consultants is one way of preventing these regressive forces from gaining the upper hand. Individuals from outside the organization usually possess a very different frame of reference, and their vision will be considerably less distorted by the existing organizational dynamics. They can provide more of an overall view and warn about potential sources of trouble. Board members in particular can play a critical role; selecting a strong, independent board that is really willing to enforce its auditing role rather than just acting as a rubber stamp is one of the best ways to keep an organization on course and prevent it from losing touch with reality.

Another useful countervailing force can be participation in top executive training programs. These programs can provide a nonthreatening environment in which leaders can discuss their working experience with colleagues and professionals exposed to similar problems; such situations will enhance reality testing. Mutual comparison of potential problem areas may provide leaders with a revelation, and insight is the first step toward constructive change.

A Shared Responsibility

Leaders and their employees are like partners in a dance: The experience can be very exhilarating, but the dancers can also fall over each others' feet. Both parties carry a heavy responsibility for the interchange to work. To make this possible, they must be willing to listen and have respect for each other's point of view. This requires a certain amount of self-knowledge and a preparedness to reflect on their actions. Empathetic listening becomes a *sine qua non* to a real understanding of the leader-employee dialogue. Thus in spite of all the countervailing forces mentioned, in the end it is the relationship of equity, consistency, and trust that will make for frank interchange between leaders and employees and will constitute the strongest force in preventing regressive behavior in leadership. And given the nature of power in organizations, making this relationship work is the real challenge for all concerned.

Selected Bibliography

For a more detailed discussion of the pitfalls of leadership, see my book *Prisoners of Leadership* (Wiley, 1989), which will appear in late spring. Other books I have authored, coauthored, or edited deal with the same subject emphasizing unconscious dynamics. For example, *Power and the Corporate Mind* (Houghton Mifflin, 1975; Bonus Books, 1985), which I coauthored with Abraham Zaleznik, is a clinical interpretation of power and pathology in organizations and leadership. In *Organizational Paradoxes* (Tavistock, 1980), psychoanalytical concepts are applied to the study of leadership behavior, organizational stress, work disorders, and careers. *The Neurotic Organization* (Jossey-Bass, 1985), coauthored with Danny Miller, integrates psychiatric and psychological findings and insights with management theory to reveal the underlying causes of organizational problems. In this book, individual, interpersonal, and group behavior and decision making are examined in a clinical context.

I edited *The Irrational Executive* (International Universities Press, 1984) to counter the rationalist model in management. The articles in this book were compiled to counter this bias in management theory by demonstrating how unconscious processes influence decision making. *Unstable at the Top* (New American Library, 1988), coauthored with Danny Miller, is an effort to demonstrate how a CEO's personality is reflected in strategies, structures, and cultures of his or her organization. In this book, we present the five most common "neurotic" organizational types, all of which relate closely to five common problematic personality styles in CEOs that we have labeled "Dramatic," "Suspicious," "Detached," "Depressive," and "Compulsive." Finally, my article, "The Leader as Mirror: Clinical Reflections" (*Human Relations,* forthcoming, 1989), shows how—particularly in situations of crisis—leaders turn into mirrors reflecting what we ourselves want to see.

Another book that takes a clinical look at leadership is Abraham Zaleznik's *Human Dilemmas of Leadership* (Harper and Row, 1966), a pioneering study illustrating the different personality conflicts between leaders and employees. In his article "Managers and Leaders: Are They Different?" (*Harvard Business Review,* May–June 1977), Zaleznik illustrates how leaders are of a different psychological type than managers. And in his forthcoming book *The Managerial Mystique* (Harper and Row, 1989), he takes another look at the vicissitudes of leadership.

Among the many insightful books by Harry Levison that touch upon the topic of leadership are *CEO: Corporate Leadership in Action* (coauthored with Stuart Rosenthal, Basic Books, 1984) and *Executive* (Harvard University Press, 1981), both of which present a psychoanalytic view of leadership behavior.

In his book *The Gamesman* (Simon & Schuster, 1976), Michael Maccoby emphasizes the narcissistic dimension of leadership by describing a new type of corporate leader. A more basic, conceptual view of narcissism can be found in Heinz Kohut's work. Excellent descriptions of the idealizing and mirroring transference reactions are presented in his book *The Analysis of the Self* (International Universities Press, 1971); the article "The Disorders of the Self and Their Treatment: An Outline" (coauthored with Ernest S. Wolf, *International Journal of Psychoanalysis,* 59, 1978); and "Creativeness, Charisma, and Group Psychology" in *The Search for the Self: Selected Writings of Heinz Kohut: 1950–1978,* Vol. 2 (International Universities Press, 1978).

A work that complements the above-cited literature and to which the study of the irrational side of leadership behavior is central is Edgar Schein's *Organizational Culture and Leadership* (Jossey-Bass, 1985). Schein explores the way in which an organizational leader creates, manages, and modifies the organization's culture and presents a systematic approach for uncovering the beliefs and assumptions that form the basis of that culture.

Analysis

1. Why did Robert Clark become less accessible? Do you agree with the author's analysis, or are there other relevant factors?
2. How can a leader reduce the problem of "loneliness of command" so that she or he will not lose touch with reality?

3. One of the dangers of transference discussed in the case is the creation of a core of subordinates who agree to whatever the leader says. How might the leader manage the environment to prevent this from occurring?
4. How might self-defeating tendencies in a leader be known before the individual is promoted to an advanced leadership position?
5. The author of the article suggests receiving feedback from individuals outside the company, including external directors. Why might this not work?
6. How would you structure an executive training program to reduce the probability that a leader will exhibit self-defeating behaviors?

Chapter 14 Interpersonal Processes, Groups, and Conflict

Case 1. Data Processing Equipment Company

The Data Processing Equipment Company is a major manufacturer of complex data processing equipment. The company prides itself in being able to meet tight delivery schedules of customized computer equipment manufactured to customer specifications. One of its most important projects is a costly computer with specific data characteristics that it has developed for one of its largest customers, the Acme Corporation.

The project manager for Data Processing Equipment Company, Ellen Kerr, was responsible for gathering the necessary data that would be incorporated into the final design packages for various computers. Ms. Kerr had assigned the major responsibility for the Acme project to Neil Harden, an engineer who had been with the company for only six months. In that time Neil had steadily improved his knowledge of data processing packages.

As the collection process continued, representatives of the Acme Corporation visited the plant to check on the progress of the package. They met with Ellen Kerr and Neil Harden to explain what they wanted and the changes that were needed. Neil Harden believed that in these meetings he had learned the complete requirements for Acme's data package.

As the project progressed, Neil Harden continued to gather data in a timely manner, but as the deadline neared, some items were incomplete. Neil felt that a major obstacle to completing the project on time was the inability of the quality control department to meet scheduled inspection deadlines on the project. To get the quality control people to recognize the urgency of meeting deadlines on the Acme project, Neil thought it would be useful to provide them with a portion of the data package that was complete. The next day Neil met with Adam Banks, one of the quality control inspectors. Banks accepted the drawings and data after Neil informed him of the urgency to meet deadlines. He said he would do all he could to expedite the matter.

But Neil Harden was still concerned about being behind schedule. He went back to Ellen Kerr and told her that Quality Control was entirely too slow in completing its work. Neil said, "Banks wants us to do work that Acme said is not necessary. We'll never meet the delivery date if he continues to delay the inspection and approval of the data package!" Ellen Kerr, who herself had not had a good working relationship with the quality control people in the past, took Neil Harden at his word. Ellen decided to discuss the situation with John Finch, the company president.

After hearing Ellen Kerr's complaints about the quality control department's "lack of cooperation in meeting scheduled inspections," Finch decided to call a meeting with Ellen Kerr, Neil Harden, and Judy Dickson, the manager of the quality control department. He asked the three to attend a meeting in his office without telling them what would be covered.

At the meeting, the conversation quickly centered around the Acme project. Finch told Dickson that her department was delaying this important project and that this had to stop. Dickson became defensive and told Finch, "I have no idea what's going on. I don't know who is responsible for this job or its status. If you had told me what this meeting was going to cover, I would have been able to give you an accurate response. I can't give you any information until I talk to my people about this job." At this point Dickson asked to be excused. She said she could be of more help after she had more facts. Later that afternoon Finch and Dickson had a private meeting. Finch apologized for the way the meeting had been handled and asked Dickson to check into the problem.

Two days later, the Acme data package was approved by Inspector Banks in Quality Control. However, Dickson sent a memo to Finch stating that "the engineering done on this project was horrible." Dickson stated that her department had not been given the proper or complete drawings and data and that Ellen Kerr and Neil Harden had been uncooperative. She also mentioned Kerr and Harden specifically as having "very poor customer attitudes."

When Ellen Kerr received a copy of the memo, she was beside herself. She wondered whether to write her own memo to tell her side of the story.

Analysis

1. Discuss some of the causes of this conflict.
2. Evaluate Neil Harden's approach in trying to get the project completed. Would it have been better for him to wait until all drawings and data were complete?
3. Evaluate Ellen Kerr's approach. Should she have brought the president into the situation? How else could she have handled the situation?
4. Why did Judy Dickson send the memo to Mr. Finch?
5. If you were Ellen Kerr, what would you do now?

Case 2. The Informal Group at Automatic Electric

Until recently, Dan Collinsworth had been a machine operator at Automatic Electric Co., a manufacturer of industrial lift trucks. His job was dull and routine, as were most of the jobs in his area. In order to relieve the boredom, the workers would find ways of amusing themselves. Hardly a day went by without one of them playing a practical joke on someone.

A favorite activity of the informal group was to match wits with their supervisor, Joe Morgan. Although Joe was well liked by most, he was a symbol of management and was therefore the "enemy" with whom they had a running "battle." One of their favorite tactics was to play dumb whenever they were assigned a new part to produce or a different machine to work on. They would ask Joe many detailed questions about how to produce the new part or how to operate the machine. When Joe would get suspicious, they would tell him that they didn't want to take up so much of his time because they were sure he wanted them to do the job right and not make mistakes.

When Joe was not in the work area, the group often would loaf until they saw him returning. The worker who first spotted him would signal the others and they would all start working hard again. Common complaints among the workers concerned the material they had to use, the instructions sent down from the industrial engineering department, and the quality control procedures.

Dan Collinsworth had emerged as the acknowledged leader of the work group. He seemed to have natural leadership ability and was also good at devising new ways to harass Joe Morgan. Dan knew that most of the workers were quite competent and could produce more if they wanted to.

As a result of the department's poor production record, top management decided to transfer Joe Morgan to another department in the plant. An assistant foreman from another department was placed in charge, but after two weeks he asked to be transferred back to his old job. He told the plant manager that someone should be promoted from within the work group because a group member would know the concerns of the group and be aware of how they were "goofing off." The plant manager thought it was a good idea. On checking with Joe Morgan, he discovered that Dan Collinsworth appeared to be the best choice for supervisor.

Dan was approached by the plant manager about the supervisor position and had several days to consider the offer. He decided to accept the job as supervisor, partly because of the increased pay but mostly because of the challenge. When Dan told his coworkers about the "good news," he was surprised by their reaction. Instead of congratulating him on the promotion, some of his former fellow workers seemed displeased.

In the days that followed, Dan received the cool treatment but still felt that he could "shape up" the department because he knew all the tricks the group usually played. He also knew that the workers were capable of good work if they could be motivated to work for the company instead of against it. Dan couldn't believe it when, after being supervisor only one week, he caught someone trying to play a trick on him.

Analysis

1. How can Collinsworth persuade the workers to work for the company instead of against it?
2. What are the advantages and disadvantages of promoting an informal leader to the position of supervisor over his or her own group?
3. If a new informal leader emerges and attempts to maintain the old activities of the group, what should Collinsworth do?

Case 3. Advanced Electronics

Advanced Electronics manufactured a full line of consumer products built around the latest developments in electronics. Products included garage door openers, smoke alarms, solar heating units, and small household computers. These products were manufactured in three plants located in northern California in close proximity to the California Institute of Technology, the University of California (at Berkeley), and Stanford University. Each of the plants employed three hundred to four hundred people.

Plant Number 2, located just south of San Francisco, was typical of the other plants in the system. It employed almost four hundred people, about three hundred of whom assembled electronic products. The others were part of the technical staff or worked in the administrative and billing departments. The organization is presented in Exhibit 1.

Elizabeth Nesch was the senior production engineer. Her chief responsibility was to work with design engineers and detail people regarding the redesign of existing products or the introduction of new ones. She also assumed the key responsibility for moving the product from the design stage to full production. Elizabeth had joined the company when Plant Number 2 was being constructed, so she knew most of the employees from the beginning, including those in control departments and in production supervision.

With the expansion of the company's solar products, Elizabeth soon became overloaded with projects and decided that she would have to get help or risk falling seriously behind schedule. She got approval to hire a junior production engineer. After a short search Elizabeth hired Martha Galle. Martha had a BS in science from a local state college and two years of work experience in a research and development company as a project coordinator. She was twenty-four years old and had recently married.

Martha had a pleasant personality and quickly got to know other members of the technical staff as well as some of the department supervisors while following up on projects. Of course, Elizabeth had introduced her around, but she was so overloaded that she was anxious to get back to her own projects. After a quick orientation tour and round of introductions, Elizabeth said to Martha, "You'll get to know the rest when you start to work with them."

After several months, Martha really felt that she was getting to know the system and how to get things done. Then she ran into a series of problems that made her wonder if she had missed something along the line. For example, Martha was supposed to follow up with Dave Simpson, supervisor of the smoke alarm department, on the installation of new equipment for the production of a new version of smoke alarms. Dave promised her samples of the new equipment but never delivered them. Martha checked with Dave almost every day, and it was always "We've got this or that to do, but we'll have your samples tomorrow." The samples never came, and now they were two weeks late on the project.

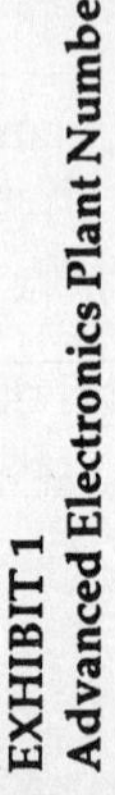

EXHIBIT 1
Advanced Electronics Plant Number 2

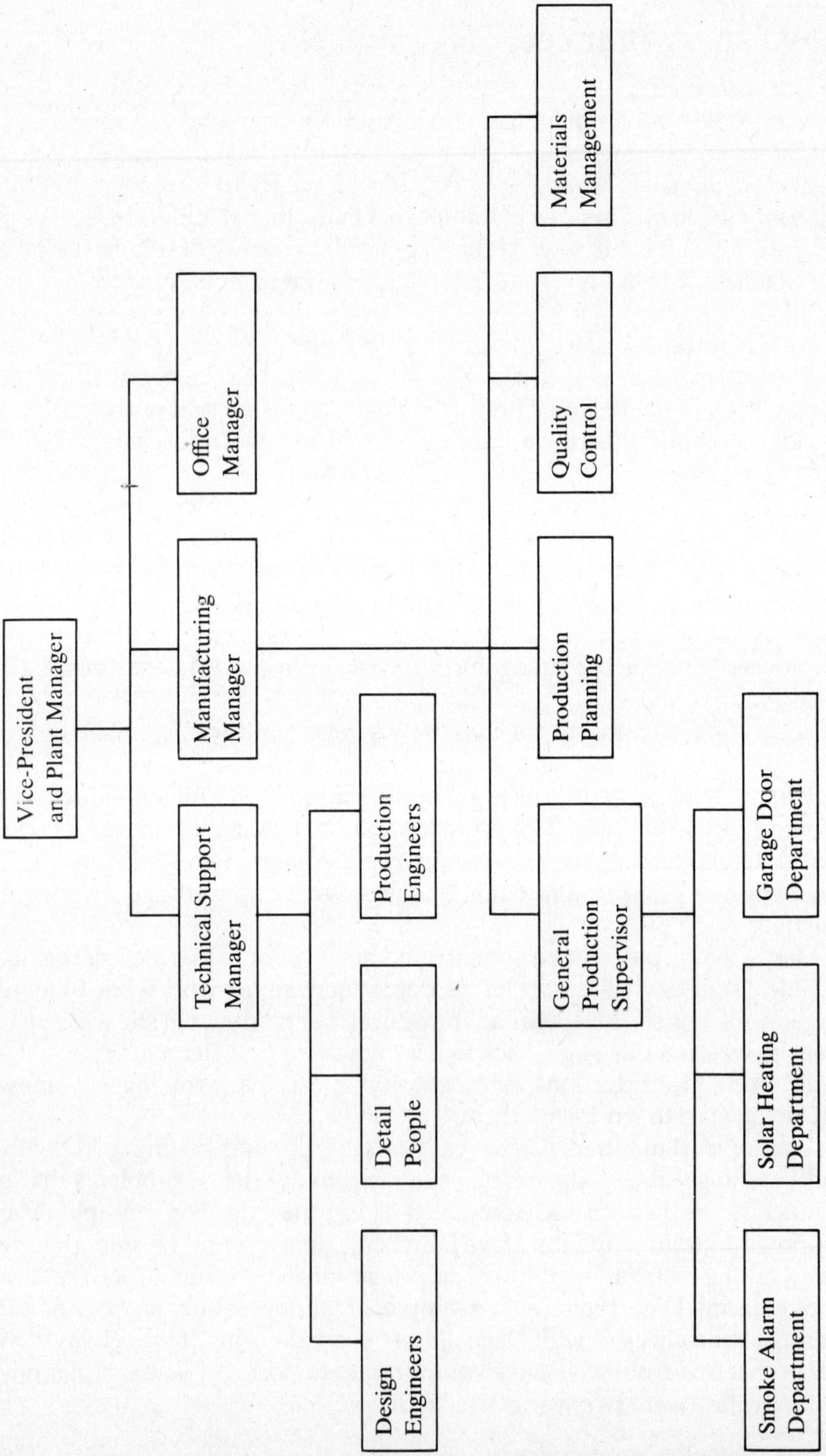

- Vice-President and Plant Manager
  - Technical Support Manager
    - Design Engineers
    - Detail People
    - Production Engineers
  - Manufacturing Manager
    - General Production Supervisor
      - Smoke Alarm Department
      - Solar Heating Department
      - Garage Door Department
    - Production Planning
    - Quality Control
    - Materials Management
  - Office Manager

In another case Martha was working with assembly line workers and the supervisor of the solar heating department. She was carrying a solar heating unit sample when she noticed that it seemed to be missing an end cap. She brought it over to Jim Dugan, an assembler, and asked to have the cap attached. With a little effort Jim managed to attach a cap. When Elizabeth saw the sample, she said, "That's the model I wanted but that cap doesn't belong on there. Anybody in the plant would know that with the cap attached, the unit will short out!"

Martha was really upset over the "wrong cap" incident and related it to her friend, Donna Kuntz, in the design engineering group. When Martha finished her story, Donna laughed and said, "Martha, I think you've been had."

Analysis

1. What did Donna mean by her remark?
2. What are the differences between Elizabeth's and Martha's situations regarding the informal structure of the plant?
3. List and briefly describe "status" factors related to Elizabeth and Martha. How would these affect their becoming part of the informal groups in the plant?
4. If you were Elizabeth Nesch, how would you have helped Martha improve her chances for success on the job?

Case 4. The Office Allocation Committee at BCW[1]

Sharon Tulley had just been named chair of the Office Allocation Committee (OAC) for Benton, Childs and Winningham (BCW), a prestigious New York law firm specializing in real estate and trust management. The OAC was a standing committee that established and carried out policy regarding office allocation and work station assignments for the clerical and support staff within BCW's twenty-five-story building in upper Manhattan. At one time the OAC did not do much. However, that ended two years ago when BCW made two major changes. First, the company went to a flextime work schedule. Most clerical and support staff had the option of working a four-day, forty-hour workweek, but each department had to be staffed from at least 8 a.m. to 6 p.m. five days a week. Second, BCW invested heavily in word processing equipment and an electronic mail system. All departments now had word processing capabilities.

As a result of these changes, two problems emerged. First, some work stations remained uncovered when everyone in a department wanted to work a four-day week with Fridays off. BCW had not yet devised a system to handle this situation. The second problem was related to the first. When the word processing equipment was installed, secretaries were given the option of learning to use the new word processing equipment or continuing with the standard typewriters. Under the four-day workweek, it was not uncommon for a lawyer or executive requesting work filed on a word processor disk to find the department staffed by a secretary who did not know word processing. The secretary trained on word processing had the day off.

New organizational policies and procedures were needed and came under the jurisdiction of the OAC. Sharon felt that it was likely that any decision made by OAC and presented to Henry Childs, the chief partner of BCW, would be accepted by him. Furthermore, since Childs was highly respected by the other partners, the decision would probably be accepted.

However, presenting the recommendation to Childs was not going to be easy. Sharon had been hired by BCW five months ago to head their trust department. Since all seven department heads at BCW were members of OAC, Sharon had attended her first committee meeting soon after she was hired. The chair of OAC at the time was Carl Kirby, a partner at BCW who also headed their real estate department. Carl had chaired the OAC for ten years and during that time had kept the committee from making few initiatives. Carl was well respected by most people at BCW. In fact, a rumor was going around that his retirement party, scheduled for next year, would be one of the best ever. It was because of his pending retirement that Carl chose to step down as chair of OAC two weeks ago and saw to it that Sharon was elected chair. About half of the current committee had also served when Carl Kirby was chair and were still influenced by him.

1. Adapted from Ricky W. Griffin and Thomas C. Head, "The Office Allocation Committee," in *Practicing Management*, 2nd ed. (Boston: Houghton Mifflin, 1987), pp. 136–137.

Sharon wondered how she should handle this situation and keep conflict at a minimum.

Analysis

1. What are the causes of these problems?
2. What conflict resolution strategies should Sharon Tulley consider in managing OAC activities?
3. How should Sharon handle Carl Kirby, the past chair of OAC?

Chapter 15 Communication in Organizations

Case 1. Bryant Pharmaceutical[1]

Recently the pharmaceutical industry has experienced rapid growth, both in the demand for existing drugs and in the development of new products. At present, the industry is extremely competitive, whereas at one time it was controlled by five or six major producers and suppliers. Its current strength has allowed companies like Bryant Pharmaceutical to become active in the development and marketing of new products. Once a small company, Bryant has enjoyed a great deal of success of late, as can be illustrated by its 40 percent increase in sales and 36 percent increase in profits over the last three years.

Although certain demographic factors have contributed significantly to the growth in this industry (most notably the aging of the American population), pharmaceutical organizations must still rely heavily on research, development, and training to be viable competitors in this market. The rapid growth experienced by Bryant Pharmaceutical caused it to modify many of its practices and policies. For example, newly hired salespeople spent the first year in a training program familiarizing themselves with the organization's various products. Considerable time was also spent on understanding a drug's chemical composition as well as its uses and potential side effects. The demand for Bryant's products increased so rapidly that the company had to reduce the training program for entry-level salespeople to three months.

Tim Hughes was hired by Bryant straight out of college after receiving a bachelor's degree in marketing with sales management as his minor. After he completed the revised three-month training program, he was assigned to sell prescription medicine to hospitals in the greater Buffalo, New York, area. This market area was precisely defined. His job consisted of setting up appointments with doctors to inform them of the new drugs that the organization was developing and filling orders for its existing products. The regional director of the upstate New York area was Cliff Young, who reported directly to Bill Willis, the district manager. The salespersons' compensation package (after they successfully completed the training program) was based on one-half commission and one-half salary for the first year. As the employee stayed with the organization and "learned the ropes," the ratio of commission to

1. This case was written by Mr. Wayne Hochwarter of Florida State University.

salary increased to the point that the employee was paid solely by commission after the fifth year.

The district manager furnished each salesperson with the list of drugs they were allowed to sell and the commission associated with each product. The products that appeared on each person's list were determined by the district manager, who was advised by the regional manager.

Recently, Bryant had developed a drug that lowered blood pressure for people who suffered sporadically from high blood pressure. During testing by the U.S. Food and Drug Administration, the drug, called Bicarbomoxy, was found to be more effective for individuals that lead stressful lives. Although the drug was found to be very effective for many patients, many medical lawyers and competing pharmaceutical companies were skeptical not only about its possible side effects but also about Bryant's refusal to describe these potential effects on the package.

Top management of Bryant Pharmaceutical was well aware of these outside concerns and criticisms. They decided that this product would be sold only by experienced salespeople and that a larger-than-normal commission would be offered as an inducement. These decisions were made with no input from anyone in the sales organization and were not communicated clearly to the sales force. Drug sales of Bicarbomoxy exceeded expectations. As a result, salespeople who were allowed to sell Bicarbomoxy made on average $20,000 more per year than those who did not.

It soon became evident that there was a significant disparity in commissions earned. This led to growing discontent among the sales force, especially with the most recently hired salespersons. Tim Hughes decided that it was about time to discuss the differences with Bill Willis, the district manager.

Analysis

1. What, if any, barriers to communication are evident in this situation?
2. Using the concepts related to group and organizational communication, how would you have handled this situation if you had been top management?

Case 2. St. Francis University

St. Francis University was originally founded as a teachers' college in the 1930s. In the 1960s, it diversified into the physical and social sciences, humanities, business, and nursing. The 1970s saw increased growth and the establishment of a graduate program in business. These new programs and the increased number of Baby Boomers resulted in an enrollment of 16,586 students in 1978; in 1962 it had been only 4,332. During this period, faculty and staff more than doubled, and new facilities expanded the campus by 50 percent. To reflect this diversity and growth, St. Francis became a university in 1978.

The 1980s saw a tapering off of student applications caused by a reduced pool of students from the school's tradition base, reduced government aid to students, and increased tuition costs due to inflation. Nevertheless, enrollment stabilized around 18,000 in the mid-1980s.

The president of St. Francis, Dr. Pam Lindstrom, was amazed at the way things had changed since she had started in 1965. Not only was there a great increase in the number of faculty and staff and in the geographical area that the new campus encompassed, but the student body also was much more diversified. Students no longer came primarily from nearly counties and cities, but from all around the state and throughout the Midwest. The graduate adult learning programs also attracted a less traditional and older student population, and minority and foreign student enrollment had increased significantly. The number of women enrolled in business programs had tripled since 1970.

The programs offered by St. Francis were considered to be of high quality and gave the university prestige in the business community. Businesses were eager to recruit St. Francis graduates. These organizations also made large contributions to the college endowment fund and sponsored various academic grants.

Although the university was thought to be in good shape academically and financially, Dr. Lindstrom was concerned that St. Francis had grown so large that communication processes were becoming overly burdensome. She often felt that she was "out of touch" with what was really going on. She also had the feeling that the various colleges and many departments didn't know what was being done in areas other than their own. She thought that it was necessary for the university to analyze the effectiveness of its communication system.

Analysis

1. What specific formal communication processes would you evaluate when analyzing communication effectiveness? Why?
2. List several communication issues that St. Francis University should be concerned with.
3. How would you improve communication effectiveness?

Case 3. Who Should Be the Secretary?

American Casualty Company was a large property and casualty insurance company. All coverages written by the company were sold through independent agents and brokers. To offer better service to these agents and brokers, American had adopted a branch office system. The branches were divided into three geographical regions (see Exhibit 1).

EXHIBIT 1
American Casualty Company

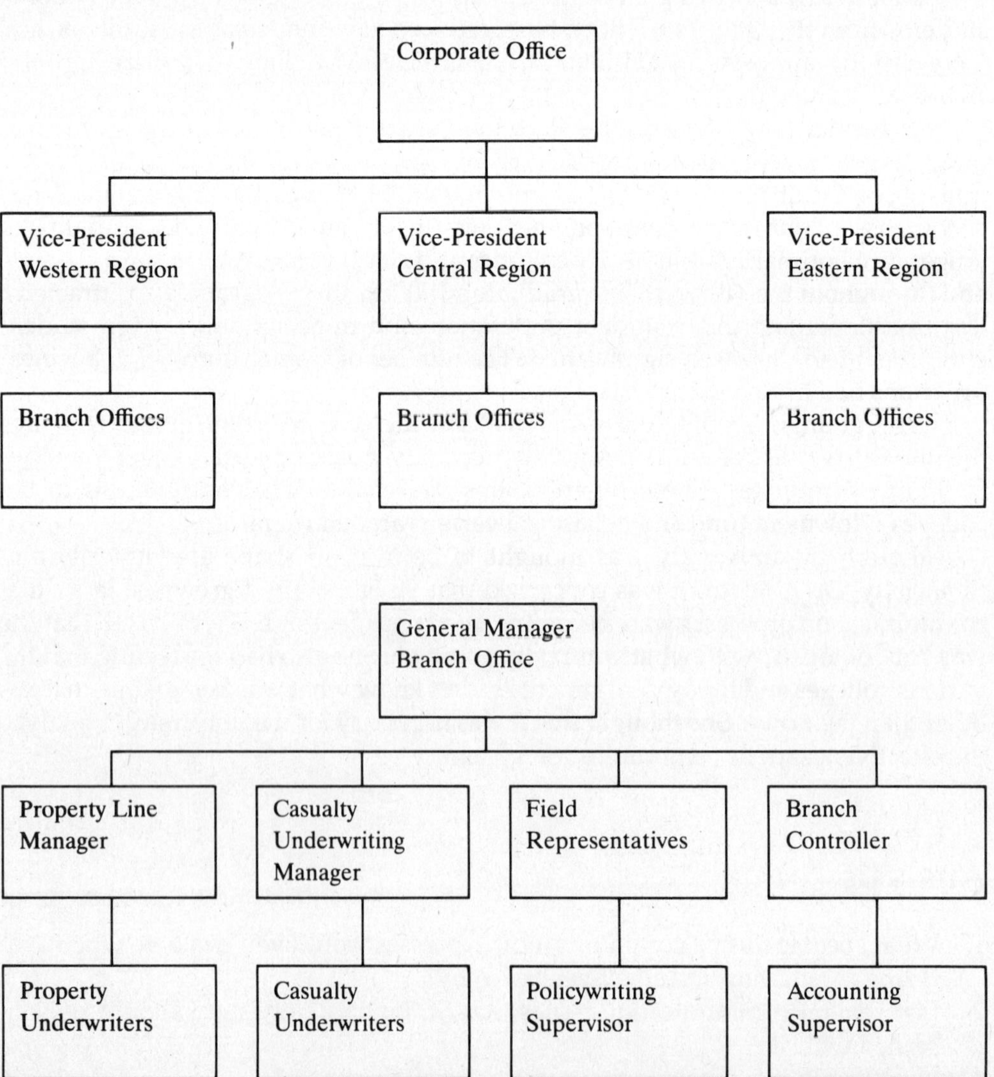

Fred Morrison, branch manager of the office in Lockwood, Missouri, was promoted to regional director of the Central Region, headquartered in St. Louis. Until a successor was selected, Morrison continued his duties as branch manager in addition to assuming his new duties as regional director. Morrison's new position required him to be away from the Lockwood office one or two weeks a month. During his absence, Carl West, property lines manager, served as branch manager. After several months, Morrison announced that he would be moving to St. Louis shortly and that West would become branch manager on a permanent basis.

Before leaving, Morrison also announced Jane Lin's transfer from field representative to property lines manager. At the same time, although no formal announcement was made, Morrison made a point of assuring his secretary, Joan Mason, that she would continue to serve in her position as secretary to the branch manager, two field reps, and Gary Kelly, who had recently been made casualty underwriting manager. No mention was made of Kathy O'Brien, who was currently secretary to the property lines manager.

Joan Mason was in her midtwenties and was viewed as a very efficient secretary. She had been the branch manager's secretary since starting with American seven years ago. Four of those were spent working with Fred Morrison, and the other three for his predecessor. Joan was well liked by everyone in the office, including Kathy O'Brien.

There was a certain amount of status attached to Joan's position. However, this prestige was somewhat reduced because she also worked for three other positions (the casualty underwriting manager and two field reps).

Kathy O'Brien had been with American for almost forty years. For the past fifteen years, she had been Carl West's secretary. She would be eligible for retirement in two years. Kathy often complained about "little things" but was usually ignored and had little influence on those with whom she worked. She and Carl West worked well together.

Everything seemed to be going along smoothly after the personnel changes. Apparently everyone seemed to have accepted the changes. It was not until Joan Mason confronted Gary Kelly that there was an indication of conflict. Joan said that she was confused and upset because of a recent incident with Kathy O'Brien. Joan had always gotten along well with Kathy. However, for several days following the announcement of the promotion of Carl West to branch manager, Kathy had completely ignored her. Then Kathy told Joan that after Mr. Morrison moved to Chicago, she, not Joan, would be the branch manager's secretary.

Joan said she told Kathy that Fred Morrison had assured her that she would continue to be the branch manager's secretary. Kathy replied that it didn't matter what Mr. Morrison said because Carl West had promised to retain Kathy as his secretary in his new position as branch manager, and "that was that."

After hearing Joan Mason's story, Gary admitted that he had never been informed of the secretarial assignments. He promised he would check into the matter and told Joan that as far as he was concerned she would continue to work for him.

Gary Kelly then discussed the problem of secretarial assignments with Jane Lin, the new property lines manager. Lin was not surprised that Kathy O'Brien believed she was to become the branch manager's secretary. Having worked with West and O'Brien for a number of years, Lin had assumed that this would be the case. However, Lin was also not aware of the discussion that had occurred between Morrison and Joan Mason regarding Joan's assignment. Gary and Jane agreed that the matter should be discussed with Fred Morrison as soon as possible.

Analysis

1. How could this situation have been avoided with proper communication?
2. Outline a course of action for Gary Kelly and Jane Lin. What alternatives should they consider before taking up the matter with Fred Morrison?
3. What would you do to rectify the situation?

Case 4. Damon Manufacturing Company

Damon Manufacturing Company is a medium-sized supplier of automotive parts. Its products are sold both as original equipment to the major auto manufacturers and as replacement parts to automotive supply firms. Sales to the replacement market are handled through wholesale jobbers and have increased steadily over the years. They now account for 65 percent of all sales and 80 percent of profits. Damon's organization chart is shown in Exhibit 1.

After a recent meeting, Rick Hernandez, a machine shop supervisor, returned to his office angry. "The boss did it again!" he thought. Rick had just been advised of pending changes affecting his department that everyone else at the meeting seemed to be aware of except him. The changes included the addition of a third shift, as well as the installation of new labor-saving equipment.

Rick's boss, Bill Hanley, was quite enthusiastic when he announced the changes at the meeting. The group included Peter Jacobs, the personnel manager; Carol Davies, the purchasing agent; and three supervisors from other departments that also reported to Bill. The other supervisors seemed to have known about both the announcement and the other information related to the group by Peter Jacobs and Carol Davies.

Rick had reservations about the company's ability to staff a third shift with the kinds of skilled workers that would be required to maintain quality standards. He also had some concern about the company's ability to deliver the new machinery on schedule. Rick had not expressed these concerns in the meeting since he had had no opportunity to discuss them beforehand. Therefore, he decided to say nothing, since the decisions had already been made.

When Rick returned to the department, Denise Fleming, one of his workers and a union steward, asked him, "What do you think about the addition of the third shift?" Rick threw his hands up in the air and walked away.

Analysis

1. Why didn't Bill Hanley discuss the proposed changes with Rick Hernandez before the meeting?
2. Why do you suppose Carol Davies, Peter Jacobs, and the others knew about the changes?
3. Suggest two reasons why Denise Fleming, the union steward, might have known about the changes before Rick Hernandez.
4. Comment on the barriers to communication that seem to exist in this situation.
5. What might be the consequences of this failure to communicate?

EXHIBIT 1
Damon Manufacturing Company

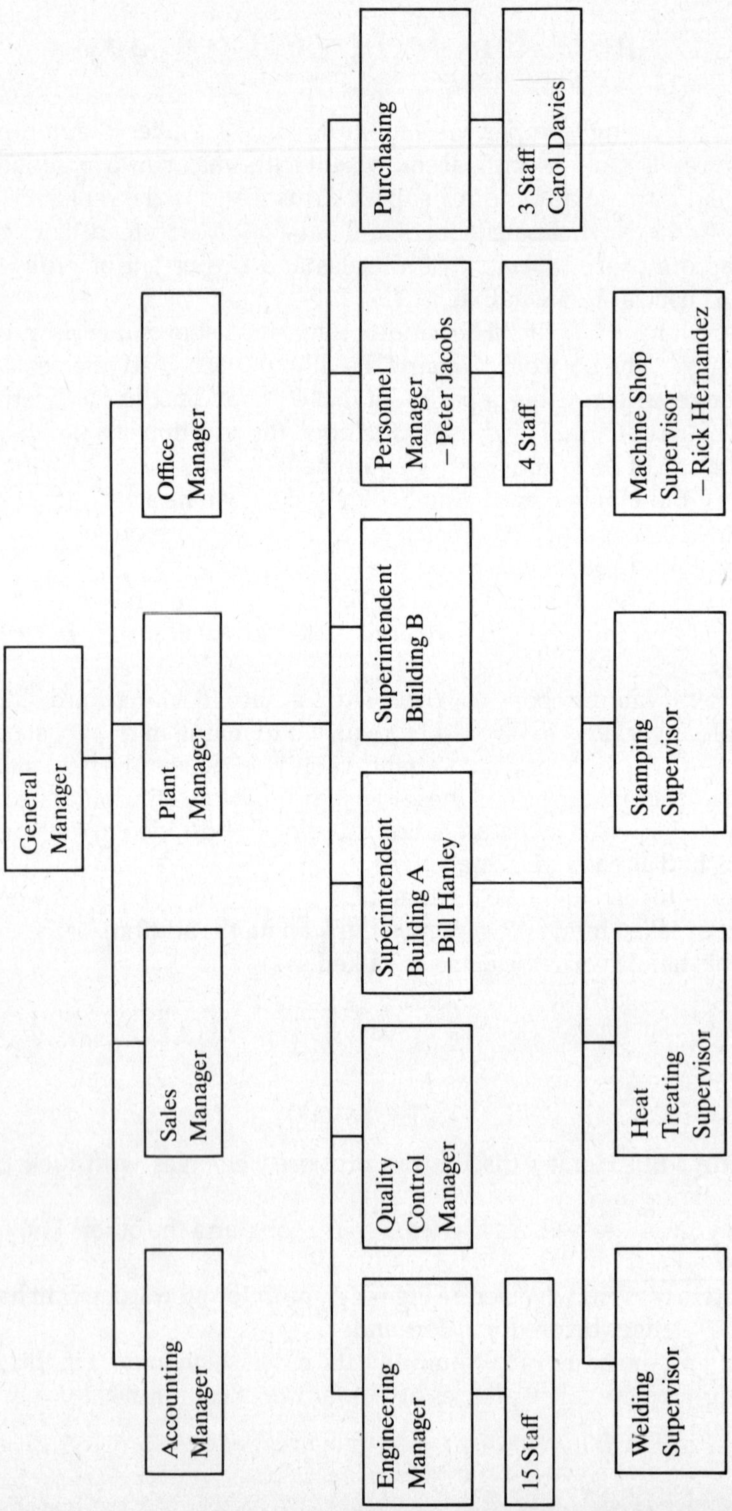

- General Manager
  - Accounting Manager
  - Sales Manager
  - Plant Manager
    - Engineering Manager
      - 15 Staff
    - Quality Control Manager
    - Superintendent Building A – Bill Hanley
      - Welding Supervisor
      - Heat Treating Supervisor
      - Stamping Supervisor
      - Machine Shop Supervisor – Rick Hernandez
    - Superintendent Building B
    - Personnel Manager – Peter Jacobs
      - 4 Staff
    - Purchasing
      - 3 Staff Carol Davies
  - Office Manager

Chapter 16 The Nature of Control

Case 1. Improving Quality at Beloit Marine

Beloit Marine makes small and large diesel and gas engines for use in boats, ships, and the static engines used to drive equipment in industrial applications. The company leader is concerned with the quality of its products. "Here is our problem in a nutshell. It is quality, quality, quality. First, we are having a hard time competing with Pacific Rim countries. We acknowledge that. However, even if we cannot compete on price, we can compete! We will do it on service and the quality of our product. The problem is, we currently have a lousy reputation for our products. The quality is terrible, the way customers are treated is terrible, and nobody seems to care. It is my job to try to improve things and try to do it before we lose more jobs at this plant."

Beloit Marine is eighty years old. It was originally designed to build the steam engines in farm equipment and the steamboats used on the Mississippi River and the Great Lakes. When steam engines declined in use, Beloit Marine switched to diesel and gasoline engines. The company now employs over six hundred employees, down from a high of one thousand employees in the 1920s. Since 1980, the company has reduced its work force by two hundred. Although wide fluctuations in employment are a given in this industry, the layoff of the last two hundred was considered a permanent downsizing of the company. There are fears that another one hundred employees will have to be laid off in the next three months.

The company is currently developing a modular engine that will be able to reduce downtime for repair significantly because sections of the engine will simply plug into other sections. A bad section can be easily isolated and replaced within a matter of minutes instead of hours. In addition, a minicomputer is being added as an option to Beloit Marine's line. The minicomputer could be added to the larger engines. It will monitor seven different engine functions and indicate operating efficiency and the need for maintenance. However, certain basic problems at Beloit remain to be settled.

"We have a control problem in three areas: raw materials, transportation reliability, and the quality of our manufacturing. Raw materials are a problem for two reasons. First, the quality is inconsistent. Sometimes we really get some quality materials from some of our suppliers—other times we get junk. The simple solution is to send it back. However, we cannot afford the raw materials inventory it would take to keep the lines running while we get a new shipment of materials. I cannot have six hundred employees playing cards while I am out trying to source a new supplier with ready material. The end result is that sometimes we try to assemble quality engines with substandard raw materials. The vendors give us a break on the price we pay to make up for the increased scrap loss, but how many machines are made that will not be as durable as we would like? How much ill will is caused when our machine breaks down? We once had a supertanker dead in the water in a hurricane because of a part malfunction. Customers do not like that much. We would not have fared very well if the supertanker had beached and spilled its oil for miles around either.

"Transportation problems relate to the quality of those who ship the raw materials here and those who ship our finished engines to our customers. I have had fits with shippers that did not seem to care. I called the railroad. They did a good job of giving us deadlines if we used only their rails. As soon as we had to use another carrier's track, we were in trouble. Instead of giving us the day the shipment would arrive, they started talking in terms of one to two weeks. Although trucks are better, they are also much more costly, and they can vary up to a week on their promised arrival time. Again, I either have to build inventories or have employees sit around waiting for materials.

"As for our own delivery service, the customers let us know in no uncertain terms when we do not live up to our delivery promises. And I don't blame them. If they have a machine down, they want to get it back working. A day with no productivity is a day without a profit.

"Our own manufacturing process is not error-free either. Our quality people have estimated that each machine has twenty-four defects. Only three of those are major, but that just isn't the level of quality that will make customers buy our product versus one that is just as good and cheaper from someone else. We have to do better, but it is difficult to see a way to make a substantial change in how we operate because much of our problem seems outside our control.

"For example, for raw materials we have over two hundred suppliers. That in itself is a problem to manage. Second, in fifty areas we only have one or two vendors that produce the parts we need. They have us over a barrel. On parts for which there are more suppliers, I think we could do something, but we will never have the clout of the automobile companies. They force their suppliers to improve their quality and force them to increase inventories to meet guaranteed just-in-time orders. We would be laughed out of the office if we proposed those constraints.

"What about our shippers? I really think the only way we can ensure dependability on the machine deliveries is to purchase our own trucks and hire our own drivers. It seems like a costly alternative, but we need to get control of our deliveries—service is that important. On the raw material shipping end, I guess we can move around until we find a reliable shipper. It probably won't be a trucker. However, that will increase our costs again.

"Improving our own manufacturing reliability is quite important too. However, it does not seem to help to hire additional inspectors. Finding the errors as the equipment leaves the plant is not helping to reduce the errors in manufacturing. We need to do something to the employees to get them to do quality work. It seems as if you can't get good hourly help nowadays. However, maybe there is something we can do to improve their work as well."

Analysis

1. What kind of control problems does Beloit Marine have: preliminary, concurrent, or postaction control? Why?
2. How might clan control be affecting performance of the work force?
3. What recommendations would you make to improve the quality of raw materials?
4. What recommendations would you make to improve the timeliness of shipments? Is there a way for Beloit to avoid purchasing its own transportation equipment?
5. What recommendations would you make to improve the quality of manufactured products at Beloit Marine?

Case 2. First Bank and Trust

First Bank and Trust was very concerned with its customers' perceptions of the bank. Surveys in the effective market area indicated that the bank was perceived as efficient but cold and indifferent to its customers. As a result, the bank was losing market share in an increasingly competitive environment.

The bank tried to improve its image through an advertising campaign. The ads indicated that it was a bank that cared. In addition, the structure of the bank was changed from a departmental structure to one with a more personalized approach. In the former organization plan, a customer would have to go to one department for loans, to another for savings, and to another for financial advice. Under the new plan, each customer was assigned a personal banker that would work with the customer for all his or her banking needs. The change in organization is shown in Figure 1. Figure 1a shows the original structure, and Figure 1b the revised structure. The result of the change was a slightly improved image, but those filling out the survey still gave a clear message: the bank was not considered a friendly place to do business.

The bank next decided to improve the interaction of its employees with its customers. Employees were paid on an hourly basis. Performance evaluations stressed the accuracy of their work and their dependability. There was little on the evaluation form that addressed the quality of their interaction with the customer.

The bank was not sure how to measure customer satisfaction with employee interaction, so it called in a consultant who was well versed in a behavioral approach to management. She advocated that the bank begin by identifying key employee behaviors. The bank first tried the approach using bank tellers.

The key behaviors were related to what the bank called "important measures" of how a customer might rate the friendliness of a teller. These key behaviors were taken from the responses that people had made on the survey when asked to explain why or why not they thought the bank was friendly. These responses were then placed on a form. An example of this form is exhibited in Figure 2. The form became a day-to-day evaluation device for checking teller behaviors.

Teller transactions were monitored using paid evaluators who were unknown to the tellers. The evaluator rated each teller's behavior, and each week the teller would receive a bonus based on his or her improved conduct. This bonus was first given for modest improvements in performance, but once behaviors on the average improved, it was given only for increased improvements in the average response rates. Currently, a bonus is given to any teller with a 90 percent response rate for each of the ten identified behaviors in a monthly measurement period. Within a month, each teller is measured at least ten times.

FIGURE 1
First Bank and Trust Organization Structure
1a—Before Personal Banker Program

1b—With Inclusion of Personal Banker Program

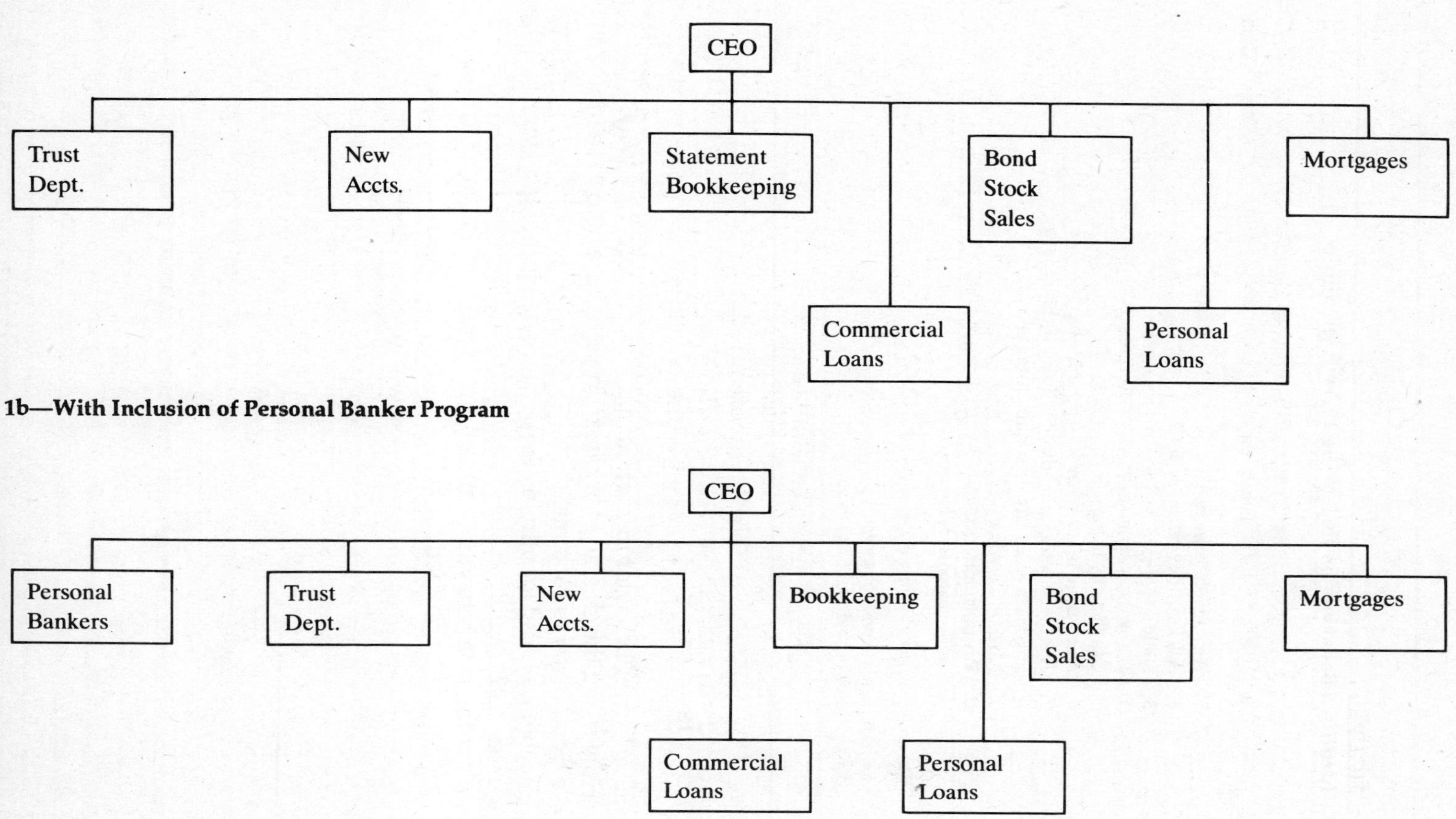

FIGURE 2
Identified Behaviors for Improving Teller Friendliness

	Behaviors	Date	Comments
_____	1. Welcome customers		
_____	2. Ask how they can be helped*		
_____	3. Smile		
_____	4. Thank the customers		
_____	5. Call them by name		
_____	6. Ask if there is any other way you can help		
_____	7. Ask if you can give candy or balloons if child is present		
_____	8. Engage in small talk while processing entry*		
_____	9. No gum chewing		
_____	10. Pay attention to customer—no talking to other tellers while customer is being served		

*Do not use same wording each time.

X = indicates behavior observed
O = indicates behavior not observed

Analysis

1. Is employee behavior important in the control process? Why?
2. How might the change in organization structure help to reinforce employees to respond better to customers?
3. In what ways did identifying employee behaviors help to improve the emphasis on service?
4. What form of behavioral control was being exhibited in the case: preliminary, concurrent, or postaction? Why?

Case 3. General Homebuilders, Ltd.

"You know, most people think that I spend most of my time building homes. The truth is that I spend a bunch of time trying to figure out what is going to happen in the market. Home building is very competitive and I simply won't make much money if I am not on top of changing conditions. More than half of the homes I build are on speculation, commonly called in the business a 'spec house.' A spec house is built without a buyer. The builder speculates that the house can be sold. If it can't be sold above cost, the builder takes a loss. And if it can't be sold immediately when it is completed, the builder pays construction rates on the building.

"Those construction rates are now at 12 percent, and mortgage rates are less than 10 percent. On a $180,000 home, you are talking about over $3,000 per month principle and interest. This does not even include what you paid for the land. I nearly went bankrupt in the mid-1980s because I built a number of spec homes I could not sell: I wasn't watching the changes in the industry. Interest rates increased, and at the same time, the demand for houses in the price range I was selling declined. There was an oversupply of houses, as many other builders were offering spec homes in the same price range all at the same time. In the community as a whole, there were more than 1,000 houses for sale in the $180,000 price range when only 100 houses in that price range were sold in the past six months. At that rate, it would take years to sell the stock of houses in that price range. Luckily, conditions improved and I sold the homes before I had to take a huge financial loss. But ever since that time I watch the trends very closely.

"General Homebuilders is my company. I own it. I built it and I have over a million dollars invested in it. All that money is in cash or property. I am a general contractor. I don't own any equipment, have no inventories, have very few employees. I provide a service. I contract with the crew that digs the hole for the foundation. I arrange to have a crew put in the foundation. I contract with a crew that frames the structure. And so it goes until the house is complete. On a routine home, I negotiate with over a dozen crews and deal with over fifty suppliers.

"My profit is won or lost on how well I can provide a timely product that a customer wants. I will do a custom-built structure if I can, because there is a nearly guaranteed buyer once the home is completed. However, I like to do spec houses more than custom houses, because sometimes custom homeowners can be a pain. It adds another variable that might get in the way of scheduling and profits. With a spec home, the home is done before there is a buyer, and the buyer purchases the home 'as is' or with only minor changes.

"So what are my worries? First, the interest rate can be a big factor in sales. A high mortgage rate kills off the demand for the product. How fast can rates change? Well, it takes up to six months for me to build a house. Rates could change enough in that time to have me sitting on 2 million dollars worth of inventory without a chance of selling the units for a profit and with my building loan acquiring a heap of interest expense that is payable monthly.

"Scheduling is a problem. A crew wants to be busy. They don't make money unless they are building homes. If I can't keep them busy they will find someone else to work for. Once they find someone else to work for I lose control of scheduling. So I want to find a steady stream of work for the crews that I contract.

"Product costing is a pain. I don't have inventories, so I am at the mercy of prevailing market rates of the materials that I buy. That isn't a problem with spec houses as I pass the cost on to the buyer. It is a problem in a custom house because I normally set a fixed cost for the price of the home. I eat any surprise cost overruns. In six months the price of anything can change dramatically.

"The availability of materials is related to my scheduling. If I can't obtain the materials for the framing crew, they start late. If they start late, the heat sub (subcontractor) moves on to another location. Or if the heat sub is late, we may find the plumber has blocked the best flow passages for the heat duct work, so heating and cooling systems are less efficient.

"What about the market? I have to figure out if people want big houses, little houses, condos, townhouses, affordable (between $100,000 and $150,000) housing or upscale (between $150,000 and $300,000) housing. I won't build spec houses that are much above $200,000 as that is putting too much money into a house that has a small number of buyers.

"What about my competition? I have to consider that too. I drive around just to see what is available and when it will be done. There are a dozen good independent builders in the area and another dozen that make poor quality homes. However, strangers to the area don't know the difference. A new house looks like a new house. It isn't until you have lived in a house several seasons that the lack of quality construction will show through. Many buyers only look at a house as something they will occupy for just a few years. Hence, poorly constructed cheap homes are a major factor hurting my sales. I have to know what is out there and match needs with what is being provided. Then I find that segment of the market where I can be strongest. That changes every time interest rates change, customer wants differ, and the competition makes different homes."

Analysis

1. Should General Homebuilders monitor other variables in the environment in addition to controls it may have of its own operation? Why?
2. What should General Homebuilders know about the general population? Why?
3. What should General Homebuilders know about its competitors? Why?
4. What should General Homebuilders know about its customers? Why?
5. What should General Homebuilders know about the industry and trends in the industry? Why?
6. Is General Homebuilders' monitoring a part of what we think of as the controlling function of the manager? Why or why not?

Case 4. Controlling for Performance and for Appropriate Conduct

Global competition will be the focus of many companies in the future. As *Fortune* says, this is the era of possibilities.[1] The barriers to trade in Eastern Europe and the Soviet Union are falling in dramatic fashion.[2] The potential markets in those areas both for consumer goods and for consulting services are excellent.[3] The Pacific Rim markets and Japan are providing a score of opportunities for United States companies that was not dreamed possible only a decade ago.[4] United States companies are truly entering the global economy with a vengeance. We are experiencing a resurgence of industry and marketing might in the United States that hasn't been evident since the 1940s.

What does this mean to the employees of companies? Clearly companies are going to demand more and require a different breed of worker.[5] Workers are going to experience more pressures and more stress than ever. Job expectations and life expectations will be heightened to new levels, which poses a lot of problems for the employee that wants to follow life in the fast lane.

It could be expected that employees may feel greater pressure to achieve these higher goals. This may lead to a temptation to cut corners and to engage in unethical actions. Actions such as bribery, falsifying reports, and deceptive marketing practices will pose an even greater hazard for companies in the 1990s. Controlling ethical behavior will be a major challenge of the 1990s. While statistical quality control and other specific service dimensions of performance have been more quantified and made measurable, controlling ethical conduct is as illusive as ever. The problems in 1989 and 1990 concerning trading on the Chicago Financial and Mercantile markets is evidence of the difficulty of legislating ethics. It is a simple fact that when greater and greater demands are placed on an employee for increasingly greater accountability for performance, dangerous shortcuts may be taken.

A second complex problem facing business regarding controlling ethical behavior is trying to safeguard those who speak out against unethical or unsafe practices in the organization. These people are called "whistle-blowers." Part of the challenge for managers in the 1990s is to establish some form of organization structure that will encourage employees to speak out about unethical practices in an organization. The structure should allow internal problems to be handled by the organization without the whistle-blower's going outside the organization.[6] External whistle-blowers can harm the organization's image and can cause expensive legal action.[7]

1. "The Era of Possibilities," *Fortune*, January 15, 1990, p. 42.
2. Brett Duval Fromson, "Investing in Communism's Collapse," *Fortune*, January 15, 1990, p. 64.
3. Thomas A. Stewart, "Penny for your Thoughts, Comrade?" *Fortune*, January 15, 1990, p. 72.
4. Carla Rapoport, "Can You Make Money in Japan," *Fortune*, February 12, 1990, p. 85.
5. Brian O'Reilly, "Is Your Company Asking Too Much?" *Fortune*, March 12, 1990, pp. 38–46.
6. "IRS Whistle-Blowers Vent their Frustration," *Chicago Tribune*, July 27, 1989, Sec. 1, p. 10.
7. David Clutterbuck, "Blowing the Whistle on Corporate Misconduct," *International Management*, January 1980, pp. 14–18.

Reprisals against whistle-blowers are common. A recent Congressional investigation learned that engineers were demoted after they complained about unsafe procedures in the operation of defense equipment. In a similar situation, employees were fired after they complained to a newspaper of hazardous conditions at a manufacturing plant. These two examples are fairly representative of what can easily happen to the individual who complains about an organization's conduct.[8] Given these fears, many employees fail to report unethical or hazardous behavior, leading the organization into even more serious problems (death to employees or customers, disaster to the surrounding community).

Organizations in the 1990s will face three major issues regarding ethical conduct: (1) promoting ethical conduct, (2) controlling to ensure that employee's conduct is appropriate; and (3) protecting those who speak out against unsafe and unethical business practices.

Analysis

1. As a manager, what steps would you take to ensure that there is proper conduct by employees?
2. What steps would you take if you were a manager to ensure that whistle-blowers are protected?
3. How can a top official monitor and control procedure and behaviors of subordinates?
4. What general steps are needed for an effective control system?
5. How can an official determine if charges of whistle-blowers are true or just revenge by disgruntled employees?

8. See Fred Luthans, Richard M. Hodgetts, and Kenneth R. Thompson, *Social Issues in Business*, 5th ed., New York: Macmillan, 1987, pp. 524–525.

Case 5. Harold's Hamburgers

Harold's Hamburgers was a regional fast food restaurant in Michigan. The restaurant was popular with people that lived in the area year-round as well as with those who made it their summer home. Its appeal was so strong that it opened a second unit on the north side of Chicago. That too rapidly became a success in the upscale, uptown area. There was great pressure for Harold's to open additional units around the area, but the owner, Harold Walker, was reluctant to do so because he did not want to do anything that might destroy the image he had developed over the years.

As Harold put it, "I sell hamburgers. What is so different between the various chains' hamburgers? Nothing! A hamburger is made of beef. It is fried. You put it on a bun with a bunch of other stuff and you sell it. I do it a different way. The end product is something that is special and something that attracts customers. And we do a good job at it. Do you know that we attracted over 100,000 customers into this location last year and we are only open nine months a year? That is quite a few hamburgers. We attract people from Indiana, which is over an hour away. They don't come here for the environment. They come for the food and knowing that the service is going to be fast and friendly."

Harold was correct. Although the facility was not unappealing, it was relatively plain. There were wood tables and a long bar. There was a patio with about a dozen picnic tables, some with umbrellas. The restaurant was in an area of older homes with a railroad track running behind it. It was on a lot with several trees, but it was obvious that people did not come for the scenery.

In an interview, Harold had much to say about his business. "We do try to create an eating experience for our customers. We want them to be comfortable in an environment that is like home. We have three large screen televisions for them to look at and a video game room where they can send the kids. Our serving staff wear polo shirts and slacks—nothing fancy. The food comes out in baskets or paper plates, and our hamburgers come out wrapped in paper. This saves time and money on cleanup and adds to the image a down-to-earth place. We don't mind if you are in construction boots or docksiders, a swimming suit, or a business suit.

"We have had some problems at our Chicago location. In fact, we changed locations a couple of years ago. The old location was too run down. We had a couple of customers killed in the place on a late Saturday night when two guys tried to rob the whole place. It was a mess. Right after that I decided it was time to move. The Lincoln Park area was becoming more upscale. So I thought it would be a good idea to go more upscale in our restaurant. But I don't know. It may be too upscale. I don't feel comfortable in it and I don't see many of our regular customers there. It does appeal to the yuppies in the area. We also get many DePaul students as customers. But, I don't know—it really isn't me. I guess it is with my kids, and they are the ones that are managing the place. I'm not much for the Jim McMahon look—you know, dark sunglasses on a string and wild haircuts. But shoot, I'm fifty-five. I will let my kids worry about that location. I am busy enough with this location and I get a three-month vacation in the winter down at Key West. Who can complain?

"The only thing I insist upon at both restaurants is that the food is of a consistent and good quality. I don't want my boys in Chicago changing the way those hamburgers are cooked. That's still why people come to our places, and I am not going to let anything hurt the image that I have spent twenty years creating. What happens at our Chicago location affects our sales here in Michigan, because at least 30 percent of our summer customers are from the Chicago area. I don't want them badmouthing the Michigan place because they have had a bad experience in Chicago. This goes for food and it goes for the service and treatment that they receive while they are a customer. I have had to fire some of the Chicago staff right on the spot because they were ignoring the customer and not moving fast enough for what I require.

"I don't think many people realize the importance of service to the survival of a restaurant. If the servers were not doing their job (fast service and checking to make sure the order is right and what is hot is hot and what is cold is cold), we would be out of business in a week. We spend a lot of time letting the servers know what we expect, and I don't mess around with them if they refuse or cannot do the job. My business is too valuable."

Harold then discussed whether he had considered marketing his hamburgers directly to customers through retail outlets such as food stores. The hamburgers would be quick-frozen and sold ready to defrost and heat. Harold said, "White Castle does that. I know White Castle. Some of those people are my friends. But I am no White Castle. I had some Chicago outfit trying to have me do the same thing as White Castle. But they could not guarantee that the product would taste the same because of the freezing involved. In addition, we might have problems with those stores where we might have some partial freezing or freezer burns. Freezer burns occur when the product sits in the freezer too long. The result is a decrease in the quality of taste, appearance, and texture. In addition, I have seen how poorly some customers cook. They slap the hamburger on a cold grill or frying pan. That is no way to cook a hamburger. And guess what, those people wouldn't have a good Harold Hamburger experience and they would blame us, not the lousy way they cooked the thing. No, there is no way I am going to stake my reputation and that of my restaurant on some lousy cook and some retail clerk who could care less about the quality of my product. I want to be responsible to make or break my reputation, not to some people who don't care about me or cooking properly."

Harold was right. He had an excellent product.

Analysis

1. Is control important in the restaurant industry? Why?
2. How does a restaurant owner control customers' image of the restaurant?
3. How might a restaurant owner develop a control system for server behavior?

4. How might a restaurant owner develop a control system for the quality of food prepared?
5. Was Harold right in his concern for the image of his food if it was sold in retail food outlets? Would the end consumer blame the product when it was not prepared correctly?

Chapter 17 Operations Management, Productivity, and Quality

Case 1. Lextronix Radio

Ramona DiBurro, plant manager of Lextronix Radio, an electronics company that manufactured car radios, did not understand what was wrong. Productivity was down 7 percent, product quality had increased from two to five rejects per hundred, and absenteeism had been on the rise. What was especially troublesome to Ramona was that just six months ago new equipment had been installed to increase production efficiency. In addition, the workers had been trained in how to use the equipment properly. They had also been given a 7 percent pay raise because of the anticipated productivity increases.

Since the planned productivity increases hadn't been realized, Ramona DiBurro felt something had to be done to improve the situation. She decided to hire Rick Reardon, a management consultant, to get an outsider's view. The following interview took place:

RICK. When did you first notice the production problems?
RAMONA. About two weeks after the new equipment was installed. I figured it would take a little time for them to get adjusted to the new system—so it didn't bother me much. But six straight weeks—something is wrong!
RICK. Ramona, why do you think this happened?
RAMONA. I really don't know. The new equipment is much more efficient than the old equipment—that's for sure. In fact, we expected productivity to go up about 20 percent. We even gave the workers their fair share by increasing their wages by 7 percent. On top of that, now the work is easier.
RICK. How so?
RAMONA. Well, in the past, the workers had to leave their work stations and go to a central location to obtain additional electronic supplies and hardware. There would often be three or four workers waiting for supplies at any one time, and it took ten to twenty minutes to get the materials. On the average I would say that most workers had to waste their time going there at least three times a day, and occasionally they would chat with one another for a few minutes. Another thing is that the workers no longer have to spend their time tediously soldering some of the components together—we decided to have a separate small group do this operation. I always thought some of the workers were a little weird the way they would compare how

cleanly their components were soldered. They even got on someone's case for a sloppy job. Now they can spend more time doing their work instead of wasting their time visiting each other's work stations comparing work. They have plenty of time to talk about their work when they go bowling together on Wednesday nights or go to Duffy's Tavern.

RICK. Were there any other changes?

RAMONA. Well, the major one was the way the partially assembled radios were moved from one work area to another. In the past, they were placed in boxes near the work station and moved three times a day from one work station to another. Now, with the new machinery, they are stored and moved automatically from one work area to another. This also cuts down on workers spending ten or fifteen minutes talking to the people at the other work stations.

RICK. How did your pay scale compare with that of other companies in the area before the 7 percent raise?

RAMONA. Oh, we were always very competitive in pay and fringe benefits. Now I'd like you to tell me why we're having all these problems.

Analysis

1. What factors are responsible for the workers' performance? What are some related problems?
2. What should Ramona DiBurro do?

Case 2. Why Black & Decker Is Cutting Itself Down to Size[1]

Few people paid attention when Black & Decker Corp. announced a $9.5 million restructuring charge this summer. The company said it was preparing to "significantly reduce worldwide manufacturing capacity." At most, one analyst suggested, the total write-off might exceed $100 million.

Hence the surprise when, on Nov. 12, Chairman Laurence J. Farley unveiled a major restructuring involving an after-tax write-off of $205 million and a spate of plant closures and retoolings. The move is an effort to adjust to a powertool market where Black & Decker's sales strategy and products had become increasingly out of place. Wall Street took the news calmly, knocking down the company's shares only ¾, to 20.

It would be hard to argue that dramatic action wasn't called for. In announcing the plan, Farley revealed that the company's plants were operating at just 50% of capacity—barely enough, one analyst said, to cover the company's fixed costs. The charge will result in a $158 million loss for the year ended Sept. 29, compared with earnings of $95 million in the same period last year. Excluding the write-offs, earnings fell 51%, to $47 million in that year, despite a 13% increase in sales to $1.7 billion. That increase, however, is the result of Black & Decker's acquisition of General Electric Co.'s small-appliance division. Powertool sales were flat.

Too Good To Replace

In part, the Towson (Md.) manufacturer is a victim of its own success. The company can now make motor tools that are 25% smaller and more powerful than its old products and that last for years. Sales growth has slowed "because the consumer doesn't need to replace them," notes Dean Witter Reynolds Inc. analyst Joel H. Krasner.

Imports from Japan and West Germany also played a part. Japanese powertool maker Makita Electric Works Ltd. began the assault by stealing a chunk of Black & Decker's 20% world market share in professional tools. By blanketing warehouse home centers frequented by a growing number of tradesmen, Makita has "attacked us in between our consumer and professional power-tool area," Executive Vice-President Alan W. Larson said last summer. Black & Decker, by contrast, has relied mainly on hardware stores and mass merchants.

More important, the Japanese undermined the company's traditional strategy of making customized products for specialized markets. Instead, the Japanese sold

1. This case was prepared by Christopher Eklund. Reprinted from the November 25, 1985 issue of *Business Week* by special permission.

standardized products worldwide. Makita's threatened assault on the consumer tool market, where Black & Decker holds an estimated 42% share, finally forced its U.S. rival to adopt a "global" manufacturing and marketing strategy. It's a big step: The company's eight design centers once produced 260 different motor sizes. When the shakeup is over, there will be just two design centers, and the number of motor sizes will be reduced to a handful.

Into the Kitchen

Although it is only now taking charge, Black & Decker's efforts to transform itself are already under way. Last summer the company consolidated its unwieldy U.S. marketing operations. It has also merged its consumer and professional tool manufacturing units. Analysts contend it has already won back lost market share in professional power tools and checked its slippage in the consumer market, where it remains No. 1.

The slimmed-down Black & Decker has other challenges ahead. For one thing, it must persuade consumers to buy small appliances under the B&D label—a name long associated with the workshop, not the kitchen. And as other U.S. manufacturers can attest, fending off import competition—even after drastic action—is no sure bet.

Analysis

1. Instead of cutting capacity, what other options might have been open to Black & Decker?
2. Was this an example of effective operational planning? Why or why not?

Case 3. What Went Wrong at Fremont Appliance Corporation?

Sharon Rheingold, vice-president of human resources for Fremont Appliance Corporation, was elated after leaving the meeting. She had finally convinced top management to support her idea to improve productivity through work redesign. She had emphasized to the group how redesigning the work process from a highly repetitive production line approach to one in which each worker would assemble one of Fremont's many small appliances—toasters, electric can openers, coffee makers, ice cream makers, and blenders—would provide the workers with more autonomy, challenge, and variety in their work. In her presentation to management, Sharon stated that the redesign would increase productivity and quality while decreasing absenteeism and turnover. She also stressed that the cost savings associated with improvement in these areas would more than justify the investment in the project.

To convince management to try something new, Sharon knew that she would need to have valid information to support her ideas. Therefore, for six months Sharon had her staff obtain documented cases from professional periodicals. She also corresponded with other company personnel managers who had done work in this area and whom she had come to know through her involvement with the American Society for Personnel Administrators (ASPA). Through this approach she was able to prepare a detailed financial estimate of the expected costs and the return on investment.

Since this was such a new approach for Fremont Appliance Corporation, management was reluctant to change its work processes. However, thanks to Sharon's convincing presentation, it finally decided to permit a work redesign project in one of the seven plants. The project would be evaluated after one year, and if the results were as positive as Sharon predicted, Fremont would consider expanding the new work processes to other production plants.

Knowing that the choice of plant would be crucial to the project's success, Sharon chose the plant in Memphis, Tennessee, which was also the site of company headquarters. She felt that this choice was an important political move that would show off the plant in the coming months. In this way management could see firsthand the results of the new work processes.

To get the project moving, Sharon met with Jack Taylor, the manager of the Memphis plant, and with his production supervisors to inform them of the upcoming changes. The plant was closed for a month so that changes could be made in its layout to facilitate the new work design. During this time, supervisors and employees attended a month-long training session at company headquarters that fully briefed them on the new production methods and other required changes.

During one of the training sessions, John Doyle, a production supervisor, pointed out that the workers were a tightly knit group and often enjoyed the opportunity to talk with one another while working on the production line. John said, "It looks like the new way of doing things will prevent people from socializing." Sharon responded, "That's exactly right. Instead of spending time gabbing with each other, they will now get work satisfaction from the increased challenge, autonomy, and variety in the job itself! They'll be able to see the whole product assembled by them. That's what motivation is all about!"

After the plant was in operation for four months, absenteeism and turnover had actually increased by 5 percent. Product quality had decreased by 4 percent and productivity by 7 percent.

Analysis

1. What went wrong?
2. What assumptions did Sharon make regarding worker needs?
3. What alternative methods could have been used to improve productivity and quality?

Case 4. Sun 'N Surfboard, Inc.

Sun 'N Surfboard, Inc. is one of the largest surfboard manufacturers in the United States. Located in Santa Monica, California, the company was founded in 1963 by Bill Sanderson, a former industrial engineer. As in most new businesses, sales and profits grew slowly. It wasn't until 1966 that the company started showing profits. After that sales and profits grew rapidly. Bill felt he had learned from his mistakes and from the night courses in business he had been attending. In addition, he was able to keep his key employees by offering them competitive salaries, good working conditions, and a familylike atmosphere. An organization chart is shown in Exhibit 1.

Barbara Beatty, the marketing manager, was responsible for much of the increase in sales. Two sales managers responsible for supervising the regional sales representatives reported to Barbara. The sales reps called on various retail outlets and dealers located largely on the West Coast and Hawaii. Ken Stills, the production manager, was responsible for designing and producing a wide variety of high-quality surfboards. Four supervisors responsible for the major operations of cutting, painting, assembly, and shipping reported to Ken.

As president, Bill Sanderson was primarily involved with general financial matters, material purchasing, and product design. Bill credited much of his success to four factors: (1) innovative surfboard designs, (2) high-quality products, (3) an aggressive sales force, and (4) low manufacturing costs.

The manufacturing process began with cutting the fiberglass, wood, and other materials to specifications. The cut material was then put in portable storage bins and transferred to the paint department. After the required painting, designs and glossing were completed and the materials were put on a conveyor and sent to the assembly department. Once assembled, the surfboards were brought to the shipping department for final inspection, packaging, and shipment. Near the shipping dock was a small storage area that was usually filled to capacity with current inventory.

To maintain high quality, all workers in the production departments had to perform their tasks properly. In fact, they took it upon themselves to check if any problems or errors occurred. If a worker found any problems with the production process, he or she would immediately contact a supervisor, even if the cause of the problem was not in his or her department. Bill felt that such open communication was the best way to catch production problems early.

About a year ago, Bill heard about some new cutting equipment that could increase the productivity of the cutting department by 25 percent. After some discussion, Bill decided that it was a good investment and had the equipment installed. He also made sure that the workers in the cutting department were trained in the proper use of the new equipment and tooling.

Three months after the equipment was installed, a number of problems occurred. Some retail outlets notified Barbara Beatty that several of the surfboards they received were in poor condition. They complained that the painting was not glossed to the high finish that was characteristic of Sun 'N Surfboard products. Also, the

EXHIBIT 1
Sun 'N Surfboard, Inc.

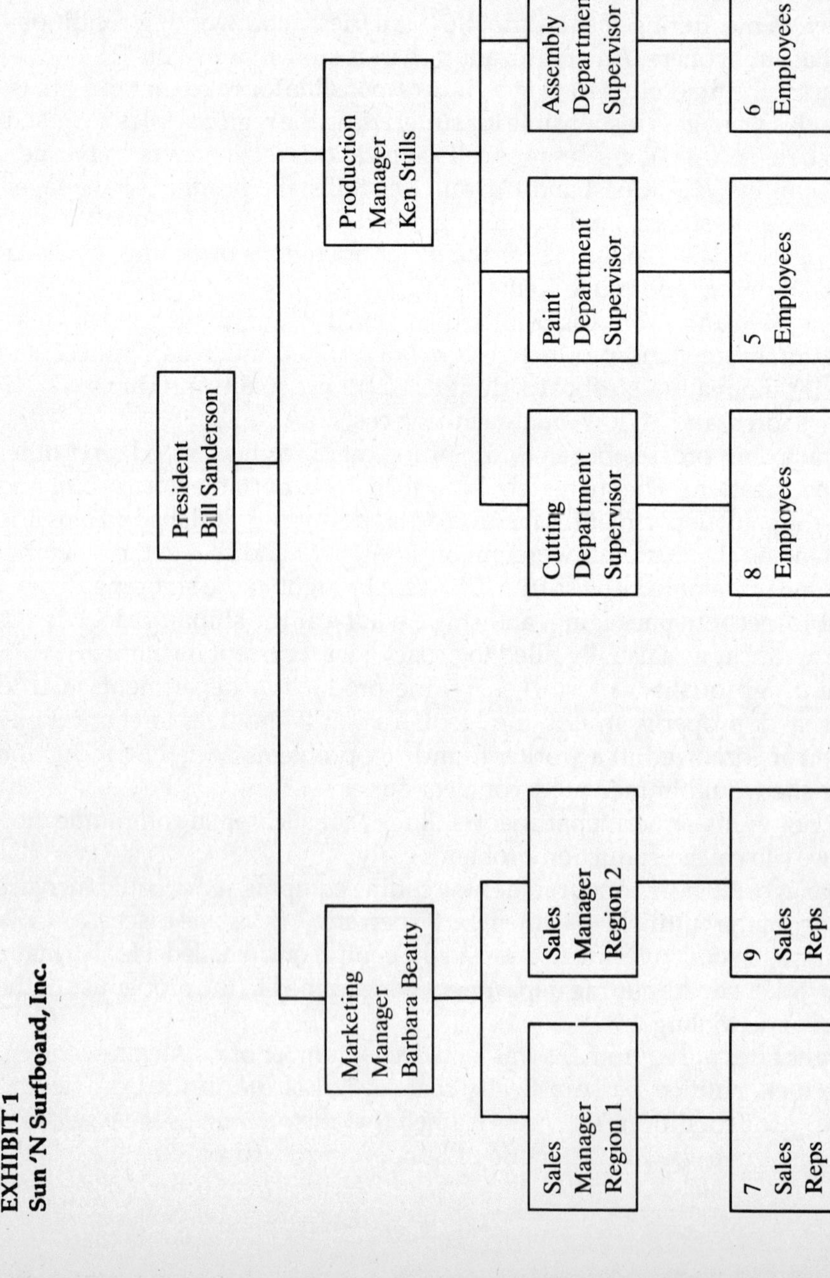

decals were not secured properly, and some were even assembled in such a way that they were a quarter-inch out of alignment. In addition, there were complaints that some surfboards had been scratched during shipment.

Bill was extremely upset. He immediately called a meeting with Ken Stills and his four department supervisors. During the meeting, Bill learned from the supervisors that the workers were not talking as freely with each other as they once had. Since the new machines had been installed, it seemed that the workers in the other departments felt rushed to keep up with production. They also felt that the workers in the cutting department had it too easy. Because of all this, workers in different departments were not cooperating with each other as they had in the past.

Bill wondered how things went wrong. On paper the investment in the new cutting machines should have increased productivity and improved quality, yet both seemed to be worse than before. To make matters worse, the workers seemed to be upset.

Analysis

1. What went wrong?
2. What would you suggest Bill do now to improve productivity and quality?

Chapter 18 Managing Information Systems

Case Introduction. Pittsburgh Supply[1]

Pittsburgh Supply was a retailer of office supplies in a 100-mile radius around Pittsburgh, Pennsylvania. The company had thirteen stores, one warehouse, and over a dozen vans that were used to deliver supplies from vendors to the warehouse, from the warehouse to the retail outlets, and from the retail outlets to the customers if they wanted their order delivered. Pittsburgh Supply was founded in 1956 by two brothers, Mark and Alex Phipps. They began in a rather run-down part of Pittsburgh with a thousand dollars of their own money. They focused on telephone business with a fast response time as opposed to walk-in business. Because of their phenomenal growth, Mark and Alex were now worth over $5 million each. Both of their families had been involved in the business full-time since 1970, and they had hired JoAnn Kreshof ten years ago because they were impressed with her ability to schedule the vans. Before she came they had been using twenty vans; now they were transporting twice as much with only twelve vans.

Mark Phipps was the president of Pittsburgh Supply as well as the chief marketing officer. Thus he was concerned with the sales staff and product marketing. Alex, as chief operating officer, was more concerned with purchasing, record keeping, and inventory analysis. JoAnn Kreshof was in charge of distribution and reported to Alex. Mark's wife, Maureen, was in charge of the personnel function and also supervised thirteen store managers. She did the hiring, firing, and training of personnel. Alex's wife, Alison, administered contracts with the vendors and large customers of the company. She had her JD from Harvard and was able to run a very small private practice because of her reputation in contract law. Five of the Phipps families' children were employed in the company. Three were store managers, one was a buyer, and one was a delivery driver. Last year one of Alex Phipps's grandchildren started working for the company as a stocker. Hence three generations of the Phipps family were now involved in the business.

The company was successful because of three major factors. First, it prided itself on speedy delivery. Three classes of service were available. Priority 13, the top priority, meant that the product would be delivered to the customer within one hour

1. This selection provides introductory material to all the cases in this chapter. Hence, it should be read before any of those cases are covered.

after it was ordered. This service was available 24 hours a day and had a flat surcharge of twenty dollars. Priority 1 service involved the shipping of the product by 10:30 a.m. the next day. This involved a service charge of ten dollars. Normal deliveries were promised within three days with no service charge for deliveries if the order value exceeded one hundred dollars. A ten-dollar shipping charge was assessed if the order was less than one hundred dollars.

Second, the company was very service oriented. Although the stores were open from 6 a.m. to 6 p.m. Monday through Friday, the company still had the 24-hour service already described. It also demanded that each of Pittsburgh Supply's employees would always be courteous and friendly. Order takers answered the phone by the third ring, and the customer was treated as a friend, not as a potential thief or nonpayer as in some of the other supply houses. Pittsburgh Supply was serious about its commitment. An employee could be fired on the spot for swearing in front of a customer.

Third, the company felt it had the best cost control system in the area and also the best purchasing team; hence it could offer products at a very competitive price even though it offered much better than average customer service and terms. Although the products were competitively priced, Pittsburgh Supply gave an additional discount based on the volume of orders that a customer made during the year. A 1 percent rebate was given for annual purchases of more than a thousand dollars and rebates up to 10 percent for annual purchases over ten thousand dollars. The rebate system seemed to motivate customers to maintain their service with Pittsburgh Supply even though they might obtain some cheaper sales products at a competitor's store. Last year alone 100 customers received 1 percent rebates, and 10 customers received 10 percent rebates. Last year more than 550 (or 50%) of Pittsburgh's customers received rebates based on the volume of their sales ranging from 1% to 10%.

Mark and Alex still had concerns about the business. Although the company was very successful, they also knew many other companies in this business that used to be successful. Some of these companies seemed to lose the drive to excel and meet the needs of the customer. Mark and Alex did not want that to happen to Pittsburgh Supply. In addition, the business supply industry was very competitive in both prices and service. Recent industry trends did not encourage an independently owned organization like Pittsburgh Supply. Large conglomerates were getting into the industry and using a K mart approach to marketing business supplies. The purchasing power, name recognition, and financial resources could make life pretty miserable for an independent retailer. However, Mark and Alex felt that they could compete on service, since not one of the mass merchandisers had ever been service responsive. That service component was hard to deliver; yet, if a company could do it, it could sustain much competition based on price. Customers were tired of no service and low prices.

Alex and Mark felt they could remain very competitive if they worked at it. Part of what they wanted to do was to develop an information system that would help them keep a handle on the operations and business environment they were facing. Construction of this system was their next project.

Case 1. Pittsburgh Supply Part 1: Customer Information System[1]

Pittsburgh Supply really knew little about its customers. Currently, Mark could tell you who the largest customers were, but that was about it. He made sales calls on the procurement officers of many of the larger companies, and then he called upon the various people who might initiate the order. The latter calls were to inform the customers about the priority service system and how to expedite orders. But Mark knew little about the consumption patterns of any of the customers and how those patterns might have changed over the years. There was no formal mechanism to determine the relative importance of service over price. In addition, there was little sense of how well Pittsburgh Supply was meeting the customers' product needs.

Currently, as in most stores, customers would receive a catalog of products. They would order a product by filling out an order blank. The order blank would be processed and when filled would be placed in the accounts receivable file. An invoice would be sent out each month to a customer showing standard industry discount terms for early payment. An additional charge was added to the bill if it was not paid within thirty days. No further information was gathered on a customer beside a standard credit report. Mark wanted to know more. Currently, he did not even have access to the historical sales patterns of a customer.

Mark saw a few things wrong even with the current system. First, he had little information to help him as he called on a customer. Second, there was no way to determine what additional products a customer might want and Pittsburgh Supply did not offer.

However, Mark saw a bigger problem. Although the business had grown over the past years, Mark had no sense of how the company was doing compared with the growth in the total market over the same period. For example, if sales of business supplies in the area had increased by 80 percent while Pittsburgh Supply's sales had increased by only 40 percent, Pittsburgh Supply would have more to be concerned about than if the industry had only increased by 20 percent. Mark didn't know. In essence, Pittsburgh Supply did not even know if it was as competitive as it thought it was, and that could pose some big problems for the future of the company.

Mark felt that customer information was needed on a timely basis and in a level of detail that would give a sales representative a clue as to a customer's current status. Mark recalled how he had a sales meeting with one customer not even knowing that the customer was fuming over a billing error. Instead of helping the customer, the sales representative had shown a lack of concern and knowledge. That had made the customer even more angry.

Mark was not sure what else he wanted from this information system. However, he did feel that he wanted to measure customer satisfaction not only in terms of attitudes but also in terms of real dollars and sense. Mark believed that he needed

1. The introductory case at the beginning of this chapter should be read before this case to obtain background on the situation described here.

some way to alert the sales staff when there was any problem between the company and the customer. The sales staff might be the only humans that the customer would know face to face at Pittsburgh Supply, and it would be better to have the sales representative work to resolve problems than to have problems simmering and antagonizing the customer unnecessarily. Mark seemed to be looking for a means to build an information base centered around the sales representative that would let the representative know what was going on with the customer and what the recent history of sales had been.

However, Mark seemed to want to go further than that. He wanted to empower the sales staff to "do what was needed" to resolve problems between the company and the customer. In this manner, the sales representative would become more of a link between the customer and the company and would create a stronger bond between the customer and Pittsburgh Supply. Although this "empowerment" notion really did not involve the information system design, it did have implications for company policies and the ability of the sales representatives to have access to information and key decision makers.

Analysis

1. Why would knowledge of customers' previous consumption patterns be important to a company?
2. How could Pittsburgh Supply determine whether it was meeting customer needs?
3. Why should a manager have market share data when making decisions?
4. Advocate an information system to meet the company's need for information on problems between the customer and the company.
5. Why do you suppose Mark wanted to empower the sales representatives? What problems might occur with locating decision making with the sales representatives?

Case 2. Pittsburgh Supply
Part 2: Financial Information System[1]

Pittsburgh Supply had very little information on its financial performance. The current system could tell the owners how well the company was doing as a whole, but that was all. Even then, the information was provided on a conglomerate basis with very little to indicate how well the company was doing. For example, the company received only a monthly statement of income and expenses, along with a monthly balance sheet. Alex and Mark really needed to have more information than that if they wanted to make better decisions about the company. The following reflects an interaction that occurred while they were discussing their concerns.

ALEX. You know that we do not have cost information on each store. We do not know if a store is making money for us or not. That bothers me. We have to use our resources better if we are going to remain competitive.

MARK. It goes deeper than that, Alex. I can't even tell you what products make the most for us. I can't tell you which products sell and which sit there on the shelves. We need that information if we are going to decide what products stay and what products should be discounted until we sell out.

ALEX. I agree with you, but I think we need to be more qualitative than that. I do think we need that sort of information, yet we also need to make some qualitative decisions about whether a product would stay or go. I wish we had some data that would look at how the product was purchased. I hate to drop a product if it tends to compliment a product line. Even if it does not sell, it still may help to stock the product. For example, our philosophy is service. That means stocking products that customers need and stocking a full range of products, not just the top sellers. That is what some of the discounters do, and we should have a competitive edge beyond that. So, I agree with you, we need the data, but the bigger question that I have is, How do we distinguish between those products that are dogs and those that we ought to keep around in order to balance our product line?

MARK. I agree, and that's something that we simply need to think through as we are developing this information system. What data do we need to make intelligent decisions about products, costs, and services? We don't want to design a system that isn't going to help us do that. I had a computer wiz in here five years ago that designed a supersystem that was user unfriendly and complex and provided information that I really couldn't use for decision making. I don't want to go through that nightmare again.

ALEX. Boy, I remember that, and I agree, I don't want to go through that either. But that's part of the problem. It's easy to design an information system, but it's tough

1. The introductory case at the beginning of this chapter should be read before this case to obtain background on the situation described here.

to decide what you want in it and how you are going to present the data in a way that will be helpful.
MARK. Well, what sorts of data do we need?

The two of them came up with the following list:

Marginal contribution for each
- Store
- Product
- Store by hour open
- Product by size
- Sales less cost of goods sold for each store
- Sales/labor cost by each store
- Sales/rent per square foot for each store
- All above data reported on a weekly, monthly, and yearly basis

Sales by
- Average size of sale: by each store and by each hour by each store
- Customer: by average size of sale for each customer and by when each sale occurred

Costs
- Average cost of each sale
- Distribution costs per sale
- Labor cost of each sale

For our company
- Sales and costs compared with our competition
- Sales and costs compared with a discount chain
- Financial ratio analysis for our company
- Ratio analysis for our competition
- Ratio analysis for the average discount store

Although it was not an exhaustive list, Mark and Alex felt this sort of information would provide important data for managerial decisions on pricing, stocking, and the pricing of services. It would help Pittsburgh Supply remain competitive and be more proactive in the market.

Analysis

1. Why would having cost/revenue data on each of Pittsburgh Supply's stores be valuable in making decisions in the organization?

2. Alex advocated that qualitative dimensions be used in decision making. If that is the case, why bother with developing information systems?
3. Why is marginal contribution used instead of allocation of overhead? (Think back to your principles of accounting class.)
4. Should only accounting and financial data be used in determining store success? What other data might be considered?
5. Suggest a means of collecting some of the data that Mark and Alex have proposed.

Case 3. Pittsburgh Supply
Part 3: Distribution Information System[1]

Pittsburgh Supply had a distribution wizard in the form of JoAnn Kreshof. She really had a gift for understanding distribution systems. The staff at Pittsburgh Supply believed that if JoAnn were an air traffic controller there would never be a delay at an airport. It was amazing how she understood people and equipment.

Distribution at Pittsburgh Supply involved scheduling the twelve vans that the company owned. JoAnn had to schedule the vans so that products from vendors were shipped in a timely manner. She also had to schedule loading so that vendor trucks would not be delayed if they were shipping the product to the warehouse. In addition, JoAnn had to schedule shipments to the stores from the warehouse. Direct deliveries to the customer from Pittsburgh Supply were also her responsibility. Some of these shipments, about one hundred per day, were under the Priority 13 schedule, which involved a time limit of two hours from when the order was placed to when it was received by the customer. Priority 13 service was provided 24 hours a day seven days a week (including holidays). All this scheduling was done with only twelve vans, less than one van per store. JoAnn's analysis gives a better picture of the variables and parameters that were considered in distribution.

"My biggest challenge is the Priority 13 service. However, it is not as unpredictable as you might expect. I can guess on target for about 90 percent of the items that will be requested, who will request them, and when. Because our stores are relatively evenly located in the area, I can actually keep an inventory of some of the Priority 13 items that I think we will need. Some supplies may be already on the trucks. Hence, when a request comes in, we phone the truck, and if they have the supplies requested they make out the order on the truck and deliver it. If they don't, we have the nearest store prepare the order. If the nearest store doesn't have the product, we keep searching until we find it—even if we have to buy it from a competitor. It may seem strange, but we have 95 percent reliability on this service. This means that in only 5 cases out of 100 do we fail to make the two-hour deadline. In over half of the orders, we are there in forty-five minutes.

"Other shipments are more routine and can be planned. On rare occasions we will have to rent a truck, but normally I can visualize the route a truck will take on deliveries and then order it to pick up supplies from our vendors. We have worked with our vendors extensively and have what I call a just-in-time system. We have standing orders for products, but we demand that we receive shipments on an order within 24 hours of placing the order, and that means either you bring it to us within that 24 hours or you get it into our truck. We want to know if there is going to be a delay in loading our truck. We will be flexible, but only to a degree. I will not have my drivers sit around for more than fifteen minutes or the vendor will get grief from me. In the same vein, when we ship to the customer we avoid getting tied up in long

1. The introductory case at the beginning of this chapter should be read before this case to obtain background on the situation described here.

lines waiting to get processed: in most cases, we bring the order in the front door. In large orders we wait, but not for long. Again, after fifteen minutes, I tell my drivers to get on the road and mark the shipment "unable to deliver because of customer unloading dock back-up." We have the supervisor on the loading dock sign the notice, the delivery representative tells the consignee about the problem, and we are on the road. I have to admit that unloading dock supervisors do not like to sign this order and are more apt to expedite the shipment, particularly because they know the consignee has been called and so will be breathing down their neck. That helps us keep on time.

"We give each driver a schedule and routing for the day, putting in some slack time to cover for Priority 13 shipments. The drivers keep a log of time spent that indicates how they have or have not kept to the schedule. We are in cellular phone contact with each driver about twice an hour. Hence, we know where each van is and can redeploy it if we need to in order to make delivery or pickup schedules. Because we have snow and hills, each van has four-wheel drive.

"I get to know the drivers. I know those who are going to be slow and those who can cover more of an area. I know which companies are going to take longer for a pickup or delivery than others. I know which routes are going to take longer to cover because of road construction or congestion. The knowledge comes with experience and the ability to conceptualize what is going to happen in the next hour and the next four hours. It may be a gift, or it may be from spending the summers with my aunt on the railroad. She was a train dispatcher, and I would spend days with her at work entranced by the excitement of her craft and her ability to keep the trains moving. When I come in each morning, I visualize the whole day. I know what it will mean if it is a Friday (heavier road traffic); I know what it will mean if it rains (slower travel times). I even check the weather radar for the area so that I will know about what hour it will start to rain or snow.

"I guess all I need is a system that will do what I do in my absence. We have no system. Everything relies upon me. Although I enjoy doing this, I think we ought to have some more formal system or computer system that could generate the routings for the day and monitor the situation. I would like to spend more time on other things rather than putting out fires on a daily basis. I would also like some cost system so we would know what deliveries are costing us. I would like to be able to simulate other routings to see if we can improve productivity."

Analysis

1. Given the tight delivery schedule, why doesn't Pittsburgh Supply just buy additional vans?
2. If there are so many variables involved in distribution systems, is it practical to develop an information system? How valuable would it be?

3. How could you measure the effectiveness of a driver given all the variables involved in shipments?
4. How would you suggest Pittsburgh Supply develop a management information system (MIS) for distribution? How would it even begin?
5. Can nonroutine decisions such as the distribution decisions faced by Pittsburgh Supply be made routine through the use of an MIS format?

Case 4. Pittsburgh Supply
Part 4: Productivity and Quality Control Information Systems[1]

Pittsburgh Supply needed a better means of tracking the productivity of its employees and the times when it had a problem with a product or a sale. This was the focus of a meeting between Mark and Alex as they continued their discussion of a management information system.

ALEX. Let's first consider each of these items as separate and distinct things. I really think after our discussion of financial information systems that we can progress much faster if we consider what sorts of goals we might have in each area and then develop an information system that can provide us with data for meeting those goals.
MARK. That sounds reasonable. For productivity, I think we are really meaning the productivity of the employees and that of each store. How do I measure productivity? It is through sales per square foot in a store. However, that's a little illusory in our case because so much of our service is an interconnected system. We need to think of each store as a warehouse, particularly because so much of our service is through phone orders. So we need to think of the sales of the whole system.
ALEX. No, I disagree. If you want to treat each store as a warehouse, that is fine with me. However, we still need to consider the sales per square foot that are made out of each unit. Even if the sale is taken at our central phone location, we can still determine where we are shipping the order from and that becomes a sale for that unit. We need that information because we need to know if the store is located in the right place. If not, we might consider closing it and moving it to a better location. We cannot ignore the importance of location because we need good service to be competitive.
MARK. I see, and I agree. However, we may ship from a different location, not the store that is closest to the customer. Hence, maybe we should look at some other criterion.
ALEX. Maybe, or maybe we should also look at some other information source. What if we look at the delivery points for our sales and make sure we locate near those points?
MARK. That sounds like a good idea as long as we compare the cost and revenue from that location. As you know, the rental rates for stores are quite variable. If I am going to locate in the Baldwin or Gateway Center areas, it is going to cost me more than the Western Avenue area. I want to be able to balance that cost with the revenue generated at each location.
ALEX. That sounds reasonable. What about looking at the productivity of each employee? What are you considering in that measure?
MARK. To control costs we ought to have some measure of the number of employees that we have at a given location. Dividing the sales by the number of employees

1. The introductory case at the beginning of this chapter should be read before this case to obtain background on the situation described here.

would give us some information for comparing each store's productivity per employee. We might consider additional staffing at stores with higher sales per employee and reduce staffing at those with lower sales per employee.

ALEX. We can assess the productivity of drivers in the same fashion looking at the volume that they have carried.

MARK. Well, maybe for a start. However, their volume might be colored by the length of their route or how slowly they complete the route. The congestion downtown might reduce the productivity of a driver; however, stops may also be closer together. Then again, smaller businesses may order less than some of our major clients along I-79. I almost think we should rely on JoAnn's judgment. But we might want to still measure volume just to know when we may want to modify our routes to equalize coverage.

ALEX. Agreed. What about quality control?

MARK. Well, this has been one of my major concerns. We do not have a good tracking system to determine how satisfied customers are with our service, price, and friendliness. However, I don't want to cover customer information systems because we have already covered that area. My concern is how we get a system that will record when a customer was not happy and what we did about it.

ALEX. Well, I agree. It's almost like we need two systems: one to measure customer satisfaction and another to measure when we have a problem and how we resolved it. So many things seem to fall through the cracks. We need some reporting system and some responsibility assigned to ensure that these problems do end in a positive experience for the customer.

MARK. We also need some means of checking the quality of the shipments from our vendors. We really don't check much on the quality of products. When we do have a problem, we don't have a way of tracking it back to get it remedied, and we don't keep a file on vendors to pull the plug on those that do not want to adhere to our quality standards.

ALEX. Agreed. But how do we measure this? What information should we ask to be designed into the system?

MARK. Well, I am not looking for a statistic here. I guess I am looking for a process to monitor the situation. Each case might be different, but we still need to track it.

ALEX. You're right. It's similar to my need to measure the on-time performance of my vendors and how many times items were back-ordered. Although some suppliers can tolerate back ordering, we normally do not want to have large amounts of money in inventory protecting our vendors. Hence, we want to know when we are having a problem and how often that problem occurs. Right now we do it by my memory, but we are adding roughly twenty-five vendors per year and stocking more than one thousand items. My memory is good, but not that good.

Analysis

1. Why might it be appropriate to design information systems around the goals of the organization?
2. Why would sales minus cost per square foot of store be an effective measure of productivity? Why not?
3. Why is the productivity of a driver harder to measure than the productivity of other jobs in the organization? Should their performance not be measured?
4. Why might it be helpful to have quality control information on incoming products? Is it important even if there are few problems with quality control?
5. Is simply measuring problems per vendor an effective means of comparing vendors? Why or why not?

Case 5. Pittsburgh Supply
Part 5: A Comprehensive Management Information System[1]

Pittsburgh Supply wanted to develop a comprehensive management information system (MIS). It knew the areas it wanted to consider: customers, finance, distribution, quality of performance, and quality control of its products. A complete management information system should be concerned with providing information to the appropriate people in a timely fashion. After considering the different relevant dimensions of information, the management team of Mark and Alex next needed to consider how to blend all this together into a system that would integrate the information needed by the various decision makers in the organization. Mark wanted the sales representatives to have greater power in resolving problems. Therefore they would need to have greater access to information or to people who would have the information. After some discussion, Alex and Mark agreed that the sales representative should be able to work with the customer to resolve problems, but could act only as an advocate of the customer in arguing before other units at Pittsburgh Supply. The final decision in resolving disputes would be Mark or Alex, with input from all parties involved. Hence, the basic information system would be plugged into Mark and Alex. Reports might go to other units as needed. For example, the financial information would be shared with the chief financial officer.

However, there still was some concern about whether the information system would be worth it. One argument related to how JoAnn evaluated driver performance. Both Mark and Alex felt she could evaluate performance better under her way than by using a few measures generated by a statistical report. There were so many variables to consider in her job that the cost of a complete system would not be worth the value it would provide. However, it was agreed that the company needed much more information than it currently had and that a management information system was desired.

Previous consultants had all talked about MIS systems in terms of expensive computers, but the current consultant had only talked in terms of how to best gather and provide the information needed. In certain cases, the focus was not on a computer system but on a simple reporting system that could be managed by a pencil and paper.

All in all, although they felt they did not have all the data they desired, Mark and Alex felt they had a good balance between needs and desires and the cost of the new system. But they knew that as their company changed they would require additional information and that an MIS system would need to be revised as needs change.

1. The introductory case at the beginning of this chapter should be read before this case to obtain background on the situation described here.

Analysis

1. What does it mean to have a comprehensive management information system? Does it mean a computer-based system?
2. Why do you suppose the consultant advocated a noncomputerized information system for part of the process?
3. Are Mark and Alex correct about not developing a system to help JoAnn? Why or why not?
4. Why were Mark and Alex concerned about who would receive the information from the MIS?
5. Were Mark and Alex correct in having only themselves receive the MIS reports? Why or why not?

Chapter 19 Control Techniques and Methods

Case 1. Midwest Tool & Die: A Division of RayCor

Midwest Tool is a small manufacturing plant that makes molds used in plastic extrusion. The company also makes machines for stamping operations and other sheet metal processing operations. The processes involved in both activities are relatively complicated and result in varying amounts of scrap loss. In addition, since each die and tool is a relatively unique product, there is a high degree of variability in the estimation of costs.

Midwest Tool & Die was acquired by RayCor, a holding company mainly involved in buying and selling companies. Over the years, the RayCor conglomerate has acquired over twenty-five companies, ranging from a dude ranch in Wyoming, to a soft drink bottler in Kentucky, to a toy manufacturer in Indiana, to a coal mine in West Virginia. It seems, at first blush, that RayCor is in the business to maximize shareholder wealth. The long-term survival of any of its subsidiaries is secondary. RayCor has to meet an immediate return on investment and needs to do whatever is necessary to maximize that investment's value for sale. It generally owns a company for a little less than three years. The longest ownership has been ten years, and the shortest, one and a half years. Midwest Tool & Die has been a part of RayCor for six months. R. C. Davis is Midwest's chief operating officer.

Midwest is currently having some problems with RayCor. R. C. Davis articulates the problem as looking at the budget and not at reality. "We have been in trouble with the home office ever since it acquired us. It seems as if it has no sense of this business and doesn't care to know. It only harps at our ability to stay on budget and on plan. This business is not conducive to that sort of mindless budget watching.

"What we do is meet the customer's needs. We want to make money at it, but our first job is to work with the customer to ensure that we have a quality product. Sometimes that takes more time and resources than we planned. We get it back in the billing or in future orders from a satisfied customer. However, if we get greedy at the front end or make a product that fits the specifications in the original plan without meeting the need for change along the way, we end up losing the customer in the long run. That isn't worth it, and that is not how things are done in this industry.

But first let me tell you how we do things in this industry, and then you can be the judge.

"A person comes to us with an idea. He or she wants an estimate of the cost. Well, here is a product that we have to build from the ground up. We start with a drawing. A draftsperson makes a multidimensional series of drawings, and the tool or piece of machinery is then made. Well, if the drawing isn't correct, we can't charge the customer. And many times, we build a machine and find out that it is not sufficiently reliable because of design problems. Again we fix it. We charge some of that to the customer in future orders, but many times we have to absorb the cost ourselves. We do keep accurate records of costs for each job, and that affects our future pricing estimates on new orders and our pricing of additional orders of existing units. In the long run we come out fine. We make a profit and keep the good will of the customer. However, because of who we are and how we operate, we do not have consistent profits. Our costs can dramatically change over a year.

"For example, we set up standard cost and labor usage on machine "X." We look at the material it should take to make the unit and the labor we should use. Materials are budgeted in terms of standards. Material cost is one standard, material use a second. Same with labor used: we set standards on the cost of labor and its use. Well, if we run into problems with a unit, we are going to be way over in labor usage and we could run into problems with material use and cost. This is true particularly if we run into a situation where we have to redesign a part after it has been partially built. We like to set the standards to guide us and we need to correctly allocate costs for current and future billings, but we never consider them hard and fast goals.

"We never have been that close to budget when it comes to nonmanufacturing expenses either. When opportunities occur, we take advantage of them. Last year, some of our sales staff was in China for two months drumming up business. We had a host of orders that would be paid for next year. However, last year's sales costs were crazy compared with our budget. But that is this business, and we do what we need to do to meet the needs of the customers.

"However, RayCor does not agree. It wants us to be much more accountable and keep within the budget. They really do not want to listen to how we operate. They want us to look good on paper, and financial ratios and budget compliance look a lot more tangible than customer good will. We will never look the way they want. In good years, we will be over budget on manufacturing expenditures, and in bad years we will be overbudget on the nonmanufacturing expenditures. Our net income figure will be highly variable. We will not be able to control it. Some years we will be way over our goal; other years we may take a loss. Those who do not know this industry do not like the variability. Those who do realize that it is just the pattern of the industry. RayCor does not know the industry. It wants to see a consistent pattern of increasing net income. Because it is in it for the short run, it cares little about customer good will or long-range perceptions of quality and service. That is something that the new owner will have to worry about.

"So here I am, stuck in the middle. How do I convince RayCor that it needs to look at something else besides profit and loss figures and whether we are over or under budget? How do I frame things so that RayCor realizes the strength of this company, before it destroys us?"

Analysis

1. Does R. C. Davis have a point? If so, what is the value of a budget if it can't be used for control?
2. What should R. C. Davis do?
3. With the degree of variability in Midwest Tool & Die, would another type of budget be better than what they have, that is, one fixed budget for the year?
4. How might R. C. Davis get a better measure of the strength of Midwest Tool & Die than just the profit and loss statement? What sorts of things might he measure?
5. Is RayCor wrong in insisting upon accountability for Midwest?

Case 2. Wyoming Wonders

Wyoming Wonders sells various pictures, post cards, and Christmas cards that depict scenery in Wyoming. The company has been in operation for the past ten years and is an acquisition candidate of Martin and Michele Mobley. Before they purchase the organization, Michele and Martin want to have a good sense of its financial aspects. How does Wyoming Wonders compare with other similar organizations?

Although their task is difficult, Martin and Michele have managed to compare Wyoming Wonders with the figures that an investment counselor obtained from four other organizations that sell art primarily through mail orders. Most of Wyoming Wonders' sales are conducted through mail orders, but the company seems to have a unique product and clientele that are hard to compare with those of other mail-order companies.

Balance sheets and income statements for Wyoming Wonders appear in Tables 1 and 2. Tables 3 and 4 show the percentage balance sheets and income statements. Table 5 illustrates the ratio analysis obtained from the investment counselor.

The Mobleys have had too little experience to interpret what the financial figures mean and have asked that you interpret the data for them. In addition, they wonder what other sorts of information they might want to obtain before making a decision to buy. They have posed the following questions to you as their consultant.

Analysis

1. Is Wyoming Wonders as profitable as the industry? What figures support your answer? What has been the trend over the past three years?
2. Does Wyoming Wonders have a higher level of liquidity than the rest of the industry? What figures support your answer? What has been the trend over the past three years?
3. Should we be concerned about the amount of debt that Wyoming Wonders has compared with the debt of its counterparts in the industry? Support your answer. What has been the trend over the past three years?
4. What cautions should we take when interpreting the data?
5. What other aspects of Wyoming Wonders should we look at before deciding to buy?
6. How can ratio analysis be used as a control tool in this case?

TABLE 1 Wyoming Wonders
Comparative Balance Sheets, 19x1–19x3

	Fiscal Year Ending October 31		
	19x1	19x2	19x3
Assets			
Current assets:			
Cash	$ 20,000	$ 50,000	$ 50,000
Accounts receivable (gross)	140,000	300,000	500,000
Inventory	40,000	100,000	200,000
Prepaid expenses	—	50,000	50,000
Total current assets	$200,000	$500,000	$800,000
Fixed assets:			
Machinery and equipment	120,000	150,000	160,000
Depreciation	(20,000)	(50,000)	(60,000)
Total fixed assets	$100,000	$100,000	$100,000
Total assets	$300,000	$600,000	$900,000
Liabilities and Owners' Equity			
Current liabilities:			
Notes payable	—	—	$200,000
Accounts payable	$100,000	$200,000	100,000
Accrued expenses	50,000	100,000	100,000
Total current liabilities	$150,000	$300,000	$400,000
Owners' equity:			
Common stock	100,000	200,000	350,000
Retained earnings	50,000	100,000	150,000
Total owners' equity	$150,000	$300,000	$500,000
Total liabilities and owners' equity	$300,000	$600,000	$900,000

TABLE 2 Wyoming Wonders
Comparative Income Statement, 19x1–19x3

	Fiscal Year Ending October 31		
	19x1	19x2	19x3
Sales	$500,000	$2,000,000	$3,000,000
Returns	(10,000)	(50,000)	(50,000)
Sales before disounts	$490,000	$1,950,000	$2,950,000
Discounts	(10,000)	(50,000)	(50,000)
Net sales	$480,000	$1,900,000	$2,900,000
Cost of sales	400,000	1,000,000	2,000,000
Gross profit	$ 80,000	$ 900,000	$ 900,000
Operating expenses	20,000	800,000	800,000
Net income before taxes	$ 60,000	$ 100,000	$ 100,000
Taxes	10,000	50,000	50,000
Net income	$ 50,000	$ 50,000	$ 50,000

TABLE 3 Wyoming Wonders
Percentage Balance Sheets, 19x1–19x3

	19x1	19x2	19x3
Assets			
Current assets:			
Cash	6.7%	8.3%	5.5%
Accounts receivable	46.7	50.0	55.5
Inventory	13.3	16.7	22.2
Prepaid expenses	—	8.3	5.7
Total current assets	66.7%	83.3%	88.9%
Fixed assets:			
Machinery and equipment	40.0%	25.0%	17.8%
Depreciation	(6.7)	(8.3)	(6.7)
Total fixed assets	33.3	16.7	11.1
Total assets	100.0%	100.0%	100.0%
Liabilities and Owners' Equity			
Current liabilities:			
Notes payable	—	—	22.2%
Accounts payable	33.3%	33.3%	11.1
Accrued expenses	16.7	16.7	11.1
Total current liabilities	50.0%	50.0%	44.4%
Owners' equity:			
Common stock	33.3%	33.3%	38.9%
Retained earnings	16.7	16.7	16.7
Total owners' equity	50.0	50.0	55.6
Total liabilities and owners' equity	100.0%	100.0%	100.0%

TABLE 4 Wyoming Wonders
Percentage Income Statements, 19x1–19x3

	19x1	19x2	19x3
Sales	104.1%	105.3%	103.4%
Returns	(2.0)	(2.7)	(1.7)
Sales before discounts	102.1	102.6	101.7
Discounts	(2.1)	(2.6)	(1.7)
Net sales	100.0	100.0	100.0
Cost of sales	83.3	52.6	69.0
Gross profit	16.7	47.4	31.0
Operating expenses	4.2	42.1	27.6
Income before taxes	12.5	5.3	3.4
Taxes	4.2	2.6	1.7
Net income	8.3%	2.7%	1.7%

TABLE 5 Wyoming Wonders
Ratio Analysis

	19x1	19x2	19x3	Industry
Gross profit margin	16.7%	47.4%	31.0%	25.0%
Operating profit margin	12.5	5.3	3.4	15.0
Net profit margin	8.3	2.7	1.7	10.0
Return on assets	16.7	8.3	5.6	25.0
Return on equity	33.3	16.7	10.0	40.0
Current ratio	1.33	1.67	2.0	2.0
Quick ratio	1.07	1.33	1.5	1.0
Debt to assets	50.0	50.0	44.4	50.0
Debt to equity	1.00	1.00	0.8	1.0
Fixed asset turnover	4.9	79.0	29.0	50.0
Total asset turnover	1.6	3.2	3.2	10.0

Case 3. Route 23

The Wesley Construction Company (WCC) was making its first bid on a state contract to resurface and widen State Route 23 near Granger. The standard bid that WCC normally made allowed for a generous construction period. These sorts of bids were lower than the accelerated time bid, which was used when the state wanted a section of road built within a tight construction schedule. The state called for these kinds of bids whenever the construction would cause major disruptions and the state wanted it done as fast as possible to minimize traffic delays. In the Route 23 construction, the road was a major link between a town of 185,000 people and several bedroom communities.[1]

This was the first time that WCC was bidding on an accelerated contract, and that concerned the owner, Phyllis Schmitz. Although the accelerated contracts paid at a higher rate, there was a penalty clause that would reduce the construction company's revenue if it did not complete the project on time. The penalties could eat up much of the profit if there were prolonged delays not related to weather. Phyllis met with her partner Buff to discuss how they might approach the problem so that she would feel comfortable with making the time commitment on the accelerated bid.

BUFF. It really is not a problem. I have done these sorts of things before with new home construction. It just takes a little planning.

PHYLLIS. Well, you went to college and you're the sorority member, so tell me what to do.

BUFF. Well, it's so simple even you could figure it out. The approach is called the Critical Path Method, but I have also seen it called the PERT approach.

PHYLLIS. What does PERT stand for?

BUFF. Project Evaluation and Review Technique.

PHYLLIS. It sounds like something we can't afford.

BUFF. Well, it's free, and all it takes is brainpower. We both have the construction experience to plan what we need to do. All it takes is some planning and paper and pen. We can do that.

PHYLLIS. Well, you know planning is hard to do in construction. You never know what sorts of problems you are going to have. You can run into bedrock, have a machine break down, or have a subcontractor who doesn't meet the schedule, and then you are in trouble.

BUFF. That's true, but at least you will be able to try to reduce some of the variability using PERT. Here's how it works. First, let's list everything we need to do to get the job done. Then we need to put things in the order in which they have to be done. If there are things we can do concurrently, we list those. We then draw a map that depicts each activity and how long it is expected to take. For our sake, we fix a time for each activity. Even though it may vary, we give our best estimate. Then we connect

1. A bedroom community was one in which most of the residents work in a larger community even though they live and sleep in the smaller community.

those activities in a sequential order. When we are done, we have a critical path showing the total time the process will take. It is critical in that this path must be followed if all the parts of the job are to be done on time. We then know which tasks we need to keep on time to keep the whole job moving.
PHYLLIS. OK, let's try it out and see what we come up with.

They developed the PERT diagram shown in Figure 1. The various activities are described below the diagram, and the times required to complete those tasks are indicated in days and appear in the diagram in parentheses. Although the PERT chart did not guarantee that the job would be done on time, Phyllis agreed that it would be valuable in developing an estimated price to use for the bid. They now knew the number of crews and equipment they would have to allocate on the job, the number of subcontractors they would have to use, and the time parameters they would have to meet. In addition, they had a goal to strive for which they could then use as a milepost of their progress during the project. At any time they could compare the elapsed time on the contract with the planned time, and they could react to problems much sooner than before.

Analysis

1. Which is the critical path in Figure 1? Why?
2. What is the maximum time Phyllis and Buff could wait before starting activity 7? Why?
3. How much can activities 1-3-5-7-9 be delayed while still allowing the project to be done on time?
4. How can the PERT approach be a planning tool? How is it a control tool?
5. If there are events that cannot be planned, as Phyllis discussed, how can PERT be of value?

FIGURE 1
Buff and Phyllis's PERT Chart

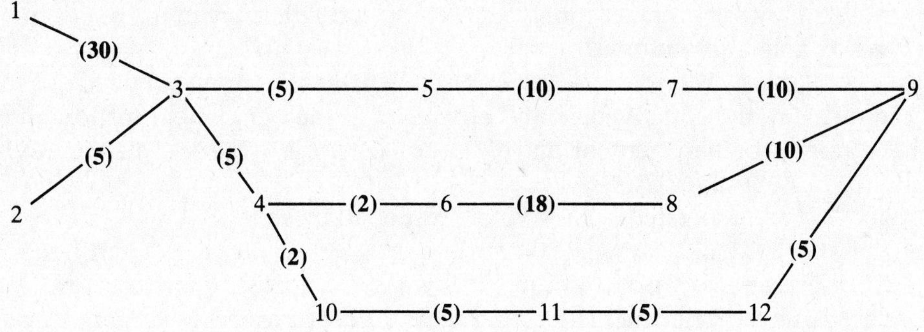

Activity Description

1 Environmental impact statement
2 Survey
3 Primary grading
4 Bridge work approach grading
5 Concrete forms & reinforcers for concrete
6 Steelwork for bridge supports
7 Paving
8 Deck work on bridges
9 Detail work; fencing; striping
10 Retention pond digging
11 Rough grading of retention pond area
12 Sod work and heavy gravel fill of erosion areas

Case 4. Human Resource Management at Cole International

INTERVIEWER. How do you measure effectiveness and efficiency in the use of human resources at Cole International?

LOUISE JOB, DIRECTOR OF CORPORATE PERSONNEL. Well, that is a three-pronged question. We can measure the effectiveness and efficiency of the personnel function, of personnel's training of management, and of the use of people in the organization. Which should we talk about first?

INTERVIEWER. I am interested in how you consider all three.

JOB. OK. Let's first look at how we determine problems out in the departments. Job dissatisfaction can show up in a number of ways. We measure three distinct ways: voluntary turnover, grievances filed, and requests for transfers. Voluntary turnover is calculated by the number of individuals in a unit who left without being fired or laid off divided by the number of employees in the unit. A voluntary job termination occurs when the employee quits the organization as opposed to being fired or laid off. We keep track of this statistic for the company as a whole, for each division, and for each department in the division. We look for problem spots where voluntary turnover is abnormally high or low.

INTERVIEWER. That indicates a problem with the supervision?

JOB. No, not necessarily. It could very well be a random event, maybe a disgruntled employee who is creating some discontent. No, I would say that it only indicates that we may want to look around some and ask questions. I have been in the business too long to make quick decisions without knowing the situation.

INTERVIEWER. Good point. What else do you use?

JOB. In the same manner we look at the number of grievances filed divided by the number of employees in a unit. We further look at how the cases were resolved. Again, this indicates that we ought to take a closer look. We have many supervisors whose job is to make some major changes in their unit, and those supervisors are going to create some unhappy employees. We know that one employee filing a grievance will lead to other filings. Requests for transfer to different departments are handled in a similar fashion.

INTERVIEWER. How do you measure effectiveness and efficiency in employee utilization?

JOB. Well, for example, here is what we do in the human resource department. We first define the department in terms of activities that need to be done. For example, part of our department is involved in employee screening. We interview potential employees, do preemployment testing, and do a reference check. We standardize the amount of time that it takes, on the average, to process one employee. We then consider the number of people we will be screening in a given period and estimate how many people one employee can screen. By dividing the number of people to be screened by the number of people a personnel specialist can screen in a given period, we get some sense of our needs for that activity. This process is called workload analysis. From this analysis we can determine the number of employees we need to allocate to that function. This process is repeated for each of the functions in the human resource area. We then have some sense of how many employees we need for the full department.

We use cross training and a pay-for-knowledge approach extensively. Hence, our people can perform many more functions than those in many human resource departments.

INTERVIEWER. What do you mean by pay-for-knowledge?

JOB. This approach bases an employee's pay on his or her skills, not just on his or her current job. So, for example, if we have an intake specialist who is also trained as an interviewer or benefits counselor, we will pay that employee for the highest basic pay rate of those functions. In this case, it is the rate for a benefits counselor. Now, the employee may not even be in that job or may not have ever been in that job, but if he or she has those skills, we will pay that rate. The end product is a highly trained staff.

INTERVIEWER. Isn't it expensive to pay employees at a high rate and only use them for less costly jobs?

JOB. Sure, but we gain in the flexibility of the work force. If we have to move employees from a higher-paying job to a lower-paying one, they do not get as upset because they will be paid at the higher rate. In addition, the pay-for-knowledge concept is designed to show that the company cares about developing its employees. If they work to learn new skills, they are rewarded. They are happier with the company, and we end up with a better-skilled work force. We do not have the problems we had before with losing a key employee and having a minor disaster while a new employee filled in and learned the job.

INTERVIEWER. What other statistics do you look at related to your function?

JOB. We are charged with employee safety and health. As part of that function we look at two statistics. One is called the accident frequency rate. That is calculated as the number of accidents divided by the number of labor hours worked in a unit. A second statistic, accident severity, looks at the time lost with each accident. That statistic is calculated as the hours lost to accidents divided by the number of hours worked in the unit. Both are then multiplied by 1,000 to move the number to a more readable index instead of something out in the minute decimals. As with turnover statistics, we compare both these statistics on a companywide, division, plant, functional unit, and department basis. We want to locate problems, not just wonder about them.

We also make a once-a-year safety audit of each department. We compare federal standards with those of the unit to determine where we need to make improvements to comply with our best interpretation of their latest regulations. We think we are prepared if they inspect our facilities.

Analysis

1. How can the statistics that are calculated become a control mechanism?
2. How can the statistics that are calculated become a planning tool?
3. Are federal compliance reviews for safety and health a form of control? How?
4. Does Louise Job's definition of voluntary turnover consider those cases in which the individual quits because of a spouse transfer? Should that be considered voluntary or involuntary transfer? How could she determine if the employee quits because of factors on the job or factors off the job?
5. How could Cole International assess the success of the pay-for-knowledge program?

Case 5. Sears and the Retail Industry[1]

Sears needs to make some changes to stay competitive. The company is losing market share. In 1971, it had 44 percent of the share of the market of the top five retailers, followed by J. C. Penney with 21 percent. By 1988, Sears's share of the market had dropped to 29 percent, with K mart at 26 percent and Wal-Mart at a close 20 percent. While K mart's revenues have increased nine times since 1971 (from $3.1 to $27.3 billion), Sears's revenues have only increased three times (from $10.1 to $30.2 billion). Sears's selling and administrative expenses eat up 30 cents of every dollar of revenue that comes into the stores, versus K mart's 22 cents and Wal-Mart's 18 cents. Sears's retail group earnings have dropped at an annual rate of 7.7 percent for the last five years, and overall earnings are relatively flat.

Sears has been criticized for having too complex a decision-making process that slows competitive decisions. Its information system is regionalized and does not seem to provide timely reports to buyers and corporate headquarters. The system is extremely slow and not very innovative. Consider Wal-Mart's decision making at its headquarters in Bentonville, Arkansas. All regional managers meet once a week on Thursday to look at sales and make immediate decisions on pricing and promotions. Changes are then communicated by satellite to all one thousand stores on Friday.

Sears is beginning to respond to some of its problems. First, it has reduced prices to become more competitive with the discount retailers such as K mart and Wal-Mart. In addition, it has begun to merchandise brand name products. It is also moving to an everyday low price strategy, hoping to increase traffic in its stores and reduce advertising expenses.

The true test of the CEO, Ed Brennan, will be how much he can reduce selling and administrative costs. Sears will not be able to compete until it gets its costs in line. This will entail, by some reports, the elimination of literally thousands of jobs in order to slim down the corporation. Part of the plan is to close fourteen regional offices and sell the corporate image, the Sears Tower in Chicago, the world's tallest building. Sears is attempting to ensure that the name will stay with the tower, but most buyers balk at that idea.

Job cuts are particularly hard at Sears because there has been an unwritten law that Sears will protect good employees for life. However, if Sears cannot improve its sales per square foot in the store, it has few other options. Brennan needs to gain control of a selling machine that is out of control and not responding to the needs of the customer. As some put it, the company is unfocused and unsure of the market it wants to serve.

1. This case is adapted from Amy Dunkin, David Woodruff, and Dean Foust, "Little Price Tags are Looking Good to Big Retailers," *Business Week*, July 3, 1989, p. 44; Walecia Konrad, Brian Bremner, and Russell Mitchell, "As Price Tags Shrink, So Will the Daily Newspaper," *Business Week*, July 3, 1989, p. 44; and Brian Bremner and Michael Oneal, "The Big Store's Big Trauma," *Business Week*, July 10, 1989, pp. 50–55. The author has also drawn on his experiences with several large retail and fast food restaurant organizations.

What happened? Why did Sears lose its dominance over the retail market? Did Sears change, or did the customer? The answer seems to be both. In the mid-1970s the appeal of Sears as a one-stop shopping place was replaced by the appeal of specialty stores such as Toys R Us, Fretters, Highland Appliance and Sound Stores, and specialty clothing stores. In addition, the discount retailers were hurting Sears because they were more concerned with price. The private brands of Sears, such as Kenmore, seemed to be less innovative than other brand names, and customers could not find a good selection of brand names at Sears. In addition, although Sears did have an extensive service and repair system, there were complaints that friendly and prompt service was the exception rather than the rule. Although Sears did spend more on advertising than its competitors (3 percent of sales revenue versus 1 percent for Wal-Mart), it didn't seem to make much of a difference. It all added up to strong consumer discontent, a comparative reduction in Sears growth, and a significant loss of market share.

What needs to be done? Sears needs to get closer to its customers, and it needs to identify its strengths in the market. For example, McDonald's compares its customers with national demographics provided by the Bureau of the Census. It knows that it attracts a higher percentage of those who are over eleven and under forty-five years of age. Knowing that, it can focus its advertising on that segment, and if that segment is not large enough to meet sales goals, it can target other markets. However, a company needs to first maintain its appeal to its current customers so it doesn't lose that base. These surveys ought to be done for each Sears store to determine if there are differences in the market for that store. In addition, census data can be compared to determine differences in the effective market area of the Sears outlet: these differences may pose additional product mix opportunities not available in other Sears outlets.

Issues such as the quality of sales staff and service need to be addressed. Just as other retail stores are concerned with their images (see Case 5.3 in this text), so must Sears be concerned with the full experience that customers have when they shop at Sears. Having low prices and brand names will not be enough to attract customers if the sales staff is rude or uncaring or if planning a delivery time is a nightmare.

What of advertising? As Sears reduces its expenditures on advertising, it needs to ensure that the return for the advertising dollar is high. The use of focus groups or preview groups to assess the quality and impact of an advertisement or a campaign ought to be addressed. Again, since Sears needs to create a consistent image, it must take much more care in building its advertising approach. And it will have to do much more than make promises; it will have to create a different in-store environment that meets the needs of the consumer.

Although Sears might be considered too big and complex to be adaptable, it looks like it must adapt if it is going to maintain its leadership in the market.

Analysis

1. What statistic should Sears use to measure progress in its turnaround strategy?
2. Why should Sears not just look at sales increases as a major indicator of its strength in the market?
3. How can Sears find out if a particular approach might have market appeal before trying it out on the whole market?
4. What measures besides customer satisfaction can Sears use to assess the effectiveness of its advertising strategy?
5. How can focus groups help to assess an advertisement's effectiveness or to improve the image of Sears?

Chapter 20 Entrepreneurship and Small-Business Management

Case 1. Hamburger Haven

Mary and Hank Lane met in San Francisco in 1970 and quickly discovered that they shared a common interest in food. She liked to cook and he wanted to own his own restaurant. They married and pooled their meager financial resources. With this money they leased a small building in a desirable location, remodeled it themselves, and opened the first Hamburger Haven in June 1972. The restaurant had seating for eighty people and a limited menu. Mary and Hank soon settled into a routine of eighteen-hour days. Hank acted as the greater, broiler man, and cashier while Mary handled all of the cooking chores.

From the start, they attempted to set themselves apart from other places identified with hamburgers by adding blintzes, crepes, and flaming desserts. They offered personalized service at low prices, which was possible because they were doing all the work. Their restaurant caught on rapidly, and the Lanes found themselves confronted with the problem of success: a growing and demanding clientele, a more complicated menu, and an exhausting work pace with little or no time off.

A decision had to be made. To implement more innovative design and decor ideas, the Lanes knew they would have to expand to new locations. This change meant they would have to hire other people for management roles to whom they would have to delegate authority, something they had not tried before. Despite the risk that others would succeed using their formula of high-quality food, personalized service, and low prices, the Lanes decided to go ahead with their expansion plan. They designed a management system that included a complex training program for all new employees, a manual of work rules and procedures, and a control system that kept Hank Lane in the field almost continuously visiting various Hamburger Havens.

By the mid-1980s, twenty units had been established and more were being planned, moving outward from a California base to the West Coast, Arizona, and then Illinois. In each new location, the basic design and decor were maintained: bright red seats, dark paneling, white silk walls, thick red rugs, chandeliers, and paintings on the walls. At some locations special features were added, such as a patio, greenhouse, library, or art posters. Few of these features would ordinarily be associated with a name like Hamburger Haven.

With the expansion of units also came an expansion of the basic menu to over one hundred items. This further tested management's ingenuity. To serve all of the items without pricing itself out of business meant management had to recruit, screen, and train cooks who could handle heavy, complicated workloads and would take the initiative to maintain rigid control over the portions. Another requirement was excellent table service. Here, the Lanes tested potential waitresses for such personality traits as dependability, adaptability (for scheduling purposes), and caring.

As the success of the chain continued and the distance between various units increased, management had to take additional care to ensure an overall system of control while recognizing local differences and allowing for creativity. For example, in checking out a potential new unit in Scottsdale, Arizona, a research team of management trainees interviewed merchants and suppliers in the area. They performed pricing calculations based on locally bought ingredients for the Haven menu and for others that would need to be shipped in from elsewhere. The team then "comparison shopped" at competing local restaurants to determine prices, menu choices, and service quality.

By 1988 Hamburger Haven had over thirty units and the Lanes had put in place a sound management team. Each year for the past five years an annual planning retreat has been held. This year Hank felt that some portion of the meeting should be used to critically evaluate the company's management practices since its inception. He felt that this historical evaluation would be useful for planning what to do in the 1990s.

Analysis

1. Evaluate the management of Hamburger Haven in the functional areas of planning, organization leadership, and control.
2. What are the entrepreneurial qualities exhibited by Mary and Hank Lane?
3. What should the Lanes do to ensure continued success?

Case 2. The Leather Shoppe

Michelle Matthews and Lisa Levitt were roommates during their sophomore year at UCLA. They both liked the laid-back California lifestyle and found that they had many other interests in common, including a fondness for leather. They quickly became good friends. After much discussion during the following two years they decided that they would like to open a leather shop in the Los Angeles area. Michelle felt she had some expertise in business operations since she had majored in marketing and had worked part-time for various retailers. Lisa was a skillful and talented designer.

On graduation they decided to obtain sales positions in retailing so they could save money for their business venture and at the same time get valuable retail experience. While working they continued to research possible locations for their leather store. After two years they found a desirable location and decided to secure a bank loan.

Michelle felt she had to be prepared to answer the questions that the loan committee would ask. She had to demonstrate that the store would be profitable. She therefore estimated the costs of operating the store, including material costs, store rental, labor, equipment, and advertising.

During their research, Michelle and Lisa found that the markup on leather clothes was between 100 and 300 percent, depending on quality. They figured that they would need two full-time sales clerks and would need to invest a minimum of $100,000 in sales stock to start the business. Of course, they would need another $100,000 for other operating costs to have sufficient time to reach the break-even point. Inventory turnover would be critical to ensure sufficient flow and profitability. Michelle felt that after the first year of operation they would be able to make an after-tax profit of 25 percent on sales. She realized that she might not have figured in all costs but felt that the 25 percent provided a cushion for these costs as well as for Lisa's and her salary.

Michelle felt that she was prepared for the upcoming meeting with the loan committee. One week before the meeting, she was discussing her ideas with a group of friends at a local cafe. One of her friends, Joan Warden, who had also majored in business, listened to Michelle's proposal for the loan committee. At the end of the informal presentation, Joan said, "Michelle, is that all you're going to present? I'm surprised at you! Don't you remember the discussion about planning in our principles of management and business policy courses? Your estimates of costs and sales may be accurate, but they're only part of the picture. If you really want to impress the bankers and get the loan, you'd better be prepared to talk about other issues related to the planning function. This way you'll show them that you've done a lot of homework and are really ready to manage a business, not just sell clothes."

Analysis

1. What should a business plan include that Michelle has not included?
2. What planning and organizing issues should Michelle and Lisa agree upon before establishing the Leather Shoppe?

Case 3. Allegré Fashions

Alice Allegré, owner and manager of Allegré Fashions, wondered what was going wrong with her business. Over the past year, she had been receiving many customer complaints about product quality. Two of her top accounts had even canceled some orders because of what they felt were excessive delays in delivery. Until now her four-year-old business had been running smoothly.

Alice felt it was time to get some outside help. She had heard about the management assistance programs that were offered through the Small Business Administration. When she inquired, she was put in contact with Diane Blakely, a member of the Active Corps of Executives (ACE). Diane had over fifteen years of experience in the fashion business and volunteered some of her time to ACE to help out struggling small businesses. When the two met, Diane wanted to know more about Alice and Allegré Fashions.

Alice had graduated from college with a degree in fashion design in 1978. She then hired on with a major design company to gain experience. During her first two years her quality work on various design projects resulted in many diverse, challenging assignments. Between 1980 and 1984, she was involved in designing innovative fashions; making contacts and purchasing fabrics from various suppliers; meeting clients to discuss special projects; and coordinating the design, cutting, and sewing of specialty orders.

After one of many ten-hour workdays in the summer of 1985, Alice asked herself why she was working for a company when she could be putting in the same time for her own design business. After all, she had a sound technical background and over six years of experience. Besides, she was hard working, ambitious, and willing to take risks. Yet she was realistic enough to know that "Rome wasn't built in a day." It would take several years of hard work to get her business off the ground.

The following summer Alice requested a $50,000 business loan from a local bank. This amount plus the $20,000 that she had saved would be enough to get her started. The bank was impressed with Alice's education, experience, and solid reputation in the industry and gave her the loan.

By November of 1986 Alice had set up a small design shop, which she called Allegré Fashions. She hired a secretary, one pattern cutter, and two sewing machine operators. Alice felt it was crucial for her to develop a good reputation with prospective clients. Her goal was to provide quality designs at competitive prices while also giving good service. From her previous contacts, she was able to secure several small orders.

Clients were very pleased with the work of Allegré Fashions. By the summer of 1987, Allegré Fashions had attained a reputation for high-quality, moderately priced fashion wear. Orders increased by 70 percent from the past year, and the number of clients doubled to twelve.

To keep up with the increased production, Alice hired another pattern cutter and two more sewing machine operators. She found herself spending more time designing the fashions. She also spent more time than she liked visiting fabric suppliers and prospective clients. All of this was taking her away from supervising the day-to-day operations of the business.

By the summer of 1989, Alice began to receive a few client complaints about product quality and delays in receiving orders. Since she was concerned about service, she immediately called and apologized to the clients. However, by the end of the year, she had received more complaints than ever. Finally, one client canceled an order and vowed she would not deal with Allegré Fashions again. Another top client suggested he might cancel if things did not improve.

Alice held an emergency meeting with her employees to tell them about the complaints and find out what was going on. She was told that some of the machines were in need of maintenance, that some of the fabric had imperfections, and that one of the fabrics was already out of stock. After the meeting she received an anonymous note stating that some of the employees were taking long lunch breaks and slowing down when Alice was not around. It was at this point that Alice contacted Diane.

Analysis

1. Identify the sources of Alice's difficulties in the areas of planning, organizing, leading, and controlling.
2. If you were Diane Blakely, what specific actions would you recommend that Alice take?

Case 4. Schiller's Ski House

Pat and Barbara Schiller had just opened Schiller's Ski House, a small sporting goods store that specialized in ski equipment and accessories. They also handled equipment and accessories for other winter sports like snowmobiling, tobogganing, and sledding.

The Schillers had invested their life savings of $25,000 in their business, along with a $70,000 loan from the Small Business Administration (SBA). With the SBA loan, they had agreed to use the services of an SBA consultant from the Service Corps of Retired Executives (SCORE), retired executives who offered free business advice to small businesses. The Schillers were put in contact with Matthew Plunk, a retired business executive with much retailing experience.

During Matthew's initial interview with the Schillers, he discovered that when Pat and Barbara had incorporated the business, both had agreed there would be no boss. "We share authority and responsibility equally here," they told Matthew. The Schillers also advised him that in the interests of equality each of them could independently make decisions and set policies regarding the management of the store. Each could give orders or instructions to the store's two employees with the understanding that, if any employee had questions or problems, he or she could appeal to either owner for help or advice.

Pat said, "We are too small a business to be overly concerned with such things as objectives and policies at Schiller's. Our objective is to take each day as it comes and try to increase our sales volume. As for policies, we handle each situation as it develops—because each situation is different. And whoever is here will decide how best to handle it. If the employees get different answers or advice at times, it doesn't really matter that much. Right, Barbara?"

"That's right, Pat," Barbara said, and added, "As for any market research to determine what our store's potential might be, we think that's for big stores. We have neither the time nor the help to do this. All we can hope to do is work hard and try to meet customer needs."

After Matthew observed Schiller's Ski House in operation for the better part of a week, he discovered that many problems centered around the lack of direction and planning that Pat and Barbara had described in the initial interview. The store also lacked basic control procedures. For example, Matthew noted that Pat and Barbara often took cash from the only cash register to cover incidental expenses, including meals and drinks consumed during the store hours. At the end of the day one of them counted and balanced the cash receipts against the register totals. Inevitably the cash register was short, and each day the sales clerk was notified of the shortage amount. As a result, Matthew observed that the clerks felt mistrusted. They hesitated ringing up sales for fear of being accused of either theft or inaccurate sales transactions. In talking with the two employees, Matthew noted that their morale was low and both were thinking of quitting soon.

Analysis

1. What basic management principles are being violated by the Schillers?
2. List the common causes for failure among small businesses that are occurring at Schiller's Ski House.
3. If you were Matthew Plunk, what would be your advice for Pat and Barbara Schiller regarding their equal sharing of authority and responsibility?

Chapter 21 Managing in the International Sector

Case 1. Marketing Angel Dolls

JAN BYER. (CEO, Delray Toys, Ltd.) OK, let me understand this. You are telling me that we cannot sell our Angel Dolls in this country. Is that correct, Harry?
HARRY STONE. (legal counsel, Delray Toys) That is correct. This is based on an order by the Consumer Product Safety Authority. They seem to think that the coloring process used to make the beads on the doll may not be safe.
JAN. What do you mean, *may* not be safe?
HARRY. Well, they want to suspend our sales in this country until they have a chance to explore the process used in developing the dye that we use on the beads. They are just not sure if it is safe.
JAN. Haven't we told them that the dye is formed from an ancient process that is secret except to the tribe of Indians that make it? In addition, that process is part of their religious culture and they will not release how it is done because of religious reasons. Haven't we turned over all the test results we have had to assess the safety of the dye? You know that the popularity of the doll is mainly because of its authentic Indian design and colors. We can't change that or we will hurt the authenticity of the product. In addition, I don't want to make changes: I have seen no evidence that the product is unsafe, regardless of what Ottawa thinks.
HARRY. I've turned over all our reports and cooperated with the National government as well as the Territorial. However, it looks as if we will not be able to sell the doll in this country until we can take the injunction off. That may take six months.
JAN. Six months. Do you know how much inventory we have tied up in those dolls? What do we tell the tribe? If they do not have the dolls to count on it will mean one half of the tribe's annual income is lost. And for what purpose? To please a government that is overprotective? We and the tribe should suffer for some bureaucrat?
HARRY. Well, it is more complex than that. A child had toxic poisoning who had one of our dolls. However, no one has been able to find the source of the child's poisoning. It could have been anything. Lead paint on the walls, something up off the ground—who knows? Ottawa just wants to be sure.
JAN. And we suffer and the tribe suffers. What are our options?
JANE. (marketing manager) Well, while we are precluded from selling in this country, we can still sell the product abroad. We might be able to shift our advertising efforts

to Europe, Africa, and the United States. I think we have the biggest potential in the United States.

HARRY. I know what you are saying is legal, but is it ethical?

JAN. Ethical? Wouldn't it be unethical for us to walk away from a tribe that needs economic development? Isn't it ethical to our shareholders and employees to survive as a company and sell these dolls? Isn't it ethical to sell these dolls at a reasonable price, which is the result of our low-cost production methods?

HARRY. I guess, but you tell me what you think would happen to our stock price if you saw a headline that read "Delray Toys sells unsafe Angel Dolls to other countries."

JAN. The doll is not unsafe.

HARRY. Ottawa recalled it. You tell me what the consumer is going to think. You tell me how much goodwill we will lose. People trust us. That is a fragile commodity and I think what you are saying we should do will demonstrate that our customers shouldn't trust us.

JAN. Fine. Give me some concrete evidence that the product is not safe and I will act. But to base our decision on some bureaucrat who is upset because we can't reveal a production process, and because we refuse to change to a process that we can define. What is the world coming to?

HARRY. I don't make the rules. I just think the adverse public relations may not be worth the cost.

JAN. So a tribe has a hard winter. For what purpose?

Analysis

1. Is it legal to market Angel Dolls to a foreign country if they meet the legal standards for that country even though it is illegal to market them in the home country?
2. In general, is it ethical for a company to sell a product to a foreign country if the product is illegal to sell in the country it is manufactured?
3. What if it is inconclusive that the product is harmful?
4. What is the role of the producing country to protect other countries from questionable products? What if it means lost jobs as the producing plant moves to another country to produce the questionable product?
5. What is the obligation of countries to work together to set uniform standards for pollution, product safety, and health? Why is it in the interest of a developing country? Why would it be of interest to a developed country?
6. What would you do if you were Jan?

Case 2. Plastic Suppliers, Inc. (PSI)[1]

Company History

Plastic Suppliers, Inc. (PSI), commenced operations in April, two years ago. The company was an offshoot of its founder's lifelong dream of owning his own business by providing services which he enjoyed and was considered to have been highly qualified to do. At the onset he was named as the Chief Executive Officer (CEO) and the two other people who joined him were part owners and heads of the various functions within the organization. All three were friends who had worked in the plastics business as technicians for many years and shared the founder's personal objective of being their own bosses.

Mr. Edmunds, the founder, had a sixteen year working experience at IBM, where he started from the bottom and worked his way up until he became Head, New Products Division. Despite his position with IBM, Mr. Edmunds's entrepreneurial spirit could not hold him down to a job at a prestigious internationally acclaimed company like IBM. Therefore, after some sixteen years experience at IBM, he, and two of his friends with the same technical background, invested their lifetime savings in a small company, Plastic Suppliers, Inc. (PSI), and started operations in McAllen, Texas.

Several advantages accrued because of the choice of location in South Texas. First, the founder Mr. Edmunds was a native of South Texas. Second, most of the existing plastics injection molding outfits were located in the northeast or midwest USA and the nearest (a very small facility) was in Dallas, Texas some 550 miles to the north of McAllen, Texas. Thirdly, the maquiladoras were located just across the border in Mexico, some 12 miles away. Maquiladora plants are usually one half of twin plant operations, where parts and technical operations are performed on the US side; and manual operations are performed on the Mexican side. . . . Mr. Edmunds realized that the maquiladora industry was a rapid growing industry, with a need for various manufactured parts for its many operations requiring parts made out of plastic.

Having a supplier that was close to the maquiladoras could cut delivery time enormously. Inventory levels could be kept low (thus resulting in lower investments in inventory and all the pluses and minuses of JIT—Just-in-Time inventory methods). The distance alone was an advantage for PSI as a supplier. If for any reason, problems

1. This case was prepared by Dr. Walter E. Greene of Pan American University, Edinburg, Texas. Research assistance was provided by Mark E. George and Carminia D. Oris, graduate assistants, Pan American University. This case should be the basis for class discussion rather than to illustrate either effective or ineffective handling of an administrative situation. In Susan Wiley (Ed.), *Annual Advances in Business Cases*, 1988. Published by the Midwest Society for Case Research.

occurred about the supplied parts, customers (maquiladoras) had the convenience of easily crossing the border into the USA and correcting the problem(s).

Maquiladors chose suppliers from the U.S. rather than Mexico primarily due to higher quality and service available. Finally, in the Rio Grande Valley region of Mexico alone, there had been a forty-three (43%) percent increase in maquiladoras in the nine year period 1978–1986, increasing from 49 to 70 plants. Mr. Edmunds had projected, barring any drastic changes, a ten percent (10%) annual growth rate for PSI, with ninety-five percent (95%) derived from the Mexican maquiladoras.

During the first two years of operation, growth had been tremendous. The first operation was equipped with four 150 ton plastic injection molding machines (similar to the plastic injection molding machines that make toy soldiers, etc., only much larger). Four months ago, four additional machines had been installed, three additional 150-ton and one 500-ton machine. The plant had been expanded to accommodate the new equipment and the work force had grown from the original three to a work force of eighty-six.

Company Objectives

Aside from Mr. Edmunds's personal desire to run his own business, the company had one major objective. All three agreed that the company was to become a full service supplier of plastic injection molding parts to local manufacturing firms on both sides of the border, i.e., in U.S. plants and in the Mexican maquiladora operations.

An organization chart is shown in Exhibit 1. PSI was Mr. Edmunds's dream of a lifetime, he had worked hard and put his lifetime savings into founding PSI. As a technician his major concerns were meeting client specifications and providing quality services and products. His cohorts were also technicians who wanted to be their own bosses. PSI found a niche in the market and grew at a tremendously fast pace during its first two years. As was common with entrepreneurs, they outgrew their original investments, and venture capitalists from both U.S. and Mexico stepped in and provided much needed capital.

Products and Services Provided

PSI had three profit generating departments: Engineering, Tooling and Production. The Engineering department created mold designs, the Tooling department made the actual molds and mold repairs, and the Production department ran the mold to produce the various plastic parts.

Although each department's function could be considered a continuous flow from mold design to parts production, clients came in needing one or two or all of the

EXHIBIT 1
Organization Chart—Plastic Suppliers, Inc.*

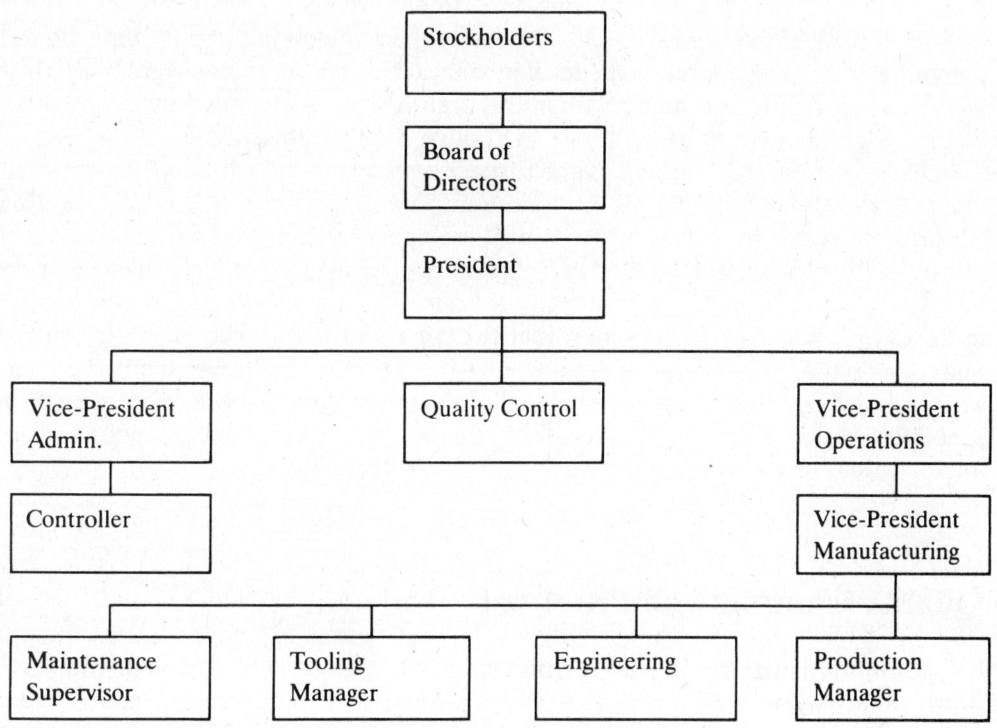

*Prepared from a report issued to third parties, customers, suppliers, and prospective investors.

services that PSI offered. Some clients had their own molds (which they brought down from northern U.S. locations, so that delivery would be faster) so all that PSI had to do was produce the plastic parts and maintain the molds. Other customers came with specifications for the part that they wanted to produce, so PSI had to design and make the mold, then produce the parts. Added to all these functions, PSI was also capable of rendering local delivery services following the purchase of its own small delivery van.

The Engineering department was responsible for designing the molds that would be used to make the parts. Its head was one of the original three that started the business. He had two assistants preparing drawings showing all details of the mold. The drawings were made through a computer (CAD/CAM—Computer Assisted Design/Manufacturing) thus making the task easier than when done manually. Designing the molds required highly skilled people, unavailable in the local job market area.

The Tooling department, supervised by one of the three founders, made the molds based on the drawing specifications from the Engineering department. Making a mold took anywhere from a couple of weeks at the very least to three months or more. Skilled personnel were a must for this department because of the complexity of the tasks involved. However, as was the case with the Engineering department, skilled personnel were unavailable in the local job market. After the molds were built, they were moved to the production floor for preliminary testing. If any flaws were discovered, the molds were sent back to Tooling for adjustments.

Adjusted and tested molds were turned over to the Production department manned mostly with semi-skilled operators. The only skills required under this department, were in setting up the machine specifications to turn out the right number of plastic parts. Knowledge of cycle times, water levels, etc., was an important factor. Apart from this the machines did most of the work. Each machine was manned by a worker who saw to it that the parts were produced according to the quantity on the specification sheet and that the machine did not run out of water. This task did not require any special skills. Normally the only way big production schedules could be met was by second shift operations in the Production department, and on rare occasions even a third shift (24 hour operations).

Quality Controls and Problems

Mr. Edmunds realized that Quality Control was of the highest priority with maquiladora operators. Since PSI produced plastic parts which form part of larger components, all parts had to fit perfectly (e.g., one of PSI's customers, which used a large portion of PSI capacity was a maquiladora plant which required the plastic parts for automobile seat belts. This maquiladora plant produced all seat belts required by one of the big three U.S. automobile manufacturers). This required strict measurement and material quality controls. Therefore a QC department was added.

Frequently, problems arose concerning a work order. Usually time schedules were set up to insure that the parts got to the customer on time and to maximize the utilization of personnel and machines. However, delays could, and did occur often, caused by any of the following factors:

1. Too much time spent on designing the molds (Engineering), or in making the molds (Tooling), or in producing the parts (Production).
2. Sometimes parts did not conform to QC standards, and then each of the departments blamed the other department for the failure.
3. Sometimes the molds broke or did not work correctly even if they passed QC checks.
4. Finally, machine breakdowns were a much too frequent problem.

Economic Environment

PSI's economic environment was greatly influenced by the fact that it was situated in the Rio Grande Valley of South Texas. While the U.S. national unemployment rate was about 7% as was the state of Texas, unemployment in the valley area was between 15 and 18% during this period. Starr county (one of the four counties in the valley) had the dubious honor as being one of the four poorest counties in the U.S.A. with an average annual income of $3,300. Poor health, low educational achievement, and limited job opportunities characterized this region. The local economy was highly influenced by what happened to the oil industry and the Mexican economy. Mexico's rate of inflation during the first years PSI was in operation was 160% and had averaged over 100% for each of the past three years.

Most Mexicans residing near the border brought business to the area by purchasing goods on the U.S. side of the border. With the Mexican peso devalued a few years earlier, the high rate of Mexican inflation, and the bottom dropping out of the oil market, followed by the killing freeze that had destroyed the valley's citrus crop three years before, business on the U.S. side of the border was basically at a standstill.

Unfortunately, in view of the area's past economy, local banks were geared to agriculture, oil and small retail type establishments. The failure rate of Texas banks during this period had been one of the highest of any state in the U.S.A. Bankers were scared, and in addition, none had any experience with manufacturing establishments like PSI.

Public officials in the region exhorted the development of a manufacturing sector. With high employment, firms of any kind were encouraged to relocate to the valley from the industrial north. Aware that the economy had to become multi-faceted to lessen the impact of drastic changes in the local economy, a strong desire developed to encourage the manufacturing sector to grow in the valley region.

Fast Expansion

Rapid expansion was triggered by the increased demand from maquiladora operators. At the onset, PSI was doing small jobs and one big project (to manufacture bag handles). One machine was devoted entirely to the plastic handles. The other three machines were almost always idle because of small production runs. Then when the word spread that PSI was located in the valley, jobs came pouring in. Two maquiladora plants, Zenith Televisions and TRW (seat belts) alone took practically all of the original capacity. Expansion was inevitable, and the four additional machines were acquired.

The Production department's capacity in terms of machine hours had more than doubled over its first two years. The personnel complement had increased from three to eighty-six employees. The number of machines had grown from four to seven 150-ton, plus one 500-ton plastic injection molding machines. Raw materials were stacked in boxes alongside the machines due to lack of storage space. A small nearby warehouse had been leased for extra storage space. A small office for the Engineering department had to be added due to overcrowding in the administrative office.

Financial Problems

During the first twenty months no accurate financial reports were maintained. The new stockholders were concerned about the lack of accounting information to support decision making. The original bookkeeper was just that, a bookkeeper. Mr. Earl, a CPA with consulting and work experience in one of the major accounting firms, was hired almost seven months ago.

Mr. Earl set up the accounting system from scratch (see Exhibit 2). As the controller, he performed functions like financial sourcing, financial information analysis and general accounting. He did manage to secure several short-term and long-term loans. Cash flow problems had beset PSI from the start. Collections were very late. To meet current expenses (such as payroll and regular monthly payments) short term loans had been obtained. However, as loans matured, interest and principal payments became too high for PSI to handle. Eventually the debt grew so large that the debt to equity ratio and the debt to asset ratio precluded conventional debt financing. Long term loans were hard to come by because of the banking system's reservations about lending to manufacturing organizations.

When job costs were derived and compared against the revenues by Mr. Earl, it was discovered that PSI was barely making a profit on most of its contracts. In the absence of cost standards and a cost accounting system, the price quotations given to clients were not enough to cover costs of manufacturing the parts. A consulting team was hired to determine the standard costs for labor, raw materials, and overhead and to also set up a system to monitor expenses on a per job basis. The study was finished three months ago. However, the resulting cost accounting system was not implemented because Mr. Edmunds, the CEO, was too busy searching for more sales and financial sources to borrow from.

With the existing plant already filled to capacity, management had plans for a bigger facility that could accommodate twenty plastic injection molding machines in the Production department and officers for each of the departments. The number of jobs had increased, the company was producing at maximum capacity, therefore management believed that the proposed new facility was a must, and no financing was available.

EXHIBIT 2
Plastic Suppliers, Inc.

BALANCE SHEET*

ASSETS

Current Assets		
Cash	$ (8,689)	
Accounts Receivable	146,547	
Inventory	266,449	
Prepaid Expenses	3,765	
Deposits	579	
Total Current Assets		$ 408,651
Fixed Assets		
Autos and Trucks	$ 75,880	
Furniture and Fixtures	14,191	
Equipment	2,084,960	
Building	283,246	
Less Accumulated Depreciation	(98,470)	
Land	81,383	
Leasehold Improvements	49,525	
Less Accumulated Amortization	(3,186)	
Total Fixed Assets		2,487,529
Total Assets		$2,896,180

LIABILITIES

Current Liabilities		
Notes Payable	$ 152,049	
Accrued Payable	22,590	
Taxes Payable	91,519	
Other Payable	52,421	
Current Portion of Long-term Debt	343,487	
Deferred Income	67,771	
Total Current Liabilities		$ 729,837
Long-term Liabilities		
Mortgage Payable	$ 361,154	
Notes Payable	1,694,265	
Total Long-term Liabilities		2,055,419
Total Liabilities		$2,785,256
Stockholder's Equity		
Common Stock	$ 466,575	
Paid-in Capital	579,236	
Treasury Stock	(180,432)	
Retained Earnings	(754,455)	
Total Stockholder's Equity		110,924
Total Liabilities and Equities		$2,896,180

*Taken from a report issued to third parties, i.e., suppliers, bankers and prospective investors.

EXHIBIT 2 (continued)

PSI
Income Statement
For the year ended December 31

	Department			
	Production	Mold Build	Repairs	Total
Sales	$120,000	$140,000	$ 34,000	$294,000
Cost of Sales				
Materials Used	68,345	20,496		88,841
Direct Labor	32,492	123,932	566	156,990
Overhead	31,433	26,058	3,515	61,007
Total Cost of Sales	$132,271	$170,486	$ 4,081	$306,838
Gross Profit	($ 12,271)	($ 30,486)	$ 29,919	($ 12,838)
General and Administrative Expenses				
Payroll				$ 108,232
Maintenance				24,289
Depreciation				36,114
Amortization				1,213
Rents and Leases				311
Insurance—Assets				7,887
Travel and Entertainment				11,546
Shipping				507
Taxes				741
Consulting Fees				30,428
Office Supplies				7,324
Telephone and Telegraph				5,622
Mail/Postage/Courier				2,596
Electricity and Water				19,835
Fuel and Oil				122
Contributions and Donations				51
Licenses and Permits				491
Memberships, Dues and Subscriptions				1,418
Total General and Administrative Expenses				$258,728
Operating Income				
Less Other Expenses (Revenues)				($271,565)
Financial Expenses				
Other Expenses				42,083
Net Income				3,824
				($317,471)

Change of Management

Mr. Edmunds relinquished his position to Mr. Earl just one month ago. Mr. Edmunds felt that the administrative duties were too much for him to handle and all sort of paper work was piling up in the office. Besides, Mr. Edmunds was a technician and not fond of paper work, and Mr. Earl had done an outstanding job of compiling PSI's financial statements.

Almost immediately, conflict of opinions arose about strategic policies between Mr. Earl and the partners.

At the board meeting this morning, Mr. Earl tendered his thirty-day notice of resignation. Mr. Edmunds stated in the meeting that he would not resume duties as CEO, as he had more than he could handle generating sales (technical marketing).

Takeover Problems

Aware of the financial problems of PSI and of their prospects as a maquiladora supplier, one of PSI's newest clients had become interested in acquiring PSI. This client was one of the larger maquiladora operators and it was its intention to integrate vertically and thus ensure an adequate supply of plastic parts at cheaper prices. This potential acquirer saw a definite advantage of a supplier located as close as PSI. In an attempt to prevent the takeover, the existing stockholders had infused additional equity of approximately twice their original investments. Despite this, PSI still needed additional financing to start the new facility.

Analysis

1. What specific strategies would you propose to solve PSI's financial problems? Are there alternatives to local bank financing? If so, what types are available (equity or loans)?
2. What was the bank failure rate in the United States? In Texas?
3. What is the basic problem you foresee for the company as the result of having a customer base composed of 95 percent maquiladoras?
4. What can you suggest to solve the personnel problems? Does the maquiladora operation really take jobs away from U.S. workers, as some claim, or does it merely relocate jobs away from the Northeast to the Southwest, as others claim?
5. What strategies should PSI take to protect itself from any drastic changes in the maquiladora industry? From changes in the Mexican or U.S. political situation?

Case 3. Kolbe Foods, International

"We have a problem, and that is how to compete when there isn't a level playing field. We want to be an international food distributor, but we aren't going to be put in a position where we are guaranteed to fail." This statement was made by the chief operating officer (COO) of Kolbe Foods, Dr. Mary Stuart. She has been the COO of Kolbe Foods, International for the past five years and has been in the food distribution business for the past fifteen years.

Kolbe Foods, International is a division of Kolbe Foods, a major food distributor and wholesaler in the United States. Five years ago, Kolbe Foods decided to enter the foreign market and create an international division. Mary Stuart was appointed head of that division because of her experience in the industry. However, no one in the company had any previous business experience with international trade and distribution.

Kolbe International was designed to meet a growing need for a variety of foods for institutions. Potential was seen in the number of major construction projects worldwide and the need to provide quality foods for construction teams in remote locations. Kolbe International wanted to provide whatever foods an institution desired. For example, if an American school in India wanted American-style meats and vegetables, Kolbe would supply it with American-grown products. If a construction crew in Egypt wanted French food, Kolbe again would meet that need. Kolbe did not want to compromise the quality of its product by offering local substitutes because there were often extreme differences between meat grown in one country and that grown in another. The differences could be caused by the staple diet of the animal or the procedures used in processing and storing the product.

Stuart described what happened with deliveries. "Here is our basic problem in a nutshell. We ship the product from Europe or America or wherever. It gets to the country our customer is in, hits customs, and sits there sometimes for months—that's right, months. We once had a truckload of meat that sat so long in one developing country's customs office that we had to dig a hole and bury it because the meat was so bad—container and all, twenty feet deep. We didn't even open the container. All that food, rotten. Why?

"Let me tell you why. Some people think it's because the country is inefficient and bureaucratic in handling customs. But talk to other businesses and see what they say. They won't say a word until they know and trust you. Then they will tell you that the way to get through the red tape is to pay someone off. You pay the border guards, you pay the customs officers, you pay the inspectors. For a sum they will ignore any law. If you want to kill your chances to sell in their country, report the bribe to the officials. The system goes on and on. If I want to move my product, I must hire a local delivery firm. If I want them to ship the product, I had better be ready to bribe the company, bribe the drivers, and bribe the local police. It is unreal. It's no wonder there is little economic progress in some of these areas.

"What happens if we bribe someone? We have to report it to our government. And if some nosy newspaper obtains the report through the Freedom of Information Act, then we look like the bad, crooked company trying to subvert justice in the poor underdeveloped country. Hence we are abused if we bribe, but we don't do business if we don't. Our reputation is getting beat up either way. It's getting so bad that we may get out of the international trade business or at least trade only with countries that do not live by bribes. But if we do that we're not serving our customers very well, and that's why the division was created in the first place."

The reporting requirements that Mary described are part of the compliance laws that U.S. companies face under the Foreign Corrupt Practices Act of 1977. The Foreign Corrupt Practices Act (FCPA) makes it illegal for companies that are registered with the Securities and Exchange Commission (SEC) to "influence foreign governments or officials through payments or gifts."[1] Violators of the act can be assessed a $1 million fine. The Securities and Exchange Commission enforces and administers the FCPA.

Stuart expressed the dilemma in this way: "What we need is some way to level the playing field. If we are required not to pay bribes, then we are not meeting the general business practices of some countries. However, we need to meet the needs of our global customers. We have had to do some very fast dancing to meet the law and the needs of our customers, and I'm not very comfortable with what we have to do."

Although it was not clear what was being done at Kolbe, there had been rumors that some companies were simply developing joint ventures with companies in foreign countries that had fewer restrictions than U.S. firms. In a joint venture, an agreement is made to provide services or products to a third party. If Kolbe was doing this, it would have been contracting its food services to a separate company that was organized outside the United States. The fee paid by Kolbe would cover the cost of the food and the costs associated with handling the food. Kolbe would not want to know if part of the handling cost was the price of bribes or part of the profit to the subcontractor. That was not relevant to Kolbe. It would only be concerned that the customer received the product in good condition and in a timely fashion. Although subcontracting like this increased the cost of doing business for U.S. firms, it enabled them to meet the needs of their customers.

Analysis

1. Is it fair competition for U.S. firms to be forced to subcontract work to foreign suppliers to meet the FCPA provisions?
2. Is it ethical for a U.S. company to circumvent the law in this manner?
3. How can the United States govern what U.S. companies do in a foreign country?

1. H. Baruck, "The Foreign Corrupt Practices Act," *The Harvard Business Review* (January–February 1979), 33.

4. Is it legal for a foreign country to bribe a U.S. company?
5. For what other reasons might a U.S. company want to subcontract with a foreign company?

Case 4. Becoming a World-Class Competitor

"We needed to be a world-class competitor—it was as simple as that. And we wanted to do this in the United States if we could, not in Mexico, or Japan, or Singapore. That depended on many variables coming together to make the climate right for us here. It was a question of economics and of being competitive: we wanted to stay in business and make money for our investors. Personally, we preferred using U.S. employees, and we currently do, but not without many discussions on this question. So before making the commitment we had to know that we could produce our product in this country.

"Our company manufactures high-tech products: cellular phones and a host of other high-technology devices. So do the Japanese, the Koreans, the Chinese, and the Germans—it is clearly a global economy. So we had to figure out how we could do it better than the other guys. Specifically, we wanted to know if we could make a product (1) that customers wanted, (2) that could be made at a competitive price, and (3) that we could sell to our customers abroad.

Making a Product the Customer Wanted

"First, we used market research to find out what customers wanted, not just in the U.S. market, but also in Europe and the Pacific Rim countries. Our product would have to match what was needed abroad; we couldn't be content with a local following that could be attacked by our global competitors.

"So, we asked people to describe the product they wanted and needed. In this way we learned a lot about the nature of our potential customers and what sorts of things they cared for. This went beyond the product's usefulness to everything else it meant to them. We asked about reliability, servicing, and terms of sales, about features on the product, current uses, and how the customers might visualize using the product in the future. We also looked at a host of demographic and psychographic analyses to obtain the age, income level, type of job, family size, and geographical location of each respondent.

Making the Product at a Competitive Price

"From the market research we did and our own desires to make a quality product, we decided that our product would have to be very reliable. Now I am not talking just public relations prattle. I mean we wanted to produce a product that would be such that only one in a hundred would break down in a year of extensive use. I wanted none to leave the company that were not in 100 percent workable condition.

If we could not establish ourselves as the quality producer, we would not be able to remain competitive and still produce in the United States. It was as simple as that. There was no way that we could underprice some of the foreign competitors because some of them were getting big subsidies from their governments. Labor cost in many cases was one-third of what we could pay. So we had to move toward quality and service.

"However, we could not produce the product as we had in the past: now it was necessary to improve quality and also lower production cost. So we decided to plan for computerized technology and robotics. The goal was not to put employees out of work, but to become competitive enough that we could put more people to work. The simple truth was that if we couldn't be competitive we wouldn't employ anyone. Computerization and robotics could give us quality tolerances that we never dreamed were possible. We used all the buzz words at our plants: *just-in-time inventory processing, quality control computer processing,* and *statistical process control systems.*

Could We Sell in Foreign Countries?

"Our final question was whether we could sell in enough foreign countries. The notion that there is anything like free trade out in the world is bunk. The advantages that we give to foreign producers in this country are incredible. Look at the clothing industry. Large retailers give better terms for products made overseas than they do to domestic producers. Think of it! We are making it easier for foreign nationals to get employed in their country and making it harder for people to get a job in the United States. Although we have fairly moderate tariffs and trade restrictions, other countries are bending over backward to show why we cannot market our product in their country. In one Pacific Rim country, U.S.-made clothing was not accepted because the material was "too coarse for their consumers." Was this theory tested in the market? No. In fact, the black market for the product demonstrated that there was a desire and a market. But not to the officials of the country. Is that free trade? Not how I see it.

"Anyway, we did strong-up front work trying to break down some of the trade barriers for our product. We pushed in the foreign country, and we pushed for Washington, D.C., to push for us. We bugged whoever might help and whoever would listen until we were comfortable that our product would sell.

"What did it get us? We now sell over one-third of our product to a country that has been our strongest competitor. We employ thousands of workers, people we didn't employ before. I think we did all right."

Analysis

1. Why is being competitive central to success in a global economy? On what basis can a company compete?
2. Why is market research important in defining a competitive niche in a foreign country? What things would be looked at when researching a country?
3. What does the speaker mean by saying the company can't compete on price? Isn't price a factor all the time?
4. How could Washington help to ease foreign trade restrictions?
5. Why couldn't a competitor use this company's technology and apply it in a less costly labor environment and introduce a cheaper, similar product?

Chapter 22 Managing with Ethics and Social Responsibility

Case 1. Business Out Front on Schools: Unprecedented Activism, from Execs Through Ranks[1]

When Harris Trust and Savings Bank last month launched its drive to recruit employees to run in the Chicago school council elections, some longtime political activists in minority communities branded it an attempt by the downtown business community to take over the schools.

But Amanda Spencer, 30, and Nelida Rodriguez, 31, who last week completed the first phase of the bank's school council candidate training program, could care less about that.

Spencer, who is black, is a single mother with a 9-year-old son, Kedron, at Beulah Shoesmith Elementary School in Hyde Park–Kenwood. She works as an auditor at the bank.

"My concern is not with that political garbage," she said. "My concern is to help children."

Rodriguez's sons, Jonathan and Jason, will attend first grade and kindergarten, respectively, this fall at Diego Elementary, a magnet school in Logan Square. She echoed Spencer's sentiment in stating her plans to run as the community member of the school council at Richard Yates Elementary, her neighborhood school.

"If that school turned around, I'd send my kids there," she said. "Now you have police cars all around. There's shootings going on."

Spencer and Rodriguez are the first soldiers of what organizers in the Chicago business community hope will be a small army of corporate employees running in local school council elections Oct. 11 and 12 for the 595 schools in the Chicago public school system.

The 11-member councils were mandated by the 1988 school reform law. Each council will have six members elected by and from parents at that school.

The effort by business is setting a national precedent, the organizers say. Nowhere

1. Merrill Goozner, "Business Out Front on Schools: Unprecedented Activism, from Execs Through Ranks," *Chicago Tribune*, August 7, 1989, Sec. 4, pp. 1, 7.

else in the country has business moved so far beyond the usual verbal entreaties to improve urban public education that, at best, are accompanied by token programs.

"The plain fact is that Chicago's first decent chance at universally good schools could crash on the rocks of indifference if parents and community residents don't get involved—and get involved fast," Harris Bank Chairman B. Kenneth West said last month in launching the recruitment drive.

The blue-ribbon downtown business groups not only lobbied for a school reform law and a tax increase to finance changes in the system but also created a well-funded political organization to get enmeshed in the nitty-gritty of school governance. Their three-year campaign is unprecedented in a city where business' usual political involvement could best be described as here today, gone tomorrow.

The motive, they admit, is self-interest, though not the jobs-and-contracts calculus that has dominated Chicago politics.

"The economic future of Chicago is absolutely dependent on producing a viable work force," said Joseph Reed, president of Leadership for Quality Education and a member of the interim school board. "If we don't do better with the class of '93 than we did with the classes of '86 through '89, our businesses are in deep trouble."

The leadership organization, an offshoot of the Civic Committee of the Commercial Club and Chicago United, has a membership roster that reads like a Who's Who of corporate Chicago. Many of the firms have large downtown work forces.

Reed, 61, retired early from his post as regional vice president of American Telephone & Telegraph Co. to take on full-time leadership of the organization. It has a $500,000 annual budget and six full-time staffers.

The group, with its close ties to corporate foundations, also has raised abut $600,000 to fund local school council organizing by neighborhood groups. Using a 5-member panel of foundation executives to screen proposals, the group recently chose 25 groups to receive $25,000 each for organizing. That 125 groups applied for funding also fed charges of an attempted corporate takeover of schools.

Reed met with Rev. Jesse Jackson recently to smooth ruffled feathers. "We cleared the air about Leadership for Quality Education," Reed asserted.

"He doesn't like people with money doing what he's been beating the drum about for years. He sees us as Johnny-come-latelies in this while he's being labeled as antireform. He has a legitimate beef," he said.

Still, some minority community groups and even the Parent Teacher Association continue to grumble about the business community role in the school reform effort. They are doing their own organizing for the coming elections.

"What we have is the prospect of competition," Reed said. "That's what will produce the turnout."

The common theme of all the groups, Reed said, is viewing parent involvement in schools as key to improving the system. The school reform law gives the local school council the right to hire principals on performance contracts after developing a three-year plan for improving the school.

"The centralization of the bureaucracy created a staff-driven operation. We need a customer-driven operation," he said. "It's messy. But I'm convinced it's the wave of the future."

Designs for Change, a school reform advocacy group, is briefing corporate trainers on how to teach school council candidates from business what's expected of them and how they can win. Don Moore, of Designs for Change, takes credit for convincing business leaders that parent involvement and decentralized power was critical to improving the schools.

"We argued that it was parallel to their own businesses," he said. "The system had to cut out middle managers and make the local manager the key person."

The Designs for Change training curriculum, used by 28 organizations around the city, was adopted with only slight modifications by Harris Bank. Last week, the first batch of 80 bank employees who said they want to run for the local school councils completed the first nine hours of training, all on company time.

"We cover the 10 ingredients of an effective school; we teach them skills for a collaborative work process—how to work in a group," said Karen Stoeller, vice president for training and development at the bank. "We give them practice on interpreting information and how to write a school improvement plan for a typical Chicago school."

The newly elected local school councils will have 90 days to write their first three-year plans.

A second phase of the training will be about how to get elected, which at Harris will be run by Diana Nelson, vice president of community affairs. Nelson was a Republican state representative from Western Springs from 1981 to 1985.

"We'll teach them why the goal is to reach each voter three times, what a piece of literature should look like and how to give a successful coffee," she said.

"It will be a grass-roots campaign structure. I don't think they'll need to do much fundraising, maybe ask 10 friends for $50. You don't want to look too flashy or your neighbors will look at you suspiciously," she laughed.

It remains to be seen how successful the business organizing drive will be. Harris and Amoco Corp., whose chief executives have actively participated in the school reform effort, have their training programs underway.

Continental Bank will kick off its program Tuesday. But the company is requiring that employees take most of the training classes on their own time.

Leadership for Quality Education has invited representatives from 1,000 businesses from throughout Chicago to a breakfast meeting Aug. 24 in the Chicago Hilton & Towers to brief them on how they can help recruit local school council candidates from their employees. The group hopes 300 to 400 chief executives or their designees will attend.

Analysis

1. Do you agree with the claim that this sort of program is an attempt by local business to influence area schools? Does business have this right?
2. In what ways could a business influence the decision making of local boards?
3. Why should business be concerned about local schools anyway? Shouldn't their role be confined to making a profit?
4. Is using the Design for Change training curriculum giving an unfair advantage to some candidates over others in school board elections? Is it fair that these programs are open only to employees of the sponsoring organizations? Should they be open to anyone?
5. Given the shift from centralized to local school boards, do you think that the quality of programs will increase or decrease? Why do you think Chicago went to a more decentralized structure?

Case 2. Can a Good Lawyer Work Part Time? Women Lead Push for Alternative[1]

Lane Hammond worked part time for three years before assuming her current job as corporate attorney for the telecommunications firm U S West Inc. in Englewood, Colo.

"Part time at a corporation means 20 to 30 hours a week, instead of between 42 and 55 hours a week," said Hammond, 40, a graduate of the University of Denver Law School. She's married to an attorney and has two children, age 7 and 4.

Hammond doesn't work for a law firm, so she's not concerned about being on a partnership track, but women who work part time often find themselves derailed when they have a family.

"Increasing numbers of women in the profession and younger male and female lawyers are interested not only in time for their families but also in other aspects of life," said Hammond, who resumed full-time work last year. "Employers will have to be much more flexible in work-time demands."

The attorney is working to make that happen: She's on the board of Lawyers for Alternative Work Schedules Inc. (LAWS), a national nonprofit organization based in Evanston that works to promote creative job options for lawyers. Hammond has been co-chairwoman of the 300-member group's part-time work committee for seven years.

"We put people in various parts of the country in contact with one another and help them negotiate part-time jobs," she said. "The desire of many lawyers to work part time is bringing additional pressure to bear on employers."

That pressure is underscored by the fact that in 1988 there were 140,000 female lawyers, 20 percent of all practicing attorneys, according to the American Bar Association. Today, 45 to 50 percent of all law school students are female, up from 33 percent in 1974. And, in 1985, 80 percent of female attorneys were of childbearing age.

Some female attorneys have devised their own solutions to the problem of balancing work and home.

Carol Kanarek, a New York lawyer, opened her own firm in 1983 with attorney Judith Wood. "I worked very long hours for a major New York law firm," said Kanarek, a graduate of the University of Michigan Law School and active LAWS member. "I left the firm because I wanted to see more of my husband. Today, so many women are drawn to the legal profession, but they don't realize how fundamentally unyielding it is."

She and Wood, who had her first child in January, work overlapping hours. "We try to do job-sharing and be interchangeable for one another," said Kanarek. "I'm in the office most of the time, but I don't work late."

1. Carol Kleiman, "Can a Good Lawyer Work Part Time? Women Lead Push for Alternative," *Chicago Tribune*, August 7, 1989, Sec. 4, p. 10.

Something is going to have to give, said Linda Marks, a San Francisco consultant who works with law firms on work options. "There simply has to be more flexibility in the workplace," says Marks, who is married to an attorney. "The 70-hour workweek expected by law firms just won't work for everybody. Women are pushing for a change, and I hope they open the door so men can walk through, too."

Marks, a board member of LAWS and co-author with Karyn Feiden of "Negotiating Time: New Scheduling Options in the Legal Profession" (New Ways to Work, $12.50), says: "I remember when women lawyers were afraid to ask for something men didn't ask for. Now, the number of women who want to negotiate part-time work is increasing."

The law profession is changing rapidly, said Sheila Markin Nielsen, an attorney and executive director of LAWS.

"The model for a lawyer has been that you are a team player and you stay as many hours as you possibly can," said Nielsen, a graduate of Lake Forest College and of Temple University Law School. "But there's a new monastic change underway, and it's coming from inside the law firms: If they want to retain the best and the brightest, they will have to accommodate them. Law firms realize it costs more than $100,000 to recruit a new attorney."

Nielsen, 40, was a litigator for the U.S. attorney in Chicago, a prestigious appointment, until she had her first child in 1983. She and her husband, a psychiatrist, have three children younger than 6.

The attorney, who also has a master's degree in social sciences from Bryn Mawr College, took what she calls "a motherhood sabbatical" from her job and plans to resume practicing law when her youngest is 3.

Nielsen planned to go back to work after a six-month leave of absence, but after four months felt that "no one could care for my child the way I wanted to do it. The bond between us was intense and exciting."

The attorney says her years at home with her children have taught her a lot. "When I go back to work, I can bring to the workplace a humanistic and broader perspective," Nielsen said. "I feel richer for it—and I feel I would enrich a firm."

The phone number for LAWS is 312-328-8818.

Analysis

1. What should an employer expect from an employee? What should an employee expect from an employer?
2. How might part-time staffing of law professionals hurt a law firm?
3. How might part-time staffing of law professionals help a law firm?
4. If the part-time option is offered to women, should it be made available to men as well?

5. If you were the partner of a law firm, how would you treat a request for part-time status? How would you handle benefits or potential promotions? Would you exclude a part-timer from consideration for partner? If each person is accountable for billable hours, how would you treat the part-timer?

Case 3. Shakeup in Sears Family: New Format Changes Old Suppliers' Relationships[1]

For years, shopping at Sears, Roebuck and Co. meant buying merchandise with the retailer's name.

Sometimes the logo was simply "Sears." Other times, the goods were sold under private labels—Kenmore, Craftsman, LXI, Diehard, Roadhandler—designed exclusively for the nation's largest retailer.

It was a very comfortable relationship for the thousands of suppliers who made the appliances, tools and tires for the retailer's stores. For a number of them, Sears wasn't just a business client, Sears was their business.

But since March, all that's changed.

That's when Sears launched a massive overhaul of its pricing and merchandising program. The company increased the amount of national brand name goods sold at prices competitive with specialty and discount stores such as Highland Superstores, Best Buy, Wal-Mart and K mart.

Sears shoppers now have a lot of new choices.

And the company's longtime suppliers now have some major competition for shelf space and customer attention.

Gene Slagle admits the change in strategy worried him.

"I was a little concerned about the increase in name brands," said Slagle, president of Glendale Hosiery of Siler City, N.C., a major supplier of Sears brand hosiery and pantyhose for more than 30 years.

Slagle's firm also makes hosiery products that are sold under private label for a number of retailers, including Mervyn's, J. C. Penney's and Lerner Stores. But about half of its annual $50 million in sales comes from Sears.

Slagle said it's too early to tell if the introduction of brands will help or hurt his business. "If the brands pull more women into the hosiery department, then it will be good for us," he said.

"Anytime there's talk of putting a competitive product on the floor there's some concern," said Ernest J. Lovelady, president of the special products division at St. Louis-based Emerson Electric Co. The $7 billion-a-year company is a major supplier of bench power tools, table saws and drill presses sold under the Sears Craftsman label.

"Sears is far and away my biggest company," said Lovelady. "In the power and hand-tools division, it is my only customer. When Sears breathes and hiccups, I feel it."

His anxiety has been unfounded, he said. "We like what we've seen so far. At least in our lines, we've had double-digit sales increases."

Because Craftsman brand is such a leader in the hardware and power-tool field,

1. Wilma Randle, "Shakeup in Sears Family: New Format Changes Old Suppliers' Relationships," *Chicago Tribune*, August 6, 1989, Sec. 7, pp. 1–2.

suppliers making those products for Sears will fare better than those making some of the company's lesser known in-house brands, said Don Longo, executive editor at *Discount Store News*, an industry trade publication.

"I think there's a danger to all these companies of losing sales," he said.

Sales at two longtime suppliers, DeSoto Inc., of Des Plaines and Whirlpool Corp. of Benton Harbor, Mich., have been hurting this year, although each maintains it's not because of anything happening at Sears.

DeSoto makes the company's Easy Living and Weatherbeater house paints. Whirlpool makes the company's Kenmore appliance line.

DeSoto's earnings fell 57 percent in the first quarter of this year from a year earlier and 95 percent in the second quarter. The company has announced a restructuring program that will eliminate about 200 salaried jobs and save the company about $10 million.

"There's no doubt that the Sears paint business has been weak this year. It has not lived up to our expectations," said William Lamey, DeSoto vice president of finance. He doesn't think the new pricing and brand name format, nor the introduction of the Dutch Boy national brand, are at the root of the slump. Sears has been testing sales of the nationally known brand in select stores.

"We don't think it's taken any market share from us," said Lamey.

Still, he says, the new format has changed the way consumers buy paint. "A substantial portion of the business was always done on sale, and people always bought it. Only time will tell whether this new 'everyday low pricing' program works."

Theoretically, Whirlpool should benefit from the new format. But so far it hasn't, although Sears has added the Whirlpool brand name to its product lineup along with others like Amana.

Earlier this month, Whirlpool said because of a decline in demand for refrigerators and freezers at Sears, the company's largest customer, it was laying off 850 workers at its plant in Ft. Smith, Ark.

The addition of the Whirlpool line in the Sears stores hasn't had any noticeable impact on Whirlpool's sales, said William D. Marohn, company executive vice president who oversees the Kenmore appliances group.

Marohn says it's the poor climate and increased competition in durable goods that's causing sales to falter, not Sears' new pricing strategy. Analysts think it's a little of both. Last week, Sears posted the weakest sales gain of all major retailers in July, a scant 0.4 percent. Its comparable-store sales fell 2.4 percent.

Demand for durables is weak, analysts said. But there is also the feeling that the novelty of Sears' new retailing strategy is wearing off and that other retailers are starting to fight back for market share.

DeSoto and Whirlpool are classic examples of the Sears-supplier relationship, which is unique in the retail industry because of the length of time and the retailer's involvement.

Sears has been doing business with Whirlpool since around 1916 and with DeSoto since the 1920s.

"We developed washing machines for Sears in 1916, and we've been doing business with them on a handshake ever since," said Marohn.

The supplier network expanded as the company's desire increased to make products under its own label to skirt a Depression-era law allowing manufacturers to set minimum prices for brand goods, explains Donald R. Katz, author of "The Big Store," a history about Sears.

"All retailers had to honor the price by law, so Sears circumvented the rule with considerable creativity by growing its own brands," Katz wrote.

In time, Sears was involved in all levels of manufacturing, from concept to owning major blocks of stocks in the supplier firms like Whirlpool, DeSoto and Glendale Hosiery.

Because of this longtime relationship, supplier concerns were a major part of discussions about the new strategy, said Matthew Howard, senior executive vice president, Sears Merchandise Group, who oversees supplier relations.

"At the time we introduced the concept, we asked all our private label suppliers to come in, and we spent several hours discussing what the impact would be on their individual businesses," Howard said.

Howard said the new merchandising strategy has not changed the company's relations with its private label suppliers.

"I think it has helped make our private label suppliers better manufacturers," he said.

The new strategy, which also includes a major shift in how Sears distributes and markets the goods it buys, puts more of the onus of a product's success on the manufacturer.

It is a challenge, said Robert Cook, president of American Yard Products in Augusta, Ga., a major supplier of lawn mowers, lawn and garden tractors and tillers for Sears. The products are sold under the Craftsman label.

"I think this [new strategy] requires the supplier to think more like a retailer, about things like marketing, rather than just bending the metal," said Cook.

Cook said he likes the new pricing format, which takes the emphasis off frequent sales promotions. "It has helped us reduce our investment in inventories," he said.

Emerson's Lovelady hopes Sears sticks with the strategy long enough to see if it works.

"If they were to change it in too short a time it would not bode well with its credibility. It certainly would not bode well for its credibility with its suppliers," he said.

Analysis

1. Does Sears have a responsibility to its captive suppliers? If so, what?
2. Does Sears have a responsibility to its customers? If so, what?

3. Why do you think increasing competition by adding brand names to compete with the Craftsman label increases sales for Craftsman?
4. Isn't it the suppliers' fault if they did not have a long-term contract with Sears that guaranteed a level of sales and price?
5. Do you think Sears should provide some help to its suppliers that suffer from the change? If yes, what do you recommend and for how long?

Case 4. Helping the Customers or Killing the Town?

The following debate reflects the views of those who like the idea of a discount chain placing a store in a small rural town and those who don't.

PRO-DISCOUNTER. It is nearly thirty miles to drive over to the next town. I would be delighted to see a K mart, Wal-Mart, or any kind of mart open a store in our town. I think one of the reasons that this town is not growing is that it doesn't have enough opportunities for work. In addition, most people now drive thirty miles once a week to buy their food and their other supplies. Wouldn't it make sense to be able to meet their needs right here? I don't like to make the hour-long drive—I can think of better things to do with my time.

Consider too, the selection you can obtain in one of those stores and how much lower the prices are than the prices in our town. I can get toys and paper goods for almost a third less than what I pay here. That makes the drive worthwhile. By opening a discounter in our town, we would be gaining an employer and saving a long drive for many people. People are already going to a discounter, but they have to drive thirty miles. And don't tell me that a discounter would hurt our local businesses—they should look out for themselves. They haven't done us a very big service through the prices they have been charging over the years.

ANTI-DISCOUNTER. I have seen how great a discounter can be for a community. In Crete it nearly killed off the whole town. It closed the drugstore (the only one left in town), the five and ten cent store, and the flower shop. The flower shop closed because of the lack of business in the downtown area. It was a shame, because each of those businesses was owned by someone in the community, not some corporate giant three states away. We didn't gain any employment because of the stores that closed. The bank lost business because the discounter only used the local bank for daily deposits. The profits from the store went three states away. Even the construction on the store went to some builder out of Missouri; it didn't even use a local work force. How did that help the town of Crete?

The store management team is not even from the area. Sure they hired the local residents to be salesclerks and stockers. But those wages aren't the best, and there isn't much growth potential in those jobs. The stores in Crete used to have charm and were friendly because you knew each person in the store. The discount store is cold and impersonal. What did Crete gain? I haven't seen much improvement. What did Crete lose? I think it lost a uniqueness and a town spirit. Now it's just like the rest of too many small rural towns. There is a dying downtown with a new discounter somewhere on the main highway. And that's what you want to bring to this town. I'm sorry, I can't see it. The cost would be too great. I don't think you really know what you are advocating.

PRO-DISCOUNTER. Should I care about a store owner that has charged more for his or her product than another store? How much should I pay for folksy service and a quaint (I define it old and run-down) store? How much should I suffer because our quaint store only has a dozen different kinds of toys for my kids compared with hundreds in a discount store? How much is it worth to me not to have choices on clothing and shoes for my family or to drive over a narrow and winding two-lane road for thirty miles to have a choice? I feel bad that the merchants of this town couldn't get together to keep the center of town alive. That's too bad, but don't tell me that I have to lose choices so that the town can give me lower-quality merchandise at higher costs. You may want to remain in the nineteenth century; I want to move to the twentieth century before it ends.

ANTI-DISCOUNTER. Look beyond just your choices in consumer goods. The discounter would be draining jobs from our town. It would take away money from the town. That money, if deposited in our bank, would help finance new construction and jobs for our people, not for some corporate giant. If we are to grow as a community, we need resources, and I wouldn't expect a chain discounter to care about our community as much as those who have lived here all their lives. Most managers of these discount chains move from store to store. How will they care about the community? The discounter is here only to make money. If it doesn't make money, it will leave, and all that will be left is an empty building, another eyesore.

PRO-DISCOUNTER. What is this about a loss of jobs? That's hogwash. The discounter will hire more employees than have lost their jobs from the nondiscounters that have closed up shop. Discounters pull people from farther around than just this town. Those people will come to our town, shop at the discounter, and maybe shop at some of our other businesses. That will create more jobs and will help the community. Don't blame a discounter if other stores haven't kept up with the needs of their customers. If I receive better value and quality from one store over another, I will go to that store. I don't care if it is a discounter or one of the stores that have been in the community for years. I just won't accept the notion that I have to suffer to keep the community the same. I don't see the current store owners suffering.

ANTI-DISCOUNTER. Well, I moved to this community because it was something special. I wanted a community that was different from the standard town with the strip development of junky stores somewhere outside of town and the decaying center core of the city as a reminder of yesteryear. That's the fate of this town if you allow a discount store to build. That's not what I want from a community, and I don't think it's what other people want. I know it will hurt property values and that it will hurt our town. I think you need to look beyond your own immediate consumer needs to the quality of life you want for yourself and your family. I think you would agree that a strip development is not what you might consider a cultural event.

Analysis

1. Is a discounter being socially responsible by opening a new store? Socially responsible to whom?

2. In what ways can a discounter hurt a community? Does this make the discounter socially irresponsible? Why?
3. How could a discounter reduce the negative effects it could have on a community?
4. Do you agree with the argument about the flow of money out of the community? How could a discounter rebut that argument?
5. How might a small retailer compete with a national chain store?

Case 5. Tradeoff in Futures Industry: Customer Safeguards Sacrificed to Growth, Critics Say[1]

Chicago's futures traders brought on much of the trouble detailed in last week's massive criminal indictments by browbeating regulators, using political muscle to get their way in Congress and refusing to make reforms that might have slowed their rise to world prominence, a number of critics said.

Former federal regulatory officials, criminal investigators and some traders all said the alleged corruption festered, in part, because the exchanges emphasized rapid growth in business volume over ensuring that customers got a fair shake.

The charges against 46 traders depict at least four pits at the exchanges as shady betting parlors in which insiders routinely skimmed money from unwitting "marks" among the investing public. U.S. Atty. Anton Valukas and the FBI expect to seek indictments against dozens of additional traders, several sources said.

They said investigators believe the alleged fraud was no pervasive that they could build cases against scores of others if they have enough time and resources.

"The exchanges always said, 'If it ain't broke, don't fix it,' " said Thomas Russo, a former top official at the Commodity Futures Trading Commission, a federal agency that repeatedly has scaled back attempts to impose new regulations in the face of opposition from the exchanges.

"Everyone is to blame," he added. "Congress and its agriculture commodities are ultimately responsible for the [CFTC], the agency is ultimately responsible for the exchanges and the exchanges are ultimately responsible for the traders."

Other experts said executives of the Chicago Board of Trade and the Chicago Mercantile Exchange have made little effort to hide their disdain for some top CFTC officials. The exchanges also have handed out hundreds of thousands of dollars in campaign contributions to allies in Congress, who sometimes have repaid the favors by siding with the exchanges in their struggles with the regulatory agency.

James Stone, a former chairman of the CFTC, said the exchanges' success in deflecting proposed regulations also benefited from a political climate in the 1970s and 1980s that favored deregulation.

"When a tremendous amount of money belonging to other people changes hands very rapidly in an underregulated environment with poor record-keeping, the temptation will get to people," he said.

Stone is convinced that tighter regulation is inevitable in the futures industry and other areas as a result of the FBI's 2½-year undercover inquiry at the exchanges, the savings and loan crisis, the stock market crash and Wall Street's insider-trading scandal.

But others said major reforms won't occur in futures trading unless there is more of an outcry from huge agribusiness and securities firms and other big customers.

1. Christopher Drew and Laurie Cohen, "Tradeoff in Futures Industry: Customer Safeguards Sacrificed to Growth, Critics Say," *Chicago Tribune*, August 6, 1989, Sec. 1, pp. 1, 18.

Steve Krisik, executive vice president of a Harris Bankcorp unit that uses futures markets, said that while he favors curbs on abusive trading, "I would also be concerned that such regulations would take a step too far and serve to dry up some liquidity."

Top officials of both exchanges insist that allegations of cheating on the trading floor have been overblown. No more than a small percentage of their 6,000 members engage in abuses, they say.

And in the wake of last week's indictments, they have pledged to clean up any wrongdoing.

Leo Melamed, chairman of the Merc's executive committee, said at a press conference last week that he will "instill the fear of God" into "a handful of immoral people."

"We know our credibility has been called into question just by virtue of the media coverage," Board of Trade President Thomas Donovan said in an interview. He said the exchange has taken many steps over the last two years to beef up its self-policing efforts.

But exchange officials also made it clear they will continue to resist more sweeping reforms, which they fear would slow the pace of trading in the most tumultuous pits and slash traders' earnings.

They especially oppose recommendations that would require more precise recording of the time of each trade and that would ban dual trading, a practice in which brokers are permitted to execute orders for customers and trade for their own accounts at the same time.

They also reject any suggestion that they hire their own undercover investigators.

Even critics caution that they do not want to destroy the century-old futures markets, which represent a vibrant part of Chicago's economy.

While many other U.S. industries have stagnated, trading at the Chicago markets has soared almost tenfold since 1975, to 221 million contracts a day, despite intensifying competition overseas.

This amazing growth has been fueled by the creation in the 1970s of financial futures, which quickly rocketed past traditional soybean, corn and wheat contracts to become the exchanges' most popular trading instruments. The exchanges, which like to refer to themselves as the last bastion of free enterprise, argue that stringent regulations would stifle such innovation.

The philosophy has fostered a "macho" culture on the trading floors. Traders, who live by their wits and stamina, second by second, are openly scornful of outsiders, especially government regulators.

Traders commonly profess no special knowledge of economics or world affairs. But their trading—in contracts covering everything from soybeans to Treasury bonds to stock indexes—affects the price of food, the level of interest rates and stock prices from Wall Street to London to Tokyo.

Major corporations rely on futures markets to protect against adverse price swings.

The Board of Trade's hiring of Donovan, a former aide to two Chicago mayors, underscored the exchanges' view of the importance of politics. Melamed also has many admirers on Capitol Hill.

But critics said exchange officials have been highhanded at times in dealing with CFTC officials, who became visibly more reluctant to challenge the exchanges as their influence with Congress grew.

In one memorable instance, Donovan lambasted then-CFTC Chairman Susan Phillips at an industry breakfast in late 1985, accusing her of "grandstanding" in holding a news conference a day earlier to announce several enforcement actions, including one against a big Board of Trade member firm.

"The chairman of the New York Stock Exchange would never have treated the head of the [Securities and Exchange Commission] that way," one industry source who witnessed the scene said.

The critics said the difficulty in restricting dual trading and improving the exchanges' systems for tracking trades illustrates the traders' clout with the CFTC and Congress. Records show that the exchanges' political arms have given congressmen more than $615,000 in honoraria over the last six years.

Shortly after the CFTC was formed in 1975, Russo helped push through a proposal to permit dual trading only if exchanges adopted a one-minute time-stamping requirement. At the time, there was no federal requirement to record the times of trades, and the proposal would have forced brokers to stamp all trades within one minute of execution to make it easier for regulators to detect wrongdoing.

The exchanges beat back that proposal and forced the CFTC to reverse another vote in 1979 in which it approved a similar rule. "My colleagues [on the commission] received many visits from industry representatives and told me they received pressure from Congress as well," said Stone, who was chairman then.

The CFTC finally approved the one-minute recording standard in 1986. But again under pressure from Congress, the agency allowed the exchanges to reconstruct trade times through the use of computers rather than actually recording all of them as they occurred.

Several sources said that the FBI agents who posed as traders have concluded that the only way to prevent some of the abuses would be to require traders to record transactions as they happen rather than reconstruct them.

The House Agriculture Committee approved a bill Wednesday that would restrict dual trading until the exchanges improve such tracking systems. A Senate committee is leaning toward requiring tougher penalties for abuses and placing more outsiders on exchange boards.

The Merc and Board of Trade also have taken a series of steps to tighten trading rules, improve surveillance and stiffen penalties.

Critics applaud these actions but say that they don't go far enough.

"The things [being proposed] today made sense 13 years ago," Russo said.

"We should have been proceeding with them then."

Analysis

1. To what extent are traders responsible for the problems at the Chicago Board of Trade and the Chicago Mercantile Exchange?
2. To what extent are the officials of the Board of Trade and the Mercantile Exchange responsible for the problems?
3. To what extent is the Commodity Futures Trading Commission responsible for the problems?
4. What is the socially responsible action for a trader who detects fraud? Why might the trader not act in this situation? What might the Board and the Exchange do to reinforce whistle-blowing by traders who detect fraud?
5. What consequences might this image of poor trading practices have for the Chicago Board of Trade and the Mercantile Exchange?